M.P. plays 'land ...
Hope ... victory par...

... was a moment of sheer triumph for Leyt...
... M.P., Mr. Ronald Buxton, on Friday whe...
... by more than 300 jubilant supporters ...
... ation in the Town Hall.

MR. GORDON
LOSES LEY...

POLITICAL FUTURE ...
JEOPARDY

...ATIVE IN BY 205 VOTES
...TER RECOUNT

...KES OPENS
...RIDGE OVER
...WAPA CREEK

...t of interest to Road
...rity for a long time

Bailey bridges
pan the world

TUTE PHUTE SAMAN SE MOTOR TAYYAR KAR LI

NEW M.P. TAKI
HIS SEAT

NOW he can add the initials ...
... M.P. after his name, Mr. ...
Ronald Buxton, 41-year-old sur...
prise winner of the sensational ...
Leyton by-election, is pictured ...
arriving at the Commons on Tues...
day to take his seat ...

THE BOOK OF RON

Ronald Buxton

THE BOOK OF RON

The Biography
of
Ronald Buxton

Antony Woodward

First published in Great Britain, 2015
by Robbie Buxton Publishing
Kimberley Hall, Wymondham
Norfolk NR18 0RT

Typeset in Sabon by Waveney Typesetters
Wymondham, Norfolk
Printed and bound in Great Britain
by Berforts Information Press

ISBN 978-0-9932314-0-7

The Children of Israel by Heaven's decree
Are to grow and increase like sands of the sea.
The Buxtons are better by birth and by worth,
The malt of the land and the salt of the earth.

Anon., c. 1900

Contents

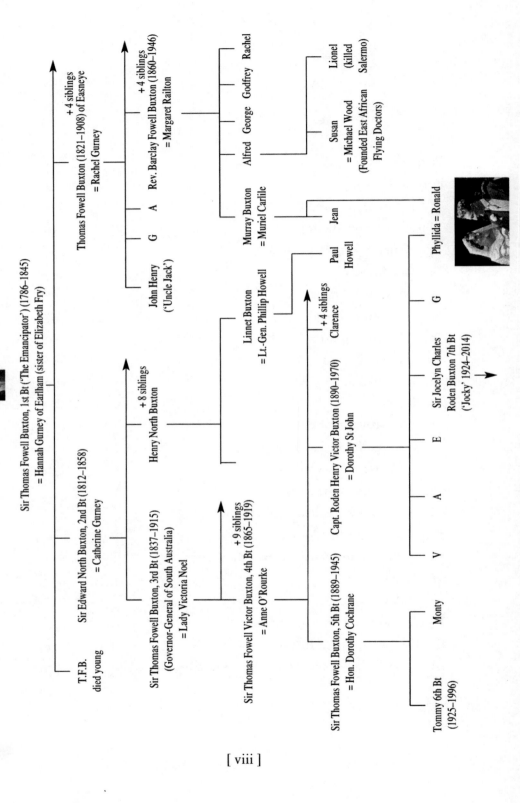

Sir Thomas Fowell Buxton, 1st Bt ('The Emancipator') (1786–1845)
= Hannah Gurney of Earlham (sister of Elizabeth Fry)

T.F.B.
died young

Sir Edward North Buxton, 2nd Bt (1812–1858)
= Catherine Gurney

Thomas Fowell Buxton (1821–1908) of Easneye
= Rachel Gurney

+ 4 siblings

Sir Thomas Fowell Buxton, 3rd Bt (1837–1915)
(Governor-General of South Australia)
= Lady Victoria Noel

Henry North Buxton

+ 8 siblings

John Henry
('Uncle Jack')

G   A   Rev. Barclay Fowell Buxton (1860–1946)
= Margaret Railton

+ 4 siblings

Murray Buxton
= Muriel Carlile

Alfred   George   Godfrey   Rachel

Susan
= Michael Wood
(Founded East African
Flying Doctors)

Lionel
(killed
Salermo)

+ 9 siblings

Sir Thomas Fowell Victor Buxton, 4th Bt (1865–1919)
= Anne O'Rourke

Linnet Buxton
= Lt.-Gen. Phillip Howell

Paul
Howell

Jean

Sir Thomas Fowell Buxton, 5th Bt (1889–1945)
= Hon. Dorothy Cochrane

Capt. Roden Henry Victor Buxton (1890–1970)
= Dorothy St John

+ 4 siblings
Clarence

Tommy 6th Bt
(1925–1996)

Monty

V   A   E   Sir Jocelyn Charles
Roden Buxton 7th Bt
('Jocky' 1924–2014)

G

Phyllida = Ronald

[viii]

Grandchildren

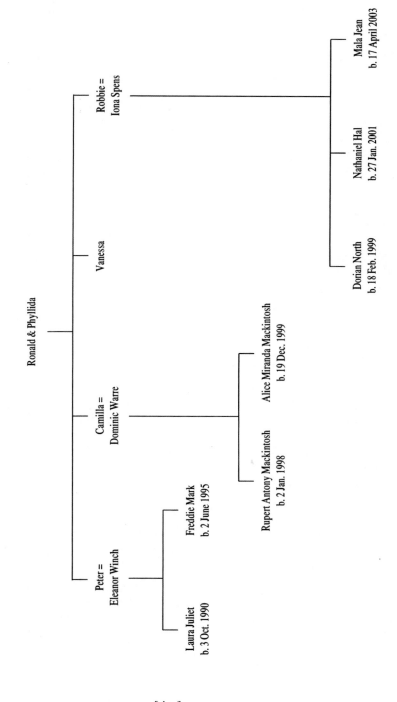

Ronald & Phyllida

Peter =
Eleanor Winch

Camilla =
Dominic Warre

Vanessa

Robbie =
Iona Spens

Laura Juliet
b. 3 Oct. 1990

Freddie Mark
b. 2 June 1995

Rupert Antony Mackintosh
b. 2 Jan. 1998

Alice Miranda Mackintosh
b. 19 Dec. 1999

Dorian North
b. 18 Feb. 1999

Nathaniel Hal
b. 27 Jan. 2001

Mala Jean
b. 17 April 2003

Foreword

LIKE MANY, I heard about Ron Buxton long before I met him. Friends of his daughter Vanessa would say 'Have you met Ron?' as if here were a subject worth pursuing. Tales would follow of a vast and freezing mansion in Norfolk, of companies across Africa, of building bridges in the middle of nowhere and barely credible flying capers – in particular a dramatic crash into the sea. There was usually mention of eccentric home improvements, in particular a double-glazing system contrived from polythene sheeting, and a home-built swimming pool.

I hardly knew what to expect when I first visited the house, Kimberley Hall, and met its owner. He didn't *look* particularly exotic. Around sixty, compact, hair like wire wool, he was wearing a grubby, fawn, many-pocketed nylon safari jerkin, so well-worn that at the front little bobbles of material had collected – his default country uniform, I would discover.

During breakfast Mr Buxton pottered to and fro through the cluttered kitchen with pliers and other tools. On one of these passes he paused by myself and another guest: 'Do you play the piano?' And to our apologetic response: 'What, *neither* of you?' Later, seated next to him at lunch, conversation started with the difficulties of surveying with eighteenth-century instruments, and ranged via water politics in the Middle East to comparative finger techniques for organ and harpsichord. At dinner that evening, during the pudding, mid-conversation with the woman next to him, he fell asleep.

Gradually, over further visits, I learned a little more about Mr Buxton. He drove an orange Daihatsu 4x4 so close to disintegration that the ground was visible through its footwells and the doors were held on with loops of bungee. When he spoke, there was a sense, in both his expression and his voice, that his mind was elsewhere. Framed newspaper cuttings from the mid-Sixties in the downstairs loos pointed to a high profile political career, but as I had been two at the time, the names meant little. Other snippets surfaced randomly. During a bout of piano moving (a quintessential Kimberley activity) he mentioned that the instrument in question, a spectacularly unwieldy grand, he had brought back from Saigon during the war. Finding it abandoned, he had his men pack it up, then carted it across India by rail. ('It was a little wider than the train. The station master at Madras made a dreadful fuss.')

On another occasion he told us how he came to live at Kimberley; how he had bought the house and park from a dissolute peer for a song. ('No one wanted houses like this at the time.') I still wasn't sure what he did exactly, except that it involved projects in parts of Africa I would be hard pressed to place on a map.

What captivated most, however, were his flying exploits. They seemed endless. The ditching incident was merely a single highlight. Whether it was a honeymoon spent air racing in Sicily, flying so low along the Nile he could see the whites of the tribesmen's eyes, or almost colliding with a passenger jet on the runway in Oslo, he rarely seemed to have made a routine transfer. He seemed to have lead a charmed life, both in the sense of it being charming (the place-names he bandied, wherever they were, conjured adventure and romance: Juba, Malakal, Wadi Halfa, Kisumu), but also in the sense of being a survivor who had used up at least his nine lives.

When I murmured, thinking aloud, that it must be amazing to be able to fly, I recall the disconcerting matter-of-factness of his response: 'Well, do it then.' As if life were so simple! But then, I was beginning to see, for Ron it was. I had not met anyone before for whom the difference between intention and execution was so trifling.

The more I got to know the Buxtons, the more cheerfully offbeat the family seemed to be. Like other guests, I got used to the minor booby-traps of everyday life: electric fences wired to the mains; Phyll Buxton's glass water jugs secured with Sellotape, ancient electric bar fires in distant bedrooms that fizzed and ticked ominously. I never got the least hint that Ron recognised me or, indeed, could distinguish between any of his children's friends, whom he regarded chiefly as a pool of labour for the unending list of tasks about the place. When, four years after buying a microlight aircraft with him, I brought up the subject of flying at breakfast one morning (admittedly, wearing glasses in place of my usual contact lenses), he blinked at me, as if seeing me in a new light: 'Good Heavens, are you an aviator?'

For a family that shared the same address, the Buxtons seemed to live strikingly independent lives. One Saturday morning in the kitchen, after a piece of toast and a glance at his watch, I remember Ron announcing 'I must be off', a comment eliciting no response from anyone. A final, head-round-the-door 'See you, then' a few minutes later prompted Robbie to ask his father where he was going. The answer turned out to be China. Similarly, when Robbie returned from his 'gap year' trip to Africa, strolling into the library after eight months away, Ron looked up from his newspaper: 'Ah, there you are, Robbie. Could you bring in some logs?'

*

This book was Robbie's idea. The youngest of Ron's four children, he thought it would be a pity if so many stories were lost to future generations. It is based on a series of taped interviews with Ron, his family and friends. In his eighties when we began, Ron had recently recovered from a bout of cerebral malaria and blackwater fever contracted in Zambia that would have killed most men half his age. It nevertheless required months of notice to secure periods of three consecutive days during which he was not abroad organ-playing, on company business or travelling.

The interviews took place in the library at Kimberley, the central room of the South Front. There, a fire burning encouragingly behind the club fender, if yielding little by way of actual heat, Ron in his favourite armchair, we sat while he fluently recounted the events of his life. Leaning back, microphone pinned to his lapel, eyes half or fully-closed, speaking in his characteristic drawl, he would pause only at my interruptions to request further explanation. My questions – about, say, mid-twentieth century British steel production, or the history of the organ – were invariably greeted with incredulity ('You don't know Marshall and Snelgrove? Really? Marshall and Snelgrove? Well I never.'). Periodically a third voice can be heard on the tapes; female, distant, mildly irritated: 'Ron, where did you put the stapler?'

As for so many of his wartime generation, expressing feelings is anathema to Ron. Asked what he *felt* when told aged seventeen of his father's death, or when his bid for Kimberley Hall was accepted, or the moment he realised he had won the seat at the Leyton by-election, and he gives an odd, slightly suspicious look and becomes as close as he gets to irritable. 'I didn't feel anything at all.' For technical details and figures, on the other hand, for rents paid, prices for hunters, cubic capacities of car engines, numbers of rail cars produced annually, his recall is exact and remarkable.

While many of Ron's qualities shine out from what follows, some risk being buried beneath the anecdotes. Amongst these are his utter fearlessness, be it in business, hunting, flying, skiing or whatever. Another is the tenacity with which he has fought for things he sometimes allows it to be thought he has had on a plate. His confidence in himself, also, is not to be confused with self-impor-tance: his entry in *Who's Who* is brief to the point of terseness, where those of lesser achievers run to columns. Sometimes this natural humility, combined with the way he makes look effortless tasks that many would find daunting (such as starting a company), makes it easy to underestimate his achievements. Also, no one can recall having heard him swear or lose his temper.

My rule for what to include has been simple: is it potentially interesting to a general reader, with no particular knowledge of or interest in Ron, in fifty years? The offbeat nature of his adventures, of course, has assisted the fulfilment of this ambition, as has the fact that he has lived through interesting times. Ron's story, and that of his family company, have unfolded against the background of a century of unprecedented technological and social change, at the start of which we couldn't fly, weld, listen to the radio, watch television and so on. Ron's life has been shaped by some of the determining events and developments of the twentieth century: Gallipoli, the Great Depression, the production of high-grade mild steel and its engineering consequences in the shape of the 'skyscraper', cinema and department store; the Second World War and in particular the Blitz and the Burma, Borneo and Malaya campaigns; the rise and fall of empire from its Victorian heyday to its final extinction in the 1980s; the demise – and resurrection – of the cult of the country house.

As for those nuggets of quirky family history that it is always pleasing to unearth, for me the most satisfying have been Charles Dickens's mention of the Buxtons in *David Copperfield*; the connection between the Buxtons and Stanley's phrase 'Dr Livingstone, I presume'; the cock-up of the sphinxes that guard Cleopatra's Needle; the use of the great Buxton seat of Easneye as the setting for the 1950s St Trinian's films (the girls duly burnt the celluloid version to the ground); and the fact that so many Buxtons have occupied a particular set of rooms in Trinity College, Cambridge that the suite is unofficially known as 'The Buxton Rooms'. These hard-won gems I would triumphantly serve up to Ron, who would nod, and say 'Yes, yes, of course. Everyone knows that.'

Casting around at the beginning for character-revealing stories and anecdotes, many friends pointed out how little they knew of Ron, apart from the single aspect of his activities that they did know. Guy Pease, however, was quick to point out: 'You shouldn't have ANY DIFFICULTY AT ALL [his caps] in filling a huge tome with endless stories of absurdities, eccentricities, affairs of state, catastrophes, emergencies and outlandish situations.' What follow, then, are the adventures of someone who has, as another friend put it, 'a nice streak of old-fashioned craziness'; someone *Tatler* (a magazine it would never occur to Ron to read) called the 'fabled' Ron Buxton. As for the anecdotes, Guy Pease was quite right. I didn't have ANY DIFFICULTY AT ALL.

A.J.T.W.

Bibles, Banks and Beer

R ONALD BUXTON WAS born into the fringes of a remarkable dynasty of Victorian businessmen, churchmen, plutocrats, philanthropists and social reformers. Examine the back of the current £5 note, and, standing on the extreme left is a tall, gentle-looking figure in spectacles and sideburns, wearing a frock coat. This is Ron's great-great-grandfather, Sir Thomas Fowell Buxton, first baronet. On the far right of the same £5 note (as prominent as the Queen is on the front) stares a steely woman, her hair done up in a coal-scuttle bonnet. This is Elizabeth Fry, 'Betsy', sister-in-law of Sir Thomas Fowell Buxton.

Two family members, one banknote – FAR LEFT: in spectacles, 'The Emancipator' Sir Thomas Fowell Buxton; FAR RIGHT: in coal-scuttle bonnet, his sister-in-law, the prison reformer Elizabeth Fry

Few of the Sovereign's subjects make it onto British banknotes – far fewer than, say, become Prime Minister or win a Nobel Prize. Even fewer have *relatives* on the same banknote. Yet here are Buxton and Fry, alongside Newton, Wellington, Darwin, Elgar, Shakespeare, Wren, Dickens, Faraday and the rest.

Yet has anyone heard of them? How did they achieve this singular honour?

*

The family line which resulted in the first Sir Thomas Fowell Buxton can be traced back to a William Buxton of Coggeshall in Essex who died in 1625. Before this, the name probably originated from the place, Buxton – the question is, which one? There are two Buxtons in Britain: the market town and spa in the Derbyshire Peak District and a tiny village in north Norfolk. The Buxtons may have originated from either.

For heraldic and genealogical reasons, as much as emotional ones (later Buxtons have decisively adopted Norfolk as their county), the family seems most likely to have originated from Oulton or Irmingland, near Buxton, in north Norfolk.

Thomas Fowell Buxton – hereafter TFB – was born in Essex in 1786. (The slightly quaint name, Fowell, still carried by many Buxtons, dates from 1733, when a Sarah Fowell married Isaac Buxton.)

His mother, Elizabeth Hanbury, was a Quaker, through whom he became close friends with two other prominent Quakers: Joseph John Gurney and his sister, Elizabeth Fry, who lived at Earlham Hall in Norwich. The Quakers were a quasi-Christian group officially called the Society of Friends. They were called 'Quakers' because they supposedly trembled, or 'quaked', when moved by the Holy Spirit to speak in meetings for worship.

The movement had been founded in the seventeenth century as a Christian religious denomination by those dissatisfied with the existing denominations. No one seems to know why such a stronghold of Quakers developed in Norfolk at this time, but it did. Quakers were barred, as non-Anglicans and by their refusal to take oaths (because, they declared, to do such a thing would imply they didn't always speak the truth), from joining the professions. So they went into business, chiefly banking, where many made fortunes.

Although Church of England himself, Buxton attended Quaker meetings with the Gurneys and became involved in the social reform movement being led by them. He started helping to raise money for weavers in London forced into poverty by the factory system.

In May 1807 TFB married Hannah Gurney, sister of Elizabeth and John. The union established one of the most powerful connections in the Buxton family tree. TFB's new father-in-law, John Gurney, was a partner in the then famous Gurney Bank, and a successful businessman, owning a wool-stapling and spinning factory. 'As rich as a Gurney' was a figure of speech at the time. He was also a prominent Quaker. His wife, TFB's new mother-in-law, Catherine, was a member of the Barclay banking family, and, again, a devout Quaker. A measure of the significance of this union within the family is the frequency with which these two family names, Gurney and Barclay, recur down succeeding generations.

The union also established, or re-established, a Norfolk connection for the Fowell Buxton family, which now always came to Norfolk for holidays.

MESSR.ᵗ TRUMAN, HANBURY, BUXTON & C.ᵒˢ BREWERY,

'E-NOR-MOUS profits!' – The Truman Hanbury Buxton Brewery, Brick Lane, founded 1669, and by 1873 the largest brewery in the world. Today (2015) it is an arts and media centre.

The influence of TFB's mother, Elizabeth Hanbury, didn't stop there. In 1808, through her maternal connections, aged twenty-two, he started working at the East End of London brewery, Truman, Hanbury & Company in Brick Lane. The Black Eagle Brewery, rebuilt around 1724, was already an East End landmark.

The brewery brewed and popularised 'porter' beer, a dark brown malt beer, heavily hopped, that had become popular in the eighteenth century with London's street and river porters – hence its name. A kind of weak stout (in fact, the word 'stout' comes from the name used to describe the stronger 'double porter' or 'stout porter' beer), porter beer was widely regarded as a more nutritious and healthy alternative to the gin which was the regular tipple of the working classes. More importantly, it was the first beer which could be brewed in massive quantities without deterioration.

Within three years, TFB was made a partner in the brewery, which was renamed Truman, Hanbury, Buxton & Co. His principled approach began to show, as the company became renowned for its good treatment of its workers, providing free schooling, and for its support of the abolition of slavery. TFB improved the brewing process, converted the works to steam power and, with the rapid expansion and improvement of Britain's road and rail transport networks, the Black Eagle label soon became famous across Britain.

Meanwhile, the profits were gargantuan. By 1835, when, on Hanbury's death, TFB took over the business and became sole owner, the brewery was producing 200,000 barrels of porter a year. It eventually employed over 1,000 people, becoming the largest brewery in London and the second largest in Britain, catapulting the Buxtons into a new class of hugely wealthy Victorian brewing families known as 'The Beerage' (a reference to the fact that political funding by brewers often drew reciprocal political favours, including honours, to the brewing industry). The fortunes made by brewers, and Buxton in particular, was noted by Charles Dickens. In chapter 28 of *David Copperfield* (1850), Mrs Micawber says:

> ... I have long felt the brewing business to be particularly adapted to Mr Micawber. Look at Barclay and Perkins! Look at Truman, Hanbury, and Buxton! It is on that extensive footing that Mr Micawber, I know from my own knowledge of him, is calculated to shine; and the profits, I am told, are e-NOR-mous!

With his 'e-NOR-mous' profits, TFB provided increasing amounts of financial support for his sister-in-law Elizabeth Fry's prison reform campaigning, aimed at getting prisoners treated more humanely, chiefly by reducing overcrowding. He became a member of her Association for the Improvement of the Female Prisoners in Newgate and his influence on her is hard to overstate. He became a surrogate brother to the Gurneys, and an indispensable ally in Fry's prison cause. Over six foot four inches tall and ponderous, they affectionately nicknamed him 'the elephant'. On Fry's side, when disaster struck the Buxtons, and four of their eight children died of whooping cough in five weeks around April 1820, Fry comforted and supported them. (Another child died later of consumption.)

Of Fry's daunting purity of spirit the Reverend Sydney Smith wrote in 1821: 'We long to burn her alive. Examples of living virtue disturb our repose and give birth to distressing comparisons.' But her influence doubtless rubbed off on TFB. In 1818 he became MP for Weymouth and Melcombe Regis, and began his vigorous campaigning for the abolition of slavery (amongst other areas of social reform).

Surely it was William Wilberforce who did that? Wilberforce had abolished the slave *trade*, in 1807. However, the Slave Trade Act did not outlaw slavery itself. It left 800,000 British slaves for whom the new legislation changed nothing, mainly in the sugar plantations of the West Indies. TFB took over as leader of the abolitionist movement after Wilberforce retired in 1825, mounting a profoundly unpopular campaign, fighting ideas and interests entrenched enough to include even the Church. His efforts culminated in the

Slavery Abolition Act of 1833, which saw the final and complete abolition of slavery anywhere within the British Empire and the founding of Freetown in Sierra Leone, West Africa, to make a home for returning slaves.

Even after achieving this, TFB campaigned on, urging the government to make treaties with African leaders to try to abolish the slave trade there. (In 1841 a team was even sent to the Niger Delta, though the party suffered so many deaths from disease it was recalled.)

'The Emancipator':
Sir Thomas Fowell Buxton, Bt,
1786–1845

A curious side-effect of this campaigning was the gift to popular culture of one of the English language's immortal phrases. According to the Victorian missionary David Livingstone, he was inspired to go to Africa solely by TFB's arguments that the African slave trade might be effectively destroyed through 'legitimate trade' and the spread of Christianity. Had he not been so inspired, had he not joined the expedition to search for the source of the Nile that, after six years without word, prompted the *New York Herald* to send the journalist Henry Morton Stanley to investigate, Stanley would never have said those four words on encountering the missing missionary in 1871. But for TFB's inspiration, we would not have the phrase 'Dr Livingstone, I presume?'

TFB was also a vociferous opponent of capital punishment, and although he did not accomplish its abolition, he helped to reduce the number of capital crimes from more than 200 to eight.

'The Friend of the Negro' – LEFT: Sir Thomas Fowell Buxton's statue in the north choir aisle of Westminster Abbey. RIGHT: The Buxton Memorial Fountain, commissioned by TFB's son, Charles Buxton MP, and created by Samuel Sanders Teulon, 1865. In Parliament Square until 1949, it was subsequently moved to Victoria Tower Gardens.

For his abolition achievements TFB became known as 'The Liberator' or 'The Emancipator' and in 1840 was created a baronet. The coat of arms he took (see p. v) features an African, and a motto taken from Ecclesiastes 9:10, much quoted (and followed) by his descendants: 'Do it with thy might'.[1]

When TFB died in 1845, a statue of him was erected in Westminster Abbey, 'THE FRIEND OF THE NEGRO', with a replica in the cathedral at Freetown, Sierra Leone, where large numbers of freed African slaves settled. He was also commemorated by a memorial fountain in Parliament Square, now moved to the House of Lords garden – and, from 2002 to 2014, with his sister-in-law Elizabeth Fry, on the £5 note.

*

'The Liberator' was the founding father of a formidable dynasty of Buxtons, many of whom gravitated to Norfolk to buy country seats – among them Bolwick, Catton, Earsham, Horsey, Hoveton St Peter, Shadwell and

---

1 In the twentieth century, added by some Buxtons to the underside of raised lavatory seats in their country houses.

[10]

Wiveton.[2] To these, in due course, Ron Buxton would add perhaps the finest: Kimberley Hall, near Wymondham.

Over succeeding generations, Buxtons married into other powerful Norfolk Quaker families (interestingly, though, never converting to become Qakers themselves). These included, alongside the Gurneys, such banking names as Birkbeck, Hoare and Barclay. By the second half of the twentieth century, these families sprinkled so many areas of East Anglian life they were being referred to as the 'Norfolk Mafia', cropping up in institutions like Anglia Television, the Norwich Union Insurance Company, the University of East Anglia and Barclays Bank (which, some Buxtons will tell you, should be called Buxton Bank).

Because wealthy Victorians tended to have huge families, the Buxton family tree sprouted densely (there are more than eighty living second cousins). Bright, educated, energetic and driven, many rose to public prominence. Amongst the fifteen Buxtons listed in the *Dictionary of National Biography*, thirteen are directly descended from The Liberator. Six are classed as politicians, four as philanthropists. There are two governor-generals (South Australia and South Africa) and a distinguished medical entomologist.

Other Buxtons exhibit a maverick streak. Anthony Buxton, practical joker, in 1910 helped mount 'the most famous hoax in history': an official inspection of His Majesty's Home Fleet flagship, *Dreadnought*, with the hoaxers dressed (alongside Virginia Woolf and others) as Abyssinian princes. Then there was the diplomat who became the first Lord Noel-Buxton, who wore a beard to cover the scars of a Turkish assassination attempt in Bulgaria and had a street in Sofia (Brothers Buxton Street) named in his tribute. His son, the second Lord Noel-Buxton, waded into the Thames near Westminster Bridge in 1953 to prove the Romans once crossed this way – to find himself nearly drowning and swimming for his life. Angela Buxton, born in 1934, was an All-England tennis player. Many Buxtons are obsessed with shooting, none more so than the distinguished conservationist, Aubrey, Lord Buxton of Alsa, co-founder of Anglia Television and the World Wildlife Fund.[3] Similarly

2 Seven of the owners of these seats are depicted in separate portraits in the dining room at Kimberley Hall.

3 A Buxton noted for, apart from his important wildlife conservation and television work, his assiduously pursued social and royal connections: 'Seldom better illustrated', his *Telegraph* obituary noted, 'than when he and Peter Scott flew out to make a film in Iran in 1976. The Foreign Secretary Jim Callaghan and a party from the Foreign Office also happened to be on the plane, paying an official visit. As the aircraft taxied to a halt, some distance from the terminal at Tehran, the Foreign Secretary's party prepared to disembark for their official reception, but as Buxton later recalled: "As soon as the door opened, a very important general covered with gold braid and ribbons entered the aircraft, marched smartly past Callaghan and straight down to us and saluted. We were taken swiftly off the aircraft on to a red carpet and then a limousine, while the aircraft door shut and the Foreign Secretary and all the passengers were taken to the airport buildings. He was just going to see the Foreign Minister, but Peter and I were going to see the Shah."'

conservation-minded are John Buxton, of Horsey Hall in the Norfolk Broads, who filmed programmes for Anglia TV's hugely popular *Survival* series; and Cindy Buxton, Lord Buxton of Alsa's daughter, a documentary film-maker made famous when she had to be rescued by the British Navy from South Georgia (where she was filming penguins) at the outbreak of the Falklands conflict in 1982.

So many Buxtons have similar or identical names and titles (even, occasionally, marrying other Buxtons) tracing their antics can be confusing. A glance at *Burke's Peerage and Baronetage* reveals a second Buxton baronetcy, a Sir Robert John Buxton ('of Shadwell', 1753–1839), Norfolk-based, who, like TFB, was both an MP (for South Norfolk) and campaigned for the abolition of slavery *and* prison reform. There are several Lords Buxton: Baron Noel Edward Noel-Buxton, a Socialist in the House of Lords; not to be confused with Sydney, first and last Earl Buxton (1853–1934), grandson of The Liberator and former Governor-General of South Africa; and (just mentioned) the life peer Lord Buxton of Alsa.

Despite these complexities, the family tree can be simplified, symbolically, into two halves. With The Liberator's children it effectively splits: one branch follows the direct line of the baronetcy, godly and less business-orientated; the other branch, the so-called 'Easneye Buxtons' (see below) who retained control of the brewery and remained, in general, more business-driven. The 'Easneyes' became so-called because they ploughed their brewing fortune into a vast new family seat called Easneye Park. It is their side which eventually produces Ron Buxton.

Things are never clear-cut, of course. Both sides married into great banking families, while the Easneyes, for all their supposed materialism, produced numerous committed churchmen, missionaries and philanthropists. Within the family these different threads have tended to be simplified into the phrase 'bibles, banks and beer'.

*

It was The Liberator's third son, Thomas (1822–1908) – Ron Buxton's great-grandfather – who decided to give the Buxton family solid foundations in society by converting his brewing fortune, and his wife's banking fortune, into a country seat.

'To the English merchant or industrialist,' Mark Girouard has written in *The Victorian Country House* (1979), 'working twelve hours a day, disciplining and denying himself, fighting for survival in the commercial jungle, there was increasingly present the vision of a quiet harbour at the end – an estate in the country, a glistening new country house with thick carpets and plate-glass windows, the grateful villagers at the doors of their picturesque cottages, touching their caps to their new landlord, JP, High Sheriff perhaps, with his sons at Eton and Christ Church and his clean, blooming daughters teaching in the Sunday school.'

No doubt something of this kind was in Thomas Buxton's mind (given that later he became both a JP and High Sheriff, and sent his sons to Harrow and Trinity College, Cambridge). Perhaps, growing up in the long shadow of his father's fame, and lacking the public presence of his brothers Edward or Charles, both of whom were MPs, he wished to leave his own mark for the family.[4] After leaving Cambridge, he followed his father's and older brother's example and married a Gurney – Rachel, the fifth daughter of Samuel Gurney (whose second daughter had already married Thomas's older brother Edward). Samuel Gurney was reputed to be 'one of the richest commoners in the country', nicknamed 'The Quaker Rothschild'.[5] Thomas also entered the family brewery, where, with his two brothers' involvement in political and other aspects of public life, it fell to him to handle most of the running of the business. Having had ten surviving children during eighteen years at Leytonstone House, Leyton, Essex (an address that would prove significant for Ron a hundred years later – see chapter 15), Thomas and Rachel were spurred by the relentlessly encroaching suburbs to build somewhere new for themselves. In 1866, Thomas bought land in Hertfordshire.

The Easneye (originally Isneye) Park Estate, near Ware, included farmland, fields and thick woodland. Here, 'on a hill that King Alfred had held against the Danes' (or so the sales particulars declared), Thomas commissioned the Quaker architect Alfred Waterhouse to design a new mansion that would properly reflect the Buxtons' place in Victorian society.

Waterhouse was on the cusp of fame. Specialising in one of the fashionable styles of the moment, the Gothic Revival, he had already executed prestigious commissions for the new Cambridge Union Society building, new buildings at Gonville and Caius College, Cambridge and Balliol College, Oxford, and big public works like Manchester Town Hall. Within five years he would design The Natural History Museum, for which details like the terracotta tiles he used at Easneye were an important stepping stone.

For the new house, no expense was spared. Reflecting the almost possessed confidence of the age, in which agricultural rents were rising on an apparently relentless agricultural boom, and a well-defined class hierarchy which meant servants were cheap, over the next three years Easneye grew like a vast palace of red brick and terracotta: a hectic medley of turrets and chimneys, pointed arches, pointy roofs, stepped gables and cross-patterned brickwork. 'Rather harsh and unsympathetic in general effect' was Pevsner's conclusion in the Hertfordshire volume of his *Buildings of England*.

4 See Davies, R. E., *The Buxtons of Easneye: An Evangelical Victorian Family and Their Successors* (2006, revised 2007).
5 Verily Anderson, *The Northrepps Grandchildren* (1968), p. 193.

'Easneye was Valhalla' – Easneye Park, Ware, Herts, completed 1869, the architect
Alfred Waterhouse's stepping stone to The Natural History Museum

Along with fifty bedrooms, every fashionable late Victorian appurtenance of country house living was present – smoking room, library, billiard room, downstairs cloakroom – complemented by every convenience of new technology: baths and sinks with hot and cold running water, vitreous-glazed sanitary ware, flushing lavatories, central heating via titanic boilers connected by miles of pipes to great iron radiators. An army of staff, naturally, was required to run it.[6]

Easneye was part of the last hurrah of Victorian country house building, a cathedral to what Mark Girouard called 'the specifically Victorian atmosphere of earnestness, unencumbered wealth, and almost unbelievable deference', their making a 'mixture of piety, snobbery, romanticism, idealism and pretentiousness'.

In 1866 the family moved in. For two generations Easneye would become the fulcrum (or, in Ron's word, 'Valhalla') for the wider Buxton family, a meeting place and headquarters for events and celebrations; a sanctuary to which family could return from religious or military campaigns in far-flung corners of the earth. Here Ron's grandfather, Barclay Buxton, the youngest of Thomas's five boys, would grow up in a household devoted to God and the Bible.

Despite the mythopoeic significance it acquired in the minds of the Buxtons who grew up knowing it, Easneye was soon to share the fate of so

6 Butler, two footmen, house porter, two lady's maids, three housemaids, cook, housekeeper, nurse, laundress, three kitchenmaids, coachman and two grooms. Outside staff included gardener, gamekeeper, dairy manager, dairy maid, shepherd and several general and agricultural labourers.

many other country houses built during this wildly over-optimistic period. The place had been running for little more than a decade when the agricultural slump of 1879–94 brought the country house building boom to an abrupt halt. The First World War, then the Second, dispensed two more death blows, leaving houses like Easneye, with their acres of roof and gloomy panelled interiors, in Girouard's words, 'stranded monsters', beached by the disappearance of the low-waged serving class that their size demanded and their design presumed.

Easneye passed to Thomas's eldest son, John Henry (Ron's Great-Uncle Jack and Hannah Gurney's favourite grandson), then to his son Henry, who was the last Buxton to live there. He did so in markedly different circumstances from his grandfather, occupying just a few rooms on the ground floor. When Henry died in 1947 the estate passed to his son John (Ron's second cousin), but by then postwar Britain was a different world. Easneye, with its fifty bedrooms, epitomised the insane overconfidence of another century and the key question was: what on earth to do with such a liability?

It took until 1964 to find the answer. Some forty years earlier, Ron's Uncle Godfrey had founded a missionary training college in South London. Following various mergers, by the early 1960s this had become the All Nations Missionary College, accommodated in a dilapidated house in Taplow which it had completely outgrown. Still on the council, at a meeting Godfrey diffidently produced a faded sepia photograph of Easneye. Would the College be interested in 'this place in Hertfordshire that my grandfather built'? After negotiations with John, Easneye was made over and the All Nations Christian College remains there today.

Just before its relegation to institutional use, Easneye enjoyed one burst of limelight. Its severe appearance, combined with its easy access from London, made it the perfect choice when the film director Frank Launder was hunting for a location to set a new Ealing-style comedy about an anarchic girls' school. In 1957, Easneye made its screen debut as St Trinian's. It was the first of four black-and-white classics written by Sidney Gilliat (based on the Ronald Searle cartoons), starring George Cole, Joyce Grenfell, Alastair Sim, John le Mesurier, Syd James and Terry Scott.[7]

*

Barclay Buxton, Ron's grandfather, was nine when the family moved to Easneye. He had the red hair that regularly appeared in the Fowell Buxton line and took his unusual Christian name, Barclay, from the Quaker cousins

7 *The Belles of St Trinian's* (1954), *Blue Murder at St Trinian's* (1957), *The Pure Hell of St Trinian's* (1960) and *The Great St Trinian's Train Robbery* (1966).

[15]

'Come along now, girls …' LEFT: Easneye on the St Trinian's prospectus.
RIGHT: Torched by the girls, from *The Pure Hell of St Trinian's* (1960).

who had founded Barclays Bank.[8] He also, it soon transpired, had his
grandfather's height. Six foot two-and-a-half inches, he quickly proved
himself a formidable performer both as a sportsman and in the classroom. At
Harrow he was the first boy in the school's history to win the Gold Medal in
Mathematics twice. He also played fives for the school in his first year (an
accomplishment no doubt assisted by Easneye having its own court). At
Trinity College, Cambridge, he graduated as Senior Optime in the
Mathematics Tripos and won a double blue at tennis (going on to play at
Wimbledon). He was also, in 1881–2, a founding member of the Hawks'
Club, the private members' club eligible to those who had represented the
university at sport (i.e. had a blue or half-blue), and whose maroon and gold-
striped tie rests across many a once-lean City stomach.

After Cambridge, Barclay, like his older brother Arthur, took holy orders.
As the youngest of five boys – so with no expectation of inheriting – this was
hardly an unusual career choice of the time. In Barclay's case, however, it was
prompted not by force of circumstance, but profound calling, as his youngest
son Godfrey Buxton notes:[9]

> Business was open to him on the largest and most profitable scale, as his
> father had proved and his brothers were to prove; he saw in them and in his
> forebears how fruitful a Christian business man or member of Parliament

8 'The Fowell Buxton red hair. I asked my mother where this came from. She said she believed it
was in the Gurney family and not in the Buxton. That certainly one or two of his Frys (*sic*)
generation had it notably Mrs J. Cunningham.' So runs a hand-written note in an ancient leather-
bound volume of *The Buxtons of Coggeshall and Essex*, owned by Bridget de Bunsen Buxton of
Horsey Hall.
9 B. Godfrey Buxton, *The Reward of Faith in the Life of Barclay Fowell Buxton 1860–1946*
(1949).

could be for Christ and how much effective philanthropic and gospel work such a man could do. Yet he had quietly settled to the conviction that God was calling him to be ordained and to find some large needy parish in which to work, though he realized that it must cut him off from the life that was bound up with Easneye, the estate, shooting and games.

His decision, Godfrey goes on, 'was strongly contested by some whose advice and goodwill he valued. Was it the best use for Christ of his clear brain and good looks to be buried where these gifts might not be appreciated ... ?'

Having decided to get ordained, and having stayed up at Cambridge an extra year to do so, the Reverend Barclay Buxton began to re-shape his life accordingly. Drinking was an early casualty. Shortly afterwards, the decision whether or not to continue game shooting prompted some vexed soul-searching – particularly as Barclay was an outstanding shot.

In 1886, aged twenty-six, he married Margaret Railton, daughter of the architect William Railton, designer of Nelson's Column. (His design won a

'Clear brain and good looks' –
The Reverend Barclay and Margaret Buxton (*née* Railton), 1936

competition held in 1838; previously he had been a finalist in an earlier competition to design the new Houses of Parliament, for which Charles Barry's design was chosen.)

Barclay was offered numerous livings in England, but after various curacies, in 1889, decided to join a church mission to Japan. And there, apart from a few brief trips home to Easneye, was where he and Margaret lived for the next twelve years.

That same year, however, was important for another reason: in July their first surviving child was born, a boy. They christened him Murray Barclay Buxton – Ron's father.

2

A Very Fine Example

FOR THE FIRST seven years of his life, with his parents in Japan, Murray Buxton was brought up by his Aunt Ethel at Easneye. In 1898 he was sent to an English preparatory school, and in 1902, when his brother Alfred (three years younger) joined him, he moved on to Repton. In the absence of their parents, school holidays were spent at Easneye with their grandparents and Aunt Ethel.

As the two youngest boys, George and Godfrey, neared school age, however, Barclay and Margaret decided to return to Britain, perhaps for ten years or so, to see them through. In 1903 the Buxtons took a house at Widbury, a few miles from the Easneye estate.

There the Reverend Barclay Buxton brought up his family in circumstances of extreme and all-pervading godliness. Consider the following regime, taken from a biography of his father, *The Reward of Faith in the Life of Barclay Fowell Buxton*, published by Godfrey in 1949:

> Before breakfast at eight a.m., we would go for a few minutes to his study, when he would read us a verse and we would each pray if we wished. That began to teach us to pray aloud. At breakfast we would recite a verse of Scripture ... After breakfast came family prayers, with a hymn, a reading, and a prayer ... at ten a.m. [we] would rush in ... for twenty minutes' Bible study round the dining-room table.

This environment would have its effect on the four children when they grew up. But meantime Godfrey's writing gives an idea of life at Widbury. It is as notable for its tone as its content:

> What kind of home, then, did my busy parents give us all? Perhaps it is significant to mention how great a shock I received when I first stayed away with friends and met quarrelling in the home between my host and hostess. I had never seen this in my home. At meals and in general conversation there was literally no criticism of others. In later years, if for some reason I asked my father for his opinion on someone, and an unfavourable comment was given, it made me all the more alert: and in course of time I would find how right he had been, and that he had gone to the root of the matter without any bitterness. How much unprofitable and harmful petty criticism passes in the general

conversation of the Lord's people! I am glad that our home was never tarnished with it.

Yet father was a disciplinarian, both in the leadership of his fellow workers and at home. He had the largest and also the most beautiful hands that I ever saw … But at times he applied [them] in no uncertain measure to that portion of the anatomy provided for the purpose, while we squealed for mother as our only hope in a day of evil. Father rightly believed that his form of punishment was best, for it is over and done with at once, and relationship is restored. But it must be just and it must be most evident that the parent has not lost his temper. Then the child, knowing what is just, accepts it as such, and no breach is created between the offender and the one who carries through the correction.

The fact that father did not speak critically does not mean that he did not assess what was good and what was unprofitable: so that our lives were in fact shielded from many surrounding influences, yet were not cut off from healthy contacts. Father gave us the joy of outdoor recreation, so that we really did not want to bury ourselves indoors in stuffy dark theatres, cinemas or at dances. And what terrific games of tennis we had! Father's tennis was superb, his low drives one after the other, exactly where he wished, were perfect. I believe that until father was over sixty, Murray, who had been captain of the Trinity College Lawn Tennis six, never managed to beat him. Though I played him until he was about seventy, I never beat him.

Widbury had a good kitchen garden and orchard; and as it was a new house, there was plenty to do cutting down trees and shrubs, which we loved. Father could drop the biggest tree exactly where he wanted. George had a donkey and coster cart, on which he would stand upright as he drove the mile to the station for luggage, or to the gravel pit on grandfather's estate. There were two ponies, Khaki and Snowdrop, so we learnt to ride with all that this imparts of discipline, courage, decision and regular care of the pony itself.

Grandfather, and later our Uncle John Henry, let us shoot and fish on the Easneye estate, especially down at Mardocks … Best, the shepherd, would show us the Hampshire Down flock, each one of which he knew by sight, or we would go to see the huge farm horses.

Such, then, was the world in which the teenage Murray grew up. Because *The Reward of Faith* amounts to 274 pages of adulation to the point of hero-worship by Godfrey of his father, it is hard to get a realistic impression of the Reverend Barclay Buxton or Margaret (who scarcely rates a mention). Ron remembers his grandmother as 'rather severe, not good with children' which possibly says enough.

Plainly, Barclay Buxton was a charismatic man (photographs display an almost saintly countenance), but it seems hard to believe that he was not, to his sons, somewhat remote, and that his absence in Japan during his children's formative pre-school years cannot have had its effect.

For there is no doubt that their upbringing did affect the children: all four boys elected to become missionaries. Of the four, Alfred would become a missionary in Africa[10] – abandoning (and, interestingly, not entirely to his father's pleasure) a place in medical school to do so. George went to work on a missionary farm in Kenya, planning to join Alfred, but war interrupted, he returned to join the Royal Flying Corps, and was killed. Godfrey intended to go to South America as a missionary, but while serving as a captain in the Duke of Wellington's Regiment on the Western Front, a shell fell on his billet. The shrapnel damage to his legs was so bad he was invalided out and had to walk with two sticks for the rest of his life. Unable to become a missionary, he became instead the Commandant of the Missionary Training Colony in Britain.

Murray, too, nearly became a missionary. Academically gifted, after Repton he followed in the footsteps of his father and grandfather to Trinity College, Cambridge. There he played hockey for Cambridge (for some reason never getting his blue) before leaving in 1911 with a First in Natural Sciences.

On coming down, he worked for a year with a firm of chartered accountants to gain business experience; then, for some months, as layman in a London parish church – torn between the traditional Buxton careers of businessman or churchman. By 1913, it seems, he had made up his mind. Aged twenty-four, he accompanied his parents on the newly-completed Trans-Siberian Express to Japan, where Barclay was resuming his work and where, it seems certain, Murray would have joined his mission.

World events, however, intervened. On 28 June 1914, the heir to the Austro-Hungarian throne, Archduke Franz Ferdinand of Austria, was assassinated in Sarajevo, and the world toppled into war. Murray decided his rightful place was fighting for his country.

*

Murray's war service is relevant only in so much as it impinged on Ron's life. Having returned from Japan (eastwards, via America, following European developments), Murray enlisted with the territorial battalion of the Norfolk Regiment – 'The Norfolks' – reaffirming the long-standing Buxton connection with the county.

While Murray was still undergoing basic training, in 1915, the Norfolks were sent to Gallipoli with the Mediterranean Expeditionary Force. After all

10 See Norman Grubb's book, *Alfred Buxton of Abyssinia and Congo* (1943).

the talk of this being a new kind of highly mobile war, the Western Front had stalled into a hopeless, bloody stalemate in the Flanders mud. The brutal war of attrition had seen the losses of hundreds of thousands. Desperate somehow to break the stalemate Winston Churchill, as First Sea Lord, championed a rearguard action. A campaign mounted by sea from the south would attack the Dardanelles from the Mediterranean. That way, he hoped, the Allies could push north, and get the war moving again.

Captain Murray Buxton, 1915

It became the most notorious decision of Churchill's career. The first attempt to take the Gallipoli peninsula succeeded only in making that place-name synonymous with Ypres, Loos and the Somme as bywords for military incompetence. Shortly afterwards the 'Sandringham Company' of the Norfolks, recruited from the King's estate at Sandringham, became reluctantly famous when, on 12 August 1915, it became isolated during an attack and massacred. A myth grew up that the company had advanced into mist and simply disappeared (a story that was in 1999 made into the BBC TV drama *All the King's Men*).

After the disaster of the Dardanelles campaign, the survivors of the so-called Mediterranean Expeditionary Force were evacuated at the end of 1915 (the only successful part of the campaign) and regrouped in Egypt, merged with the forces there and renamed the Egyptian Expeditionary Force. General Archibald Murray arrived to take command. The new force's duties were to guard the British Protectorate of Egypt, but soon they began to push their defences of the Suez Canal into the Sinai Peninsula and by 1917 extended their area of operation into Ottoman Palestine, specifically the ancient coastal town of Gaza. For many centuries, Gaza had been the gateway for armies travelling along the coast to and from Egypt and Palestine. To prevent a modern, mobile army from outflanking this fortress, the Turks formed a defensive line from Gaza inland to Beersheba, thirty miles south-east.

The First Battle of Gaza, in March 1917, would go down as one of the more notable Allied fiascos of the war. The commander, General Charles Dobell, opted (a decision which cost him his job) to withdraw his troops just as they were in a position to seize victory. The Turks, encouraged by their

[22]

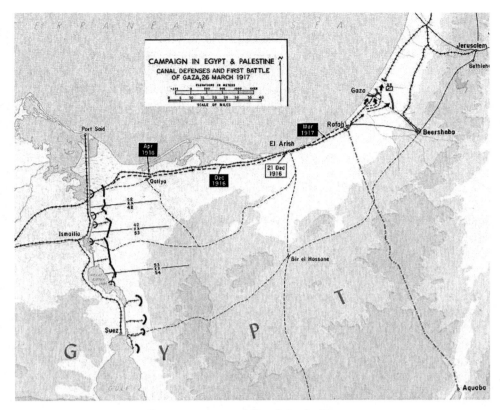

Incompetence and Death in the Desert
The Battles of Gaza, March and April 1917

widespread success, resolved to stand firm on what became known as the Gaza-Beersheba line, so that by the time the British renewed their assault, the Gaza fortifications were stronger than ever.

Captain Murray Buxton arrived to serve on Brigade Staff in Palestine in April 1917. His first excitement had already occurred, on New Year's Day 1917, when, aboard Cunard's *Ivernia* en route to Alexandria from Marseilles, in a heavy swell, the ship was torpedoed. It was 10.45 a.m.

> I was reading in the Library when suddenly a terrific explosion took place and the next thing was the sound of debris falling. Of course everybody knew what it meant … as I left the door, the officers who were on deck by the explosion came rushing through … with their faces all over black so that proved it.

So he wrote home to his father two days later. Fortunately the *Ivernia* took more than an hour to sink, allowing most of the troops aboard to be picked up by a trawler. 140 men and 6 officers were drowned.

Murray was joined by his younger brother George, now a second lieutenant in the 5th Territorial Battalion, just in time for the Second Battle of Gaza, 17–19 April. If the previous Battle of Gaza had been a fiasco, the second one inflicted a British defeat almost as bad as Gallipoli. The Norfolks suffered 75 per cent casualties, an attrition rate matched only at Ypres and on the Somme.

Moving across open country towards the Turks, General Murray issued the incomprehensible order for Murray Buxton's battalion to advance directly into Turkish machine-gun fire. About 1,100 men were killed (resulting, afterwards, in General Murray's dismissal). Murray Buxton, one of the few still left alive, went forward to attend to the wounded. A mile in front of the British line, he was hit by the machine-gun fire. With his femur shattered, bleeding profusely and in acute pain, he sheltered in a shell hole until, after dark, he could finally be rescued. For his action he was later awarded the Military Cross. His citation read:

> For conspicuous gallantry and devotion to duty as brigade intelligence officer. When communications with the front line had broken down, he made his way through heavy fire of every description to an advanced position, from which he collected and sent back important information. He afterwards acted as guide to a search party, and set a very fine example throughout.

Three months later, George, who had also miraculously survived the campaign, transferred to the Royal Flying Corps. In due course he was posted 'missing', then 'killed in action' over enemy lines beyond Passchendaele.

For Murray, a wretched few months in Cairo followed, in which he had to fight to stop his leg being amputated due to the bad surgery when his bone was set. In the end, a pin was put in his knee where he had lost the joint, and his leg was saved. His knee was stiff and his right leg was several inches shorter than the left, requiring a built-up boot for the rest of his life. Remarkably, he remained able to play tennis and golf to a high standard.

By the war's end, the Barclay Buxtons had, of their four boys, lost one and had two badly wounded. For the boys, like so many of that generation lucky enough to survive, the war robbed them of their youth and left daily reminders of what they had endured in wounds that never fully healed. It is risky to speculate on the psychological consequences of being involved in one of history's most brutal confrontations, but it seems safe to assume there were plenty. For those involved in the campaigns like Gallipoli and Passchendaele that became bywords of military iniquity, it must be assumed that the deepest wounds carried from the war were not physical. If psychological recovery to a great extent depended on the ability to bury unpalatable memories, and if this produced a severer generation of fathers and a generation both more serious and less able to communicate with their children, then probably it was a small price to pay for being alive.

*

Fortunately for Murray, his parents had decided in 1917 to return to England from Japan for good. By the time he was home, they had found a house in the village of Hoddesdon, five miles south of Easneye. With the death of Murray's grandfather, in 1908, the estate was now in the hands of Barclay's eldest brother, John Henry Buxton. It was now to Hoddesdon, his parents and the familiar, comforting embrace of Easneye, that Murray returned to convalesce for the remainder of the war.

In fact, despite the reassuring proximity of Easneye, for Murray his spell at Hoddesdon was significant more for the proximity of another house: Ponsbourne Park, home of Sir Hildred Carlile, Bt, and Lady Carlile. Murray had grown up with the Carlile children: their son, Hanbury, and their four daughters, Dora, Beatrice, Muriel and Ciceley, all of whom had been sent to finishing school in Dresden. Now it was the third Carlile girl, Muriel, known to everyone as 'Mew', who caught Murray's eye. Mew was affectionate and (Ron's later description) 'pretty, if not beautiful'. She loved art and drawing, and being in the country. As his leg gradually mended, and his fitness returned, Murray began to court her. In the spring of 1920 they became engaged to be married.

The two families were remarkably well-matched. Like the Buxtons, the Carliles had amassed a large fortune as Victorian industrialists; in the

Happy couple: Murray and Mew, three years before Ron's birth, Spring 1920

[25]

Carliles' case from thread-making.[11] Like the Buxtons, the Carliles combined their business flair with piety, probity, a social conscience and generous philanthropy. Like the Buxtons, the Carliles were consolidating their position in society, in the Victorian tradition, with a mansion house, land and title – a generation or two more recently than the Buxtons. Sir Edward Hildred Carlile, Muriel's father, had been created first baronet of Ponsbourne Park, Hertford, just three years earlier, in 1917.

The Ponsbourne Park estate comprised 760 acres of undulating, wooded countryside with, at its centre, a 1720 house. The place had previously been owned by Hildred's uncle, James Carlile, who after running his own thread-making firm in Paisley, Scotland (then the world centre of thread-making), had successfully presided over the vast expansion of his father's Yorkshire-based firm, Jonas Brook & Brothers, due to their patented method for twisting thread. James Carlile put his wealth to work enlarging and renovating Ponsbourne in the style of a Regency villa.

Following the death of his first wife, however, in 1892, he evidently decided the place was too big for him. He remarried and built a much smaller dower house, completed in 1897, which he called Ponsbourne Manor. Here he moved, in 1906, selling Ponsbourne Park to his 54-year-old nephew, Muriel's father, Hildred.

Hildred was born in 1852, the second son (of four, plus, eventually, eight sisters) of a merchant in the City of London. His career had followed the trajectory of many Victorian high-achievers: a career in industry followed by politics, public service and philanthropy. After St Albans School, in 1876, aged twenty-four, he married the beautiful Isabella Hanbury (coincidentally a descendant of Elizabeth Hanbury, mother of Thomas 'The Liberator' Fowell Buxton, whose family had owned the Brick Lane brewery). He joined Jonas Brook & Brothers, rising to become a partner. The company's patent for twisting cotton into 'Paisley thread', which had driven the firm's expansion under his Uncle James, in due course led to the company being taken over by J. & P. Coats Ltd (later Coats Viyella PLC, the world's largest thread manufacturer), bringing Hildred a fortune.

In the early 1900s, in his fifties, as a director of J. & P. Coats, Hildred went to Russia to open factories (all subsequently nationalised in the Revolution). Family stories passed down via his daughter Cicely (pronounced 'Sice-ly') tell of wild winter adventures, such as an occasion when he was chased on his sledge by wolves. Around the same time, in 1906, he bought the Ponsbourne Park estate from his uncle.

11 Despite the origins of the name suggested by a poem in the 'Carlisle' archives which begins 'Near Carlisle's towers so high and strong / There lived a brave and warlike knight / Who from the town derived its name / And claimed much land within its sight' the 's' disappeared – Carlisle's Family History, compiled by Nicholas Carlisle, 1771–1847.

Eggs, beans and crumpets: Sir Edward Hildred Carlile, Bt, at Ponsbourne Park, about 1910

Ponsbourne reflected the settled and distinguished figure that Sir Hildred now became. Never a place that could be called beautiful, contemporary photographs portray the stiffly controlled formality of the times. Walls are so covered by ivy and Virginia creeper that barely a brick can be seen. Low, slightly sinister, sun shades hood the south and west windows. The manicured grounds are terraced, with shorn and rolled lawns and endless formal borders crammed with bedding plants. At the centre of these Edwardian tableaux, archly posed and cutting a Wodehousian figure in cap and knickerbockers, stands Sir Hildred himself.

Ponsbourne Park was run on a grand scale – grander, even, than Easneye. There were never fewer than twenty indoor staff and numerous gardeners. There was even a golf course. Amongst the names of the wealthy and fashionable guests gracing the visitor's book over the following years was the Australian soprano Dame Nellie Melba – from whom the peach Melba takes its name.[12]

12 The dessert was invented in 1892 by the French chef Auguste Escoffier for a dinner at the Savoy thrown by the Duke of Orléans following Dame Nellie's performance of Wagner's *Lohengrin* at Covent Garden. In an ice sculpture of a swan (a swan featured in the opera) Escoffier placed peaches on a bed of vanilla ice cream topped with spun sugar, later modifying the topping from sugar to raspberry purée. Rumour had it that the dessert was created especially for her because she loved ice cream, but dared not eat it, believing it would affect her vocal cords. The peach Melba, by having ice cream as only one element in the whole, would not be so cold, thus not harming her precious vocal cords.

Sir Edward Hildred Carlile (1852–1942) by Sir Arthur Cope R.A.

The same year he bought Ponsbourne, Hildred stood as Unionist MP for St Albans, returned unopposed. He held the seat for the next thirteen years, the last nine on the House of Commons Accounts Committee. Innumerable positions in public service followed: notably JP for Hertfordshire, the West Riding and Huddersfield and Honorary Colonel of a company of the King's Own Yorkshire Light Infantry Regiment, culminating in a knighthood in 1911. A war spent working for the Red Cross was followed by a baronetcy in 1917, CBE in 1919, and High Sheriff of Hertfordshire in 1922.

Hildred's greatest contribution, though, was to women's education. In memory of his mother, Maria Louisa, a gifted linguist and musician who died in 1908, he made a bequest to Bedford College, London. Bedford, founded in 1849, was a higher education college specifically for women. In 1900 it had become part of the University of London. For Christmas 1913 Hildred donated the princely sum of 100,000 guineas (equivalent to nine million pounds today). It was the largest gift ever made for women's education, and made possible the establishment at Bedford (now co-ed and part of Royal Holloway College) of chairs in botany, English, Latin, and physics.

Through his elder brother, Wilson, he was also a vice-president of the Church Army.

*

Wilson founded the Church Army. Like the Buxtons, the Carlile family's approach to religion was no more passive than their approach to business.

As a teenager, Wilson had informed his family that he would earn his first £20,000 (a stupendous sum at the time) by twenty-five. Joining his grandfather's company, Jonas Brook & Brothers, due to that relation's failing health, he soon found himself more or less in charge. The result was that by twenty-five he had, in fact, vastly exceeded his stated ambition. The following year, however, in 1873, the Great Depression arrived. His new-found wealth evaporated, causing him such mental turmoil he had a breakdown. Confined to bed for weeks, questioning the purpose of life, Wilson read W. P. Mackay's *Grace and Truth* (a contemporary how-to-live-your-life guide) published the previous year. It changed his life.

On his recovery, his father took him into his firm. At the same time Wilson joined the Plymouth Brethren and started working with drop-outs and vandals around the Brethren's meeting place at Blackfriars. Soon after, confirmed into the Church of England, he began assisting at the Islington rallies organised by the American evangelist Dwight L. Moody and gospel singer Ira D. Sankey. These regularly exceeded 5,000, and Wilson, who from an early age had been musically gifted, played the harmonium to accompany the singing crowds. In the process he decided to become an evangelist himself.

Taking holy orders, he was ordained a deacon in St Paul's Cathedral and, in 1881, the Reverend Wilson Carlile was accepted as a curate. It soon struck him, however, that churches were little more than 'resorts of the well-to-do', and that if the Anglican message were to reach the working classes, more assertive action was required. Convinced this was best done by lay people of the same class as those they wished to convert, Wilson resigned his curacy and set about banding together 'soldiers', 'officers', and working men to take the word to the slums.

The 'Church Army' was born. It was 1882.

It was an 'army', Wilson said, because it would wage war against sin and the devil. And it was a time of wars – the Franco-German war was not long over and the Boer War was about to begin. The Church Army would also provide a counterpoint to the Salvation Army, founded four years earlier (also in London's East End), which was linked to the Free Church. The Church Army was emphatically Church of England.

The idea took time to catch on and, in places, met considerable resistance – both official, in the form of obstruction by those who saw the idea as threatening the Church's traditional role, and by violence in the slums. On several occasions Wilson was injured, once so badly he nearly died. But then his most violent opponents, he said, often became his greatest converts.

In 1885 the Church Army was approved by the Convocation of Canterbury. The following year Wilson opened a small training centre in Oxford where working men, at no cost, could become full-time evangelists. In due course this moved to London's Marble Arch where the Church Army's headquarters was established.

Organised around the unit of the parish, the Church Army grew rapidly across Britain. By the turn of the century it was a major force within the Church of England, significantly expanding lay opportunities there, while its influence on the evangelistic side was enormous.

Unquestionably, its social work – providing care and shelter for the destitute, long before the Welfare State – alleviated much misery. Its appeals for money and low-interest housing loans became a precursor of the housing association movement. Most significantly, it publicised the plight of the truly poor to middle-class Anglicans in the suburbs who otherwise would have remained comfortably oblivious.

In 1927 it went international, first to the USA, then, over the following decades, to Canada, New Zealand, Australia, Jamaica and East Africa. Celebrating its 130th anniversary in 2012, the Church Army's current president is Archbishop Desmond Tutu.

The Church Army's success brought Wilson honours from both Church and State. In 1906 he was made a prebendary (a kind of canon) of St Paul's Cathedral; in 1915 he was awarded an honorary DD by Oxford University; in 1926 he was made a Companion of Honour. His three unmarried sisters – the 'Miss Carliles' – he roped in to do 'battle' alongside him. Plus, of course, Hildred. Hildred and Wilson remained exceptionally close all their lives. They died on the same day, 26 September 1942, aged ninety and ninety-five respectively. Wilson was buried in St Paul's. Their obituaries appeared side by side in *The Times* of 28 September.

*

So the Buxtons and the Carliles were a match indeed: two Home Counties families; two fortunes generated at the hub of a mighty empire; two baronetcies, created in almost identical trajectories of Victorian gentrification, and two formidable new (or newly-appointed) country mansions. Both families were driven as much by religious belief and social conscience as their business skills; both were savaged by the war, one having lost its only male heir. And both achieved the remarkable honour of having a direct forebear buried or remembered in Britain's most celebrated churches: Muriel's maternal great-uncle in St Paul's, Murray's great-grandfather in Westminster Abbey. These were the backgrounds Murray and Muriel brought together when they married on 30 June 1920.

The couple set up home in London, taking a terraced house in South Kensington at 51, Evelyn Gardens. In October Muriel announced she was pregnant, and on 10 June 1921, she gave birth to a baby girl. They christened her Jean Carlile Buxton.

Obituary

PREBENDARY CARLILE

FOUNDER OF THE CHURCH ARMY

Prebendary Carlile. C.H., D.D., founder and honorary chief secretary of the Church Army, died at his home at Woking on Saturday at the age of 95. Three hours earlier his brother, Sir Hildred Carlile, first baronet of Ponsbourne, died at Tunbridge Wells at the age of 90.

When he was 90 years old Prebendary Carlile was congratulated by the King and Queen and informed that their Majesties " join with your many friends in hoping that you may be spared to continue your splendid work." Dr. Lang, then Archbishop of Canterbury, the chairman of the Prison Commissioners, the Chief Metropolitan Magistrate, and many others paid tribute to the Church Army, but the founder said that not enough praise had been given to the workers, among whom were people who had been even worse than outcasts. He had had influential support and money, " yet there are still criminals, people sleeping out, people who do not say a prayer or go to church. Why has there not been a greater result ?." In a letter to *The Times* he gave thanks for the gifts which

would help to establish the new Church Army hostel in London for youths from the distressed areas.

Born at Brixton on January 14, 1847, Wilson Carlile was the eldest son of Edward Carlile, a prosperous merchant of Scottish ancestry, whose family had been in business in Cheapside for many years. His mother was a member of an old Yorkshire family, Wilson, her name, being given to her first child. His parents were staunch Nonconformists, his father being a deacon at Stockwell Congregational Chur . . . . ile en . . . grandf . . . a li . . .

among the gifts was a lamp given by 23 ex-convicts, five of whom had been sentenced to death. At the end of his watch-chain he had about 50 small souvenirs, all given him by men to whom he had ministered in prison and who had asked him to pray for them. He was made a prebendary of St. Paul's in 1906 and a Companion of Honour in 1926. In 1936 he started what he called " News Teams," groups of Church members, mostly young, working under the control of their parish incumbent, to spread the news of the value of Christianity in their daily lives.

Mrs. Carlile, who was Miss Flora Vickers, was married to him in 1870. In spite of much ill-health she was a constant support and encouragement to her husband. She died in 1925, leaving five sons.

SIR HILDRED CARLILE

BENEFACTOR OF BEDFORD COLLEGE

Sir Hildred Carlile, Bt., C.B.E., younger brother of Prebendary Carlile, died at Bishops Down Grange, Tunbridge Wells, on Saturday at the age of 90, three hours before his brother.

Born on July 19, 1852, Edward Hildred Carlile was educated privately in England and abroad. At one time he was a partner in J. Brook and Brothers, Meltham Mills, Yorks, and a director of J. and P. Coats. The family's ancestral connexion with the cotton industry dated from the middle of the eighteenth century, when an ancestor, John Carlile, began to organize the production of sewing-thread at Paisley.

Sir Hildred Carlile, who was created a knight in 1911 and a baronet of Ponsbourne, County Hertford, in 1917, was formerly a captain in the 2nd West Yorkshire Yeomanry Cavalry, and afterwards commanded the 2nd V.B. West Riding Regiment. From 1906 to 1919 he sat as Unionist M.P. for the St. Albans division of Hertfordshire, of which county he was High Sheriff in 1922 ; he had inherited the estate of Ponsbourne there in 1906. For war work in connexion with the Red Cross in the last war he received the C.B.E.

He was deeply interested in education, was a governor of Haileybury and Aldenham schools, and, above all, was a princely benefactor to Bedford College at a time when that institution had entered on its new home in Regent's Park and was badly in need of endowment. At Christmas, 1913, he gave the sum of £105,000 towards the endowment fund, in memory of his mother, Maria Louisa Carlile (1826-1908), a proficient linguist and musician, the mother of many children, and for a number of years treasurer of M.A.B.Y.S. It was conveyed to the college through the medium of Lord Haldane, the Lord Chancellor. Sir Hildred Carlile also served the college in other ways; but this gift was believed to be the largest individual gift ever made for the education of women in this country. Some 10 years previously, Dame Margaret Tuke records in her history of the college, Mr. Acland had said at a meeting of the council, " What we need is not gifts of £5, or £20, or £100, but £100,000 ! " The idea then seemed vi . . .

There is no heir to the bar . . . . Carlile having lost his . . . France in 191 . . . was Isab . . . f Litt . . .

Died on the same day: Wilson and Hildred Carlile's double obituary, *The Times*, 28 September 1942.

Murray, meanwhile, as he convalesced, had been considering his future. Had his circumstances remained the same as when the war began, no doubt his inclination would have been to revert to becoming a missionary. With a pronounced limp, however, permanently requiring a stick, this no longer seemed an option. Besides, he now had others to think about. As his father had done twenty-five years before, he agonised. There were alternative ways to dedicate himself to God; he could take holy orders himself. And of course there was Mammon. Intelligent, educated, disciplined, already acquainted with the workings of a balance sheet, like so many Buxtons before him he could thrive in business. But what kind of business?

Here an opportunity arose through his new wife. One of the many consequences of the war was that it had removed almost an entire generation of young men, so that many family businesses found themselves with no male heir. It so happened that Muriel's uncle-by-marriage, husband of Hildred's third sister, Aunt Beatrice, was a venture capitalist called Sir Thomas Sturmey Cave. Cave owned the majority share in a casting and structural steel company called Henry Young & Company, in just such a position. It was an interesting company, operating at a time when new building methods promised a huge demand for structural steel. But the ageing directors were looking to retire. Word soon filtered through the Carlile family that Muriel had acquired a dynamic new husband who might be just the man. Henry Carlile, Cave's nephew, suggested Cave speak to Murray.

So a meeting was arranged between Sir Sturmey Cave and Murray Buxton, and Cave told him about his company. How, Cave wondered, did Murray feel about a career in engineering?

3
Henry Young & Company

THE COMPANY THAT Sir Sturmey Cave wished to discuss with Murray had started life half a century earlier, in 1871, as an iron foundry, its success built on Britain's imperial success. The last three decades of the nineteenth century found the British Empire, the largest in the history of the world, at its zenith: the peak of its size, operating at full throttle, irrepressible and indestructible. By the 1870s British schoolchildren were learning not just how much of the world map was pink (denoting British control), but that the sun never set on British soil. Through its colonies, territories, dominions, protectorates, dependencies and mandates, Great Britain controlled a quarter of the earth. British railways crossed India and Africa. British interests spread from the Antarctic to the Arctic Circle, from Pitcairn to Palestine. British schoolchildren learnt that Britain led the world in ... well, everything really.

After being the cradle of the Enlightenment, then launching the Industrial Revolution, Britain had enjoyed decades of more or less continuous peace (the *Pax Britannica*) and economic prosperity. Ours was the world's most advanced economy, the most politically sophisticated constitution. London was the largest city in the world. We had invented the postal service, the steam engine, the canal, the screw-propeller, the iron-hulled ship, the railway, rubber tyres, the spinning jenny, the flushing lavatory, photography, the sewing machine, the bicycle, the telegraph, Tarmacadam, the underground railway, the typewriter, the electric tram, X-rays and an almost endless list of other things. We'd built the world's longest tunnels, widest-spanning suspension bridges, tallest viaducts. We had prophets and thinkers like Darwin, Disraeli and Cardinal Newman. We had zoos full of exotic wild animals imported from (our) jungles, deserts, plains and mountains. We had found the source of the Nile, named the tallest mountain, and catalogued the animal and plant kingdoms, the rocks, the clouds and the wind. The Evangelical movement was spreading Christianity and fair play, 'educating the natives of Borrioboola-Gha', as Dickens's Mrs Jellyby put it in *Bleak House*, 'on the left bank of the Niger'.

Our enlightened liberalism meant we were the first country to abolish slavery, to care for the poor, to introduce state education for every child, to oppose capital punishment. Since the 1870s the empire had expanded so rapidly the statistics and reference books simply couldn't keep up, becoming freighted with addenda and footnotes. We were, in almost any area you cared to name, incomparably, incontrovertibly, top dogs.

And yet. As the century wore on, and began to draw to a close, somewhere deep down (perhaps as we embarked on the second Boer War) there seemed to be some faint sense that it couldn't last – that these glorious days might, just might, be numbered. The most obvious sign of this doubt was in an urgent desire to start commemorating our imperial heroes: our conquering generals, great admirals, elder statesmen, our thinkers, reformers, explorers, inventors, engineers. How? By placing statues of them on plinths in the many new parks and gardens being laid out in our rapidly expanding towns and cities.

Nowhere was this more the case than in the capital and hub of the world – London. London's population was doubling every forty years. If its days on top really were numbered, what could be more crucial than to commemorate this moment? To set it in stone, so to speak – or, more accurately, cast it in bronze?

Cast in bronze: A typical commission for Henry Young & Co.

The result was an insatiable desire for cast figures to adorn the new civic spaces – especially from the London boroughs and wealthy regional centres such as Bristol, Liverpool, Manchester and Dublin. Nor were statues required only of those with the highest profiles. There was a general wish to commemorate by the families of the innumerable entrepreneurs made wealthy by the booming culture, whether it was for manufacturing cloth, mining coal or importing guano. All were anxious to see some permanent memorial to their success.

Which was how the enterprising young founder Henry Young made his name. Young was a gifted metalworker and forger. He could cast molten iron and bronze, via moulds, into columns or brackets, and could forge more malleable wrought iron into ornate gates or railings. The company archives do not record how they met, but, in 1871, with the financial backing of Sir Thomas Sturmey Cave, Young and Cave set up a new forge and foundry in Eccleston

Street, Pimlico, to exploit the insatiable demand. They called it Henry Young & Company. (Its name was changed in 1900 to H. Young & Company Ltd.) A surviving photograph reveals Henry Young to have been a dapperly handsome man with a high, determined brow and dark, shining dark hair to match his black beard.

Young swiftly began to forge a reputation for himself. He undertook a wide variety of general work, such as ornate wrought iron railings, balconies, balustrading, gates and lamp standards, some highly elaborate. But it was his particular skill at casting that led to civic commissions such as the tall, intricate, three-headed cast-iron gas-lamp stands that still grace Trafalgar Square and the Thames Embankment.

Henry Young

These, however, were not what made his name. Young's greatest skill was casting bronze sculptures and memorials. Generally, cast statuary was 'hollow cast', a process whereby molten metal was poured into a two-part mould, then poured out again to leave two hollow shells which could be joined (like chocolate Easter eggs). This method, originally developed for the production of lead toy soldiers, used vastly less material than solid casting, and produced a much lighter, less costly result. Young, however, devised a way of reducing the thickness of castings further while maintaining the structural integrity of the finished sculpture – thereby dramatically reducing the cost. As a result he was in constant demand.

Almost everyone knows his work from those years, whether they are aware of it or not. Endless examples of the imperious, walrus-moustached, if anonymous, figures that strut and preen in the capital's squares, parks and gardens were his. Best known of his countless commissions are the two bronze sphinxes and bronze plinth for Cleopatra's Needle on the Victoria Embankment. The 60-foot, 186-tonne red granite obelisk was donated by Mehemet Ali, Viceroy of Egypt, to the British in 1819. Cut from the quarries of Aswan in about 1475 BC, and having stood for centuries in Alexandria, the giant monolith completed an eventful journey to Britain (it was nearly lost in a storm in the Bay of Biscay) and was finally erected in 1878 – along with the two bronze sphinxes that flank it.

Unfortunately, the superintending site engineer was evidently not versed in Egyptology, for the two sphinxes, also cast by Henry Young, were mounted

LEFT: Still lighting Trafalgar Square RIGHT: Regarding, not guarding – the wrongly-
facing bronze sphinxes, Cleopatra's Needle, 1878

facing the wrong way. As installed, they demurely face the Needle, whereas
their intended purpose is to face outwards, as the Great Sphinx of Giza does
the Pyramid of Khafra – to *guard* it.

Henry Young & Company expanded rapidly, especially as casting was only
a part of the business. All the new civic spaces and parks required fine
wrought and cast iron street furniture, from lamps and railings to park
benches. And this was just the start.

To accommodate the explosive growth of empire, new buildings of all
kinds were needed: public buildings to cope with the ever-mounting
administration, and buildings to express civic pride and the Victorian belief in
self-improvement: town halls, hospitals, infirmaries, public swimming baths,
museums, public libraries, covered markets. Then there were private
buildings such as banks, hotels and restaurants, and new kinds of industrial
buildings such as railway stations (the directors of the separate railway
companies vying with each other for grandeur and magnificence), power
stations, water works, sewage plants, parcel-sorting offices and breweries. All
these new buildings were beginning to use, in ever greater quantities, two
materials: cast iron and wrought iron.

*

The story of Henry Young & Company requires some explanation of
building construction techniques at the end of the nineteenth century, and the
technological changes that were about to transform them.

Building in towns and cities was changing. Until the Great Fire of London
in 1666, London was a wooden city. All buildings were timber-framed, the
frame being in-filled with whitewashed wattle-and-daub or brick, the result
resembling the black-and-white 'half-timbered' buildings that can still be seen
somewhere in every British town. Following the Great Fire, however, all

buildings within the devastated area – and, more gradually, those beyond it – were replaced with walls of non-combustible brick or masonry. The supporting frame was still timber, but now usually hidden behind plasterwork, as in a typical Georgian terrace. The walls were load-bearing, which meant they had to be thicker at basement level, gradually becoming slimmer with height, which was limited to a maximum of nine or ten storeys. The span of a room was limited by the size of available timbers. With the exception of further fire-based refinements (such as recessing timber sash windows behind brickwork) and various stylistic flourishes, this was how most buildings continued to be built for two centuries following the Great Fire.

Towards the end of the eighteenth century, however, cast and wrought iron began to be used for industrial buildings. Iron was more fire-resistant than wood, but building with it had its problems. Cast iron was strong in compression, but poor in tension. This meant it could shoulder enormous weights, but was brittle. (If dropped or stressed, it shattered like china.) In short, it was good for columns, but not for beams. Wrought iron (which contained less carbon) was softer, more malleable, and better for beams. So, gradually, the first iron frames appeared: using cast iron pillars, with wrought iron beams, often supporting brick arch floors, but still with external load-bearing masonry carrying a proportion of the vertical load. The many warehouses in mill towns and docklands converted for 'loft living' in the 1980s were all built like this.

Iron frames allowed these industrial buildings much wider internal spans than timber frames did. They consumed much less space on lower floors by allowing for slimmer walls. They added at least a storey or two on top. And, crucially for storage buildings, they were less fire-prone. By the 1870s such iron-supported warehouses were common. Their appearance was timely because, in city centres, a new kind of building requiring similar properties was called for – a kind of super-shop. It was called a 'department store'.

'Department stores' began by agglomeration. Drapery stores gradually expanded, buying and colonising neighbouring shops. Whiteley's in Westbourne Grove was the first, with seventeen separate 'departments' by 1867. Barker's of Kensington by 1880 had encompassed fifteen neighbouring shops. Harrods, similarly, by 1883. The Army and Navy Store started as a co-operative in 1872. Jenner's, in Edinburgh, was by 1890 Scotland's largest retail store. Mostly these stores were ramshackle affairs: conglomerations of interconnected buildings. With their rabbit warren layouts and inflammable stock, they were tinder boxes (and many did burn: Harrods in 1883 and Jenner's in 1895). It became clear that a new kind of shopping required a new kind of building, one that enclosed more space and was less fire-prone.

Structural ironwork was called for – masses of it.

Work poured in to Henry Young & Company from architects commissioned to design these new buildings.[13] If the adoption of all-iron superstructures by the building trade began as a gradual process, it was soon accelerated by a further dramatic development. In 1858 the British engineer and inventor Henry Bessemer patented a method of making, cheaply and in quantity, *steel*. Steel had always been tricky and very expensive to make, and then only in tiny quantities, because of its high melting point. Using monsoon winds to act as blast furnaces, small amounts were produced in India, China and elsewhere. Steel was known to have extraordinary properties. It made the light, resilient sword blades that could hold a sharpened edge. Bessemer used the oxygen in air blown through molten impure iron or, 'pig iron', to burn off the impurities.

As a construction material, steel was the Holy Grail. It combined the compression strength of cast iron with a tensile strength that bordered on the miraculous. It was light and pliable. It could be rolled and punched. By different heat treatments, or varying the carbon content, or adding other metals, it acquired wildly different and wonderful characteristics: from stainlessness (for cutlery), to the 'blued' resilience of gun barrels, to super-hard knife or tool blades, to springs, wire or magnets.

Quality control issues, however, slowed steel's adoption by the building trade. Despite Bessemer's process, it was not until the French engineer Pierre-Emile Martin devised a slower, more controllable system (the 'Siemens-Martin open-hearth process'), in 1875, that mild steel of consistently reliable quality became available. Even then, mild steel beams tended to be used initially only in conjunction with more familiar cast and wrought iron. Most commissions specified a combination of the two metals. The photograph below, of the basement of the Piccadilly Hotel, shows columns or stanchions of cast iron, supporting the 'new' mild steel beams. Regarded as still unproven, the British Board of Trade restricted mild steel's use in structural engineering until 1877. Even so, Britain was way ahead of the Continent. The first major all-steel structure in Britain was the Forth Rail Bridge, built between 1883 and 1890, but its exact contemporary, the Eiffel Tower, was still being built in wrought iron.

Across the Atlantic there were no such reservations. There, mild steel's building potential prompted a building revolution. It was driven by two inventions which would shortly transform almost every city across the world.

The first innovation was so revolutionary, so overturning of the fundamental syntax of building that had existed for centuries, it can be hard to

13 One such commission, in the early 1870s, was from the architect Alfred Waterhouse for the construction of a new Town Hall for Manchester: a civic cathedral with a 280-foot bell tower. The same busy architect had just overseen the construction of a mansion in Hertfordshire called Easneye Park for one Thomas Fowell Buxton – all parties, of course, unaware that one day H. Young & Company would be owned and run by Buxtons.

Iron meets steel: basement of the now almost completely demolished Piccadilly Hotel, showing cast iron stanchions (uprights) supporting the 'new' mild steel beams

grasp that it is hardly more than a century old. Since the Pyramids and the Parthenon, the essential elements in the structural vocabulary of any building had been the column, the beam, the load-bearing wall and, later, the arch and the dome. Now, at a stroke, these were rendered obsolete – by the *self-supporting structural steel frame*. The strength of steel meant that, if it was erected into a lattice-work, then that *sine qua non* of every previous built structure, the load-bearing wall, became irrelevant. Suddenly, building a ten-storey building didn't require ground-level walls seven feet thick. In fact, there was almost no limit to the height a building could be: height was limited only by how many floors people were prepared to climb.

And that was where the second innovation came in: the lift. Lifts, or versions of them, had been around for ages, but everyone was terrified of them. Then, in 1854, at the New York World's Fair, Elisha Otis staged a spectacular demonstration. From his new 'safety passenger elevator', as he called it, halfway up a tall tower, he ordered an axe-man to cut the hoisting rope – the only thing holding up the platform on which he stood. The platform fell only a few inches before a special mechanism halted the falling elevator. This, plus the development (also from steel) of wire rope, finally convinced people that lifts were safe.

These two developments were united in Chicago in 1884–5. The Home Insurance Building was only ten storeys tall, unexceptional even by the standards of the day. But its architect, Major William Le Baron Jenney, created on the top four storeys the first load-bearing frame of structural steel. It became known as the 'Chicago skeleton'. As British engineers worked on

[39]

the Forth Rail Bridge, American engineering had made its first tentative step into a new building realm: the sky.

In Britain, the death of Queen Victoria in January 1901 heralded the end of one era and the dawn, technologically, of an exciting new one. Within a year, Marconi would be transmitting wireless messages across the Atlantic, cars would be appearing in the streets and, a year after that, the Wright Brothers would conquer heavier-than-air powered flight. For structural engineering, the possibilities offered by lifts and steel frames were elegantly demonstrated by a new building completed in 1902 on an awkward triangular site in Manhattan between 23rd Street, Fifth Avenue and Broadway. The Fuller Building – soon rechristened the 'Flatiron Building' – was, at 285 ft (87 m) high, one of the tallest buildings in the city. It depended for its structural strength entirely on a steel skeleton. A new term began to be used to describe this new building; a nautical one, borrowed from the small triangular sail on sailing ships that is set high above all the others: the 'skyscraper'.

The advantages of building with a steel frame were endless. It was cheap. It could be prefabricated, so assembly on site was quick. Partition walls on each floor no longer had to be vertically continuous with load-bearing walls beneath, so the internal space of every floor could be arranged in almost any way. Yet gaining acceptance for such a sharp break with building tradition took time. This, plus early quality control issues, meant it was not until 1909 that London County Council finally acknowledged that the thickness of external walls might safely be reduced if a steel skeleton were introduced.

By that time, good quality mild steel was readily available from British mills, and Young's could supply almost every kind: high tensile, rolling, 'I' beam joists, angles and channels. From its foundry and wrought iron work of just a few years before, the company metamorphosed into one of the leading structural iron and steel companies in the south-east, moving from its original Pimlico foundry-cum-machine-shop to a fully-fitted works off Nine Elms Road in Battersea which incorporated heavy drilling, riveting, sawing, punching, shearing and cropping equipment, a quarter-mile long 'fabrication shop' and a big stockyard served by giant cranes to unload the raw steel arriving by Thames barges.

The list of buildings for which H. Young & Company supplied and assembled structural iron and steel by 1910 makes remarkable reading. (See box p. 41.) As well as these, other successful 'lines' included breweries and seaside piers. In the company's books by this time were no fewer than nineteen breweries, from Maidstone to Ormskirk, and piers for Eastbourne, Worthing, Ryde, Sandown and Ventnor.

By the First World War this new industry was still finding its feet. Universal standards were being settled upon and implemented. Some steel mills attempted to set up their own construction arms, prompting bitter accusations of price favouritism from independent firms. Competition became intense. In the wake of industrial action, the first official trade associations began to form – to settle wage rates and conditions and attempt to raise steel prices. One of the earliest of these, established in 1913, was the London Constructional Engineers Association, of which H. Young & Company's principal shareholder, Sir Thomas Sturmey Cave, became the first chairman.[14] The Association attempted to initiate standardised forms of contract, drafted by solicitors, to instigate industry standards, and to adapt and expand the syllabuses of engineering qualifications to take account of structural steel.

The First World War had little effect on this vibrant new industry. Urgent initial work constructing arms and munitions factories surprisingly quickly gave way to business as usual. (Despite a supposed moratorium on inessential building, some surprising landmarks survive, such as Heal's in Tottenham Court Road, built in 1916.) The structural steel industry supplied infrastructure to the Army in France. It built railways and port facilities, hospitals and workshops, and amassed vast quantities of prefabricated bridging and pontoon equipment (copied from French designs by Gustave Eiffel) in readiness for the new, modern highly-mobilised war everyone was assured lay ahead – only for it all to become an embarrassment as the two sides became bogged down in trench warfare.

After the Armistice, following a fleeting postwar building boom, steel construction, like the rest of manufacturing industry, became mired in the

14 The LCEA was amalgamated in 1936 with the six other regional structural steel associations, into the British Constructional Steel Association – of which H. Young & Company remains the second-oldest member.

Depression. About the time Sir Sturmey Cave was buttonholing his wife's new nephew-by-marriage, the future for the iron and steel industry looked bleaker than at any time since Cave had got involved with it. Remarkably, Young's were still doing well enough to open a new headquarters at Thorneycroft House, Smith Square, complete with drawing offices and accounts department – something Sir Sturmey no doubt made much of to Murray, to indicate just what an outstanding opportunity H. Young & Company presented.

*

Such, then, was the background that Colonel Sir Thomas Sturmey Cave would have sketched to 32–year-old Murray Buxton. The firm had no heir. Henry Young was dead and his son Harvey had decided to make his way as an independent consulting engineer.

And so, in 1921, Murray made his decision. He decided to join the board of H. Young & Company as managing director. Still recuperating from his war wounds, knowing not the first thing about structural engineering, he joined a business with an ageing board seeking retirement, in the midst of a Depression. Having taken his decision, it was symptomatic of the man that he did not follow up on it half-heartedly. Emerging from three years of academic study, a year's accountancy and four years bloody slaughter culminating in a severe leg wound, he enrolled for evening classes to prepare for the exams of the Institute of Structural Engineers. After a full day at his new Smith Square workplace, he took a taxi back to Evelyn Gardens in time to glimpse Muriel and baby Jean before supper. Then he sat down to study Differential Calculus, Structural Mechanics, Metallurgy, and the other subjects specified by his new calling – determined, as in everything he did, to make a success of it.

Which was just as well. For in November of the following year, 1922, Muriel announced she was expecting another baby.

4
Fine Hands

'Isn't it simply splendid to have a *son*! We are delighted! He is a splendid baby, with flaxen hair and lovely blue eyes, weighing 7lb 6oz. He arrived with a shout of joy at 1.30 am this morning and slept all the rest of the night after having thoroughly surveyed us all.' So Murray Buxton described his new offspring, still unnamed, in a note to his mother dated the morning of the arrival, 20 August 1923. He added: 'He has got fine hands; nurse says he is like the Carliles, the doctor says he is like my father, so it is a good mixture!'

No name had yet been settled on. Were the baby to be a boy, 'Gervase' had been the name under consideration, after the man who had saved Murray's life when he was wounded in Palestine. But in the end it was not to be. 'Ron' it was, though who chose this name or why is forgotten. For his second name, like Jean, he took that of his mother's family: 'Carlile'.

The Buxtons' boy was entering a world adjusting to monumental changes. Five years after the Armistice, Britain was still in recovery. Science was piling one miraculous discovery onto another: from Einstein's Theory of Relativity to television and the splitting of the atom. Telephones, X-rays, cars, frozen food, passenger flying and radios were catching on. Indeed, BBC Radio broadcasting had just begun. Stanley Baldwin was Britain's recently-elected Prime Minister. In America, Prohibition was at its height. Howard Carter was unearthing treasure after treasure from the tomb of Tutankhamun in Egypt. Lenin lay dying after a stroke in Moscow, as Joseph Stalin jostled for power.

The Buxtons' life at 51, Evelyn Gardens resumed its routine, the usual quiet of this tall brick terrace, with its white porches and windows, now punctured by another baby's cries.

While Murray worked tirelessly, by day at H. Young & Company's offices, learning about the structural steel business, by night at his engineering evening classes, Muriel's life was as interrupted as any mother's with two children under three. It was a pleasant enough existence: Jean and Ron were pushed around in a big double pram by the nanny, and much time was spent in the communal garden at the back of the house. Even so, it was an urban existence far from Muriel's own childhood at Ponsbourne. At regular intervals she promised Jean and Ron – and herself – that they would soon move to the country.

Murray's evening classes paid off the following year when he sat and passed the examinations for the Institute of Structural Engineers. This

LEFT: Ron, aged three, on the beach; RIGHT: almost four

allowed him to add the letters 'M. I. Struct. E.' to his MC, MA (Cantab). He was now, officially, an engineer. Without pausing, he enrolled for evening classes for the examination of the Institute of Civil Engineers, a more demanding qualification because of the more all-embracing nature of the subject. By 1925, the letters 'M. Inst. C. E' were also added to the lengthening set of decorations and qualifications that followed his name.

It was a bad time to be joining an engineering company. Manufacturing industry, particularly, was crippled by the Depression. Unemployment in 1923 had passed one-and-a-half million for the first time, a situation which in three years' time would culminate in the General Strike. Aggravating the situation, underlining the fact that Britain was still a society of two halves – the working classes and the rest – for others life seemed just fine. The 'roaring' Twenties were beginning to roar. Jazz and swing filled the airwaves on the new radiograms. Driving was catching on, with the Austin Seven most popular of the new mass-produced 'baby cars' and petrol at just two shillings (about 20p) a gallon. The Duke of York and Lady Elizabeth Bowes-Lyon were four months married: it was the time of Evelyn Waugh's Bright Young Things.

In fact, as manufacturing companies went, Henry Young & Company was weathering the situation better than most. This was because the Twenties saw the explosion of a new leisure activity that had first emerged before the war: cinema – or 'kinema' as it was known.

Here was a way even the most badly affected by the Depression could, for a few hours, escape. For a tanner (6d), the cinema-goer could enjoy, as well as the main feature, advertisements, a cartoon, newsreel and a supplementary feature.

As entertainment went, excitement had never come so cheap. Cinema-going became a national pastime. Many went not once or twice a week, but three or four times. It was the heyday of the silent film. *Felix the Cat* appeared in 1923; Mickey Mouse followed within five years. Epics of the era included Westerns, romances, Fu Manchu thrillers, horror and disaster movies. But most of all (as always in bad times) it was the era of the comedy: Charlie Chaplin, Buster Keaton, the Keystone Cops and Laurel and Hardy.

Movies, of course, needed cinemas. And cinemas needed structural steel, hundreds, sometimes even thousands, of tonnes of it.

By the First World War, Britain probably had 3,500 first generation, purpose-built Edwardian 'picture palaces' – cinemas such as, in London, the Electric in Portobello Road or The Gate in Notting Hill. But these quickly proved to be nothing like big enough. The epics released during the war, such as D. W. Griffith's *The Birth of a Nation* and *Intolerance*, turned out to be 'events' that could fill large theatres for weeks. No West End cinemas were big enough, so the biggest London theatres, even Covent Garden, were hired and hastily adapted. By 1921 there were 4,000 cinemas, yet the average seating capacity was only about 600. American block booking systems, whereby cinemas were booked for set periods, made greater numbers of prints of popular films available, so that films could be shown more widely and benefit from bigger advertising campaigns. Wherever you lived, it now became possible to calculate how long it would be before a particular film reached your local cinema. Film exhibitors began to cotton on to the fact that it was possible to fill cinemas with two, three or even four thousand seats, as the Americans had been doing for years.

Through the 1920s more and more live theatres turned to movies, most never switching back. (In the West End, this was when Leicester Square became London's film centre.) But converting theatres was unsatisfactory. Too much precious space was wasted on scenery which, in a purpose-designed building, could be seats. The first 'super-cinemas', American-style movie palaces, began to spring up in regional towns: the Regals, Ritzes, Astorias, Roxys, Regents and Plazas. In London, in 1927, just such a commission came the way of H. Young & Company: for the New Victoria Cinema in Vauxhall Bridge Road.

The year was a highly significant one, for 'talkies' had just arrived (the first, appropriately for the Jazz Age, entitled *The Jazz Singer*). Talkies closed down many regional cinemas, which could not afford to wire for sound, but in the capital and the big towns sound provided a new impetus for the latest cinemas. In London, central sites were so expensive that architects won or lost contracts according to how many seats they could cram into tight spaces. The site of the New Victoria had cost its developers an astronomical £250,000. For such a gamble to pay off, seat numbers were critical. The

New Line Cinema, Victoria, 1929 – ABOVE: H. Young & Company's 70-ton girder is brought down Vauxhall Bridge Road on a Sunday morning. BELOW: The girder in place.

architect Ernest Wamsley Lewis won the commission by squeezing in more than 3,000. The stalls were taken down to basement level, the side gangways were pushed under the flanking streets, and the foyer was sandwiched in above the ceiling of the stalls below a vast balcony. The structural demands of such a complex plan were enormous. One of the riveted girders that H. Young had to fabricate and install was 102 feet long, nearly 9 feet deep and weighed 70 tonnes. Its size meant it had to be delivered on a Sunday morning, when there was less traffic to be blocked by the traction engines.

When the New Victoria opened in 1930 it caused a sensation. Hitherto, cinemas had been utilitarian versions of theatres. Most people had no direct contact with the joys of the Deco style they had read about in the papers (other than, perhaps, spotting a Bugatti car in the streets).

Now, for the price of a cinema ticket, they too could enjoy a dose of the *zeitgeist* – in the form of walls with concealed, coloured lights controlled by dimmer switches, shining from ice cream cones (or were they Olympic torches?). Cascades of glazed stalactites descended from a giant central dome, hung with 40,000 bizarre spheres introduced by the 'acoustician' (now an important member of the design and technical team). Fountains of glass in niches beside the stage, and a 'sea' of seats whose backs formed a wave pattern (Wamsley Lewis had declared that his auditorium would resemble 'a mermaid's palace') completed the picture.

The Expressionism divided opinion. 'People don't want this sort of thing: they want marble columns, gilt and mirrors. This won't pay,' declared Sidney Bernstein, a cinema mogul (who later founded commercial television). Pay it did, however, at least for a decade or so. 'The New Victoria, which opened in 1930, represents a turning point in cinema design,' says Richard Gray in *Cinemas of Britain*. 'The revolutionary design introduced Modernism to Britain in a popular form.' It was just one example, if an important one, of the many cinema commissions won by H. Young & Company over this period.

∗

While Murray Buxton built the buildings of the age, Muriel yearned to move to the country. Growing up at Ponsbourne Park had meant fields and fresh air. That was where her heart was, and the same was true for Murray, who had grown up in similar circumstances at Easneye and Widbury. In 1927 Muriel finally made good her repeated promises to the children. With Jean aged six, and Ron four, Murray bought a house near Sevenoaks in Kent, from which he could catch a train to London each day. It was called Britain's Lodge.

Britain's Lodge was a big, detached house of a kind springing up along the principal rail routes into London – for this was the dawn of the Commuter Age. With its tall, overhanging gables, bay windows, decorative 'Tudorbethan' timberwork on the front, it reflected the English nostalgia that developers were eagerly tapping into on behalf of London's fast-expanding middle classes and their desire to live 'in the country'.

The house sat in substantial grounds and presented a picture of romantic rusticity. Its walls, in the fashion of the day, were cloaked in ivy. Its hedges were heavy with honeysuckle and rose briars, its borders planted Gertrude Jekyll-style and its lawns immaculately mown and rolled. (The late 1920s saw the arrival of the first mass-produced petrol-driven lawn mowers.) There was

[47]

Romanticised rusticity – Britain's Lodge, Sevenoaks, 1927. With its nostalgic
Tudorbethan timbering and large grounds it was a villa for the 'commuter age'.

a tennis court and a field. Most importantly, the house sat in countryside,
bordering the Runge family's estate, Montreal Park – yet the journey from
Sevenoaks station to Charing Cross took just 53 minutes.

Britain's Lodge quickly became home to a thriving community. As well as
various indoor maids there were Miss Evors, the nanny, Ellis the gardener and
Miss Usher, the governess. A wire-haired fox terrier called Drip soon arrived,
then Rosie the donkey, and a Shetland pony called Darkie (collected by
Murray one Saturday in the back of his Armstrong Siddeley car) not to
mention Flip and Flap the ducks. Jean was sent to a local day school,
Kipington, while Ron learnt to read and write at home with Miss Usher under
the Parents National Education Union (PNEU) system. Both children, it soon
emerged, were bright.

It was a happy time. Despite a strict and godly regime – grace before meals
and prayers after breakfast, for which the servants were brought in – there
was always plenty to do. A spiral staircase led through a hole in the floor to
the nursery on the top floor, where there was an indoor swing. Outside, there
were fields and woods and streams to explore, and endless trees to climb
(both Jean and Ron were great tree-climbers). Granny and Grandfather, the
Barclay Buxtons, were quite close at Tunbridge Wells, where the Reverend
Barclay had the living of Holy Trinity Church.

At weekends the family would go for walks or rides. In winter Ron would
watch Murray set off to shoot, in tweeds and plus fours, at Montreal Park
where he had taken a gun. On Sundays they would walk across the fields to
church at St Nicholas, Sevenoaks. At bedtime, we may safely assume, Jean

and Ron were read the new children's story that was sweeping the nation: *Winnie-the-Pooh*.

There were only two blemishes to this otherwise enchanted scene. First was Muriel's recurring chest troubles or, as it was then known, pleurisy. This inflammation of the lining of her lungs gave her constant chest pains and breathing difficulties. It made her prone to chest infections, and when they came they led to coughing fits and shortness of breath. She caught fevers and chills easily. (Penicillin on prescription, the routine cure for such a condition today, lay two decades in the future.)

The other blemish was Murray's absence. The children saw their father only at weekends. Every morning Murray would be gone by eight, dressed in

The Buxton Family, 1928

[49]

the regulation metropolitan subfusc of bowler hat, striped trousers, black jacket, polished Oxfords and rolled umbrella, returning after the children were in bed. This might not have mattered – it was hardly unusual – had Murray been more accessible to the children at weekends. But having had a strict Victorian upbringing himself, he now inclined to something similar for his own children. Reserved and distant, he was at his most relaxed on Saturdays, when he permitted himself his weekly pint of beer at lunch. Even then, he could never have been called warm or playful, and when he tried to be friendly, he did not communicate well. Fortunately, Mew was the reverse: a highly affectionate mother.

Periodically there were weekend trips to relations, such as Grandfather Hildred at Ponsbourne Park. These trips were exciting for their glimpse of a lifestyle of a different order. The ritual with the servants at Ponsbourne, especially, made an impression on Ron, where there were ten gardeners and twenty indoor servants. At prayers, every morning, everyone assembled in the hall and a harmonium was played to accompany hymns. On departure the family would visit the servants' dining room and solemnly shake hands with everyone, saying: 'Thank you for all you've done for us.' Less often, the family would visit Great Uncle Jack at Easneye.

In the summer there were tennis parties. Despite being lame, Murray remained a dangerous opponent, a trait inherited by Jean. There were also seaside holidays: at first to Littlehampton, near Bognor, staying in lodgings with Miss Evors; later, to Woolacombe in Devon, where there was surfing; to Port Eynon in South Wales, usually with Uncle Godfrey's children, Joanna and Christopher (four years and six years younger than Ron respectively) and Alfred's son, Lionel; and to Bude, in Cornwall.

The family photograph albums vividly recreate the period: stiffly formal images, the women in elaborate dresses and hats, Murray and the men with close-cropped hair, suits, collars and ties, despite the heat. Murray, especially, cuts a severe figure. Still sporting his clipped, military moustache which he had grown during the war, it seems to say: 'Keep your distance.'[15] The photographs clearly depict, for those who encountered Ron later in life, one of his most characteristic expressions: a quizzical wrinkling of the nose and narrowing of the eyes with the mouth slightly open, as most people appear when about to sneeze. It was firmly in place by the age of three.

*

15 Moustaches were a military fashion, and many well-known moustaches of the period were hangovers from the war. Harold Macmillan first grew his trademark moustache in 1915. His brother officer, Osbert Lancaster, was ordered by his Colonel to grow a moustache – to which he responded: 'What colour, sir?'

Aged seven, Woolacombe, 1930

By the late Twenties, Murray Buxton might have congratulated himself on making a success of his new career. From a standing start, knowing nothing about engineering and without company experience, as managing director he had steered H. Young & Company through a potentially disastrous postwar Depression, winning some prestigious contracts in the process. Young's order book was, if not full, at least doing fine, and the future looked promising. Perhaps this was the reason why the other directors chose this moment to drop their bombshell. They wanted out. They wished to sell their shares.

It was a difficult moment. Murray had very little money himself, so buying out the other directors without a loan was impossible. Should he borrow the money? Yes, things seemed to be going well enough, but Murray knew he was still inexperienced. By 1928 he was still only thirty-nine. Was the company sustainable? What had already become abundantly clear was that structural steel was a highly fickle business. The industrial and commercial building trades were at the mercy of the economy, utterly dependent on public confidence: so much so that it was no accident that most structural steel companies were not listed on the Stock Exchange. They were not reliable enough. They tended, instead, to be family-run concerns which, to survive and prosper, depended on a judicious balance of engineering versatility allied to ruthless accounting. Many succumbed because they fell down in one of these areas.

There were other factors to consider, too. Jean was seven and Ron was five. Both would be going away to school shortly. There would be school fees to pay. Was it responsible for Murray to saddle himself with a large loan?

On the other hand, it was a huge opportunity. Yes, it might require specialised skills, but if anyone had those, Murray did – his first six years at H. Young & Company proved it. He decided it was worth the risk. He went to see his cousin, Robin Barclay, a senior director and scion of Barclays Bank. He secured a loan and bought out the other directors.

As 1928 became 1929, and the New Line Cinema opened, to great acclaim, it seemed the right decision. There was optimism in the air. The big Bentleys won at Le Mans. Britain won the Schneider Trophy air race. New steel football stands were being commissioned for the outskirts of many regional cities. Directly alongside the Nine Elms works in Battersea, the adjacent site was being cleared for a vast new power station. Giles Gilbert Scott's edifice would be the largest brick-built structure in Europe and the biggest power station in the world. Yes, everything seemed to be going well. One of the biggest musical hits of the year would be Leo Reisman's 'Happy Days Are Here Again'.

Alas, the happy days were not here for long. On 24 October 1929, Wall Street crashed.

5
Multum in Parvo

IF THE ECONOMIC outlook looked black, from the children's perspective something far worse loomed: boarding school. The year Wall Street crashed, 1929, Jean finished at Kipington and was dispatched to Belstead in Suffolk. A couple of years later Ron, too, was wrenched from the cosy embrace of Miss Usher and the happy contentment of Britain's Lodge. He was sent to Hawtreys, on the north-east coast of Kent.

Hawtreys was in Westgate-on-Sea, a grim town perched on the chalk cliffs above the Thames Estuary a few miles west of Margate, on the peninsular known as the Isle of Thanet. It was a bleak, unprepossessing place of gloomy housing estates and concrete bus stops, damp and windswept, surrounded by cabbage fields, looking out over the grey North Sea. When the railways arrived, Victorian entrepreneurs had tried to launch the town as a seaside resort serving London, but without success. By the 1880s most of the proprietors were bankrupt, so property was available cheap. The result was that the town began to attract schools. Low rents, fresh air plus a railway station presented an irresistible combination. School after school opened, until at one point there were twenty. Of these, many struggled with few pupils before closing. Of the survivors, the largest was Streete Court, opened in 1894 by John Vine Milne, father of A. A. Milne. The most successful of the rest were Wellington House – not to be confused with, a mile or two along the coast, Wellesley House – and St Michael's, which was soon after re-christened Hawtreys.

St Michael's had opened on 29 September – St Michael's Day – 1869, in Slough. The Reverend John Hawtrey, an Eton housemaster and Old Etonian, with Eton's permission, removed the lowest two years of the school (which then took pupils from the age of eight) to buildings in neighbouring Slough where the new institution's main purpose became the preparation of pupils for Eton. St Michael's was amongst the first of a number of 'preparatory schools' dedicated to supplying the top public schools, many of which appeared around this time. It quickly became known as *the* feeder school for Eton.

John Hawtrey's son Edward removed the school to Westgate-on-Sea early in 1883 and when he died (by which time Old Boys included the architect Detmar Blow, the Prime Minister Stanley Baldwin, Field Marshal Lord Alexander, W. Somerset Maugham, and the artist and stage designer Oliver Messel) the name of the school was changed to Hawtrey's [fairly soon dropping the apostrophe – hence Hawtreys throughout this text].[16] Here, in September 1931, for the Michaelmas term, Ron arrived to begin his formal education.

Ron at Hawtreys

The school was still owned by the eighty-year-old widow of Edward Hawtrey, one of whose daughters had married the present headmaster, Frank Cautley, an ex-county and England cricketer. There were around eighty boys, housed in, according to one Old Boy's account, 'a hideous collection of red brick villas' on both sides of the Margate-Wesgate road, connected by a gas-lit subterranean tunnel.

With the emphasis firmly on discipline and sport, the school was old-fashioned and tough even by the Victorian standards prevailing in English prep schools at the time. Compounding compulsory games was a lack of internal plumbing (boys washed in tin hip baths) and a restriction on parents being allowed to visit more than once a term, at half-term. On Sundays – mindful, perhaps, of the scheduled destination for its charges – the boys wore Eton suits, Eton collars and top hats. Bowler hats were worn for travelling on the train to and from Victoria Station. 'Symptomatic of the acceptance by parents of the school's reputation as a nursery for Eton', commented Donald P. Leinster-Mackay in *The Rise of the English Prep School* (1984), 'was an incident described by Colonel Ansell when he was due for corporal punishment:[17]

The Head Porter arrived in Mr Hawtrey's study with what looked like a birch broom: the noise it made was worse than the pain, blood drawn in a few places, but worst of all my mother found as extras on the bill: one birch, ten shillings. A very expensive besom.

Ansell left only thirteen years before Ron arrived. Another old boy's account, just a few years before Ron's time, describes arriving as a new boy:[18]

Derek always remembered that his mother kissed him and his father simply shook his hand and walked away. The boy was left alone – again.

16 The school moved at least twice more before, in the 1990s, merging with Cheam near Newbury, Berkshire.
17 Colonel Sir Mike Ansell, *Soldier On* (1973).
18 Stephen Mansfield, *Derek Prince – A Biography* (2005). Derek Prince became an international bible teacher.

Immediately, though, the new students were herded into a room to have the 'procedures' explained to them. It was a pitiful scene. Several dozen nine-year-olds, many already in tears, stood at attention while the school's policies were explained. One boy could stand it no longer and finally cried out, 'I want my mummy.' Other boys began to cry aloud in sympathy. Derek did not cry, but it was just at that moment that he felt it again: that paralyzing, gnawing loneliness, the feeling that would become his enduring memory of Hawtrey's.

And so it was for Ron. After the carefree days at Sevenoaks, being taught at home by Miss Usher, with the run of the garden and fields, Hawtreys was unutterably lonely and miserable. It was the first time Ron had been away from home and he hated it and felt desperately homesick.

*

Things at home, however, were not so rosy as Ron may have remembered. Following the Wall Street Crash, the market for structural steel collapsed. H. Young & Company faced the second disastrous slump within ten years. Having just borrowed heavily to buy out the rest of the board, one of Murray's first tasks, in order to save the company, was the unpleasant one of laying off most of the workforce. Many had been there for decades. Just twelve remained at Thornycroft House in Smith Square, with a similarly skeleton staff across the river at the Nine Elms works. To make matters worse, Muriel's coughing fits and chest were worsening.

The one gleam of hope, from the company's standpoint, was that structural steel was, finally, catching on. Two new office developments in London, one either side of the Thames, significantly aided this process, advertising the astonishing speed with which a steel frame enabled new buildings to go up: one was the Unilever Building on the north embankment, the other the Shell Building on the south. Both these structures were erected in less than five months.

Across the Atlantic, simultaneously, the Empire State Building, 1,454 feet high, the tallest building in the world and one of the largest constructions ever undertaken, with 102 storeys and 50,000 tons of steel in its frame, was erected in just six months. Newsreels in the cinema were full of its lightning progress, with breathtaking, vertigo-inducing images of steel stanchions so high they were above the clouds, being bolted together by fearless, gravity-defying Mohawk Indians working without scaffolding or safety harnesses. It was the supreme advertisement for the wonder, glamour and modernity of the building industry's new super-material.

And it worked. By the end of 1931, H. Young & Company had won two high-profile commissions. The first was for the Gaumont Palace cinema in

LEFT: The Hammersmith Apollo; RIGHT: Shepherd's Bush Film Studios, 1931

Hammersmith, an order for over 1,200 tonnes (today's Hammersmith Apollo). Then another order arrived, for 1,200 tonnes, to erect the Shepherd's Bush film studios at Lime Grove. On its sound stages Alfred Hitchcock would soon make *The Man Who Knew Too Much* (1934), *The Thirty-Nine Steps* (1935) and *The Lady Vanishes* (1938). These, in time, would be followed by hundreds of other film and television productions, including, in 1963, the first series of *Doctor Who*.

Another prestigious commission followed shortly after, for the rebuilding of a Chelsea department store. This would prove highly significant. The store, founded in the nineteenth century by a Welsh draper called Peter Jones, had, on his death in 1905, been bought by John Lewis. Now Lewis's enlightened son, Spedan, having converted the company into a giant partnership involving every member of its staff, turned his innovative mind to the architecture of his flagship store. Hitherto, new London department stores, even if they employed structural steel frames, stuck religiously to a conventional stone or brick façade. Most ended up resembling vast country houses like Longleat, and were freighted with imperial symbolism.

Now Spedan Lewis, working with the architects Slater, Crabtree and Moberly, broke decisively from this convention by using the steel frame to do something no other British building had done before; something only possible *because* of its steel frame. They dispensed with masonry walls entirely, replacing them with – glass. The island site for the new Peter Jones building was awkwardly-shaped, abutting the west side of Sloane Square. The amalgam of previous buildings was replaced with a single unified structure with a snaking glass façade which smoothly and exactly followed the site's footprint. The building would not only rely completely for its structural strength on H. Young & Company's steel frame; it would flaunt the fact. Its walls would not only be non-supporting, they would *hang* from the frame, like curtains. The new Peter Jones would be the first 'curtain-walled' glass building in Britain.

It was revolutionary. And as the precursor of every steel-and-glass office

The King's Road: crowds wave as the just-crowned King George VI passes H. Young &
Company's partially-erected steel frame for the new Peter Jones building.

block that would soon follow, in every town and city in the country, it was a
cultural landmark. Clearing of the site began in 1932, and by Coronation
Day, 12 May 1937, the steel frame was almost complete. A rare photograph
from the Young's archives shows the just-crowned King, George VI
(following Edward's abdication in favour of Mrs Simpson) sweeping out of
Sloane Square and up the King's Road on his journey from Buckingham
Palace to Windsor, passing the partially erected steel frame as the crowds
cheer and wave.

Peter Jones's sleek, futuristic glass shape seemed to epitomise the machine-
made future. As one of the defining aesthetic features of Modernism was this
impression of being machine-made, the Peter Jones building became a torch-
bearer for the movement.

Yet, in truth, H. Young & Company's steel skeleton was anything but
machine-made. Every beam and girder was laboriously hand-crafted in a
process that had more in common with Victorian boiler-plate-making and the
Steam Age than some nebulous Machine Age.

Young's work progressed as follows. First, technical engineering drawings

Britain's first curtain-walled glass building, 1938: Peter Jones, a glimpse of the future compared to the antiquated cars around it.

had to be prepared for every part. Once completed and checked, these blueprints would be sent down to the template shop where exact templates would be prepared. Materials would then be selected from the stockyard, a place stacked with raw mild steel in girders, sheet and plate from steel mills in Newcastle, Scunthorpe and the north-east, arriving by rail or sea followed by Thames barge. These materials would then be cut, sheared, punched and drilled, using hand-operated heavy machinery, then riveted or welded according to the templates. For joining steel, the rivet was still king. Although welding (using oxygen and acetylene gas) had been invented around the turn of the century, with electric arc-welding soon after (the *Titanic*, completed in 1912, was one of the first welded steel ship's hulls), structural steel for buildings, with all its constituent beams, brackets and fittings, still tended to be riveted. Every individual girder, however simple, required dozens of rivets. Once completed, checked and painted, the order was delivered to the site where it was assembled like Meccano. Accordingly, it was hardly surprising that John McAslan, architect of Peter Jones's 2004 revamp, compared Crabtree's 1930 design, with its heavy steel frame, to that of a well-worn ferry of the period.

Somehow, though, the laborious work that had gone into its skeleton was forgotten when viewing the finished building. It was an instant triumph. Alongside its Victorian and Edwardian neighbours, and the cars with their running boards parked in Sloane Square, the new Peter Jones looked other-worldly in its modernity. Its interior was light, airy and open-plan. Its

[58]

significance, in the history of both architecture and structural engineering, was officially recognised in 1969 when it was listed Grade II*.

*

For Ron, meanwhile, life at Hawtreys remained anything but futuristic. His first three years were characterised by unremitting misery and homesickness, not assisted by the action of Holmes, his father's confidential male secretary, whose task it was at the start of each term to drop him at Victoria Station to be met, along with other boys, by the headmaster. Holmes seemed to take a sadistic pleasure, when saying goodbye, in squeezing Ron's hand so hard it made him cry; a dreaded ritual at the end of a dreaded journey. 'My poor hand' Ron would later say, in a rare display of emotion.

Once back at the school, things were little better, though they were less bad for Ron than for many. The brutal regime run by Frank Cautley was infinitely worse for those who weren't bright or good at sport. Fortunately for Ron, it quickly emerged that he was extremely bright, and the teaching, undeniably, was good. He also had his moments at sport. Summer terms were least bad. Cricket, given he was an ex-county player, was the focus of Cautley's enthusiasm, and Ron was in the school eleven. Besides, fine weather found a seaside resort, however lapsed, at its best.

Apart from this, Ron's prep school life offered two other sources of pleasure. One was that every pupil was allowed his own garden. The other – a particular solace through the winter – was the piano. Ron had started lessons when he arrived and was showing considerable promise. Musical talent ran in his mother's family: Great-Uncle Wilson was, it may be remembered, playing chords on the family piano before the age of three, and spent his twenties accompanying Dwight Moodie at his evangelical rallies before he founded the Church Army. Grandfather Hildred and Aunt Cecily were also accomplished pianists.

There were, however, disturbing changes at home. At the end of his first year at Hawtreys, in 1932, there was a drama involving Grandfather Hildred. By now Hildred was eighty, widowed, and being looked after at Ponsbourne Park by Aunt Cicely, his widowed youngest daughter. In an appropriately Agatha Christie turn, his butler, after being served notice, mounted a revenge arson attack, arguably an attempt on Sir Hildred's life, by setting fire to the house.

The attempt was foiled, but Hildred's passion for Ponsbourne was over. His only son, Hanbury, had been killed in the war, lost flying over the Western Front. As a result, there was no male heir to inherit the place and the baronetcy, just his four daughters. His family seat, of which, those fifteen years earlier, he had so proudly been created baronet, meant little or nothing now. It was, too, a vast place for just him and Aunt Cicely. She persuaded him

[59]

to sell so that they could move somewhere smaller.[19] The estate, one of the fixtures of Ron's childhood, was put on the market, and in due course Sir Hildred and Cicely moved to a new, smaller house called Bishop's Down Grange near Tunbridge Wells, then a favoured town for the retired looking to settle.

Muriel's health, too, was deteriorating. Her coughing fits came more frequently and her chest infections lasted longer. Doctors suggested that a contributory factor might be the heavy Wealden clay on which Sevenoaks sat, which meant the air was perpetually damp. The Buxtons should consider moving somewhere drier.

Murray and Muriel decided to take this advice, and in the process move nearer to London. Murray, as his work schedule became ever tighter, was frustrated at wasting more than two hours each day commuting.

Muriel undertook the house-hunting with her father, Hildred. In due course, she found somewhere suitable near Woking, Surrey. It lay on the Bagshot Sands, so promised drier air, while its proximity to Waterloo meant Murray's daily commute would be cut almost in half. When he saw that his daughter liked it, Sir Hildred – always generous, and with cash to spare following the sale of Ponsbourne Park – wrote out a cheque for the asking price of £6,000. In 1935 the family moved.

Holywell, built in 1906, had a friendly, rustic cosiness. Brick, with tall chimneys, tile-hung walls, white casement windows and bow windows beneath protruding gables, it had something of Lutyens and the Arts-and-Crafts about it. With its clipped yew hedges, rose-clad trellises and large (four-and-a-half acre) garden with wonderful views towards the Hog's Back, it was not without charm. But for Ronald and Jean, it was a retrograde step. Unlike Kent, Surrey was built up. There were no fields and woods to explore. The nearest thing to real countryside was the golf club.

Meanwhile, the very innocence and English charm that Holywell so determinedly sought to evoke, of peace and rural tranquillity, was beginning to look distinctly under threat. Mainland Europe was coming to terms with an unwelcome new boisterousness from one of its largest member countries. In Germany, the death of Hindenburg, in August 1934, had cleared away the last remaining hurdle to total power for Adolf Hitler, who now decreed that the title of President would henceforward be abolished. As Germany's head of

19 As a result of the sale of Ponsbourne, and the fact that two of Muriel's sisters died *d.s.p.* (without children), most of Ron's greatest material benefits (in the form of portraits, furniture and china) came from the Carliles. Five years after selling Ponsbourne, Hildred bought a yacht, the steam-powered *Andrea*. A considerable yachtsman and member of the Royal Yacht Squadron, Hildred had won numerous prizes at Cowes (including a 100-piece Crown Derby dinner service). *Andrea*, with her crew of twenty, made many journeys, including crossing the Atlantic. After owning her for just a year, however, in 1938, Hildred suffered a massive stroke leaving him unable to speak, so *Andrea* was sold.

'Wonderful views towards the Hog's Back' – Holywell House, Woking, 1935

state, he declared, he would be known as Fuehrer and Reich Chancellor. In March 1936, with the occupation of the Rhineland, the papers were full of 'The German Threat'. Weekly cinema newsreels showed startling footage of massed rallies of uniformed soldiers marching like automatons beneath swastika banners and floodlights, with, at the centre, the diminutive, shouting Austrian dictator. His long face, with its cow's lick of hair and toothbrush moustache, was becoming disagreeably familiar.

*

For the Buxtons, once the upheaval of the move was over, a more settled period began. The change from clay to better-drained Surrey sand really did seem to improve Muriel's health. Murray bought a neighbouring cottage so that Ellis the gardener and his wife could accompany them. Mrs Ellis did the cleaning. As for Murray, by the mid-Thirties, despite the economic situation, he was again hitting his stride.

Competition from other structural steel contractors, especially in London and the Midlands, was his chief bane. The same companies jostled for almost every tender in the London area: chiefly Dorman Long and Powers and Deane Ransomes. In Birmingham there was Marshall and Snelgrove. Once again, however, Murray's natural business acumen asserted itself. In a frenetic burst of activity, he formed an alliance with structural steel companies in Manchester and the West Midlands, so that if a contract that was too big for

Young's to handle alone came up, it could rapidly be subcontracted out. And big contracts, increasingly, did come up.

In the mid-1930s, H. Young & Company opened regional offices in Exeter, Coventry and Guildford. In 1935 Murray struck a deal with arch-rival Powers and Deane Ransomes, whereby the two companies took shares in each other, bringing in more business. In the process, Sir John Powers's son, Eldon, and Murray became friends.

By this time the company was completely outgrowing the Nine Elms works in Battersea. The Powers family owned a site at Lea Bridge, Leyton, in the Hackney Marshes of north-east London, just off the main route out of London heading east. In 1936 they sold this to Young for £15,000. The sale would have a considerable bearing on the future of the now twelve–year-old Ron.

The new Lea Bridge works, Leyton, 1936

In 1937 Murray founded the Durham Steel Works on the Team Valley Estate in Gateshead. Because it promised jobs in a region of high unemployment – the previous October had seen the Jarrow March, when 200 protesters marched from the neighbouring town of Jarrow all the way to Westminster to highlight the 68% unemployment in the area – he was able to attract substantial government grants. So now the company had works in Battersea, alongside the new power station, in Leyton, and in Durham.

To this tally, during these hectic interwar years, another of Murray's deals needs to be added. Shortly after getting married, Murray's father-in-law Hildred, a freemason, introduced him to No. 5 Lodge. Two centuries old, it consisted chiefly of London professionals – distinguished doctors, surgeons, lawyers and architects. Visiting Jersey on a contract, and dropping into the masonic lodge in St Helier, Murray met the Provincial Grand Master, a lawyer called Richardson, who urged him to start a steel company on the island, partly for the tax advantages, but also because there was much potential work. The result, in 1935, was the Jersey Steel Company. After slow beginnings, interrupted by the war, the company would thrive. The Richardsons became friends and remained so for three generations.

By the Coronation, in the summer of 1937, Murray Buxton headed a company that was fabricating more than 3,000 tonnes of steel annually. The two London works employed over 100 men. More than sixty draughtsmen worked at the Pimlico Head Office, which had expanded to a full floor of Thorneycroft House. Steel fabrication was now just a part of the service H. Young & Company offered, which included providing advice, design and assembly on site. As governing director, Murray's schedule included opening new offices, controlling contracts, checking drawings, supervising fabrication, visiting sites, while always liaising closely with the accounts department. ('Old Powell', the company secretary, was good at watching the interests of the family, to make sure the Powers family did not try to wrest control.)

The company was run on strictly hierarchical lines. Ordinary employees had little insight into areas of the company beyond their immediate arena, whether or not they had served for twenty years or more. Photographs from contemporary company leaflets hint at the discipline, deferential respect and manners. One, of the bare-walled drawing office, shows the waistcoated draftsmen perched at their drawing boards on high wooden stools. The studious silence is almost palpable.

Another document in the archives offers a glimpse into management techniques of the day. In the contemporary equivalent of a corporate away-day, a tradition had developed in the 1920s whereby, every October, a staff outing was organised for the twenty-five most senior managers. The 'entertainment' comprised a five-mile staff walk to Oxshott Heath and back from The Bear at Esher. As it was intended to be a race, however, not an idle stroll, entrants were formally handicapped according to their previous year's performance. After the race, there was a celebration dinner, the printed menu card spiced with structural steel in-jokes:

There were toasts ('His Majesty the King', 'The Chairman', 'The Firm') followed by presentation of a cup to the winner, speeches, and a musical programme, mainly by employees, finishing with everyone singing round the piano.

THICK, bitumastic
OXTAIL SOUP
slenderness ratio over 200'

FRIED FILLET OF SOLE
machined top and bottom with TARTARE SAUCE welded on

ROAST BEEF with YORKSHIRE PUDD. *wired on*

or

ROAST CHICKEN
limb small, painted one coat BREAD SAUCE

BAKED and BOILED POTATOES, sawn to shape, not burnt

PEAS stencilled both sides

CAULIFLOWER in bloom

FRESH FRUIT SALAD in 4 ton lots

APPLE TART to template

The mounting success and reputation of the company under their dynamic governing director, combined with his inviolable integrity, meant Murray Buxton was becoming a considerable industry figure. As well as being chairman of H. Young, and Powers and Deane Ransomes, and the Horsehay Company, he was invited onto the boards of several other steel companies (including Brown Bailey's). In response, perhaps, to this increased standing, he promoted his bowler hat to an Anthony Eden-style black trilby.

To Jean, and more especially Ron, he presented a daunting role model. His Victorian views about how children should be brought up meant the children were seldom, if ever, praised or encouraged, and they never developed a remotely friendly or close relationship with their father. It may be assumed that, by the time he was twelve, Ron regarded his rarely-seen, distant, reserved, godly, authoritarian father with appropriate awe.

*

However much he disliked Hawtreys, Ron was thriving there. By his last year, 1936, despite being smaller than most of his contemporaries, Ron was consistently near the top of the school academically, and performing well on the playing field. On the piano he could play 'Für Elise' and other

Murray Buxton

straightforward pieces. Critically, he was liked by Frank Cautley, who repaid his achievements by making him head boy.

For the next step of his education, Ron's name was down for Harrow. That was where his grandfather Barclay had been, and Ron had been guaranteed a place. He was also down for Eton. The chance of a place at Eton – it went without saying, according to Ron – was better than the guarantee of a place at Harrow, so during the Christmas term at the start of his final year, he attended Eton for interviews. Following this, he was placed on the house list of a housemaster called Mr Pole. (Getting accepted onto a house list, as opposed to applying via the collecting pool of the General List, was an important step to admission.) Dramatic news arrived, however, shortly after his visit. Mr Pole had been killed, along with three other Eton beaks, in a freak mountaineering accident in the Alps. With Pole's entire house list washed out, it looked as if Ron would end up at Harrow, until Murray found him a place on the house list of a new, young housemaster called Dick Young, whom Murray had known at Repton.

It was still by no means a foregone conclusion that Ron would get in. A critical part of his application, in addition to passing the Common Entrance exam, was the report supplied by each boy's prep school headmaster, which

'*Multum in parvo*': head boy of Hawtreys, aged thirteen, 1936

testified to the quality of the applicant's character. Frank Cautley chose an elegant and felicitous Latin phrase to describe his small star pupil: *multum in parvo* – 'much in little'.

The school plainly agreed. During the summer of 1936, Murray Buxton received a letter informing him that Ron had been accepted into Eton.

6

'An Unusual Boy'

THE ARMSTRONG SIDDELEY would have been full to bursting for the journey to drop thirteen-year-old Ron at Eton for his first term in January 1937. As well as Mew and Murray in the front, and Ron behind, chafing awkwardly in his new school clothes – short black 'bumfreezer' jacket, waistcoat and pin-striped trousers, starched collar and studs pinching his neck – there was his trunk, crammed, as every new boy's was, with neatly folded and name-tagged clothes ticked off on endless checklists. Many of these had been collected on earlier missions to Eton outfitters for measuring and fitting. There was a padded Ottoman chest for storing games kit, a 'boot box', an easy chair. There were even curtains, as at Eton every boy, right from the start, has his own room.

In this matter of domestic accommodation, Eton differs from all other public schools. There are no dormitories. From the first day, every boy has his own private bedroom-cum-study, complete with fireplace and coal scuttle (in 1937 the houses had yet to be centrally heated). In each room was a fold-down steel bed, a desk or 'burry' and a chair. Everything else had to be supplied by the new tenant, with the result that the first day of any term at which new boys arrived (Michaelmas in the autumn and Lent in the winter) resembled a furniture-removing convention, as boys, parents and servants battled up and down staircases loaded with cargo.

Waynflete House was a large, detached Queen Anne-style red-brick building off the east side of Eton Wick Road, one of more than twenty houses that were each home to around fifty boys. These, along with 'College', where the seventy or so King's Scholars resided, made up the pastoral accommodation of the school. Here, as in the colleges of a collegiate university, boys lived, ate and did their 'extra work' (homework). His room was each boy's private sanctuary. Ludovic Kennedy, a contemporary of Ron's, describes a typical example:[20]

On the walls boys hung pictures of whatever they fancied. Thorburn's game birds were always popular, as were prints of Peter Scott's ducks; others preferred photographs culled from movie magazines of Hollywood stars like Carole Lombard, Ginger Rogers, Constance

20 *On My Way to the Club, An Autobiography*, Collins, 1989.

Bennett. Here one slept and studied and, with one or two other boys, made up a mess for daily high tea.

After Hawtreys, Eton seemed vast. Instead of 80 boys, there were over 1,200. Eton's Head Master at the time was Claude Elliott,[21] but more influential on Ron's day-to-day life were his classical tutor and his housemaster. The title alone, 'classical tutor', reflects the emphasis of the curriculum for the early years, when Latin and the classics, plus, for the brighter boys, Greek, were mandatory, plus English, French, history, maths and science.

Ron's classical tutor was Walter Hamilton, a brilliant classicist who went on to become Master in College at Eton (responsible for the King's Scholars), Headmaster of Westminster School, then Master of Magdalene College, Cambridge. He took responsibility for Ron's academic studies in his first two years. Pastoral care, meanwhile, was down to Ron's housemaster, R. A.Young, ('RAY', in Eton parlance, where houses were known not by the name of the building, but by the housemaster's initials). Dick Young was a senior housemaster of the old school: a mathematician who had kept wicket for England. Unsurprisingly, RAY was a strongly cricketing house, come the summer, when, in sporting terms, Eton divided, about equally, into those who played cricket ('dry bobs') and those that rowed ('wet bobs'). The tables in the downstairs dining room had more than their share of school cricketing trophies.

For most boys, starting at Eton was an intimidating experience. There was not only a new town with widely-dispersed school buildings to navigate, but all the rules and arcane traditions of a centuries-old institution. There was a new vocabulary to acquire – 'beak' for master, 'dame' for matron, 'half' for term, 'division' for class, and so on. After a fortnight, there was the 'colours test', in which every new boy was tested on the twenty houses' 'colours' ('RAY – green and blue quarters', for example).

For Ron, there were various additional obstacles. Because he was rated as bright, having scored highly in Common Entrance, he had been allowed to arrive a term later than most new boys. Thus, while they were already settled in and had made friends, Ron had to start afresh, a term behind. Being a later arrival also meant he was one of the most junior boys in the house, lowest in the hierarchy of fagging so continually prey for the most menial and time-consuming tasks and errands dispensed by the senior boys. Placed in high divisions, unlike the blunter minds at the bottom of the school, he also had to learn Greek, a subject which – again, unlike many – he had not studied before.

Physically, Ron was small. Boys at Eton tended to be taller than average (it

21 'A non-entity whom we never saw' – RCB.

was not unusual for eighteen-year-olds to be six foot six or more), but even by normal standards Ron was shorter than most. By a brutal school rule, until a boy was five foot four, he was not permitted to wear a tailcoat. Through no fault of their own, therefore, shorter boys were singled out not just by their size, but their uniform too. Naturally, everyone in a short 'bumfreezer' coat longed for the growth spurt – normally sometime in their first year – that would allow them to graduate to tails: a kind of visible acknowledgement of progress to adulthood. Ron did not graduate to a tailcoat for two years, well after most of his contemporaries.

He was also plagued by poor health. To anyone knowing Ron in later life this aspect of his early reports makes scarcely credible reading. There are repeated references to his lack of energy and poor general robustness. His second term he returned late after catching measles. His third, he missed more time due to appendicitis.

Notwithstanding these hurdles, Ron says he enjoyed his first term at Eton more than any other of his school career. Perhaps it was a relief to be away from Hawtreys and nearer home. His attitude, however, was regarded as suspect. In his first year reports he was repeatedly upbraided for idleness ('his written work is scandalous'), shyness ('outstandingly inconspicuous'), messiness ('he can't even fold a sheet of paper in too (sic) neatly and his handwriting is horrible') and insolence (not removing his top hat or taking his hands out of his pockets when talking to beaks).

Certainly his intellectual preferences were emerging. Mathematics he found easy, an ability perhaps inherited from his paternal grandfather. (Barclay Buxton, it may be remembered, was the first Harrovian in the school's history to win the Gold Medal for Maths twice, going on to graduate as Senior Optime in the Mathematics Tripos from his year at Trinity, Cambridge.) Ron tolerated classics, but detested Greek and French ('It has been a great and largely unsuccessful struggle to get any good and worthwhile work from him'). Eton reports, with their combination of waggish phrase-making and sly viciousness, may reflect beaks' attempts to impress each other as much as being an accurate reflection of progress; whatever their truth, it was the end-of-term exam ('trials') results which really counted. Here, from the start, Ron excelled, performing well or magnificently, bordering first class or, in the summer, first class bordering distinction.

Notwithstanding these results, Ron's manner grated enough for his house-master RAY, a mathematician, to feel it necessary to assert his loyalty. 'I find it very hard to understand why almost all the masters who have taught him have some very pertinent criticism of his attitude – we have had passive, off-hand, casual, mouse-like, passive resistance, and now a host of other things ... I shall soon feel that I am about the only one who takes a non-gloomy view of his character and qualities, and that may be the reason why he works well and cheerily during the four hours he comes to me.' Unsurprisingly, to Ron, RAY was wonderful.

Nevertheless, one imagines Murray Buxton going through his son's reports, making the careful pencil notes on Holywell writing paper that still remain with some of them, summarising the salient points ('RJB considers he has greatly improved ... no manners ... must try to please and be polite to others ... very stubborn and strongwilled ... thinks the only thing that matters is himself ...'), before asking his son in to discuss them.

In 1938, his second year, Ron took up the organ. His piano lessons had continued since Hawtreys, and he was inspired to take the step by the College Chapel organist, Dr – later Sir – Henry Ley, an ex-professor at the Royal College of Music whose playing at morning service impressed Ron greatly. Usually boys were not allowed to play the vast Hill organ in College Chapel, but Ley liked and rated Ron, so gave him a try. Ley affirmed what Ron already knew, 'If you want to learn the organ, first learn the piano.' Ron's lessons continued in Lower Chapel, with Ley's assistant, Percy Higgs, where he was photographed.

Playing Lower Chapel Organ, 1938

His enthusiasm bemused RAY. 'I shall always remember him as the first boy to ask leave ... to examine the organ in a church in Slough. I can not begin to compete with him in this branch of knowledge, but I am pleased to have a House with such a wide variety of tastes.'

Around this time Ron also played the piano for an improvised jazz band. The trumpeter, a couple of years older and son of one of the housemasters, was Humphrey Lyttelton. Masters at the Music Schools would bang on the doors during their jamming sessions and bellow: 'Stop that noise.'

By his third year, bumfreezer and fagging behind him, Ron was coming out of himself. He had made friends he would keep for the rest of his life: Quintin Curzon (whose room on the top floor of the house became a regular meeting place), Michael Cooper ('inherited the best beat on the Wye, and would shout at us when we canoed down it'), Andrew Caldecott and Alan Ball (both, later, directors of Lonrho). Two names with whom he would later sit in the Commons were James Ramsden and Bill Brewis, though his relationship with the latter had unpromising beginnings. In his second summer, while practising his batting in the nets, a fast ball struck Ron's foot. Swearing in anguish, he found himself briskly reported to Dick Young, whose response was: 'You can't talk like that. You'll have to be beaten.' In those days, it was the house captain's task to execute disciplinary sentences dispensed by the house master, so the task fell to Bill Brewis.

Ron's exam results continued to be exceptional or near-exceptional, and with more freedom to choose how to spend his free time, apart from music, his main extra-curricular activity became the School of Mechanics. There he found time to make what RAY called 'the attractive-looking boat which he took away behind your car'. 'He has looked very much fitter,' his house master added, 'with more colour in his cheeks, and more signs of cheerfulness.' 'His capable brain and attractive character ought to be appreciated by all who meet him' reported his classical tutor George Tait. 'The only time I got angry with him was when he took away his boat without showing it to me.'

Tails at last: 'RAY' house photograph 1939

Such aptitude and enthusiasm for subjects impinging directly on his father's business can only have delighted Murray, however hard he found it to show it. During the school holidays, Murray took Ron to visit H. Young & Company sites, so he could see what the company did and how it worked. Later, Murray got an old turner called Todd to teach Ron how to use a lathe, and he bought Ron a treddle-operated machine. Ron, however, finding he was still not strong enough to work the treddle effectively, bought an electric motor and fitted it instead. Oddly, this demonstration of initiative and resourcefulness, when discovered, only had the effect of angering Murray. So, while his father may have been clear in his mind that a suitable heir for the family engineering business was moulding itself, Ron remained less certain. He would make up his mind in due course.

*

By the time the boys returned for the Michaelmas half 1939, Hitler had invaded Poland and Britain was at war. Ron was now just sixteen, starting in the fifth form. World events had been creeping up on the cloistered world of Eton. The evacuation of 1.5 million children from Central London was almost complete. Air raid shelters had been dug in the gardens of each of the boys' houses. Staff had begun to be called up, or leave of their own accord to do so, and khaki uniforms had become a common sight. Every household had been issued with a hand-operated stirrup-pump and long-handled shovel to deal with incendiary bombs. (Memories of the Spanish Civil War and Guernica were still fresh.)

With war declared, no one knew what to expect. The government had prepared for 100,000 casualties during the first few weeks. Hospitals had been cleared, cardboard coffins prepared, lime pits dug for the dead. But all that happened was … nothing. No air raids, no invasion, no 'Blitzkrieg', in this, the phase that would become known as the 'Phoney War'. Apart from all the excitement – relief, almost – of finally being at war, the only bombardment was with new regulations. A national register was being completed for identity cards to be issued by the end of October.

Blackout regulations arrived: going out on cloudy or moonless nights after 'lock up' at 6.15, as the days shortened, was to stumble into a world of inky blackness not seen since primeval times. Vehicles with dimmed-out headlights had to be avoided. Houses and shops in the High Street painted the edges of their windows black, as even the slightest chink of light prompted heavy fines.

At home, Murray and Mew had to take in evacuees at Holywell. As it happened, this did not change things much, as they had already been putting up a family of German Jewish refugees. The company, on Murray's direction, had built a steel-framed underground shelter in the garden.

For Etonians, the most significant effect of the war was, following the sounding of air raid sirens, firewatching duty. This took place from the roof of New Schools, a two-storey range of Victorian classrooms near the centre of the school. Almost the sole wartime concession to daily life was that boys no longer had to carry a top hat. This was partly due to wartime shortages, but it was a tradition that was never revived. Instead, boys carried gas masks in tins.

Eton took its war role seriously, as befits a school that had earned nearly twice as many Victoria Crosses as any other. Joining the Combined Cadets Force or Corps became mandatory, and everyone knew they would be going straight into one of the services on leaving. Captain Cave came down from the Rifle Brigade (later the Royal Greenjackets) on a recruiting mission and Ron and many others duly signed up – though as it happened, when the time came, Ron's services would be mandated elsewhere.

Meanwhile, from his own perspective as a sixteen-year-old, life was looking up. The last term of 1939 saw Ron win a prize for organ playing, while collecting his now standard set of reports – outstanding in the subjects he liked, the reverse in those he did not. This situation was now accepted almost with equanimity by his housemaster: 'He is an unusual boy, who has unexpected things said about him, and it would be surprising if he were to receive a uniform set of reports.' Ron acquired some sporting significance as a footballer as captain of the 3rd Sine (the house football league) as well as, his housemaster noted, an affectionate nickname: 'I will leave him to tell you the nickname and the reason for it' wrote RAY tantalisingly in his report. Sadly, Ron cannot remember it.

A seated portrait of Ron taken around this time by the school photographers, Hills and Saunders, wearing the informal Eton alternative to school dress known as 'standard change' (tweed coat and tie, flannel trousers) is revealing. Compared to portraits before, it depicts a young man of undoubted confidence, head cocked quizzically; someone who plainly has an idea of himself and where he is going. Ron was going to need this growing sense of himself for what lay ahead.

*

Christmas 1939 was the first war-time Christmas since 1917. January brought rationing of butter, sugar, bacon and ham, and Ron returned to school for the Lent half to a new housemaster, Leslie Jacques (LHJ) and many further depletions to the academic staff. By the time the school broke up for the Easter holidays, and Ron headed back to Holywell, rationing had extended to meat and the first British civilian had died in an air raid in Scotland. Easter was early that year, on 24 March, and two weeks later, having overrun Denmark with hardly a shot fired, Hitler began a full-scale invasion of Norway. As the school reassembled for the summer term, with the action moving inexorably closer, one can only imagine the buzz. For an institution of boys just entering adulthood, such times could hardly have been more exciting. Britain might be facing her greatest crisis since the Spanish Armada – but at least there was plenty to talk about.

Most boys took a newspaper and, strictly contrary to school rules, many also kept radios. Ron was among them, the difference between himself and most others was that he had made his radio himself. He kept it hidden in his chimney. When this was revealed by a search, after having denied such a thing to his housemaster, he was, once again, caned by the house captain.

Each month seemed to bring a redrawing of the map of Europe, and fortunately, in the academic staff, there were informed minds to explain and discuss the developments. Almost everyone had at least one close relation or family friend serving, or who had joined the British Expeditionary Force so recently despatched to France. Rarely had European history's events had such extraordinary immediacy.

The 'Fourth of June' holiday – Eton's summer sports day that traditionally began the summer half-term – was a muted affair. Usually the day pivoted around elaborate picnics with family and friends on Eton's largest playing field, Agar's Plough. But news of the desperate retreat of the British Expeditionary Force in France was in everyone's minds, notwithstanding reports filtering through of a miraculous rescue from Dunkirk taking place even as the picnic rugs were being spread. With so many brothers and cousins enlisted and absent, and Britain's future so uncertain, celebration seemed inappropriate. That evening, Churchill made his 'We shall fight on the beaches' speech. A fortnight later, the papers and cinema newsreels brought images of German troops parading up the Champs Elysées to the Arc de Triomphe in Paris. The last capital city before London had fallen. The only possible cause for celebration, for the Buxtons, at least, was that Murray had just been elected President of the Institute of Structural Engineers – a singular honour, and for someone who had not studied engineering at university, a remarkable one.

As the summer half resumed, Ron's increasingly charming school life in the sunshine belied events unfolding across the Channel. He enjoyed cricketing success in his house XI ('an enterprising though unorthodox cricketer' – LHJ) and completed the term with a near-distinction in trials.

Three weeks before the school broke up for the long summer holidays, Churchill broadcast his 'Finest Hour' speech. 'The Battle of France is over', his determined, steely voice informed the nation. 'I expect that the Battle of Britain is about to begin.'

Would there be a next term? Would the Germans have invaded and Britain be under Nazi occupation? Amongst endless rumours circulating was one that Eton might transfer overseas, possibly to Canada, for the duration. This particular rumour became so persistent, and prompted so many inquiries, that every pupil's summer school reports included a letter from the Head Master.

> The arguments against moving Eton to Canada or elsewhere are so weighty that we have never had any intention of taking such a step, and we have in fact done all in our power to discourage individual parents from removing their sons either overseas or to places supposedly safer than in these islands.

The letter went on, in a distinctly admonitory tone, to point out that Eton was no more likely to be bombed than any district in the greater part of England and Wales, 'and is very well provided with Air Raid Shelters and A.R.P. Services.' It stated firmly that, as a 'Reception Area' for evacuated children from Central London, the effect would be disastrous 'if the impression gained ground that a district considered suitable for the children of the poorer classes is considered unsuitable for the children of the well-to-do'. While the letter stopped just short of accusing anyone who had inquired about Eton's wartime arrangements of being a coward, it left no doubt about its own position. 'It is difficult to conceive anything more damaging to civilian morale in this country than the removal of Eton overseas.'

That famously balmy summer, Ron embarked on a plan hatched with a friend a few weeks earlier. He and Jonny Vane[22] set off on bicycles up the Great North Road to Yorkshire, to Raby Castle where Jonny lived. The Great North Road, in those pre-motorway days, was the main arterial connection between north and south. Yet they found this normally congested thoroughfare almost deserted. Petrol rationing, plus fears of invasion in the south, meant no one was travelling. The only traffic they encountered for three days was the odd Army truck. North of York, Ron wheeled off to Grimston Manor, near the village of Gilling in East Yorkshire, where his indomitable Aunt Dreda (Mew's sister) lived. There he stayed for the summer, as the Battle of Britain raged down south, helping bring Uncle Tom's harvest in.

*

22 Now Lord Barnard.

By the time the boys returned for the Michaelmas half 1940, in the second week of September (a few weeks after Ron's seventeenth birthday), the Battle of Britain was almost over. Hitler's tactics seemed to have changed. Having failed to destroy the RAF or launch an invasion over the summer, he began to bomb London. On 7 September, in the late afternoon, wave after wave of bombers attacked the East End. The flashes in the sky and the distant crump and thump of high explosive could be seen and heard in Eton. Next day the papers reported that more than 300 enemy aircraft had been involved. More than 400 had been killed, another 1,600 severely injured. It was the overture to the Blitz.

Over the following weeks, the nights rumbled to the drone of aircraft engines, heralded by the rising and falling whine of air raid sirens and soon followed by the thumping of ack-ack batteries. Not that being woken by such events was especially unwelcome; for interrupted nights meant Early School (the pre-breakfast lesson at 7.30 a.m.) was cancelled. From their windows boys could watch the dark skies being carved by searchlight beams in the knowledge that, well clear of London, bombs were unlikely to fall on the school. Any planes overhead were either wildly off-course or heading home. As a concession to any danger, however, boys were moved off the top floors of houses.

As it transpired, only two bombs fell on the school over the duration, both on the night of 4 December 1940. One, a timed high-explosive bomb landed in Upper School, one of the school's oldest buildings, on the east side of the quadrangle adjoining College Chapel. The unexploded device was sandbagged and the area cordoned off, but next day it exploded, blowing in the medieval windows of the Chapel. All the glass shattered except the window above the organ. Morning prayers the following day went ahead as usual – icy, as the bitter December air howled through the shards of glass still held by the empty stone mullions. The other bomb, also high-explosive, demolished the house occupied by Ron's friend, Dr Ley. His precious piano was amongst the wreckage that lay smashed in the front garden – but the great man was unhurt.

Ron remembers the bombs. The windows of College Chapel were blanked off for the rest of his time at school, and, in due course, the timber roof was replaced by the stone-vaulted one there today. But by the time the bombs dropped and these events took place, Ron had other matters on his mind.

One full-moon night as the leaves had begun to fall, a Monday in mid-October, the familiar sirens filled the cool night air, soon followed by the frenetic roar of the ack-ack barrages. Those on fire duty could see the bombs falling, followed by the yellow stabs of the incendiaries. The following day, copies of *The Times* reported the night's activities as 'the most severe since the raids started'.

There were moments when the whistle of bombs, some apparently of the explosive-incendiary type, punctuated the barrage every few minutes, while the sky was filled with shell-bursts and the drone of German bombers attacking from all directions.

Ron was in his room next day when there was a knock, and a boy put his head round the door saying LHJ wanted to see him downstairs in his study. Wondering vaguely what his housemaster wanted, what he had done wrong, Ron made his way to the green baize door that linked the boys' side of the house to the private side. Opening it, he knocked on LHJ's study door and the familiar voice called him in. LHJ, sitting at his desk, looked serious. He asked Ron to sit down. He was sorry, he said, but he had bad news. Ron's father, he said, had been attending a meeting with Ron's uncle Alfred at Church House, next to Westminster Abbey, the night before. There had been an air raid. It was not clear why, but neither of them had sought shelter and there had been a direct hit. He was sorry to have to tell him that his father and his uncle were dead.

*

There was a joint funeral service for Murray and Alfred before the burial at Brookwood Cemetery. (Brookwood was where their father, Barclay, was buried.) The service sheet was titled *The Two Brothers* and the graveside oration was made by Godfrey, now the sole survivor of this family of four sons. His speech was reported in *The Structural Engineer*, the journal of the Institution of Structural Engineers. Running a leader about their president of just five months, it noted how Godfrey's speech 'revealed facts of which even those of us who knew – or thought we knew – Murray Buxton very well, had been quite unaware.' These included details of his heroism and wounding during the Gallipoli campaign in the First World War and his work in establishing the institution's Benevolent Fund and Staff Pension Fund. (Various medals and diplomas still carrying his name are awarded annually by the Institute for outstanding research in structural engineering.)

The article went on to mention 'his utter disregard of danger to himself which made him decline to take what he considered unnecessary precautions'. He was serious, disciplined, godly, courageous, brilliant, generous (when his brother Godfrey had decided to pursue a life dedicated to religion, Murray stepped in to pay for the education of his children, Christopher and Joanna), diligent, a gifted businessman and irrepressible achiever. A leaflet was circulated around H. Young & Company bearing Murray Buxton's photograph and a quote from the new chairman, Harold Judd (later Controller of Salvage for the war effort): 'Of few men it could be said so truly that in his company it was almost impossible to think an unholy thought or to do an unworthy action.'

To his children, however, he remained remote and strict; someone, as Jean put it, 'easier to respect than to love'.

*

When Ron's school report for the Michaelmas half of 1940 arrived at Holywell, it was not addressed, as every previous report had been, to 'Capt M.B. Buxton'. Nor did the housemaster's letter commence with the usual, businesslike 'Dear Buxton'. Instead, it was addressed to 'Mrs M. B. Buxton', and the housemaster's covering letter attempted a slightly softer tone. 'I shall not forget Ron's courage' wrote LHJ. 'I am sure he will do all that he can for you as his father would wish.'

Muriel, once Ron returned to school and she was left alone at Holywell during term-time, decided to let the house and move in with her sister Ciceley at Bishop's Down Grange. It meant both sisters could have each other's company and share the burden of nursing their father Hildred following his stroke.

Ron left Eton at the end of the summer half 1941, having sat School Certificate exams in mathematics, physics and chemistry before specialising in Mathematics for his Cambridge Entrance. He also passed his School Certificate in the organ (for which the Westminster Abbey organist came to listen). He had applied to Trinity College, the largest and most prestigious Cambridge college, and a place with which his family had a long association. It had been attended by his father, uncle and grandfather (not to mention Newton, Rutherford and Wittgenstein). Getting in, then as now, was by no means a foregone conclusion, but with Ron's academic record his chances were always good. He was accepted, and, over the long summer vacation he moved to Cambridge lodgings to be tutored in extra mathematics for the Engineering Tripos.

If leaving school and losing your father might be regarded as two of the most significant steps to adulthood for any young man, for Ron another rite-of-passage also arrived that summer. At H. Young & Company's Lea Bridge works, a new canteen had been under construction, initiated by Murray. As it neared completion it became obvious that the building would make a fitting memorial for the company's lost chairman.

A stone lintel carved with the word 'BUXTON' was set over the new building's entrance, and Ron was asked to speak at the opening ceremony. The symbolic significance of the occasion can hardly be overstated: the young eighteen-year-old pretender, fresh from school, stepping up to the platform so recently occupied by his much-respected father. Around him, a sea of overalled and cloth-capped workers, sizing up the young man they barely know, whom they have only occasionally glimpsed visiting the company with his father, yet on whom their own futures will soon depend.

It was plainly a big moment for Ron: not only his maiden speech, but a moment, in public, to assert his new role as head of the family and heir to the family company. He had to instil confidence in the company's workforce and its directors, in front of the managing director Harold Judd, his Uncle Godfrey, his sister Jean, his mother, and numerous other suited or uniformed directors and dignitaries.

In a photograph taken as he was speaking, Ron cuts an already adult figure. Speaking without notes, erect, confident, hands behind his back in what would become one of his characteristic poses, the commitment and assertiveness with which he has embraced his new role is, even from a distance, tangible. For everyone present that day, beneath the overcast East London skies, despite the extreme uncertainties of the war situation, one thing can have been in no doubt. The company might have lost its respected chairman, but in his teenage son, shortly to go up to Cambridge to read engineering, it had found his successor.

Heir apparent: Ron opens the new H. Young & Company canteen, Summer 1941.
Amongst the dignitaries, in uniform, are Uncle Godfrey and Jean Buxton.

7

A Trinity Buxton: Cambridge in Wartime

THE BUXTONS HAD a long and remarkable relationship with Trinity College, Cambridge. Enter the college via the Porter's Lodge, cross Great Court to the diagonally opposite corner, climb the steps past Hall, then continue through Nevile's Court, and, tucked away beyond, bounded by Trinity Lane, is a less familiar quadrangle, in Neo-Gothic. This is New Court, built in 1823–5. Find Staircase B4, enter the panelled neogothic doorway, and inside, on the wall, is a sight few, if any, other families can claim. A tall, varnished wooden board records, in carefully hand-lettered black capitals, the names of all the Trinity men who have occupied this particular set of rooms from 1824 until 1973. Amongst them, dominating the board, are the names of forty Buxtons, from 'Buxton, T. F.' in 1856 until the final entry – 'Buxton, R. M.' in 1973. These are the 'The Buxton Rooms'.

What is even more remarkable is that these names represent by no means all the Buxtons who have attended Trinity College during this period. Many – Ron's great-grandfather, grandfather and father, to take three – are not mentioned as, although they went to Trinity, they never secured tenure of these particular rooms. As for Ron, sadly he never even got the chance to apply. For the duration of the war New Court was let to a government ministry and no student accommodation was available there.

Cambridge, by the time Ron went up for the Michaelmas term of 1941, was a long way from the university life of Rupert Brooke or *Brideshead Revisited*. Numbers of both undergraduates and dons were much reduced. Most of the best young academic staff had been called up. Any notion of languid afternoons punting or wondering if there was honey still for tea at Grantchester were scotched by syllabuses that crammed three-year courses into two – that was if the course were permitted at all. It was considered a vast privilege that students were allowed to defer call-up. Those reading subjects regarded as of national importance – medicine, engineering, certain sciences – were granted two years, with courses diving straight into the second year and undergraduates expected to catch up as necessary.

Rationing meant there was very little food. Even at Trinity, by far the largest and wealthiest college, students felt hungry all the time – a feeling aggravated by the sense that the dons were not suffering the same privations. (At Oxford, according to the historian A. J. P. Taylor, wartime life for the dons was regarded as 'a haven of peace', with little teaching, free dinners still

The 'Buxton Rooms' – the panel in B4, New Court, Trinity College, Cambridge recording the names of some 40 Buxtons who resided there between 1856–1973*

*Thanks are due to Richard Buxton (the last Buxton to be recorded on the board, bottom left, in 1973; Ron's second cousin, once removed) who brought our attention to the existence of this panel, and whose son, when he entered Trinity, was the fifth generation of Buxtons in direct line to attend the college. (His request to occupy the Buxton Rooms was refused as the rooms are now reserved for postgraduates.)

available in College, and the unremitting flow of vintage claret and port from the college cellars unaffected by rationing.) Rationing meant that eating in Hall was compulsory, not that the meals seemed remotely adequate. After lunch Ron usually had a second lunch in a Chinese restaurant in the town.

Transport was another problem. Trains and buses operated much reduced timetables, invariably with standing room only. My unthinking question: 'Did you have a car?' to Ron prompted the most indignant response: 'A car? A *car*? There weren't any *cars*. There wasn't any petrol.' What he had, instead, was a 'splendid' bicycle, a big old one he paid five shillings for and painted blue.

He was also short of money. Since Murray's death the family's finances, largely tied up with H. Young & Company, had become extremely uncertain. It was partly for this reason that Mew had let Holywell and gone to live with her 'little' sister Ciceley at Bishop's Down Grange. Ron was on a strictly limited allowance, and despite a bursary from the Institution of Structural Engineers he had difficulty making ends meet.

These gloomy circumstances were little cheered by his first encounters with his colleagues in the engineering faculty, with whom he found little in common. There were about 200 undergraduates in the year and, while bright, almost without exception they were grammar school boys, frequently from northern England. Their values, interests and accents were a world away from Ron's.

On top of this was the relentless schedule. Unlike today's early specialisations into mechanical, electrical, structural or civil engineering – when Ron would have opted for structural – the emphasis was on a broad grounding in applied mathematics and physics. These included areas such as the theory of electricity and magnetism and its application in the design of electrical machines, circuits, and control mechanisms; the strength and properties of materials and the analysis and synthesis of structures in which they may be used; the laws of thermodynamics and their use in the design of engines for power production, traction, and propulsion; the application of mechanics to the design and manufacture of machinery; and the science of fluid motion and its use in the design of aircraft, engines and machines – most of which were never going to be remotely relevant to anything H. Young & Company did.

University life beyond the engineering faculty seemed little better. Student politics, in particular the Cambridge Union Society – usually a focal point for those with latent political ambitions, were dominated by the Labour Party. Worse, what little spare time there was for societies and extra activities was gnawed away by the war effort. Everyone had to be in the Home Guard, training at least one day a week, in uniform.

The Backs, and the Cam, and the college courtyards and Fellows' gardens were still there, of course, though in 1941 the stone spires and towers and crockets and belfries were pitted and soot-streaked, quite unlike the scrubbed, postcard-perfect face the city presents today. There was little of the social activity that normally characterises student life. Ron's accommodation that first year consisted of digs in a narrow, rather gloomy cobbled street called All Saint's Passage, tucked well away from the architectural glories of Trinity's Great Court, or even the reassuring family names of B4, New Court.

*

Ron's chief pleasure and recreation was music, and this was the one thing that truly blossomed for him at Cambridge. There was choral singing with the Cambridge University Musical Society. As a member of Trinity Choir (which numbered between 25 and 35), he sang at all the Commemorative Feasts – important less for the honour of performing than for the fact that, by gaining admission, at least he got a square meal. He sang solos before distinguished college guests: Elizabethan songs on one occasion, grace on another.

Then there was the organ. Almost no one in college played the organ. This meant Ron could have the big, four-keyboard Harrison instrument in Trinity Chapel to himself whenever he liked. The Trinity organist and Director of Music, Dr Hubert Middleton (1890–1959), former organist of Ely Cathedral, would bicycle in from his house on Station Road to teach Ron. Middleton was a Cambridge character, his style exemplified by his response to a student expecting praise for a string quartet supposedly written 'in the style of Mozart': 'You'd expect a young woman 'cellist from Girton [five miles outside the city] to take a bus into Cambridge on a wet Monday night carrying a 'cello, to play *this*?' Middleton became a good friend, asking Ron to his house and showing great kindness, in particular following the event which would overshadow Ron's second year.

*

In vacations, Ron made the difficult and tedious train journey from Cambridge to Tunbridge Wells to see his mother. Mew was always delighted to have him, but, with two widowed sisters and an 89-year-old stroke victim who could hardly speak, it was hardly a fun place to be. Besides, Bishop's Down Grange had never been Ron's home and the size of the big Victorian house only emphasised its emptiness. Jean, now eighteen, had left home to join the Auxiliary Territorial Service as secretary and driver for a general. Ron would escape to family gatherings at Easneye with Great-Uncle Jack, who was now installed in the big house, and to Mew's other sister, Aunt Dreda, at Grimston Manor in Yorkshire. Aunt Dreda and Uncle Tom's son Edward Brooke (Ron's first cousin) had given helpful advice about H. Young &

[83]

Company following Murray's death. More than a decade older than Ron, and a successful businessman, he ran John Brooke and Sons, the oldest woollen mill in Yorkshire. Aunt Dreda, too, was an admirably indomitable character. With just a single day's notice, she had taken in forty schoolboy evacuees, most of whom stayed three years.

His first Easter vacation, Ron cycled north once more, this time bound for Scotland and accompanied by an Eton-and-Cambridge friend, Pat Holden (who shortly after won a blue running the mile). They got as far as the Firth of Forth, intending to take the train further north. The naval bases there, however, meant all trains were crammed with servicemen, so they had to return.

Summer vacations had to be spent on war work. His second summer, Ron was sent, with another Cambridge friend, Gerald Hohler, to 'forestry camp' in Uttoxeter in Derbyshire. There they were put to work sawing logs and stripping bark (by hand, using a peeling spade), billeted by night in grim, unfurnished digs in ramshackle outbuildings. A few days of this and Gerald announced he could take no more. After work one evening, he mounted his bicycle and pedalled to the nearest large house. It turned out to be called Marchington Hall. Gerald rang the bell and when the door was answered, he introduced himself and, summoning every ounce of his considerable charm, explained to the owner, a Mr Longden, their predicament. It worked. Gerald and Ron were promptly asked to stay, and Dick Longden became a friend.

*

In his second year things looked up slightly. Ron got rooms in Great Court (Staircase I2, side of the great gate), one of Cambridge's prize lodgings. In his palatial new quarters – a bedroom and a large living room – he kept two pianos. One was a Bechstein grand belonging to a Russian prince called Obolenski, bequeathed to someone else when war began, from whom it came to Ron. The other was a hired upright, in due course replaced by a Fortebello instrument bought from an antique piano dealer in Cambridge (which is still at Kimberley Hall).

Cambridge finally began to deliver livelier times. One afternoon Charles (Dalgleish) announced, full of enthusiasm, that he had found a 'quandem' – a four-man bicycle. It was made, he announced, by Charles Rolls of Rolls-Royce. Charles and Ron decided that an ideal plan would be to recruit two other friends and ride it to Ely. It seemed a harmless enough mission, but for all that the expedition nearly ended in disaster. Although three could mount the quandem easily enough, adding the fourth man, it soon transpired, was a different matter. He always upset the balance. It took a lot of practising before they got it right. All went well, so long as they didn't stop, until a downhill stretch on the busy main road into Ely. At full speed they somehow lost their balance and the bike started fish-tailing wildly before they crashed spectacularly in the middle of the road. A lorry following close behind nearly ran them over. Everyone was injured, including the bike.

Such moments were highlights, and Ron's short stay at Cambridge was not an especially happy one. In September 1942 Grandfather Hildred and Great-Uncle Wilson both died on the same day (see p. 30). While Hildred had hardly been able to speak since his stroke, and they saw little of Great-Uncle Wilson, another double demise, after Murray and Uncle Alfred two years before, had the effect of highlighting how few surviving direct blood relatives his family had left. For Ron, the news also emphasised a mounting isolation from any kind of accessible male role model.

Shortly after this, in the Michaelmas term of 1942, Muriel caught another of her chest infections. These had been growing increasingly serious recently, and as the term end approached, her condition worsened into pneumonia. From pneumonia, it worsened again into her old enemy, pleurisy. There was no treatment. Penicillin had been discovered, but its pharmaceutical production was still two years off (it would be ready just in time for troops to carry it on D-Day). On 21 November, a fortnight before Ron was due to break up for Christmas, he was contacted at Trinity. Mew's condition had worsened dramatically. He hurried to Tunbridge Wells to find her only just conscious. She died later that day, less than two months after her father. She was fifty-six.

Ron was still in his teens. Nine months before his twentieth birthday, less than two years after his father's death, he and Jean were orphans.

Mew was buried in Murray's grave, at Brookwood Cemetery. Christmas 1942, accordingly, was one of the gloomiest of Ron's life. He joined Jean and Aunt Cicely at Bishop's Down Grange, a house which now lacked both its owner, Grandfather Hildred, and Mew, but which had not yet been put on the market. Nor was there any encouraging news in the papers. Britain might have fended off the Nazis during the Battle of Britain, but that was now two summers ago. In the eighteen months since then there had been nothing even approaching a victory to celebrate.

Ron returned to Cambridge in the New Year to complete his degree. He duly graduated in the summer of 1943 with a third. It was a pass degree, far below what might have been expected of him under normal circumstances. The combination of his parents' deaths, wartime conditions and the miserable slog of completing the full, arduous three-year engineering course in two years no doubt provide the explanation.

8

Captain Buxton

WHILE RON WAS sitting his engineering finals in the summer of 1943, Montgomery's tanks were engaging Rommel's panzers in the North African desert. By the subdued celebrations of 'May Week' – always at the beginning of June – Britain had recorded her first unambiguous land victory of the war. 'It is not the end,' declared Churchill. 'It is not even the beginning of the end ...'

Days later, news of the triumph of the Dambusters' raids flagged up the precise and highly effective destructive force that Bomber Command had, finally, become. Shortly after, with Ron Buxton, BA (Cantab) having attended his graduation ceremony and 'gone down' from the university, the Allies had gained a toehold in Italy. A tipping point had been reached. Three weeks later, Ron was called up.

His formal military training commenced with six intensive weeks, mandatory for all officers, known as OCTU (Officer Cadet Training Unit), at Maidstone Barracks, near Wrotham, in Kent. His fellow trainees were a mixture of graduates and non-graduates, and his induction into military life was smoothed by the unlikely figure of his sergeant. Ron took a shine to the 'marvellous' Sergeant Twitchet from the start. Far from being the bawling martinet of military folklore, Twitchet impressed his young charge with his skill and diplomacy in handling what he called 'the college cads and the working lads'.

The military routine was relieved by escaping for occasional dinners at hotels in Maidstone, or to visit Aunt Cicely at Tunbridge Wells. With Mew's death, Uncle Godfrey had become Jean and Ron's official guardian, but as neither of them could stand his wife, Aunt Dorothea, whom they found 'intolerably sanctimonious', Aunt Ciceley had become their surrogate mother. Although Bishop's Down Grange had been sold soon after Hildred died the previous autumn, Cicely had moved to a flat in a house called Boyne Park near Tunbridge Wells, which had since become Jean and Ron's base. Although they still owned Holywell, complete with the cottage containing the gardener and housekeeper, Mr and Mrs People, it had been let for the duration (to Eustace Pulbrook, Chairman of Lloyd's).

After that, it was on to officer training with a brand new regiment that Ron had never had any intention of joining. The fact was, he had no say in the matter. Having permitted him to attend a university for two years in wartime, leaving him in possession of a qualification 'of national importance', his country had no intention of leaving his choice of regiment to him. Despite having signed up for The Rifle Brigade at Eton, less than three years before, Ron was now peremptorily assigned to an entirely different kind of outfit, one that had only come into being eight months earlier: the Royal Electrical and Mechanical Engineers, or REME.

The creation of the REME – motto *Arte et Marte*, or 'by skill and by fighting' – was a response to the increasing technological complexities of modern warfare. From jeeps and radios to tanks and trucks, fighting was now a highly technical business, as dependent on machines as men. The REME's first major mission had been El Alamein, keeping Montgomery's tanks and equipment running in the horrendous conditions of dust and sand of the North African desert. Its tasks included maintenance, inspection, testing, recovery and repair of any kind of electrical or mechanical equipment. REME detachments now formed a part of every combat, service or support unit in the Army. Wherever that unit went, REME went too. Behind the lines, REME support companies worked in mobile or static workshops to repair any equipment recovered and get it back into action as quickly as possible.

The REME's officer training unit (OCTU) was at Formark Hall, Uttoxeter. There, for Ron, three months of unadulterated misery followed, culminating with a battle-camp in Snowdonia in savage January weather. From this, duly commissioned, Second Lieutenant Buxton emerged, to be posted to a REME unit in Buntingford, Hertfordshire. Here the Commanding Officer outlined their duties: the guns and vehicles they had to maintain were divided into 'A' vehicles, armoured for fighting, and 'B' vehicles, which meant lorries, trucks and the rest. There were driving courses for HGVs (heavy goods vehicles) and any unusual machines (such as recovery trucks) and maintenance courses. Most of the day-to-day work was carried out by warrant officers: peacetime mechanics who knew their jobs well. Ron was sent on a specialist course at the Military College of Science in Stoke-on-Trent to become an expert on guns: how to deal with their specific problems, how to measure performance, how to look after them and repair them.

It was the last time he touched a gun during the war.[23]

*

After almost a year of training, Ron and his company were told they were to be sent overseas. They were not informed where. By now – late spring of 1944 – the theatre of war was shifting. Churchill's 'Germany first' policy, agreed with Roosevelt, was coming to fruition. Months of nightly raids by

---

23 His service revolver, a Colt .45, plus shells, survived the war and remained in the Kimberley gun cupboard for years.

Bomber Command, and daily raids by the American 'Mighty Eighth', from the countless new airfields across Lincolnshire and East Anglia, had smashed Germany's cities and industrial heartland. Preparations were almost complete for a full-scale land invasion of France, scheduled, not that many knew it, for mid-summer. While Britain's attentions had been on Europe, however, the situation in the East had worsened disastrously. While Ron studied, the Japanese had scythed through British territories across the Far East just as Hitler's *blitzkrieg* had earlier cut across mainland Europe. The Philippines, Indo-China, Java, Sumatra and Borneo, Malaya, Singapore, Thailand and Burma had all fallen in a gargantuan land-grab as the Japanese pushed westwards, with the aim of eventually meeting the Germans and Italians in the Middle East.

In May, still ignorant of their destination, Ron was embarked with 6,000 troops on the P & O *Orion* at Greenock, west of Glasgow. Even after sailing, it was not revealed where they were bound. For two days they sailed south, round Portugal to the Straits of Gibraltar and a first glimpse of Africa. There they were met by destroyers which shepherded them through the Mediterranean towards Suez. (As the Allies now had air control of the Mediterranean, this previously hazardous leg passed without incident.)

As they sailed into ever-warmer air and navigated the giant locks of the Suez Canal, there was a sense of impending excitement and adventure. Ron was well-travelled compared to most on board. He had visited Switzerland a couple of times, once by train over a summer with his family, once again at school. Then, in 1938, seeing that war was inevitable, Murray had taken everyone to Austria and Italy for four weeks. The vast majority on board, however, had never left Britain before. Ron himself had never taken a major sea voyage. From the Red Sea they steamed into the Gulf of Aden and thence the Indian Ocean.

There was little to do on board. Ron's principal duty was vetting letters home written by the men, but as, still, no one was certain where they were headed, there was little to censor. A Captain Hill taught Ron and others bridge, which whiled away some of the time. Captain Hill also issued cultural advice should their destination turn out to be India, particularly with regard to tipping, and chillies ('Try them, they're like strawberries').

India, certainly, seemed the likeliest option. The key to whether the Axis forces managed to enact their master plan for world takeover, turned, everyone knew, on India. Chains of islands on the other side of the world were always going to be tricky to defend with limited resources, but India was different. Apart from being, in Disraeli's words, the 'jewel in the crown' of the British Empire, it was extremely well defended, at least from any attacks by sea. For the Japanese, once their forces had crossed Thailand and taken Burma in 1942, their one hope for a land-based assault on India was from the north-east. Having got there, however, they discovered that maintaining supply lines to their forces by sea through the Strait of Malacca and the Andaman Sea, a route highly vulnerable to Allied submarines, was well-nigh impossible. That was why they had proceeded with their notorious alternative plan: to build a railway through the 258 miles of rocky, mountainous jungle from Bangkok in Thailand to Rangoon in Burma. This, the infamous 'Death Railway', crossing the bridge on the River Kwai, had been completed the previous October (in just sixteen months) by Allied prisoners of war.

The railway enabled the Japanese once again to prepare for an invasion of India. As everyone had been embarking at Greenock, the battle lines were being drawn in the hill country of the north-east, along the border with Burma. All in all, accordingly, India seemed much their likeliest destination. The idea did little to buoy everyone's spirits. Captain Hill was full of the woes of the situation, and he was by no means alone in his pessimism. The country was riven by political troubles, especially in the north-east where things were coming to a head, brought about by end-of-empire instability. Gandhi's rise was compounded by British fears about the Indian National Army, a force similar in principle to the IRA, formed by Indian nationalists in 1942 (chiefly Indian expatriates taken as Japanese prisoners of war). There had been violent 'Quit India' protests in Bengal and Bihar, requiring large numbers of troops to suppress. These were precisely what the Japanese were banking on. Moreover, the densely-populated Bengal region (today divided into Bangladesh and West Bengal) had hardly begun to recover from the catastrophic famine the previous year, disastrously handled by the British administration, in which three million had died of starvation, disease and exposure. There were real fears that if the Japanese burst through, the discontent might spiral into the whole of India rising against the British.

True, things had started to go better for the Allies in the East in 1944. Improved leadership and logistics, plus growing Allied air superiority, were gradually taking effect. On 29 February US forces had taken Los Negros in the Admiralty Islands. Three weeks later, on 19 March, in one of the most daring operations of the Burma Campaign, the British glided into Japanese-controlled Burma and established a base behind the Japanese position. In April General MacArthur's troops re-took New Guinea.

And in April, too, six weeks after leaving Scotland, the *Orion* duly docked in Bombay, confirming everyone's theories and fears. It was a critical moment in the Burma Campaign. Up in the hills along the Burmese border, between April and June, everything was about to come to a head around the small town of Kohima (north-east of Imphal in the map on next page). The Battle of Kohima became the turning point of the entire Burma Campaign. It boiled down to a dug-in, immensely bloody Rorke's Drift-style stand-off between

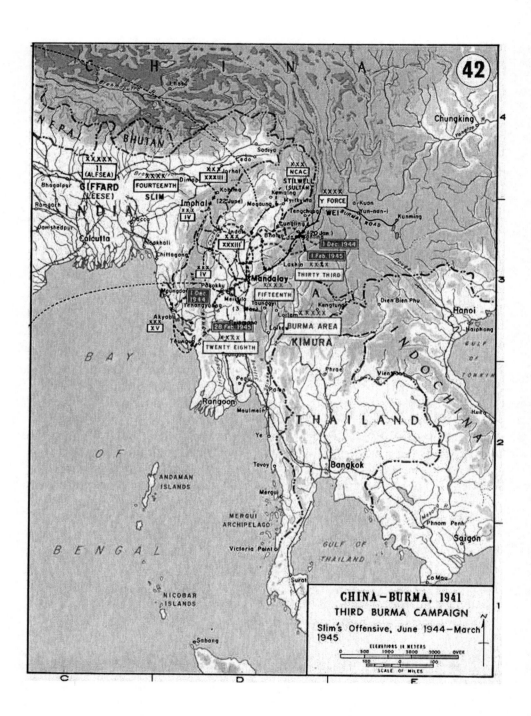

CHINA–BURMA, 1941
THIRD BURMA CAMPAIGN

Slim's Offensive, June 1944–March 1945

starving Japanese and British and Indian forces so entirely cut off they could only be supplied by the RAF. The final show-down, across the garden of the Deputy Commissioner's bungalow, became known as the 'Battle of the Tennis Court'. It would later be described by the Supreme Allied Commander, Mountbatten, as 'one of the greatest battles in history ... the British/Indian Thermopylae'.

From Bombay, meanwhile, everyone was disembarked to a transit camp outside the city. Here they discovered that Captain Hill's tipping guidance was not to be relied upon. In fact, anyone dispensing rupees according to his confident assertions was liable to be lynched.

Second Lieutenant Buxton and his men were now inducted from the British Army into the Indian Army – the Indian Electrical and Mechanical Engineers (IEME), on Indian Army pay. From Bombay they now dispersed across the country to various units. Ron was sent to Shahjahanpur, a district of Uttar Pradesh in Northern India, for a pleasant three months. There a *munshi* (tutor) came each day to teach him and the other British officers Urdu. With its Persian and Arabic roots, Urdu is not an easy language to master, but master it they had to, if they were to get a pay rise. Apart from this, he and his men repeated, exactly, the training they had so recently undergone in Britain.

*

From Shahjahanpur, Ron was eventually sent to Calcutta, to Eastern Command HQ for a staff job in administration, inspecting vehicles. There he remained – with mounting frustration and practically nothing to do – until he was finally posted for active service in Bengal in late 1944. At last he was nearing the action.

He now became part of the vast military machinery of the final stages of the Burma Campaign. One day, crossing the Brahmaputra River – three miles wide – on a ferry loaded with military equipment and servicemen, he was surprised to hear his name being called by a familiar voice. Turning round, he was greeted by none other than his old friend Anthony Gurney. Gurney was a distant cousin, a descendant of the Norfolk-based Quaker banking family into which outlying strands of the Buxtons had married several times in the eighteenth and nineteenth centuries. A year older than Ron, he had been a frequent visitor to lunch at Holywell with Murray and Muriel when he was at school at nearby Charterhouse. Now in the Frontier Force Rifles (part of the British Indian Army) Gurney had recovered from severe wounds, sustained in May 1944, during the Battle for Imphal (simultaneous with the Battle of Kohima, and part of the same turning point in the Burma Campaign). Three bullets had entered his lungs and he had not been expected to survive. Now, in the mêlée of troops and equipment aboard the ferry, he had spotted the white-stencilled letters 'R. C. BUXTON' on Ron's uniform case. It was a happy moment for them both.

With the Japanese in retreat after Kohima, the crucial Allied goal had become to push them back south through Burma as far as Rangoon (today Yangon), more than six hundred miles south, before the monsoon rains arrived in May cutting off further operations.

By the end of February 1945 Ron was still kicking his heels at the seaport city of Chittagong (best known today as the Bangladeshi ship-breaking capital of the world). Chittagong was then the main supply hub for the entire British Burma campaign, and here Ron had to wait until news arrived that Rangoon had been freed.

The Japanese were eventually defeated by lack of supplies. Their precious lifeline, the railway, was repeatedly severed by Allied bombing, most famously of the bridge on the River Kwai (a five-span steel girder bridge unlike the timber trestle structure in the eponymous film) requiring everything to be ferried.

As they retreated through the Pegu Yomas, a range of low, jungle-covered mountains between the Irrawaddy and the Sittang Rivers in central Burma near Mandalay, the Japanese were relentlessly harried by the local Burmese and ambushed by British artillery concentrations. When they reached the mile-wide Irrawaddy to find the bridge bombed, they were trapped. Hundreds drowned trying to cross the swollen Sittang on improvised bamboo floats and rafts, while Burmese guerrillas killed hundreds more. In all, 10,000 men, half the strength of the Twenty-Eighth Army, died in the retreat.

Rangoon was finally freed on 2 May. Within hours, the heavens opened and the monsoon began.

Ron and his company, after two months in Chittagong, were promptly shipped there. Now promoted captain, he was posted first to 20th Indian Division (with Anthony Gurney) under General Gracie, then to 32 Brigade in charge of the Light Aid Attachment Unit. With thirty or forty men under his command, including a sergeant who was an especially good mechanic, his task for the next four months was to recover tanks, armoured vehicles and trucks and equipment which had been damaged in combat.

Meanwhile, dramatic developments across the globe were taking place at an accelerating rate. The end of April, in Europe, had brought Hitler's suicide and Mussolini's execution. VE Day, Victory in Europe Day, was 13 May. Two thousand nights of blackout came to an end in a carnival atmosphere. Ron heard the news at Letpedan, north of Rangoon, near Irrawaddy.

Then the first week of August saw the atom bomb dropped on Hiroshima, with the second bomb dropped on Nagasaki three days later. With that, the war was over. 14 August brought VJ Day, Victory over Japan Day. The news reached Ron and his troops via the weekly military newspapers, and by the

All India Radio which blared Indian music from every village they passed through.

Although the war was now technically over, it did not mean, unfortunately for Ron, that he would soon be going home. Ending a vast global conflict was not merely a matter of ending hostilities and signing a few treaties. With millions of enlisted men, in dozens of countries, the process of winding down such a vast military operation was a protracted one, in some instances creating new military situations as power gaps appeared. After VJ Day the rate at which servicemen were demobilised rose from 115,000 a month to 171,000, with plans to release over a million personnel by December. But as demobilisation was strictly by length of service, under a 'first in, first out' rule, for Ron, having only signed up in 1943, it might be months or years before his turn came.

As a result, within a week of Japan's surrender, Ron's division, the 20th Indian, was assigned a new task. It was shipped several hundred miles by sea, to Saigon, in Vietnam, where the fighting was anything but over.

*

The situation in Saigon (now Ho Chi Minh) did not reflect the new peace in the world outside. Saigon was a city under siege by local freedom fighters. Since the 1860s, the Cochinchina region of Vietnam, of which Saigon was capital, had been a French colony. Under the French, the city had acquired Western-style classical buildings and earned itself the nickname 'the Pearl of the Far East' or 'Paris in the Orient'. In September 1940, following the fall of France, Japan and Vichy Indochina had signed an accord granting Japan the right to station troops in Indochina, and to move men and supplies throughout the region. But in 1945, with France liberated and the United States ascendant in the Pacific, Japan decided to take complete control of Indochina. French civil servants were forced to continue running things. Now, following Japanese withdrawal, there was suddenly a power vacuum, and the Viet-Minh (later Viet-Cong) spotted their chance to 'reclaim' their territory. There were almost daily attacks on the perimeter where the few French troops present, stationed to keep order, were being slaughtered by the insurgents.

As the Japanese pulled out, the Supreme Allied Commander, Admiral Lord Louis Mountbatten, rushed in the three brigades of 20th Infantry Division (of which Ron, in 32 Brigade, was now part) under General Gracie to hold Saigon temporarily for the French. On arrival, Gracie spread his brigades around Saigon to hold key points.

There were few British officers with which to fraternise. Each brigade consisted of three battalions, and each battalion had just five officers: a commanding officer, second-in-command, subaltern, a transport officer and a signals officer. Half the officers, and all the troops, were Indian. In the

[93]

evenings Ron would sometimes meet up with the French civil servants at the colonial officers' club, Le Sac Sportif, in the city centre.

Soon after their arrival, within weeks, a French general, Le Clerk, arrived with three French brigades to take over from General Gracie.

From the moment of their arrival, the behaviour of the newly-arrived French troops towards the civilian population was appalling. Apart from appearing very raw, alongside the hard-bitten and battle-hardened Punjabis and Gurkhas, the French threw their weight about, treating the local population as enemies, setting them against themselves in a way that ensured they would never be won back. Nor did the French trust or listen to the British. On one occasion they charged through a British-controlled area, ignoring the carefully-placed traffic controls, directly into an ambush. Moments later machine guns were heard as they were slaughtered.

Ron's spell in Saigon delivered one lasting memento. Lodged in a house in the north of the city near his brigade HQ, one day he was recovering armoured vehicles in the outskirts nearby. In an empty house he came across an abandoned piano. It was a grand, by the German manufacturer Haake of Hanover, sturdily made and tropically built. It seemed a crime to leave it where it was, where its fate was to be overrun by the Viet-Minh. With plenty of troops at his disposal, it was the matter of minutes for Ron to have them load the piano into a Bedford three-tonner and later, in the workshop, they made up a case for it. Thus, when they moved to their next posting, the brigade's newest item of equipment could be shipped there with them.

Within a fortnight of the arrival of the French, the 20th were broken up and despatched in different directions. (In due course, a General Service Medal would be struck for everyone who had served in the Division in Indo-China.) After his three months in Saigon, Ron was told that his brigade was bound for Kuching, capital of the jungle kingdom of Sarawak, on the island of Borneo.

Before leaving, however, at 32 Brigade HQ, the commanding officer, Brigadier Woodford, decided to organise a magnificent curry lunch to celebrate the hand-over to the French. All the newly-arrived French officers were invited. Ron rigged up generators for lighting the house. In pride of place went the brigade's newest item of equipment: Ron's grand piano. After the banquet, Brigadier Woodford called for silence. 'Captain Buxton,' he ordered, 'you will play the Marseillaise' – which he did.

*

By far the worst thing about Kuching was getting there. To do so required crossing the shallow Timor Sea – notorious, like the Bay of Biscay, for its wild weather and tumultuous seas. True to the Sea's reputation, the voyage was atrocious. It took nearly three weeks, aboard a grim Liberty ship (one of the

A Liberty ship

cheap, mass-produced US wartime steam-powered cargo vessels of which thousands were built to replace U-Boat losses). The wretchedness was compounded by an American crew who loathed the army they were carrying. Everyone was horrendously sick.

Nor were their problems over once they reached Sarawak in October 1945. As there was no deep-water berth, the Liberty ship anchored offshore and everyone had to be loaded onto lighters in nets – a hazardous business – to go ashore. Thus, Ron and his unit finally arrived in Kuching, capital of Sarawak (part of Malaysia today).

If Borneo is roughly in the shape of a teardrop, the top and most of a wide strip running down the west coast make up Sarawak, with a dent two-thirds of the way up the coast comprising the tiny sultanate of Brunei. Brigade HQ was on Labuan Island, a tiny island (and British Crown Colony) just off north-west Brunei, 500 km up the coast from Kuching. While most of the brigade immediately went there, under Brigadier Woodford, Ron, attached to the 9/14 Punjab Lancers under Colonel Hobbs, remained in Sarawak back at Kuching. His English-speaking company included only four officers and a transport officer.

The jungle kingdom of Sarawak, ruled by an English family named Brooke, was one of the more cherishably quaint bequests of Victorian empire-building. A buccaneering adventurer called James Brooke, educated in England, was awarded – or skilfully negotiated – lands with independent kingdom status on Borneo as a reward for helping the Sultan of Brunei put down a rebellion and fight piracy on the island in 1842. He thus became the

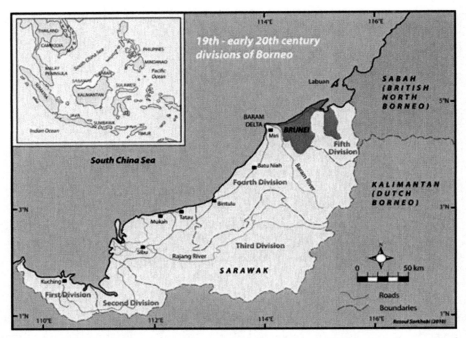

Kuching and the jungle kingdom of Sarawak – where Ron arrived in October 1945 after crossing the notoriously rough Timor Sea

first and only 'white rajah', subsequently also receiving a knighthood from Queen Victoria.[24] Thereafter the family issued their own stamps, coinage and banknotes, and displayed their own flag, remaining one of the few monarchs in the world still able to say, as Louis XIV did: 'L'état, c'est moi' ('I am the state').

Although generally benign – even, in some areas, enlightened – rulers of their singular inheritance, the Brookes were also notably eccentric. James Brooke formed his closest relationships with adolescent boys. In 1888 his successor, Charles Brooke, who expanded the boundaries of the kingdom to an area the size of England and allowed it to become a British protectorate, was an austere figure who regarded jam as 'effeminate'. When he lost an eye, making little fuss, he replaced it with a glass one from a stuffed albatross.

His son, Sir Charles Vyner de Windt Brooke, the third rajah, shared power with his nephew Anthony (ultimately the fifth rajah) in a curious arrangement of alternating six-month shifts. This was the situation, with Sir Charles himself away travelling in Australia, when the Japanese invaded in December 1941.

24 A fictionalised account of Brooke's exploits appears in Nicholas Montserrat's *The White Rajah*, in George MacDonald Fraser's *Flashman* novels, and in Joseph Conrad's *Lord Jim*, for which he was the model.

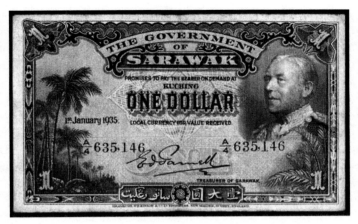

Sarawak $1 note, bearing a portrait of Charles Vyner de Windt Brooke, GCMG
(1874–1963), third and final White Rajah of Sarawak

Australian forces later liberated Sarawak from the Japanese in August 1945, just weeks before the atom bomb brought all hostilities to an end. The place, however, was left in disarray; its future by no means clear. The task of Ron's unit was to adopt a civilian role, establishing an interim colonial administration. Specifically, they also had to look after Japanese prisoners of war (I Brigade had been sent to Java to undertake identical duties there). In the meantime Colonel Hobbs, of the 14th Punjabi Regiment, was Sarawak's ruler.

Ron and Colonel Hobbs did not get on especially well, but, this aside, Ron could hardly have landed a more agreeable posting. Sarawak was a proper tropical paradise ('Sarawak' meaning 'land of the hornbills'). The heat was much less ferocious than in India or Burma and, with hostilities now at an end, military life relaxed greatly. 'The war is over,' Brigadier Woodford had declared, 'let's have some fun.' REME HQ was down on the river front and the rest of the time Ron was installed in a pleasant house on Kuching's outskirts with another captain, the transport officer, and a batman called Venkana. There they lived in considerable comfort.

Kuching and the other towns were set up-river, well inland, with the houses built in the hills. There were no roads, but Ron found a motor boat abandoned by the retreating Japanese. It had a big, old, highly unreliable Ford V8 engine which he soon coaxed into life, making possible *Apocalypse Now*-style forays up-river into the jungle interior, where there were crocodiles to shoot and some of the Dyak tribesmen still indulged in the grisly custom of headhunting. Later they made trips into the interior on foot to visit the Malay *kampongs* (hill villages) and the Chinese shophouses and Dyak longhouses.

The *kampongs* were all tremendously welcoming, as they had hated the brutal Japanese. Ron made friends with a Chinese family. Their daughter,

Suzie, they determined, was the perfect match for him and they outlined preparations for their forthcoming marriage. Admittedly, English-speaking company was limited. Ron liked the officers in the battalion of the 9/14 Punjab Regiment, but with only the transport officer sharing his house a British native, social life was inevitably limited. There was Colonel Hobbs, of course, but he had taken against Ron as a result of his travels up-country (following a mandate that 'officers will not leave Kuching without the Colonel's per-mission'). More congenial company, Winchester-and-Magdalene-educated, arrived on 14 April 1946, in the form of none other than His Highness Sir Charles Vyner de Windt Brooke, third Rajah of Sarawak, back from Australia where he had been stuck since war broke out.

Newsreel footage in the Imperial War Museum survives of the Rajah and his wife Sylvia, the Ranee, arriving back by Sunderland flying boat, being collected by launch and greeted with guards of honour by the Navy and the 9th Battalion of the 14th Punjab Regiment, plus Colonel Hobbs and Brigadier Woodford and crowds waving flags and banners. Thereafter, Colonel Hobbs and Ron set about re-installing Sarawak's ruling monarch. They saw Brooke back into The Astana, the palace on the Kuching waterfront built by the second white rajah as a wedding gift to his wife in 1870. Meanwhile, Ron found an old car, a battered American Plymouth. It had plainly seen better days, but he had his men service it, paint it gold, and put a crown on the front for His Highness to drive around in.

'The white rajah's new car is ready', from a local newspaper, April 1946. Ron second from the right.

In due course Lord Louis Mountbatten and his daughter came to stay in the mess in Kuching, and a banquet was laid on. Brooke's grand official welcome, however, disguised overtures that had already been made to him by the British government about how Sarawak and Britain might be 'marched together in the future' – in short, become part of the British Empire. In July 1946, vehemently opposed by his nephew and many of the local population, Vyner Brooke agreed to cede Sarawak to Britain as a crown colony. And so, the tiny kingdom became the very last addition to the soon-to-be-dismantled British Empire, ending a century of white rajah rule there. In July 1963 the country was granted independence, joining with Malaya, Sabah and Singapore in the federation of Malaysia – a consequence that meant that when large crude oil reserves were discovered within Sarawak's borders, all the benefit went straight to Malaysia, rather than Sarawak.

*

There was one less sunny side to Ron's spell in paradise. The Japanese prisoners were, on the whole, well-behaved. Part of the division's remit, however, was organising courts martial of those prisoners accused of war crimes. The Nuremberg Trials had already begun in Germany and, following Allied victory in the Far East, similar trials began around the Pacific Rim.

It was a laborious procedure: all evidence had to be translated into Japanese and Chinese, as most of the witnesses were one or the other. Some of the iniquities perpetrated by the Japanese on Allied prisoners of war (for whom, by definition, the Japanese had no respect) have become legendary. In Kuching, those Japanese found guilty were sentenced to death. Lesser criminals were sent to a firing squad, convened at dawn on the beach from soldiers of the Punjab Regiment. However, as the Japanese regarded the firing squad as an honourable 'military' death, they accepted this fate with equanimity: a clearly unsatisfactory situation for the most serious cases. The real punishment was to be hanged. Hanging was for criminals, and would reflect badly on their families.

Courts martial under British service law at the time took the form of a judge advocate with a panel of two or more officers sitting in judgment. Ron found himself convened for a case involving a Sergeant-Major Tsugi. A major arrived from the judge advocate's department and they sat for three weeks. The case involved a series of alleged murders of locals and repeated cruelties by the man in question, who was defended by a Japanese defending officer who spoke good English. In spite of horrifying accounts of the accused's actions, the defending officer made an unexpectedly good case that Tsugi's actions were part of his normal course of duty. It was such a good defence, in fact, that Ron and the other captain sitting saw little option but to 'allow' the man the firing squad.

The major from the judge advocate's department listened attentively to their conclusions, then delivered his verdict. 'You fools,' he said. 'This man is a war criminal. There's only one place for him: the gallows at Singapore jail!' So Tsugi was hanged.

*

After four months in Kuching, Ron moved the 500 km up the Borneo coast to Brigade HQ at Labuan Island. Although now a crown colony, Labuan Island had been established in 1848 as a base for British operations against piracy in the South China Sea, and was first governed by James Brooke, first Rajah of Sarawak. It was a small tropical island of about 75 km, in the shape of an arrowhead, lying 8 km off the coast north of Begawan. Labuan Island, on the ground, was a quintessential tropical paradise: palm trees bordered the white sandy beaches beneath cobalt skies and the green-blue waters of the South China Sea were the temperature of warm tea. For the next two months it became 32 Brigade's playground, with little to do and all day to do it.

Near the coast, Ron came across a moribund DUKW amphibious landing vehicle left by the Americans. A DUKW, or 'Duck', as they became affectionately known, was one of the more characterful pieces of American military equipment. Designed by General Motors, it was neither truck nor boat, but both. Its metal hull was boat-shaped, complete with rope fenders, but it also had six wheels with nobbly tyres and on land could carry up to five tonnes over rough or soft terrain. The 'Duck' was deployed by the thousand in the Pacific theatre to establish and supply beachheads. On roads it could manage up to 50 mph. While in water, by means of a propeller at the back, it could navigate with a full load at up to 6 mph – in other words, fast enough to water-ski behind.

Ron and his men soon had the Duck running. It was swiftly pressed into service as a tow-boat, pulling up to two pairs of skiers on makeshift skis in the form of old doors.

Later, Brigadier Woodford, a keen sailor, had the Japanese prisoners build a small fleet of half a dozen simple wooden sailing boats. He then taught the officers how to sail, and organised sailing races round Labuan Island.[25]

After two idyllic months on Labuan Island, in early June 1946, Ron was ordered back to Calcutta to await instructions. Now, of course, with a grand piano in tow, he made it without undue complications to a transit camp near Madras.

From Madras, they were bound for Calcutta by train. The difficulties of travelling with a grand piano now began to assert themselves. At Madras

---

25 A decade later, Brigadier Woodford (now CBE, DSO, Ret'd), on a sailing holiday in Cornwall, would co-crew a sailing boat with a young woman called Phyllida Buxton – the future Mrs Ronald Buxton.

Water-skiing off Labuan Island – LEFT: The dead 'Duck' revived. RIGHT: Ron water-skiing behind it, on an old door, May 1946.

station, there were problems getting the instrument loaded onto the train. It was too long, too heavy, and awkwardly shaped. After a lot of heaving and shoving getting it loaded into the guard's van, it still stuck out some six inches. The guard refused to allow the train to leave until the piano was unloaded. For some time the situation seemed intractable. It was eventually remedied, after extended discussion and argument, by the transfer of a certain amount of *baksheesh*. When he reached Calcutta, Ron finally managed to unburden himself of his awkward cargo. He left the piano with a friend he

Spot the Englishman – Captain Buxton and his men, 32 Brigade LAD Army Group, Indian Electrical and Mechanical Engineers, Labuan Island, Borneo, 1945

had met while playing the organ in Calcutta Cathedral during his previous sojourn there, and arranged for the instrument to be shipped back to England.[26]

Then he returned to the same barracks in which he had been billeted previously. The heat, stench and bustle of Calcutta were a long way from the tropical Nirvana he had so recently left. June temperatures were near 86F and 80 per cent humidity. The Indian hill stations were too remote to be reachable. There was nothing to do, few books to read, no facilities or transport. Life was maddeningly dull. Anything would be better, Ron decided. He volunteered for overseas service and was ordered to Iraq.

*

Iraq started badly and got worse. After another marathon rail journey across India to Karachi, Ron was shipped out of that Indian Ocean port as officer in charge of a hold crammed with military vehicles, mainly trucks, due for delivery to PAI Force in Iraq. PAI Force – 'Persia and Iraq Force' – was a British and Commonwealth combined forces unit formed on Churchill's orders in 1941 to take and secure the port of Basra after power in Iraq was seized in a *coup d'état* by the pro-Nazi Rashid Ali. Churchill regarded Basra as a critical future supply base for shipments from the United States and as a supply route into Russia.

Shortly after leaving Karachi, they ran into a violent storm. For several hours, in mountainous seas, the ship pitched and rolled and was thrown about. As a result, all the vehicles in the hold smashed into each other. When they eventually reached Basra, there were no port derricks on the quay, so the ship had to be unloaded using the ship's own tiny derricks, an immensely time-consuming operation. The considerable damage was compounded by rampant theft from the quayside by the Iraqis.

Ron oversaw the delivery of his battered cargo to an ordnance depot so large that it was twelve miles in circumference. Once there, stationed at a British military base at Shiba fifteen miles outside Basra, his task was to guard, maintain and run the equipment – a task more arduous than it sounds, as thieving by locals was prodigious. Any vehicle left for even the shortest time lost its wheels.

The heat was overwhelming. There was, of course, no air conditioning; just the odd ceiling fan and few of those. Even the Indian troops, used to the heat, found it unbearable. There was only one other British officer in his unit (although the Indian officers did speak English). In the stores Ron discovered stacks of tinned Spam; being pork, the Muslim officers couldn't eat it. He packaged them up and sent them home to Aunt Cecily.

26 Now in the music room at Kimberley.

Military man: Ron plus moustache, Basra, 1946

The next six months were miserable. There was nothing to do, except escape for the odd weekend to Baghdad. On one of these missions he bought a carpet. Otherwise, the only notable memento from this period was a moustache.

The heat and the boredom affected everybody. A sepoy (Indian soldier) went mad and shot his sergeant-major dead. A British officer in another unit was stabbed. There were constant complaints from the soldiers. After a few months, Ron applied for leave. As he was a member of the Indian Army now, rather than the British Army, any leave was to India, rather than Britain. It was granted – one month. He left immediately, at the end of August, for the most exotic part of India he could think of: Kashmir.

*

Ron's destination in Kashmir was the far north: the remote Gilgit Valley (now in Pakistan), with its glaciers, lakes and verdant valleys, at the western tip of the Karakorum chain of the Himalayas. Today it is one of the great tourist attractions of Kashmir, but in 1946 it was an extraordinarily remote region, tucked away between Afghanistan's Hindu Kush and Tibet. The Hunza valley of Tibet into which it runs was the inspiration for the fictional 'Shangri-La' invented by James Hilton in his 1933 novel *Lost Horizon*. Over it looms the vast, twin-peaked bulk of Nanga Parbat, at 26,660 feet the ninth highest mountain in the world.

The trip started eventfully. Steaming from Basra to Karachi the ship encountered wild weather just where the in-bound vessel had earlier, with its cargo of trucks. At one point, encountering a local sailing boat in severe difficulty, the crew were rescued and the boat was roped to the steamer. The sea was so rough it sank.

Captain Buxton, Indian Electrical and Mechanical Engineers, on leave to India from Iraq, Agra, 1946

After a brief diversion to Agra to see the Taj Mahal, Ron took a bus from Lahore to Srinagar, in the Kashmir Valley, summer capital of India's northernmost state, where he checked into the old Swiss hotel, Nedou's. After a pleasant week on one of the old houseboats on Dal Lake, he took a bus north to Bandipora where he hired a local Kashmiri servant, two riding ponies and five pack ponies in preparation for his 500 km journey through the mountains to Gilgit, capital of the Northern Area and a hill station to which British administrators repaired in the heat of the summer. The ancient city was an important staging post on the Silk Road, the ancient trade route across Asia.

Today there is a road from Srinigar to Gilgit, but in 1946 the best route was to follow the government bridlepath constructed by the British in 1880. The contractors had built bungalows every fifteen miles or so, which could be used for accommodation. En route Ron encountered another party, travelling in the same direction. It turned out to be the governor of Gilget Province (which was run by the Indian Civil Service), Paul Mainprice. Ron and Mainprice fell in together, forming a cavalcade as far as the River Indus. As

Ron's photograph of the view from the bridle-path to Gilgit

Mainprice was the governor, there was a grand welcome at each bungalow as they reached it. The intended plan, after the Kamri Pass at 14,000 feet, was to cross the Indus to Gilgit, but by the time they reached it, it was late September. The pass closed in October. With fears of imminent snow which might cut him off for weeks, Ron decided he had no option but to alter his plans. Reluctantly, he and Mainprice parted and Ron returned to Srinigar, and army life.

*

After his month in Kashmir, to be back in the heat of Iraq again was insupportable. However, not long after arriving back there, his long-awaited 'LeaB' ('Leave to Britain') came through. He hadn't been home for two and a half years. He was given three weeks.

After taking a train to Baghdad, then American bus to Mufrak in Syria – both crammed with soldiers – he continued by rail, which then still ran through Israel to Cairo (the so-called 'Medlock Route'). There, stationed in a transit camp at Port Said, he awaited a ship home.

Ron's overseas adventures, however, were not quite over. For a British national, it was no time to be in Egypt. Since the cutting of the Suez Canal by the French and Egyptians in 1869, that 100-mile link had become a lifeline for Britain to its interests in India. In 1882, concerned for the security of the canal, the British had invaded and occupied Egypt. Then, in 1936, under the

Kamri Pass, 14,000 feet. Nanga Parbat (very faint) in background.

terms of the Anglo-Egyptian Treaty, Britain had withdrawn all troops except those necessary to retain control of the canal. That treaty had been detested by Egyptian nationalists, particularly the Arab Socialist Party, who wanted full independence. But the outbreak of war had temporarily halted protests, as Britain once again took control, running a kind of British hegemony. With the war over, a wave of anti-British feeling had now resurfaced. There were protests and demonstrations, especially against the Wafd party that had supported the decision to allow the treaty. In recent months the situation had become sufficiently inflammatory for British military personnel to be advised not to go out in uniform.

This risk, however, had to be set against the chance to see the Pyramids – perhaps a once-in-a-lifetime opportunity. To visit Egypt and not do so? The idea was unthinkable. Ron engaged a dragoman (guide) to take him round the Giza complex and the Great Sphinx. Scrupulously attired in 'civvies', they set off. But as the dragoman guided Ron round, the English they were speaking evidently carried. The pair attracted the attention of some aggressive-looking Egyptian students, who began to follow them. Eventually, in the claustrophobic surroundings of the King's Chamber they found themselves cornered by a gathering crowd of twenty or so, chanting and threatening. With the exit cut off, the crowd started to approach menacingly. For the only time he can remember, Ron felt in real danger. The dragoman, however, protected him courageously, and somehow they got back outside the pyramid.

Three weeks later, still carrying the rug he had bought in Baghdad, Ron caught a boat to Marseilles. For the last leg of his journey, the train across France from Marseilles to Calais, his unwieldy luggage proved unexpectedly beneficial. The temperature plunged to below freezing. It was now January 1947. After the heat of Basra, Northern Europe in winter was always going to come as a dramatic contrast, but now, as the train headed north, the bitter cold seemed almost beyond belief. Nobody knew it, but Britain was already in the grip of what would be the coldest winter of the twentieth century. Ron and several other soldiers huddled beneath the carpet for warmth.[27] Eventually, they reached Calais, and, finally, the white cliffs of Dover, beneath sullen grey skies, lay ahead. After more than a month in transit, of sleeping in tents or bunks, Ron was finally ready to take his three weeks' leave.

*

Britain was a mess. There was no transport or petrol. The trains were crowded. Food was scarce and still rationed. Everything was broken, worn or run-down. London was still a city recovering from siege. There was rubble everywhere, from the Blitz and Hitler's doodlebugs and V2 rockets. More or less everything was rationed. The December cold snap, after 21 January, hardened into conditions of Siberian severity. On 20 February the Dover-Ostend ferry service was suspended because of pack ice off the Belgian coast. The Thames froze, marooning coal barges so people could not keep warm. With the victory celebrations now a distant memory, Britain was a shattered country, a place in monochrome, of grey skies, soot-blackened buildings, drab clothes and putty faces.

Since Ron had last been here, too, his family ties had weakened further. Few close relations as he had had when he left, now he had fewer. His cousin Lionel had been killed at Salerno during the Allied invasion of Italy in September 1943. His grandfather, the Reverend Barclay Buxton, had died earlier in 1946.

The one joy was to see Jean again. She had finished the war as a junior commander with three pips (the equivalent of captain), in her final role accompanying a general to a Continental conference on how postwar Europe would be divided. She had bought a fifteen-year lease on a house in Cheyne Row, which Ron now made his base. Since the war's end, however, Jean had not been well. Perhaps inheriting Muriel's pulmonary weakness, she had

---

27 The carpet in question still lies in the entrance hall at Kimberley.

contracted TB – tuberculosis – still a highly infectious and potentially lethal disease without prescription antibiotics available. It would take her at least a year to recuperate, during which she divided her time between Cheyne Row and Holywell.

Still, for all its gloom, London was at least better than Basra. The mere thought of returning to Iraq depressed Ron and filled him with frustration, so he visited REME headquarters to see if something could be done. There he had a bit of luck. The War Office, it so happened, was looking for a young graduate officer to join the Wartime Joint Recruiting Board, which visited universities on what today is called 'the milk round'.

So, instead of the heat and dust of Iraq, Ron's last four months of war service were spent in the infinitely more agreeable task of touring Britain's university towns in springtime. The Joint Recruiting Board supposedly consisted of a colonel, a major and a captain – the latter being Ron's new position. The colonel hardly ever showed up, so usually it was just Ron, together with one Professor Wardlaw of London University, recruiting on behalf of the Civil Service. The professor was interested only in candidates with first class honours degrees for top-level industry or the Civil Service. The few candidates meeting his exacting requirements he snapped up. For those who did not match up to his standards, but were not, in his opinion, entirely without merit, he would turn to Ron: 'Well, Captain Buxton, d'you think you could use this man?'

In June his appointment with the demob depot finally arrived. With the others appearing that day, he was given a short lecture about civilian life, issued with a cheap flannel suit (clothing was still rationed) and his war was over. Twenty-four years old, five feet nine inches tall, Ronald Buxton was at last free to do battle with the real world.

9
Escape to Africa

R ON'S FIRST MEETING with Claude Cranmer, H. Young's managing director, was, to say the least, awkward. It had always been everyone's tacit assumption that, after Cambridge, Ron would join the family firm of which his father was chairman. The seamlessness of this obvious progression, however, had been badly interrupted by two unscheduled events: the war, and Murray's death. What became painfully apparent from Cranmer, during Ron's first 'official' visit to the Lea Bridge works in May 1947, was that Cranmer had not the faintest idea what to do with him.

Following Murray's death, his brother Godfrey Buxton – Ron's uncle – and Ron had been made directors of the company. Godfrey was well summarised by the phrase 'a gentleman, a churchman, but not a businessman'. Ron was different. Here was the chairman's son, youthful, energetic, Eton-and-Cambridge-educated – something of a bird of paradise in the grey world of engineering – ambitious, independent, breezily self-assured and, following his war experiences, wise beyond his twenty-four years. He was also, since his twenty-first birthday, the company's largest shareholder, making him, effectively, owner of the company. Yet, as Cranmer puzzled, what to do with such a person?

The company had emerged from the war in better shape than most. True, Murray's death in 1940 had robbed the business of its driving force and figurehead at the exact moment when, with his election as President of the Institute of Structural Engineers, it stood to gain most. And the war years had been intensely stressful on its staff. By the nature of its work, a structural steel company was a target for enemy bombers, and for extended periods until 1943, air raid warnings were a daily occurrence: a first warning when bomber formations crossed the coastline; a second 'red warning' shortly before they reached London. At Lea Bridge, four underground shelters were constructed, plus a steel-reinforced room in the offices. In 1943 the Battersea works was almost completely destroyed by a raid aimed at the adjacent A block of the new Battersea Power Station (the first two of the famous cream chimneystacks).

On the other hand, H. Young & Company was doing useful work for the war effort, and some quick-thinking after Murray's death meant it finished the war with a number of advantages. The company accountant, Harold Judd, had stepped in as an emergency measure until (engineering being an industry of national importance) the board had been able to pull Claude Cranmer out of the Royal Engineers to take over as managing director. Cranmer was the former general manager of Powers and Deane Ransomes, one of the companies Murray had bought in 1936. He knew the industry backwards. Having started straight from polytechnic in the template shop (making the templates for the steel structures that had to be cut, punched, sheared, cropped and drilled ready for riveting or welding), he had worked his way up through the drawing office, proving himself so outstanding a designer he had ended up as head draughtsman. Combining knowledge of the business with excellent managerial skills, his selection had proved a coup. While the war meant the company's main previous source of work – cinemas and department stores – had dried up, that did not mean there was no work to be had. Cranmer's first action was to approach the War Office to tender for military contracts. His nous was rewarded when H. Young & Company won their first government order: for the manufacture of Bailey bridge panels, including over a million feet of welding.

The Bailey bridge, like the Nissen hut a generation earlier, was one of the most brilliant design ideas of the war – now heralded as a classic of military engineering. Devised by a civil engineer at the War Office called Donald (later Sir Donald) Bailey and tested in the first years of the conflict, it consisted of a steel truss bridge capable of spanning gaps of up to 60-metres (200 ft), yet that was easily portable, prefabricated and required no special tools or heavy equipment to assemble. The modular bridge elements were small enough and light enough to be handled by men and carried in trucks. Yet the bridge they made was strong enough to carry tanks. In Italy, during the winter campaign of 1944, and in France following the D-Day landings (where Allied bombing or the retreating enemy had destroyed all river or canal crossings) the Bailey bridge literally paved the way to victory. Field Marshal Montgomery later declared that 'without the Bailey bridge, we would not have won the war'. H. Young & Company would fabricate the panels, a task requiring extremely high tolerances. The completed panels could then be clipped together in the field like Meccano.

After that first order, the war had delivered a steady and increasing stream of such government contracts. In due course the Bailey panels were supplemented by the similar Mulberry harbour sections: sections of braced steel which, like the bridge panels, could be clipped together to form pontoons. Mulberry sections provided the bridgehead for the Allies to land in Normandy on D-Day.

Following the bombing of the Battersea Nine Elms works, Cranmer had shifted all production to Lea Bridge in Leyton (confusingly retaining the 'Nine Elms Works' moniker on the company stationery) where the premises were expanded and improved. Instead of the river frontage at Battersea for

'Without the Bailey bridge, we would not have won the war.' Bailey bridge panels in use.

Mulberry harbour sections at the D-Day Normandy landings

deliveries by Thames barge, Lea Bridge had a railway siding with a building running the length of the site, allowing for deliveries with spans of up to 50 feet. Four derricks stood alongside to handle the steel. The improved site worked so well that the leasehold on the ruined Battersea site was sold.

While no company was allowed to profit from war work (there was a 100% profit tax), under Cranmer's well-organised management the Lea

Bridge factory was largely re-equipped with all the heavy equipment of steel handling – giant presses, saws and angle cutters – so in the postwar scramble to rebuild and repair, H. Young & Company was poised with a decisive advantage. Soon they were taking a leading part in the postwar construction boom of a brave new world, for which houses, shopping centres and even whole new towns were planned – though in the early years steel rationing meant the company had to be careful only to take commissions with 'IS', or 'Iron and Steel Authorisation'. The steel framework for many of London and Birmingham's department stores came from Leyton, as did the steel 'skeletons' for Harlow New Town.

Into this smooth-running operation, however, it was hard to know where to place Ron. Unsure what else to do, Cranmer started him in the usual place: the drawing office. Every morning Ron would leave Jean's house in Cheyne Row in Chelsea and travel to Leyton to the distinctly less charming surroundings of the Lea Bridge works. After the finest education available, finished by three years travelling the world, it was less than the apogee of youthful ambition. Six months of this uncongenial schedule in a country still crippled by debt and rationing, and Ron was more than open to alternative diversions. And one conveniently arrived, via Jean.

Jean had for some time yearned to see the Sudan. Still British-owned, that vast country – the biggest in Africa – was the essence of the Africa of romantic imagination. Bisected by the Nile, it was tribal and colonial, a place of dust and adventure, of pith helmets, General Gordon, *The Four Feathers*, and evocative names like Khartoum and Omdurman. Jean announced she had instigated an invitation from Paul Howell, a Buxton cousin working out there for the Colonial Office. He had written suggesting they both travel out for Christmas and stay for a few weeks over the winter.

For Ron, it was not an invitation that needed to be repeated. He decided to take a break from H. Young's drawing office for three months and join Jean on a trip. Besides, who knew what Africa might yield? Perhaps there might be opportunities for the company there ...

*

Paul Howell was District Commissioner of the Western Area of Kordofan Province, in central Sudan, an area of thousands of square miles of poor scrubland between Darfur in the west and the valley of the White Nile in the east. Howell's mother, Linnet, was a Buxton (a great-granddaughter of The Liberator) whom Ron and Jean had known through childhood gatherings at Easneye. Six years older than Ron, Howell had, like him, been to Trinity College, Cambridge, where he had studied anthropology. From there he had visited the Sudan to study for his dissertation on the Shilluk tribe, in the process learning Nuer, before answering the Colonial Office's plea for young men to build the British Empire in Africa. The Sudan Political Service was at that time seen as the elite of the British African administrations – with a reputation for preferring sporting applicants, ideally with double blues.

Eldon Power arranged their flight. A family friend since Murray had bought his company (Powers and Deane Ransomes) in 1936, Power owned a third of H. Young & Company and had been encouraging about the trip from the start. In October 1947 Ron and Jean left by Dakota from London's new airport, relocated from Croydon: Heathrow. After flying to Cairo, they took the train to Luxor and Aswan, in suffocating heat. From Aswan, as roads or railways went no further, they took a boat down the Nile to Wadi Halfa (from where a vast plain opens up, stretching all the way to Juba, almost 1,200 miles further south). From Wadi Halfa, it was overland by Sudan Railways again to Khartoum where Paul had arranged for them to stay with friends of his, before taking a train into the interior to El Obeid, from where the final leg was by souk lorry. Still today a standard mode of transport for travellers across the remote and endless scrub of central Africa, lorries will carry paying passengers in their front seats. And so, eventually, after five days of travelling, they reached En Nahud, capital of the Kordofan province, where Howell was based.

Here they settled in for the next two-and-a-half months. Their stay was well-timed; effectively, a glimpse of the last hurrah of the solar-topee-and-empire-builders' way of life that was now entering its twilight years – for time

DC's Residence, En Nahud, Kordofan Province, Sudan, November 1947. Seated, centre, left to right: Ronald, Paul Howell, Jean.

was running out for the British Empire and Colonial Africa. Paul Howell's house was a typical DC's residence: a single-storey lodge thatched with reeds, with wide airy verandas surrounded by lawns. The garden was tended by two prisoners, both convicted murderers. For Ron, who had glimpsed Africa on his passage to India, and visited Cairo on his way home less than a year before, here, at last, was the *real* Africa. Here was an antidote to the gloom of postwar Britain.

Having returned from the Middle East less after almost three years away, Britain had been, in many ways, a cruel disappointment for Ron. There was a sense that the party was over, yet the bill-paying and clearing up had hardly begun. Emotionally, too, the place represented pain; the loss of his parents and home life. There was uncertainty about the future, too – except the dismal prospect of the drawing offices of H. Young & Company.

By comparison, Africa was paradise. The Sudan, with its relentless equatorial sunshine, red soil and vast skies, its brilliant light, saturated colours and exotic smells and sounds was the 'Africa and golden joys' of which Shakespeare wrote: a place to warm the soul. It represented escape from the traumas of the last few years. It was the first time Ron and Jean – now each other's only immediate family – had had time to relax together since leaving school and since the tragedy of their parents' untimely deaths. Where Ron's earlier travels in Kashmir and Cairo might have been exciting and adventuresome, they were still essentially solitary affairs. Now they had each other. Like so many of their generation who had survived the war, they were travelled and experienced – and possibly grown up and serious – beyond their years. It was a chance to cut loose and feel free in a way they never had before, to contemplate the delicious fact that, at twenty-four and twenty-six, they still had their whole lives before them.

For Jean, it was her first taste of Africa. If the headmaster at Hawtreys had chosen the epithet *magnum in parvo* to summarise Ron's character, exactly the same could have been said of her. She had left Belstead School at the age

of eighteen to join the Auxiliary Territorial Service. Small, strong, clear-thinking and forceful, her intelligent brown eyes were connected to a formidable mind which supplied both sharp wit and enabled her to grasp subjects and situations quickly. These characteristics had played their part in her swift promotion to the equivalent of captain. She was good-looking, with fair hair instead of Ron's red tinge. Already close, perhaps more so than most siblings due to the distance of their father, losing their parents so young had made them closer still.

As for Ron, perhaps still seeking role models in

his father's absence, he could not help but be struck by the responsibilities wielded by Paul Howell. Only a few years older than Ron, Howell held dominion over an area more than half the size of England. Part of the DC's role, according to Lord Lugard (who drew up the tenets for the British Colonial Service) was to 'maintain and develop all that is best in the indigenous methods and institutions of native rule'. This was the principle – of 'indirect rule', whereby the British pulled the strings behind local rulers – by which the Empire had been able to expand so vastly. It was a system that just two decades earlier had allowed for an indigenous population of 43 million across Africa to be governed by just 1,200 colonial administrators.[28] Administrators like Howell made such astonishing ratios possible. He heard complaints, solved disputes and held court as a magistrate. The Kordofan area was beset by religious and tribal tensions (still tragically present today), but with fair and determined authority Howell had gained respect and managed to maintain peace.[29]

It was all a long way from Lea Bridge. A fluent Arabic-speaker, Howell's passion and knowledge as an anthropologist piqued Jean's interest too. He told them about the Nuer tribe (previously he had been DC in Nuer country and

Camel riding, Kordofan, 1947. LEFT: Jean. RIGHT: Ron.

28 Jeremy Paxman, *Empire, What Ruling the World Did to the British* (2011).
29 Another cousin, Charles de Bunsen, whose wife was a Buxton, was also in the Sudan Political Service. He became, in due course, Deputy-Governor of Equatoria Province 1951–52.

On safari – LEFT: The Ford box-car and lorry; RIGHT: Camp at Zankor, Sudan

would go on to write a doctoral thesis about them). On one occasion Ron and Jean watched as he addressed a crowd for an hour in fluent Nuer. He also told them about the Mandari in Southern Sudan, a polygamous tribe about which, despite their numbering around 40,000, almost nothing was known and about whom no serious study had ever been made.[30] Jean could not hear enough.

They made several trips from the lodge at Nahud. It was by regular safaris that Paul kept in touch with what was going on across his vast district and helped to steer the local government and chiefs towards democracy. For these trips Paul, Jean and Ron went ahead in Paul's Ford box-car. They were followed by a lorry bringing camping kit and three or four servants. Camp would be established in the evening, often as guests of a tribal chief.

For Christmas they all travelled south by souk lorry to Shilluk country, near Malakal; then proceeded another hundred miles further south to Fangak, in Nuer country, an area to which whites hardly ever went. There they stayed with a friend of Howell's, the DC (and, later, High Commissioner of Rhodesia), Jock Duncan. They shot guinea fowl and antelopes to eat, while in the vast Sudd swamps Howell busied himself taking depth soundings for his Jonglei Canal project – a plan to divert water from above the wetlands to further down the White Nile. Meanwhile Duncan, Ron and Jean occupied themselves. One day, with some Nuer tribesmen, they took a canoe up the Nile, exploring. Somehow, in a particularly wide part of the river, the canoe capsized. The Nuer became extremely agitated – because, it turned out, crocodiles were an ever-present danger in that part of the river. Running along the banks, they formed a human chain into the water and, one by one, everyone was pulled to safety. Afterwards, there was a polo match laid on as part of the festivities.

30 Sadly, at time of writing, January 2014, bitter clashes have broken out in Juba pitting Dinka, who support President Salva Kiir, against Nuer, who back former Vice-President Riek Marchar, re-opening wounds that reach back decades.

In Fangak, Ron and Jean said goodbye to Paul Howell. From there, they continued alone, catching the post boat down the Nile to Juba (a week), then overland by bus to the Ugandan border town of Nimule. From there they took a steamer down the Albert Nile, then a bus to Lake Kyoga, picking up a train at the Kenya-Uganda Railways and Harbours rail-head to Nairobi in Kenya.

In Nairobi they met their cousin Susan, married to Michael Wood. The Woods were five years older than Ron, and had moved to Africa the year before, in 1947, after marrying during the war. They had much in common, however. Ron and Jean had grown up with Susan (née Buxton). She had the Buxton red hair and was the daughter of Uncle Alfred (and Aunt Edith), who had been killed by the same bomb that killed Ron and Jean's father. Since then, Mew had died and, in September 1943, Susan's brother Lionel had been killed at Salerno.

Susan and Michael had a house in Muthaiga. Michael, later Sir Michael, was a young surgeon who had qualified during the war under the celebrated plastic surgeon Archibald MacIndoe. (MacIndoe's pioneering techniques for rebuilding burns victims had saved many pilots horrifyingly injured in the Battle of Britain.) Over the next few years, called ever more frequently to emergencies in the bush, often in remote villages without hospitals or facilities, always requiring specially chartered flights, it occurred to Michael to learn to fly himself. Realising the difference such a 'flying doctor' could make in a place like Africa, together with MacIndoe and an American surgeon, Dr Thomas Rees, they founded the Flying Doctors Service of East Africa which later became part of the African Medical and Research Foundation (AMREF).[31] Within fifteen years it would be providing medical care over a half-million-square-mile area in Kenya, Uganda and Tanzania.

Ron and Jean also met Clarence and May (Mavis) Buxton, who owned a tea plantation near Limuru, twenty miles north of Nairobi, or 'Up Country' – colonial parlance for the fertile highlands around the Rift Valley which became an enclave for white settlers after Kenya became a British Protectorate in 1895. Again, they found much in common. Clarence, at fifty-two, by both his age and experience felt a generation older than Ron and Jean (though in fact they were the same: Clarence's father was a cousin of their father Murray). Certainly no one knew more about Kenya. Clarence had arrived in Africa shortly after the First World War to join the Colonial Service, a Cambridge graduate and a major distinguished in battle (MC and mentioned in despatches). He had been District Commissioner in Masai

31 A documentary about Michael Wood's work entitled *The Flying Doctors of East Africa* (German *Die Fliegenden Ärzte von Ostafrika*) was made in 1969 – by none other than a young Werner Herzog.

African evening: Ron and Jean in Sudan

(where he had stopped the Masai Rebellion in battle order) and, later, been DC in Kisumu too. Clarence, like Paul Howell, epitomised a deep, almost Victorian commitment to public service.

In Nairobi, Ron and Jean hatched a plan: to buy a car and drive it to South Africa and back. To convey some idea of the ambition of this plan, the one-way distance from Nairobi to Johannesburg, as the crow flies, is 2,500 miles, all by pot-holed dirt roads. As Land-Rovers had yet to be invented, the journey had to be completed in an ordinary two-wheel-drive saloon, with very limited mechanical assistance available en route. (Cars, in most parts of Africa, were still a rarity.) Ron duly found a sturdy prewar sedan, a ten-year-old 1937 Hudson 'straight eight', and they set off with two fare-paying passengers.

Unfortunately, on the pot-holed dirt roads a spring broke on the very first leg of the first day, just after they had crossed into Tanzania. It was an unpromising omen, but they limped to Arusha and managed to get it mended in the shadow of Kilimanjaro. It was their first and last mechanical problem of the entire journey. Taking it in turns to drive – Jean was an accomplished driver after spending the war driving her general about – without further incident they motored across Tanzania, visiting the Ngorongoro Crater with all its game, then on via Northern Rhodesia, to Zambia, all on dirt roads. There they visited Lusaka, then followed the Great North Road (the Zambia section of Rhodes's Cape-to-Cairo highway) south to the border town of Chirundu, then into Southern Rhodesia.

One broken spring in 14,000 miles: the £350 Hudson 'straight eight'

Here they encountered their first tarmac of the trip: two narrow strips, one for each wheel. On meeting an oncoming car or lorry, each driver moved over so that half their vehicle, or two wheels, remained on tarmac. Thus they reached Salisbury, where, for the first time on their overseas adventure, Ron had business to attend to.

*

The moment the African trip had been mooted, it had planted a seed in Ron's mind. Might there not be opportunities for H. Young & Company abroad? The possibilities of structural steel, in particular for prefabricated, steel-framed buildings that could be easily and rapidly assembled on site, must be almost limitless for undeveloped countries. Steel was light and relatively easy to transport. Precision work could be completed under factory conditions, so that in remote sites without specialised equipment or skills all that had to be done was bolt pre-formed 'kit' parts together. The 'kit building' was as perfectly suited to countries with poor infrastructure as the Bailey bridge had been to wartime. And the warm climate meant that little in the way of cladding over any steel superstructure was required.

There were other advantages to the idea of doing business in Africa, too. The map of that vast continent after the Second World War looked little different from how it had looked after the great European 'Scramble for

Africa' between 1876 and 1912. Following the 1919 Peace Conference after the First World War, Britain had claimed and got the lion's share of Germany's four colonies. Rhodes's dream of a trans-African railway from the Cape to Cairo, linking the mineral riches of the south with the strategically and economically critical Suez Canal in the north, might not (quite) have materialised. But Britain's acquisition of German East Africa (Tanganyika) supplied the last missing piece of the jigsaw that finally made it possible to travel from Cairo to the Cape on 'all-pink' – all-British – territory. More than a third of Africa's population and hundreds of thousands of square miles of territory was still, even after the Second World War, under British control: twice the percentage held by the next largest-owning power, France.

True, after the Second World War imperialism and colonialism were distinctly unfashionable. Even before the war, Britain had committed to granting India independence. Burma's independence had been granted literally as Ron and Jean drove south (in January 1948). The superpowers of the emerging Cold War were already champions of anti-colonialism. 'By the late 1940s it was obvious that self-government would come *one day* for Africa too – at least for the black African colonies directly controlled by Britain and France' wrote Thomas Pakenham in *The Scramble for Africa* (1991). 'But when would that day be? The Powers were in no hurry to leave, their better-educated subjects were too weak, despite a wide range of discontents, to make the Powers give any thought to a timetable.' And until the moment the Union Jack was lowered, the fact that large areas of Africa were British offered tremendous trading advantages.

For one, convenience. Travelling and trading within territories, colonies, mandates or protectorates of the British Empire meant English was the official language and the rule of English law applied, not to mention any number of other British customs from drinking tea to driving on the left. Senior administrative positions tended to be occupied by Colonial Service public school and Oxbridge graduates, to whom an Englishman like Ron, with just such an education, spoke (in all senses) the same language. There were also enormous currency and exchange rate advantages. Most African colonies' currencies either had their values pegged to sterling, or used sterling. Sterling at this time was a 'reserve currency' for Commonwealth countries, which meant it was the anchor currency which other countries could use as a store of value (as the dollar became later in the twentieth century), meaning favourable or preferential rates. Similarly, there were tax advantages. Taxes in African countries tended to be lower than UK taxes, so there were potentially greater profits to be made from work undertaken abroad than at home. Trading within 'pink' parts of the map also meant no import or export duties, no border, immigration or visa complications, and on it went.

Most African countries at this time had no structural steel works at all. And as for most kinds of building required for development – factories and mills, water towers, railways – structural steel was what was needed, the potential for any entrepreneur happy to spend time in Africa was vast. Almost unlimited, in fact. Inevitably the long-term future would be uncertain as British territories acquired their independence. (The eleven years from 1957 to 1968 saw a scramble *out* of Africa almost as undignified and hectic, as countries tried to withdraw before they were pushed, as the scramble *in* had been half a century before.) But that could be faced in due course. In the meantime, it all added up to a monster opportunity. And it was a first step down this road that Ron was taking with his meeting in Salisbury.

Ron had set up a meeting with the head of Barclays Bank, Rhodesia, to discuss the idea of starting the first structural steel company in the country. Of all British Africa, Rhodesia seemed most pregnant with opportunities for structural steelwork: it was needed for factories, agriculture and power stations. Many British expatriates retired to Rhodesia; it was a place where there were likely to be plenty of introductions. A few days later, in Bulawayo, Ron got together with two potential partners, Johnson & Fletcher, builders' merchants in Rhodesia, and Alpheus, Williams and Dowse, structural engineers and steel fabricators from South Africa. It was agreed unanimously that an engineering and structural steel company should be established as soon as possible.

After that, it was back into the Hudson and on to South Africa. There they visited Johannesburg and Durban, before returning, via the Victoria Falls, to Nairobi. Before catching a flight home with BOAC, Ron sold the Hudson for £350 – very nearly what he paid for it. The mileometer indicated that they had travelled 14,000 miles.

*

For Ron and Jean, the Africa trip was of momentous significance. Their own circumstances, plus those of postwar Britain, were enough to leave them hooked by that addictive continent. But there were plenty of other reasons, too. Their family had close historical ties with the place. They had grown up on stories of their distinguished forebear Thomas Fowell Buxton, abolisher of slavery and inspiration to David Livingstone. Uncle Alfred, killed with Murray, had been an African missionary. In any case, adventure and wanderlust were in their blood: from their paternal grandfather's Christian missions to Japan to Grandfather Hildred being pursued by wolves across Russia as he opened thread factories.

On their return to England, Jean promptly enrolled at Lady Margaret Hall, Oxford, to read for a diploma at the Institute of Social Anthropology, with a particular interest in the Mandari tribe. As for Ron, he discovered he had

Nairobi Airport, 1948

found a new role for himself within the company. There would be no more tedious technicalities in the drawing office. Claude Cranmer could run the UK operation – as he very capably was. Meanwhile, Ron would set up its overseas arms, specifically in Africa. In the five years before his father died, he had watched the way Murray confidently bought up, took over or set up companies. Now it was his turn. Shortly after their return, that spring of 1948, he moved out from Jean's and took a flat in St James's Place with his old Cambridge friend Charles Dalgleish. The rent was £4 a week. His career was ready to begin.

*

The following year, 1949, Ron returned to Africa and started the Rhodesia Engineering and Steel Construction Company (RESCCo), based in Bulawayo, British Rhodesia. He spent two months finding and buying land to provide the company's headquarters and factory. It was to be an ambitious concern. On the board were two directors from H. Young & Company – Ron, and Claude Cranmer – plus two directors from the South African steel company Gardener Williams, and three from Johnson Fletcher builders' merchants (a

[122]

company which already had a Gardener Williams director), all introduced by the local director of Barclays Bank. Structural machinery, including presses, drills and punches were sent out, along with, in due course, a British manager.

Ron also founded H. Young (East Africa) Ltd, based in Nairobi, Kenya, making his new friend and mentor, Clarence Buxton, chairman. The year after that Sudan Steel Construction Ltd followed, based in Jersey for tax reasons, with agents in a branch office in Khartoum. (Two years later this branch office was expanded into a small fabrication works.) These two operations would sell, chiefly, standardised, off-the-shelf, steel-framed and steel-clad buildings that could be ordered from a catalogue, fabricated in London and shipped to Port Sudan or Mombasa.

Initially these two latter companies were supervised by managers sent from the UK, but as contracts arrived to justify it, overseas factories were established with saws, drills and punches, and local labour was recruited for fabrication and erection (though larger contracts were always overseen by a UK manager).

Ron began to make regular visits to Africa, three times a year, in January, summer and autumn. Starting in Khartoum, he would then fly on down to Nairobi to visit H. Young (East Africa) and see the Woods, then proceed to Rhodesia to RESCCo. Flying in the late 1940s and early 1950s, in unpressurised, propeller-driven aircraft directly through weather turbulence at low altitudes, was, of course, a very different experience to the smooth, quiet high-altitude jet age ahead.

As if this travelling were not enough, however, Ron found time for other expeditions too. Usually these involved the same team; a mixture of his old Cambridge and new London friends: Tom Faber (of Faber and Faber, an MP), Charles Dalgleish (then still a junior fellow at Trinity), Milo Keynes (a surgeon, grandson of Maynard) and Ron. They would cram into a tiny ex-Army jeep with only the crudest of canvas roofs. Many thousands of miles were covered on these '£25 per head by jeep' trips to Italy, Spain and North Africa.

One such mission, to Morocco in 1950, almost ended in disaster. In Spain, winding up the switchbacks of a high pass through the Pyrenees, Milo Keynes at the wheel, turned to shout something to those in the back. In so doing, he drove straight off the road. The jeep overturned and, with no roll bars or seat belts, they were lucky not to be killed. They crawled out, rubbed their bruises and sprains, and, after a cursory medical inspection by Milo, righted the jeep and pressed on to Morocco – thence over the Atlas Mountains and down to the Sahara before returning home.

*

Jeepers – LEFT TO RIGHT: Milo Keynes, Ron, Charles Dalgleish, Tom Faber, in the Atlas
Mountains, 1950

Jean, meanwhile, having completed her diploma at the Institute of Social
Anthropology, began researching for a B. Litt. 'She was always clever –
cleverer than me' Ron would sometimes say. At Oxford she had come under
the influence of the eminent anthropologist Professor (later Sir) E. E. Evans-
Pritchard, a Fellow of All Souls and pivotal figure in the development of
social anthropology. In 'EP' (as Jean, like everyone else, was soon calling him)
she found an inspiring mentor. His trilogy of works on the Nuer, published in
the 1930s, were accepted classics of British anthropology. To research her B.
Litt. in 1950–2 she moved for fifteen months to live with the Mandari tribe –
which she had first encountered with Paul Howell. Mandari country was
about sixty miles north of Juba in the Southern Sudan. Nomadic cattle-
herders, the warrior tribe lived by constantly moving their open-air camps to
fresh pastures and back again, as they had done for millennia. The Mandari
had hardly been studied before, and had had only very limited contact with
white people. Jean learned to speak their dialect, Kutuk na Mundari
Mandari, and managed to get herself 'adopted' into the house of a chieftain

and his family, where she so endeared herself that they nicknamed her 'Awuk na ma Pilary' – 'The Daughter of Chief Pilary'.[32]

In due course Jean built herself a house in Mandari country. Ron bought her a jeep and a shotgun. Inside the cartridge magazine case, a card in Ron's handwriting included the following instruction:

6 shot – small, for guinea fowl, partridges, small duck
5 shot – medium, for duck etc
SG – buckshot, for defence, gazelle or other buck

When Ron later visited Jean in the Sudan, the jeep was making a terrible clanking noise. On inspection, he found it had a broken rear axle. It had been like that, Jean cheerfully informed him, for months.

British newspapers, when they got wind of Jean's adventure, were much taken by the idea of this small, pretty, English girl living alone with a tribe of giant (the Mandari are famously tall), naked, polygamous African warriors. On her return, fifteen months later, now thirty-one, several reported her exploits. Sample headlines included: 'WHERE TEN CATTLE BUY A WIFE' and 'ENGLISH GIRL'S 15 MONTHS ALONE WITH SAVAGES'. And from the bumper Christmas number of *Tit-Bits*, 1952:

Fearlessly, after learning their difficult language, she conversed with towering chieftains, some of whom have up to twenty wives. She studied their marriage customs and discovered that cattle is their only form of currency when wives are being bought and sold.

Although their warriors carry spears and bows and arrows, the Mandari are a charming, courteous people … But what queer ways of making love they have! They despise kissing – don't think it at all interesting. The young man who indulges in petting before marriage is frowned upon; the young woman who shows signs of becoming a flirt is called 'loose' and ostracized by the tribe.

When a suitor spots a pretty young girl he would like to marry, he decks himself out in vari-coloured beads, which he wears strung on wire round his waist like a corset. He puts elephants' teeth and bangles on his arms and carefully oils his ebony body all over.

---

32 Sadly, the Mandari have been in the papers for all the wrong reasons more recently. Over the last 25 years, civil war in South Sudan has claimed two million lives. Mandari herds have been targeted by militia groups and the opposing armies of the Khartoum defence forces and the Sudan People's Liberation Army (SPLA). Tribesmen were recruited into both armies. When the Dinka tribe sided largely with the SPLA, the Mandari felt obliged to fight alongside the Khartoum government. Both sides were guilty of atrocity and cruelty, with disastrous results. Today, Mandari cattle are killed wandering into minefields and Mandari herdsmen carry not spears, but 'periks' – Chinese-made Kalashnikov AK-47s – to protect themselves in this, one of the poorest regions in the world.

Then he goes to a large tent or marquee, known as Lomore, where all young girls over the age of ten sleep. Outside the marquee, the native gives a series of low whistles to attract the attention of a particular girl.

If she likes the look of him, she invites him into the tent to sleep there throughout the night – in the presence of the other girls and their suitors. But there is no love-making. The young man, Miss Buxton discovered, merely sleeps with his head nestling on the shoulder of the young woman of his choice.

And when the couple marry, after a ceremonious handing over of the dowry, which may number twenty head of cattle, the bride puts on a goatskin as a symbol that she is married. Many children are usually born, for the tribe is prolific ...

If the papers were taken with Jean, so were the Mandari: they offered 'many cattle' for her, and likewise for her jeep (for which they offered *fifty* cattle). Jean reciprocated their feelings. Becoming almost like a surrogate family to her, the Mandari became the subject of her life's work, and her time spent amongst them was plainly some of the happiest of her life. Her B. Litt research[33] was soon expanded into a doctoral thesis.[34] She took many hundreds of photographs of every aspect of Mandari life, all on fine silver

Jean (LEFT) and (RIGHT) with Mandari

33 Jean's B.Litt thesis, 'The Social and Political Organization of the Mandari' (1953) was ultimately published as *Chiefs and Strangers. A Study of Political Assimilation among the Mandari* (Clarendon Press 1963).
34 Her D.Phil thesis, 'The Religion of a Southern Sudan Tribe: the Mandari' (1957) was substantially revised and published 16 years later, after her death, as *Religion and Healing in Mandari* (Clarendon Press 1973).

Mandari women

Courting hut

Mandari battle dress

Mandari men

gelatin plates (now in the collection of the Pitt Rivers Museum in Oxford). Although she never took a permanent post in anthropology, Dr Jean Buxton became an acknowledged authority in the subject, contributing numerous papers to anthropological journals and lecturing at the London School of Economics and elsewhere.

*

Times were looking up. At H. Young & Company, Ron, naturally good at finances, perfectly complemented Claude Cranmer, who was a fine engineer but less at home balancing the books. The company was solidly profitable and expanding steadily. In 1950 a new bay was added onto the Lea Bridge works, increasing the site to four acres. The buildings were extended to allow for the handling of bigger contracts. Ron was now earning £800 a year, fixed by the board, a salary comparable to his friends in the City. He had a company car, a small blue Vauxhall 10 (Claude Cranmer, as MD, had a Rover 16). But with his constant shuttling to and from Africa, and with the vast distances to be covered once there, a more interesting mode of transport had occurred to him.

It was clear that what he *really* needed was an aeroplane.

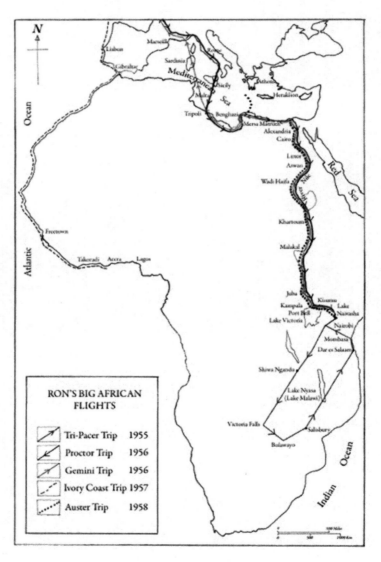

10

Flying

'So you want to fly, eh?' The avuncular figure in the clubhouse at Fair Oaks Aero Club who greeted Ron one May morning in 1952 was in his late fifties. He had a cheerful, if slightly curmudgeonly, manner. Fair Oaks was the nearest airfield to Holywell, and since their tenants the Pulbrooks had left after the war, Holywell had become Ron and Jean's weekend base. At Fair Oaks, Wing Commander Arthur, AFC – 'Wingco' to his many past students – was a club legend. An instructor since the 1930s, he had flown in both world wars and trained numerous pilots who had flown in the Battle of Britain. After helping Ron into a flying suit and helmet, Wingco led him out to an old Tiger Moth biplane standing on the grass.

Ron was strapped into the front seat, the worn canvas harness buckled over his shoulders and between his legs onto the parachute on which he sat. In a Tiger Moth the pupil or passenger sits in the front, the captain behind. Thus, unable to see the instructor, communication is by disembodied voice over headphones and the movement of the dual controls – a stick between his legs and rudder pedals beneath his feet. Once Wingco was installed in the seat behind, the fitter swung the propeller, the Gypsy engine exploded into life, and they trundled away over the grass. In no time they were accelerating for take-off, the wind in Ron's face, and moments later they had lifted smoothly off the ground and the green countryside around Chobham and the Hog's Back was unfolding beneath. As Ron adjusted to the novel sensation of open-cockpit flying, the Wingco's voice crackled in his ears. Did Ron feel all right? Ron replied that he did. 'Good.' The stick between his legs wagged sharply to the right and the docile Moth flipped onto its back. As the horizon span, Ron felt his weight transfer heavily and emphatically from the seat to the frayed canvas shoulder straps, in which he was now hanging 1,000 feet above the Surrey countryside. It was a feeling unlike anything he had felt before.

Amateur flying in England had, by the early 1950s, hardly changed for three decades. The Second World War had transformed military flying, from archaic-looking biplanes with wires and struts to sleek monoplanes like the Spitfire and even, latterly, the jet fighter (the German Messcherschmitt 262). But private flying had lagged. It was still almost in the 'barnstorming' era of the post-First World War years, when ex-Royal Flying Corps pilots landed outside villages in old Sopwiths to offer 'joy-rides' for a shilling a trip. The mere fact that, in 1952, Ron's training plane was *still* an open cockpit biplane spoke volumes.

('The aeroplane that won the war, me boy!' Wingco was fond of saying – referring, of course, to all the RAF pilots who had learnt to fly on it.)

It was not surprising, really, that Ron wanted to fly. He had grown up in an
era of airborne record-breaking: Lindbergh soloing the Atlantic in 1927;
Hinkler flying from London to Australia in sixteen days, and Kingsford-Smith
crossing the Pacific in 1928; Amelia Earhart crossing the Atlantic in 1936
and, later the same year, Beryl Markham crossing it against the wind the
other way. The Schneider Trophy for seaplanes (which gave birth to the
Spitfire) was an annual, much-publicised, event. At Hawtreys Ron would
have been surrounded by Biggles books, and at Eton that *ne plus ultra* of
airborne excitement, the Battle of Britain, had taken place directly overhead.

Flying, too, ran in the family. His father's brother, Uncle George, had been
killed in 1917, serving with the Royal Flying Corps over the Western Front.
Michael Wood, with whom Ron and Jean had stayed in Nairobi, was learning
to fly. His cousin 'Jocky' (Jocelyn) Buxton, a year younger than Ron but in
line to become, one day, the titular head of the family when he inherited the
baronetcy, had been a real 'Top Gun', a lieutenant commander in the Fleet Air
Arm, mentioned in despatches in the war, shot down in the Arctic Circle
flying Grumman F4F 'Wildcats' off carriers. Having re-enlisted with the
Royal Naval Volunteer Reserve with the outbreak of war in Korea, Jocky was
even now flying Hawker Sea Furies. With their 4,000 hp engines and 500
mph top speed, these were the fastest piston-engined fighters ever made.

Then there was the Africa effect. If anyone has the least inclination to fly,
nowhere brings it out like Africa. Africa, with its vast distances and lousy roads,
was made for flying. Indeed, after the rains, many roads were impassable. Beryl
Markham in her flying memoir *West with the Night* wonders whether it was
'well-meant wishful thinking' or 'a depraved and sadistic humour' that allowed
the government road commission to cause the erection of an 'impressive and
beautiful' signpost reading, 'To JUBA – KHARTOUM – CAIRO', as if 'the thousands
of miles of papyrus swamp and deep desert between Naivasha and Khartoum'
could be 'almost flippantly' overlooked. The giant scale of the landscape, features like the Nile and Rift Valleys, the Serengeti and Lake Victoria, were all far
too big to take in from the ground. Yet from the air everything made sense. The
scale became manageable. And for Ron, with business interests across three
African countries, manageability was everything.

Meanwhile Ron was still hanging, inverted, by his shoulder straps. The
stick wagged again, and he found himself crushed into his seat by the g-force.
Then a few moments later he was floating weightlessly between seat and chest
straps before his stomach began rising into his mouth as the Tiger Moth
cavorted and bounced around the sky in a series of ferocious spins, loops,
rolls, spiral dives and other aerobatic manoeuvres. It was not what he had
been expecting, but, so long as he could avoid being sick, it was certainly

exciting. Eventually they settled back to straight and level flight, landed back at Fair Oaks and trundled up to park outside the clubhouse. In the intense silence after the engine was cut, feeling slightly dizzy, Ron clambered out. 'So,' said Wing Commander Arthur, a gleam in his eye, 'what do you think, Ron? Do you still want to fly?'

*

As Wingco knew, to any potential aviator nothing is more exciting than a taste of the possibilities of the air. Despite his enthusiasm, however, Ron did not complete his training for another three-and-a-half years. After several more lessons at Fair Oaks, and a gap of more than a year, he decided to resume his instruction in Kenya, at Nairobi Aerodrome, in 1954. It made sense. His heart was in Kenya. That was where the Woods were, and Clarence and May Buxton. Clarence, now sixty, was Chairman of H. Young & Company in Kenya. Besides, African weather was more reliable than British weather for flying lessons (though because Nairobi Aerodrome, renamed Wilson Airport in 1963, was 5,500 feet up in the Kenyan Highlands, mornings invariably brought low cloud and poor visibility until the day warmed up and this burnt off). Also, the training aircraft in Nairobi was more advanced than at Fair Oaks: a fully enclosed, high-winged monoplane called a Piper Cub.

There were other advantages to learning in Africa, too. British Kenya (then still pronounced 'Keenya') was the romantic heart of colonial Africa; a place of big game hunting, the Muthaiga Club and the Happy Valley set which had scandalised prewar society. It was also a celebrated flying Elysium as a result of two bestselling books: Karen Blixen's *Out of Africa*, her account of a failed coffee farming venture at the foot the Ngong Hills, published in 1937; and *West with the Night*, by the Nairobi-based superstar aviatrix Beryl Markham, published in 1942.

Blixen's evocations in particular, of flying in Denys Finch Hatton's Gypsy Moth, cemented Kenya's romantic credentials. She describes the Ngong Hills just west of Nairobi Aerodrome 'perhaps at their loveliest seen from the air, when the ridges, bare towards the four peaks, mount, and run side by side with the aeroplane ... it was like having been taken into the heart of [them] by a secret unknown road.' The herds of stampeding buffalo described by Blixen were, of course, later immortalised on celluloid by Sydney Pollack in one of cinema's celebrated set-pieces. So the advantages were many, even if Ron's flying instruction was now limited to when he was out there (usually January and August). His instructor was a Yugoslav called 'Bosky' Boskavic, an ex-wartime fighter pilot. Ron went solo, a landmark moment for every flyer, after thirteen hours and five minutes, in the last week of August 1955.

To go solo is to know that you can fly; that if you put the hours in after that, your licence is assured. From that moment Ron had been looking out for

[131]

a suitable plane to buy, and the local director of H. Young & Company in Nairobi spotted something suitable at Nairobi Aero Club. It was called a Piper Tri-Pacer, a model that had recently been sweeping the private flying market. The Piper Cub, on which Ron was training with 'Bosky', while a big advance on the Tiger Moth, was still old-fashioned in one way: it was a 'tail dragger'. This meant that on the ground the body of the plane tilted back to rest on a small tail-wheel at the back (like a Spitfire). Tail-draggers, apart from anything else, were harder to land. The Tri-Pacer was the first mass-produced small aeroplane with a 'tricycle' undercarriage – three equal-sized wheels on legs holding the fuselage parallel with the ground, like an airliner. This made it much easier to land. It was part of the American Piper aircraft company's postwar drive to sell flying as being as easy as driving. The Tri-Pacer was the plane 'anyone can fly'. In place of the traditional 'stick', it had yoke-like 'control columns' because they resembled steering wheels.

It was an ideal first aircraft: a sturdy, no-frills, single-engined four-seater machine with a high wing for good visibility. Despite a squat, slightly stocky appearance that earned it the nickname in America of the 'flying milk stool', it was a not an un-pretty machine. It had a metal fuselage and fabric wings, and a Continental engine that allowed it to cruise at 120 mph for 500 miles. It had gyro instruments (a compass mounted on a gyroscope so that it remained steady however much the plane bounced about due to turbulence, vibration or incompetent flying) and a radio – neither by any means standard equipment at the time. In short, it was state-of-the-art. The plane in question was nearly new, and in August 1955 Ron bought it on the company to share with Michael Wood. Two days after soloing in the Cub, 'Bosky' checked him out on the Tri-Pacer to complete his flying training.

By going solo, Ron became airborne and independent. He could now fly alone on cross-country flights (from A to B, as opposed to the endless local flying and circuits), or as 'second pilot' with anyone in possession of a full pilot's licence. Accordingly, a whole new world of possibilities opened up; to exploit these, 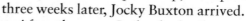 three weeks later, Jocky Buxton arrived.

After the war Jocky had taken a job as agent for Auster Aircraft in Uganda until, in 1950, Ron recruited him to work for H. Young & Company in the Sudan. In due course, when Jocky's children came to Britain to go to school, Ron re-posted him to London at the Leyton office with the aim of letting him work his way up the company, starting in the drawing office – just as Ron had done. ('Was he an engineer?' I asked, intrigued by Ron's recruitment policy. 'Not really. But he was a

Jocky

First plane. Ron with the Piper Tri-Pacer, Nairobi Airport, 1955

good flyer.') Back in England, grounded, Jocky was miserable. He hated office-bound life. He missed the travelling and the sunshine. Most of all, he missed flying. He announced he was going to leave, and when, following the start of the Korean War, an admiral contacted him to see if he would consider rejoining the Naval Reserve, he snapped up the offer. A month or so later, Ron arrived back at the London office. 'Most odd thing today,' he said to his secretary, 'Jocky wasn't in his office.' Jocky, he was informed, was aboard an aircraft carrier in the South China Sea. 'Heavens,' said Ron, 'I never thought he'd do it.' Six months later, when the armistice was signed in 1953, Ron took Jocky back to represent the Sudan office, in Khartoum.[35] It was from there that he joined Ron now.

Together with Clarence Buxton, who had by now become Ron's indispensable friend and mentor when in Kenya, the trio set off on a flying jaunt. An early stop-over was Shiwa Ngandu or 'Lake of the Crocodiles' in Northern Zambia, the bizarre English-style country house built by the monocled soldier and white settler Sir Stewart Gore-Brown (publicised in 2000 by the publication of Christina Lamb's book, *The Africa House*).

Gore-Brown's three-storey brick mansion, complete with gatehouse, tower, colonnaded porticoes, courtyards, walled garden and model village, all at the centre of its own estate, was begun in 1920 and construction work was still

---

35 Jocky later married in the Sudan, in 1960, Anne Smitherman, daughter of the British Consul there.

'The Africa House', Shiwa Ngandu
LEFT: Main front; RIGHT: Sir Stewart Gore-Brown and Clarence Buxton

under way in the 1950s. The place came about because, as a boy, Gore-Brown had wanted an estate like that of his aunt, Dame Ethel Locke King, at Weybridge, Surrey. Although he could not afford such a thing in Britain, he could in a remote corner of former Northern Rhodesia. And so it came about. The eccentric First World War colonel lived at Shiwa Ngandu from 1920 until his death in 1967, complete with butler and uniformed servants, dining every night in black tie, whether he had guests or not. Clarence knew Gore-Brown – as he seemed to know everyone in East Africa – and here they stayed for a night, shown round the curious world Gore-Brown had created for himself by its owner, who was by then seventy-two.

They flew on to Victoria Falls, Bulawayo, Salisbury, Dar es Salaam and back via Mombasa to Nairobi. The following month, October 1955, Ron passed his flight test and gained his full Kenyan private pilot's licence: his 'wings'.

And so commenced Ron's flying years. Trips to Rhodesia with Clarence. Trips to the Kapchurua tea estate in Nandi country, in which Ron had shares. Trips to Mombasa and Malindi and Lamu and Naivasha, as well, of course, as countless business trips to central and Eastern Africa. Gradually, sometimes hair-raisingly, Ron's flying experience began to accumulate. One early example was returning from a trip up-country to Lake Naivasha with his friend David Bagnall. To reach Nairobi it was necessary to climb, as he crossed the Rift Valley, to meet the much higher ground of the Kenyan Highlands where Kenya's capital sat at over 5,000 feet. In particular, he had to clear the Ngong Hills. Ron decided to fly between the peaks. As they got closer, however, something strange started to happen to the plane. It seemed afflicted by the same 'strange lethargy' that Beryl Markham described happening to her plane, in exactly this place, in her book *West with the Night*. However much Ron increased the throttle, the plane was dragged inexorably down, towards the hills and ravines below:

> When you can see the branches of trees from a cockpit, and the shape of rocks no bigger than your own hands, and places where grass thins against sand and becomes yellow, and watch the blow of wind on leaves, you are too close. You are so close that thought is a slow process, useless to you now – even if you can think.

And so it was for Ron. With seconds to spare he realised he must be caught in one of the down-draughts for which the Ngong Hills are notorious. He made a dramatic 180° about turn, away from the hills, as Markham was taught to do. He lost altitude until the valley was flat, then he climbed in a spiral until he was high above the hills and could cross them safely to get home. David Bagnall sat in silence. In fact, he said not another word until they had landed safely back at Nairobi Aerodrome, where Michael Wood had come to meet them. Pale, drawn, he found his voice at last.

'That man just nearly killed me,' he said, pointing to Ron.

'Nonsense,' said Ron. 'I just saved his life.'

*

Ron's next flying adventure came after Jocky had rejoined the company following his spell in Korea. Having an accomplished pilot as H. Young & Company's representative in the Sudan was plainly pointless if he had no aircraft. So it made sense for the company to acquire a second small plane (to accompany the Tri-Pacer in Kenya) for Jocky to have in Khartoum to cover the large distances necessary for generating new and overseeing existing business.

Ron found the second-hand Percival Proctor in Yorkshire. Designed by Edgar Percival for radio training in the Second World War, the Proctor was a rather ungainly single-engined, low-wing monoplane of which only about a thousand were ever made during its production life from 1939 to 1955. However, it was sturdily built, with seating for four, had a powerful 250 hp Gypsy Queen engine and the sophistication of a variable pitch propeller. This relatively advanced feature (usually only available on more expensive aircraft) allows the angle of 'bite' of the blades to be adjusted as the propeller spins, making it both more efficient and effective. Together with the extra power, this allowed the Proctor to cruise 20 mph faster than the Tri-Pacer, at 140 mph. After the war many ex-military machines came onto the market cheap. (This one, advertised at Leeds-Bradford aerodrome, was ten years old and cost £400.) Ron and Jocky set off together in it for Africa in August

The Proctor: Jocky with mystery brunettes, possibly at Elstree

1956. For Ron, still with well under 100 hours solo flying in his log book, it was his first major international trip from the UK.

From Elstree Airfield in North London, they flew in a series of hops via Lympne on the Kentish coast to Lyons, then Pisa, then on down the Italian coast via Naples, over Sicily to Malta. There they climbed to 10,000 feet ready for the most nerve-wracking portion of their journey: the 180 miles – nearly an hour-and-a-half – directly south across the open sea of the Mediterranean to Tripoli in Libya, North Africa. From this height, they could see land either behind them or in front of them for all but fifteen minutes of the journey.

They made the African coast without incident and headed across the Libyan desert to the nearest available refuelling spot: Marble Arch. Marble Arch (nothing to do with the one in London) was one of the world's most preposterous monuments: a vast white triumphal arch in the middle of nowhere – utterly surreal, set in a sea of sand on the main coastal road between Tripoli and Tobruk. It was built as a piece of swaggering *bragadaccio* by Mussolini: a victory arch to celebrate the Italian conquest of Libya in 1912 (unceremoniously demolished in 1970 by Colonel Gaddafi). Its sole advantage was that it was an exceptionally easily-spotted landmark, in recognition of which an air strip was constructed directly alongside it. As Libya was no longer under British administration (independence had arrived in 1952), arrangements had to be made with Shell to supply enough fuel at Marble Arch to take them the next 300 or so miles east along the coast. It was brought out to the Proctor by an Arab with two donkeys.

Marble Arch, Libyan desert. Landing strip visible below and to left of arch.

From Benghazi they flew on east along the North African coast to Cairo to join the route south into central Africa that every white man followed, the route Rhodes had dreamt would carry his Cairo-to-the-Cape railway, and that Alan Cobham had opened up for the Empire Flying Boat Service just a couple of decades before: down the Nile. They passed the pyramids, then on, via Luxor (ancient city of Thebes) to Wadi Halfa, Khartoum, Malakal, Juba, Kisumu and Lake Victoria.

A word should be said about this route. In 1941, the Australian war correspondent Alan Moorehead travelled it by Empire flying boat and in his book, *No Room in the Ark* (about wildlife in Africa), his account of the experience powerfully conveys the Africa that Ron and Jocky, travelling fewer than fifteen years later, would also have encountered:

Refuelling, fuel brought by donkey

Pyramids of Giza, from the Proctor, August 1956

There was no flying after dark, and the machine put down at some fascinating places on the way: Wadi Halfa in the midst of the Egyptian desert; Khartoum at the junction of the Blue and White Niles in the Sudan, Kisumu on Lake Victoria (the lake itself so big that you lost sight of the shore as you flew across it) and Livingstone, just a mile or two above the Victoria Falls.

Most of these stops were out-of-the-way places which had very little connection with the outside world, and so you were plunged at once into the authentic African scene. There were no familiar airport buildings, no advertisements, no other traffic of any kind; just this rush of muddy water as you lighted down on a river or a forest lake, and the boy who came out in a boat to take you to the shore was the genuine article, a coal-black African, sometimes naked to the waist. He looked as though he would have been really more at home in a thatched hut than in this strange world of flying monsters in the sky.

On the Zambezi river I recall they had to run a launch up and down the water a few minutes before the plane came in to clear the hippopotami away. I remember too, with particular vividness, a little place called Malakal on the White Nile in the Sudan, where the women of the Dinka tribe were six foot tall and as hipless as young boys. Their hair was thickly matted with grease and piled up in a marvellous coiffure high above their heads. They walked gravely along the riverbank and turned their heads away from the great flying boat on the water in the way that primitive people often do when they are confronted with something which they regard as quite miraculous and beyond all comprehension.

These scenes gave the passenger a brief but very potent whiff of Africa. He felt he was seeing the country as Livingstone and the other early explorers had seen it, and although I made this journey only once and as long ago as 1941 it filled me with an intense desire to come back.

Wadi Halfa, Khartoum, Malakal, Juba, Kisumu. These were the evocative names that would sprinkle Ron's log book over the next few years, recalling a brief era when it was possible to fly across Africa from country to country with next to no paperwork or formalities. Most of these places have changed dramatically, are no longer accessible or have even disappeared completely. Wadi Halfa, that key stop-over on the border between Egypt and the Sudan, now lies submerged beneath the waters of Lake Nasser following the building of the Aswan High Dams (completed 1964–70). Groppi's Tea Garden in Cairo, 'the most celebrated tearoom this side of the Mediterranean', beloved by the British troops of two world wars, and which would become an indispensable visit during stop-overs, had closed by the end of the 1960s.

Oddly, on this occasion Ron and Jocky were refused permission to land at Luxor, the regular and obvious next stop-over. They were told the runway was being repaired. Accordingly, they refuelled further north, at Asyût. When they over-flew Luxor, however, they couldn't help noticing, parked along the runway (which showed no signs of being under repair), twenty-five military aircraft, Illusions, parked in rows. Ron was aware of the mounting tensions between Britain and Egypt following Nasser's announcement that he was going to nationalise the Suez Canal, so when he reached Khartoum he mentioned the fact of their refused permission and the presence of the warplanes to the military attaché at the British Embassy. The following week the Suez Crisis erupted. When it did so, the RAF attacked Luxor Airport and destroyed 20–30 Illusion aircraft on the ground. Ever after, Ron wondered whether it was his tip-off that prompted this operation.

After a week in Khartoum they continued to Kenya, via Malakal and Juba and Entebbe, to Nairobi. Jocky later flew the Proctor back to Khartoum, where it was then based. Over the next few years it flew many hundreds of hours across the open plains and scrublands of the Sudan, though it caused constant airworthiness certification problems due to its wooden construction (doped fabric stretched over a timber frame). In the equatorial African climate, this made it very susceptible to woodworm – to which, in the end, it succumbed.

[139]

In the meantime, as there were still almost no private planes in the Sudan in 1956, the stationing of a plane at Khartoum Airport caused quite a stir. Ron and Jocky found themselves regarded with intense suspicion by members of the Sudan Airways office. Having seen the plane take up residence, Sudan Airways drew their own conclusions: these were clearly rivals, setting up in competition with them, intent on stealing their passengers away.

*

The hitch about keeping your planes in Africa, if you loved flying, was that when in Britain – which was still most of the year – there was no flying. This was plainly unsatisfactory. So before the Proctor was even delivered, Ron had already decided to buy another plane to keep in England. He would buy it in Africa, however, where prices were a third lower than here, then fly it home. This next plane, he decided, would be altogether more grown up. The Tri-Pacer had had its tricycle undercarriage. The Proctor had had its variable pitch propeller. The next plane would be a 'twin': it would have *two* engines.

A twin was much more reassuring in the event of engine problems – particularly desirable when your route took you over sea, desert, swamp, lion-prowled bush and mountains. Ron had come across a perfect example of what he was after at Nairobi Flying Club, going for the bargain price of £800. The Miles M65 Gemini was an altogether superior machine to the Proctor. It had an elegant double tailplane design, mildly reminiscent of the triple tailplane of the Lockheed Constellation, the handsome airliner that was ushering in a new age of civilian passenger travel. Admittedly, despite its twin engines and retractable undercarriage, its maximum speed of 146 mph was only a little faster than the Proctor, and it still only seated four. But it carried more weight, had a range of nearly a thousand miles between refuelling stops, and offered that all-important insurance against ending up as a lion's lunch.

The Gemini had two drawbacks. The first was that it was regarded by many as underpowered. Its Blackburn Cirrus Minor engines generated only 100 hp each, scarcely enough for the thin air of Nairobi Aerodrome's elevated altitude. But then that was why the plane was available for such a good price. Another hitch was that in order to fly a plane with two engines and a retractable landing gear, an additional rating was required to Ron's licence. The Gemini in question was owned by someone Ron had met at the flying club: Alec Noon, a decorated ex-squadron leader and partner in the local air charter business Noon & Pearce. Fortunately for all parties, the chief examiner for multi-engined ratings at Nairobi Aero Club happened to be none other than Squadron Leader Alec Noon.

On the appointed day for the test – both parties keen to get the formality out of the way so the deal could be clinched – all went well until Noon said: 'In the event of an engine failure, would you keep the dead engine above or below the live engine?' What he meant by this was: with the plane thrown off-balance by now being powered from only one side, would he fly with the failed engine wing slightly higher or slightly lower than the good engine wing? Now, there are plenty of minor details which may be glossed over in a flight test – to do with ephemeral aspects of airmanship, perhaps, or radio telephony. But, if there is one question that cannot ever be flunked, it is what to do in the event of an engine failure. Ron hadn't the faintest idea. 'Below,' he said.

Doubtless it was with mixed feelings that Squadron Leader Noon received this response. Standards were standards, even if they cost the examiner £800 to uphold them. There was a pause. 'Now I want you to think about this very carefully,' he said. 'I'm going to ask you once more. Following an engine failure, would you keep the dead engine above or below the live engine?' Ron took his cue.

'Above,' he said.

He passed his flight test, acquired his twin rating, and became the proud owner of a Miles M65 Gemini.

Of all the planes Ron owned, the Gemini would prove the most success-ful and long-serving; the machine in which he flew the greatest number of hours. For his first journey, back to England, less than a month after he had flown out in the Proctor, he retraced his course home, collecting, at Khartoum, an Armenian friend, Vin Vanian. Vanian, who owned a store which had been in the city 'since Kitchener's day', was a hunting friend. They had made long expeditions into the Sudanese bush to shoot kudu (a corkscrew-horned deer).

All went well until the Juba – Malakal leg, where the cloud began to close in. Lower and lower the cloud base dropped. Not having an 'instrument rating', which allows a pilot to fly 'blind' through clouds or darkness, or to climb above the weather altogether, Ron had to keep descending ever lower to remain beneath the cloud and retain visibility. This is never a happy situation for a pilot, for whom height means safety (as it allows more time to find somewhere to land in emergency). Except for taking-off and landing, pilots of small planes will always try to maintain at least 1,000 feet between themselves and the ground. But down and down came the cloud base, until Ron was forced to fly at 700 feet, then 600, then 500 ... Eventually he was flying at 300 feet, an altitude so low that it confers an unsettling sense of their 140 mph cruising speed, requiring intense concentration as ground features flashed by and the roar of the engines startled animals. Finally they reached the Nile and followed it up to Malakal.

The journey continued without further mishap, taking, in all, ten days from Nairobi to Fair Oaks. It included thirteen stop-overs and five days of solid flying. A glance at Ron's log book gives an inkling of the distances involved: Khartoum – Wadi Halfa: four hours and forty minutes; Wadi Halfa – Cairo: five hours; the final leg, Lyons – Croydon, three hours and forty-five minutes.

Ron kept the Gemini at Fair Oaks, then later at Elstree in north-west London. Two months later, in January 1957, he was setting off on his next jaunt: round the west coast of Africa to Ivory Coast. This time he was accompanied by Jocky and someone who would become one of his most frequent flying buddies: Anthony Gurney.

Gurney, a distant cousin, was a couple of years older. They had known each other from before the war when, from school at Charterhouse, Anthony sometimes came to lunch at Holywell with Murray and Muriel. During the war, it may be remembered, in East Bengal they had met on the ferry crossing the Brahmaputra (see pp. 91–2). Ending up in the same 20th Indian Division, they had seen each other on and off until both left India, Gurney finishing the war as a major. After demob they had become good friends, with Ron often spending Christmas at the Gurneys' family home, Northrepps Hall, near Cromer, where Anthony from 1953 lived close by at Manor Farm. With his upbeat demeanour and cheerful signature cry of 'Well done, well done', 'The Major' was soon a much-loved local figure.

All three were cousins within the capacious tentacles of the Buxton dynasty. Indeed, one aim of the trip, apart from visiting the Nigerian company, was to visit the statue of their ancestor Sir Thomas Fowell Buxton in Freetown Cathedral (a duplicate of the one that stands in the southern transept of Westminster Abbey).

After reaching Casablanca via the Canary Islands, they encountered an electrical problem on the ground with one of the engine's magnetos. The magnetos are part of the ignition system that generates the sparks that make an engine run. Aviation engines always have a double set for safety, which are tested as part of the pilot's take-off checks; when the principal set is switched off, the engine should keep going, albeit with a slight drop in revs. When, during his pre-take-off checks at Casablanca, Ron switched off the main ignition system, there wasn't a slight drop in revs: one of the engines went dead. There was no one at Casablanca to mend it. They pressed on.

They reached Freetown without further incident. Capital of Sierra Leone, the city was still, then, a crown colony (for another five years). After a brief visit, they flew on all the way to Abidjan, capital of Ivory Coast, a journey of 795 miles and seven hours in the air. A seven-day, 7,000-mile round-trip to Nigeria followed, landing at Lagos. On one occasion, when they were flying into a jungle strip at Potiskin in north-east Nigeria to call on the Sardoba of

Family outing: Freetown Airport, Sierra Leone 1957.
Jocky Buxton and 'The Major', Anthony Gurney, with the Gemini.

Cochatoo,[36] they burst a tyre on landing. Jocky later caught a flight from Lagos to Khartoum, while Ron and Anthony started on the long journey home in the Gemini.

Returning to Freetown, they visited St George's Cathedral to see the statue of Sir Thomas Fowell Buxton. The verger, when they explained their mission and who they were, insisted Anthony and Ron stand either side of the bust while he took a photograph.

Over the next eight years, Ron's log book records flights to Ireland, Holland, Norway, Austria, Italy, Istanbul, interspersed with Tri-Pacer and Proctor flights on African trips. The Gemini was damaged by a gale on the ground at Oulton in Norfolk. There were incidents galore: including one on the runway at Oslo, when an incoming passenger jet almost landed on top of him. There were trips to air rallies in France and air races in Italy. After the West Africa trip, however, the Gemini never went back to 'deep' Africa; its furthest flung missions were to Tunisia and Istanbul. In the end, as another wooden plane (timber frame with plywood skin) it bore the same

36 Assassinated 2005.

'THE FRIEND OF THE NEGRO' –
Marble bust of Sir Thomas Fowell Buxton, Freetown Cathedral

vulnerability to woodworm in the tropics as the Proctor. This was not what
finished it, however. In 1962 the Aircraft Registration Board declared there
was risk of glue failure, and it was sold for scrap.

It hardly mattered. By the end of the Fifties, the Jet Age was well under way
and civilian flying had transformed. It was now faster, quieter, safer, cheaper,
easier and more relaxing to get to Africa high above rough weather in the new
wave of pressurised American jet airliners like the Boeing 707 and Douglas
DC8. Not that this implied – not by any means – that Ron's flying adventures
were over.

11

The Mtwapa Bridge

HIS VISITS TO Clarence Buxton's house on the coast were one of the high points of Ron's stop-overs in Kenya. Ever since he had made contact with his cousins Clarence and May on his first visit to Kenya with Jean in 1947–8, a close friendship had developed. Soon, visiting their up-country farm at Limuru, bought by Clarence's father in 1902, was an automatic part of Ron's regular Kenyan visits. Primarily a tea plantation, the farm also grew wattle and pyrethrum (the daisy-like flower that was the source of the new 'wonder' insecticide DDT). They also bred horses. At any one time there might be 160 or more, and Ron would go riding with Clarence in the hills.

Clarence represented something special to Ron. Although apparently so bright and self-assured in his business interests, and a talented musician, in other ways Ron was still detached and withdrawn, perhaps as a result of coping with the loss of his parents so young. He had few role models at this formative period, and Clarence was precisely the kind he sought. Their identical education and similar interests meant they had much in common. Like Paul Howell, Clarence epitomised a Victorian commitment to public service. (At one point after arriving in Africa he had written home to his mother, perhaps pondering on why he had fought in the trenches: 'I don't want freedom to do nothing, but freedom to do what seems worthwhile.')

Clarence knew Kenya better than almost anyone. A popular and energetic figure, as district commissioner in Kisumu he had initiated the canoe race still held today. During his last Colonial Service post, he had hosted the first elections in Zanzibar. Altogether, he had more than three decades of African experience. In the early 1950s, as he entered his sixties, he became a father figure to Ron (his third child, Rupert, approaching thirty, was exactly Ron's age): someone who could be respected and admired and treated as a trusted source of wisdom and advice. One who, moreover, unlike Ron's own father Murray, was warm and outgoing. Most important of all, Clarence was a Buxton – 'family' – and that magical connection was emerging as a defining characteristic of many of Ron's dealings in life. When he had started H. Young & Co. (East Africa), in Nairobi, Ron's automatic choice as chairman was Clarence. Many decades later, on the other side of the world, Clarence's youngest daughter Carissa recalled Ron's reaction when, in Hong Kong, he spotted a framed photograph of her father. 'Ah, Clarence,' he said. 'My greatest friend.'

Clarence Buxton – taken around 1960, when he was in his late sixties

When Clarence had married for the second time, his new wife, May, had persuaded him to buy some land on the coast in south-eastern Kenya. South of Malindi, at Vipingo, this was part of the so-called Kenya Riviera, to which they liked to go for holidays. In due course this would become a substantial property of 200 acres, complete with a house, planted with bombax trees, and producing kapok (cotton), citrus fruit (grapefruit, oranges, lemons, limes), mangoes, coconuts and cashews. But in the early 1950s it was just scrub. There wasn't even a building, let alone electricity; just tents and, in due course, palm-fringed huts. There were remarkable caves to explore, though, and wonderful bathing in the sea. Ron loved it. It was here that he first acquired a reputation for falling asleep either during dinner (on one occasion with his tie in the soup) or immediately afterwards, often on the floor.

The one drawback to visits to Vipingo was the journey. From the farm at Limuru it was a 360-mile trip, all on pot-holed, dirt roads taking anything up to three days if the weather was bad. Nor was this the only hazard. Sometimes it was necessary to pull over and switch off the engine for two or three hours to allow a herd of 300 elephant to cross. By far the most predictable delay, however, came near the end of the journey, after the Malindi road turned north to run along the coast. Here, just before the village of Mtwapa, it encountered a wide tidal creek. Here, today, deep sea fishing tours for marlin and barracuda depart from a thriving coastal resort, but in

LEFT: Mtwapa Creek, showing existing ferry approach at foot of picture. RIGHT: The singing, rope-pulling, ferrymen.

the 1950s the place was still a tiny village, and the only way to reach it without a long inland detour was by taking a hand-ferry pulled laboriously across the creek along a rope by ferry boys 'with their minds more on the backshish for their singing than on the angry queue of waiting vehicles' Ron later wrote in the *Mombasa Times*. It was an operation which could take up to two hours on a moving tide.

The ferry was only big enough to take one lorry and a car, or two cars. So long queues frequently built up. As Mtwapa Creek approached, everyone would pray there was no queue, and hearts would sink if there were several cars waiting – which invariably there were – knowing it meant hours added to the journey.

So the idea of a bridge across the Mtwapa Creek was seldom far from the mind of a guest arriving at Vipingo. On one particular Sunday evening, however, in 1956, heading back to Mombasa after a weekend with Clarence and May, Ron reached the creek to find himself behind a queue of forty cars. He and Clarence had often discussed how sorely a bridge was needed to replace the ferry. Now, with three hours of enforced leisure on his hands, Ron took the opportunity to inspect the site as an engineer. Undoubtedly it had its problems: the river was wide where the ferry crossed, presumably so the strong current was slower. Also, the banks looked unstable. When he finally reached his trusty Tri-Pacer at Mombasa Airport Ron spent a few minutes after take-off exploring up and down the Mtwapa Creek, taking aerial photographs. To the seaward side of the ferry, near the prison on the coast, the creek narrowed onto what appeared to be a much more promising site – a site, moreover, which would provide much better road alignment than the current ferry did. The next time he spoke to Clarence about the nightmare Mtwapa crossing, it was no longer merely as an airy grievance. He had a serious proposal. 'Why don't we build a bridge?'

*

It might be imagined that Ron already had enough projects to occupy him. By the early 1950s he was running five new companies across Africa. In 1953, aged thirty, following the retirement of Harold Judd, he had become chairman of the UK parent company, H. Young & Company. Regular expeditions abroad with friends meant his passport was accumulating stamps almost as rapidly as his log book was flying hours. (He now possessed not just the 'smattering of Urdu' of colloquial exaggeration, but reasonable Arabic from his time in the Sudan, plus a decent measure of Swahili.) During his months in England, he found time to make regular appearances on the hunting fields and point-to-point courses of Norfolk. And by the end of the decade, he would be attempting to launch a political career, having got himself selected as the prospective Tory candidate for Leyton, the London borough in which H. Young & Company's Lea Bridge works was based.

This is not a history of H. Young & Company's overseas operations, but a brief summary of developments since 1948 gives some idea of how Ron was now spending his time in Africa. In that year, as we have heard, he started H. Young & Co. (East Africa) in premises on the outskirts of Nairobi. As the first steel fabrication company in Kenya, it quickly started winning contracts both at home and in neighbouring countries. A range of standardised ready-made, 'flat-pack' buildings was offered which could be chosen from a catalogue, much like those offered by corrugated-iron manufacturers in the nineteenth century. One idea with which Ron was particularly pleased was for steel-framed forms for the traditional thatched huts known as *tukls* and *kernucs* used for dwellings and schools in the Sudan. Traditionally built, with a timber frame, these tended to last less than five years before white ants destroyed them. With a light steel frame, however, which would not rust in the dry climate, clad with local roofing thatch and mud-brick walls, a far more durable building was possible.

Then Paul Howell secured the contract for the police residential quarters in Malakal, and soon after hospitals, police stations and markets, factory and storage buildings began to follow in an increasingly steady stream. Larger projects then included steel-framed cotton ginning plants (for separating cotton fibres from the seeds, so that the lint can be baled up to make cotton

LEFT TO RIGHT: Ron, Harold Judd, Claude Cranmer and Clarence Buxton at The Yacht Hotel, St Helier, Jersey, for an H. Young & Company board meeting, July 1951

goods and the seed sent to cattle feed). These were particularly popular. Most of these structures were clad in tin sheeting. Other early commissions included food-processing factories such as the coffee works at Moshe, Tanzania, and ginneries in Uganda. Operations soon extended as far as Zambia. Advertisements from the time proclaim the manifold benefits the company offered; indeed, in the phrasing of one of the headlines 'A first class job – to schedule', it is almost possible to hear the chairman's voice.

Kenyan operations, from 1952 to 1956, were enlivened by the activities of the Mau Mau uprising, when Kikuyu-dominated anti-colonial insurgents were mounting regular attacks on the British Army and the Kenya Regiment (mostly consisting of white Kenyans). Vigilance was required for construction teams working in remoter areas, and while no actual incidents occurred, there was a report of domestic staff being disconcerted to find a loaded revolver being kept on the table during dinner.

The same year that Ron set up H. Young & Co. (East Africa), 1948, he had

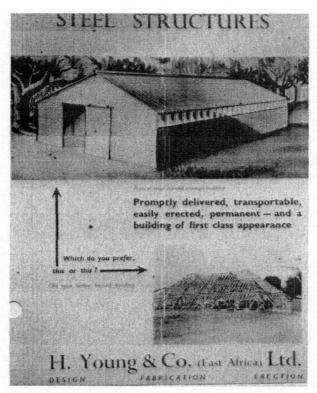

Advertisement from the 1950s for H. Young & Co. (East Africa) Ltd

also established the Rhodesian Engineering and Steel Construction Company (RESCCo) in Bulawayo. As in Kenya, it was the country's first structural steel company and it rapidly became clear it was filling a vacuum, exactly as Ron hoped. Prestigious contracts across southern Africa began to flow in, including government and mining business. By the mid-1950s the company was diversifying into building and refitting railway wagons and steam locomotives (tasks included putting main axles on roller bearings, installing new fireboxes, retooling boilers, reworking linkages and general maintenance). More importantly, RESCCo brought Ron together with someone who would play a decisive role in his later African interests: Willi Egger. Egger was an Austrian who had emigrated to Rhodesia. He came to notice following a difficult contract to build a power station at Livingstone, near the Victoria Falls which, due to his unblinkered determination, they managed to achieve.

In 1953, following a growing stream of work through agents, a small office was opened in Khartoum under the name Steel Construction Sudan Ltd. This soon expanded to a fully-equipped works site with complete erection equipment – cranes, mobile cranes, winches, ropes and tackle – plus a handful of skilled Sudanese engineers and foremen capable of overseeing projects from foundations to final cladding. Many contracts were, at least partially, grant-aided (one year in Darfur the company constructed the province's entire building programme). While there was competition from other expatriate companies, none could match the completeness of service H. Young & Co. offered, from ground works to erection.

Also in the early Fifties came the Zambia office: two existing engineering companies were bought and merged under the name of the Raine Engineering Company. In 1954 Nigeria followed. As in Sudan, at first agents were appointed in Lagos; then, in due course, a site was acquired in Apapa on the edge of the capital and Nigerian Steel Construction Ltd opened for business.

To these companies, every year, Ron would make two flying – usually, literally flying – visits: one in January, one in the summer. These were dreaded by everyone. In would bounce the young H. Young chairman, in shorts and plimsolls, his fair hair and sunburnt pink skin (as Clarence Buxton's daughter Carissa remembers him) unmistakeable against the deep established tans of his expatriate staff and the Africans. Lives would be briefly turned upside down as questions were asked and new, more efficient ways of doing things were called for: how to rearrange the workshop so the steel went through quicker, for example. Any suggestion that 'That's going to be difficult' was met with a cheerful: 'Never mind. Do it anyway.' After a few days Ron would depart, leaving routines obliterated and everyone shattered, and things would settle down again – until the next visit.

So Ron had no shortage of commitments. But energy generates energy and nothing makes time like a busy schedule. Ron had created for himself a role he was made for: as a self-starter with a natural head for business and a sharp opportunism. He had already demonstrated a formidable ability to get projects moving. He was doing exactly what he wanted. The various strands of his life were coming together: a thriving company, a satisfied hunger for adventure, flying, a love of Africa, the development of family ties, all in the pleasing knowledge that he was following a long-established Buxton tradition in making his way in that continent. This, plus his new friends and close relationships with cousins, went some way to filling the gap left by his parents, and helped bolster an already well-developed sense of self-reliance. There was an irrepressibility to this young man who knew his own abilities and was confident enough to do things his way. That he had never built a bridge before perturbed him not in the least. Life was there for the making, and he was just hitting his stride. If the folklore surrounding the energetic activities of Ron Buxton has an official beginning, it is here, in Africa, in the second half of the 1950s.

*

While the idea of building a bridge was plainly a good one, no sooner had the idea materialised than the difficulties began to emerge. On his next visit to the coast to see Clarence, Ron arranged a survey trip by boat, landing on the promontory where the bridge would eventually be constructed. Taking a cross-section, he found that the minimum gap at low tide was 313 feet – quite a distance for a single-span bridge. Owing to the depth of the creek (nearly 100 feet at that point) intermediate piers were not a practical possibility, while the fast tide in the narrows, coupled with the 40-feet high cliffs on either side, ruled out a floating bridge. The solution pointed to a suspension bridge of sufficient span to allow the piers to be set well back from the creek edge. If building a bridge from scratch was departure enough, building a suspension bridge entered a new realm of complicated, specialised and technical requirements.

The construction problems, meanwhile, soon began to look trifling alongside the political difficulties. Ten miles to the south, connecting Mombasa Island to the mainland, was Nyali Bridge, a toll bridge floating on pontoons. It belonged to Hugh Greenwood, someone Clarence knew. He was also aware that the Ministry of Transport loathed the bridge, because it was not under their control. For this reason alone, he knew, the Ministry would fight their proposal of the Mtwapa Bridge idea. Still, such difficulties were there for the overcoming, and between Ron and Clarence they had a perfect division of labour. Ron would raise the necessary capital and attend to practical aspects of the bridge's design and construction. Clarence would sort out local administration and smooth the way against opposition and political difficulties. No one knew local Kenyan politics or had contacts like Clarence's after thirty years as a colonial administrator. Finance would be raised to underwrite construction costs. A toll would be charged, and once the building costs and annual maintenance were paid, the rest would be pure profit. 'You do the engineering,' declared Clarence. 'I'll do the politics.'

The first thing – naturally – was to set up a company. The Mtwapa Bridge Company would operate separately from H. Young & Co., Ron decided, although the company would fabricate and erect the bridge. For the board, he assembled a cast of close friends and trusted advisers, also, wherever possible, 'family'. Clarence was chairman. For the board he recruited Michael Harley, a young partner in the leading Nairobi lawyers Hamilton, Harrison and Matthews. Mike Harley was five years younger than Ron and had recently decided to settle in Kenya (in 1955). They, too, had much in common. Harley was already making a name for himself in Kenyan business circles for his calm, composed manner and scrupulous honesty. They shared a background of Eton and Cambridge, and Ron regularly bumped into Michael on his visits to Kenya. Clarence put Ron in touch with a local director of Barclays Bank (East Africa) with whom he was friendly: 'Eggs' Whitcombe quickly accepted the scheme, agreeing to back it to the tune of 50,000 Kenyan pounds (rising, eventually, to 70,000).

The politics turned out to be considerable. The Governor of Kenya ruled in favour of the new bridge proposal, but the Ministry of Works, as predicted, was fiercely opposed to a team of outsiders trespassing on 'their' territory. If a bridge were to be built, they said, it should be the Ministry who built it. For a time their implacable opposition and intransigence looked insurmountable. Fortunately, however, Clarence had a card up his sleeve. It came in the form of Major-General C. C. Fowkes, otherwise known as 'Fluffy' Fowkes, chairman of the Road Authority – a quasi-governmental organisation which advised on road development, with its own legislature, run by the British Colonial Office. Fowkes promptly gave the bridge his wholehearted support. At the inquiry convened to consider the matter, the Ministry laid out its case against The Mtwapa Bridge Company. Fowkes listened patiently to the Ministry's representatives, then turned to the Director of Works. 'If they don't build a bridge, are you going to?'

'Unfortunately,' said the hapless Director, 'we don't at present have the money.'

'Well, if you're not going to build it, I don't see why they shouldn't,' said Fowkes.

The Mtwapa Bridge was approved.

*

There was much to be settled, starting with the small matter of how to build a suspension bridge. Ron's engineering degree meant he had a working knowledge of general engineering principles, but to design and construct a suspension bridge to carry heavy traffic over a fast-flowing tidal creek was well beyond his remit. There were also various structural parameters to consider. The bridge platform had to be high enough to allow clear passage for fishing vessels beneath. It also had to be constructed from steel and based around standard Bailey panels in order for H. Young & Co. to be able to handle its construction.

More surveys and some test drillings confirmed that the most suitable site for the bridge was half a mile downstream from the ferry. There the creek narrowed and there were coral cliffs leading down to the water's edge which could support piles for the two towers. Unfortunately, this site was owned by the local prison and it soon transpired that the local prison governor was vehemently opposed to having a bridge on prison land. It would, he declared, help prisoners escape. 'But if they escape, you can quickly cross the river on the bridge and catch them,' said Ron and Clarence helpfully. In the end, despite the fact that the proposed site would cost the prison its football field, the governor gave way.

Back in England, Ron paid a visit to Sir Donald Bailey, inventor of the eponymous Bailey bridge and now Deputy-Chief Scientific Officer at the Ministry of Supply. He listened attentively as Ron outlined the situation with all its problems. His response could not have been more friendly or helpful. He had his engineer do the necessary specialist calculations for an all-steel cable suspension bridge spanning 520 feet, to carry loads of up to 40 tonnes. The central suspended span would be 380 feet, with two approach spans of 40 feet on the south side and 100 feet on the north side. The cables would carry a deck of bolted Bailey bridge panels providing a single-track metalled road with a clear width of 12 feet, suspended 40 feet above high tide level.

It was a specialised design, which would involve some tricky curved fabrication for the towers. The chief engineer of the Roads Department in Kenya demanded detailed structural calculations. These Sir Donald's engineer provided and in due course Ron presented the numerous pages of advanced calculus to the chief engineer in his Nairobi office. Ron watched as he gazed at these, turning the pages blankly. The truth was all too obvious. He couldn't make head or tail of them. However, with this last formality completed, in August 1957 they were ready to proceed.

*

The procedure for erecting a suspension bridge is as follows. First, the piles are sunk for the two prefabricated towers, then the towers erected. The first cable is strung across and anchored, then the second. Once both cables are in place and securely anchored, the deck, in this case of Bailey bridge panels, can be gradually built out from either end, suspended from the cables, until eventually they meet in the middle. The towers would be fabricated at Lea Bridge and shipped out, along with cabling and suspenders, anchors and anchor blocks, but this still left a considerable amount of raw materials to find. In so doing, ever the opportunist on the hunt for a bargain, Ron had two strokes of luck.

First was the failure of the African Groundnut Scheme of 1946–54. This British Government-financed initiative, implemented by Clement Atlee's Labour Government, has gone down in history as a byword for imperial hubris and incompetence on an epic scale. The plan was to lease vast tracts – over 5,000 square miles – of land in Tanganyika, Northern Rhodesia (now Zambia) and Kenya for twenty-five years for the intensive farming of groundnuts (peanuts). Thus established, the useful cash crop could in due course be turned back to locals. Factories would be built for processing the harvested nuts and extracting the oil. Villages would be created to house workers; roads and bridges for equipment would be constructed. Hundreds of tractors, bulldozers, and other plant and machinery would be imported.

The project struck a farcical note from the start, when, before they had even left the UK, the tractors became marooned in the frozen-up Thames during the record-breaking winter of 1947, just as they were needed for clearing and planting. This initial task, too, proved harder than expected. The only practicable method was eventually discovered to be two bulldozers hauling a massive chain between them. However, when anchor chains were ordered from Britain, managers cancelled them, assuming they had been ordered as a practical joke, thus delaying the project further. Once clearing began, the baobab trees turned out to contain so many bees' nests that chronic stinging injuries became a major hazard. Having at last got the peanuts planted, it was discovered that the areas were subject to droughts, while peanuts required rainfall of at least 500 mm per year. Heavy rains, when they came, then resulted in chronic erosion of the cleared ground, in the process prompting epidemics of scorpions. By the time the scheme was cancelled in 1951, it had cost the British taxpayer £50 million and rendered swathes of Africa an unusable dust bowl. In Kenya the scheme never got going properly, though plenty of plant and materials were shipped out. The British taxpayer's loss, however, was The Mtwapa Bridge Company's gain. Ron heard that a a large cache of Bailey panels and cables was available, in Kenya, as a result of the failure of the groundnut scheme. He managed to acquire them for a fraction of their real value.

Nor was this his only lucky break. Following the end of the war, large stockpiles of redundant Bailey panels had found their way into the nation's scrapyards. Anthony Gurney, back in Britain, had been combing yards for just such booty and in the King's Scrapyard, Great Yarmouth, he came across just the treasure trove he had been hoping for. He promptly bought up everything they had, acquiring the precious, precision-engineered panels for little more than their scrap value. 'Be under no misapprehension,' clarified Ron's wife, Phyllida, describing the Mtwapa Bridge project some decades later: 'That bridge was built from bits that fell off the back of a lorry.'

Construction began in August 1957. A contract for the foundations was placed with Mowlem Construction for a scheme supplied by their soil mechanics section. Groundworks began with the sinking of the piles for the towers: groups of four 16-inch piles beneath each tower leg, sunk to a depth of 70 feet on the south bank and 55 feet on the north side. With the piling in place, erection of the towers could begin. These, each nearly 90 feet high and weighing over 20 tonnes, were guyed into position. By the end of 1957 the first of 16 main cables was drawn across the creek and fastened to the mass concrete anchor blocks. It was at this stage that the only technical hitch of the project occurred. December and January brought several weeks of heavy rain, during which one of the north bank anchor blocks for one of the cable stays subsided. After some head-scratching, the solution was found to be extra

How to build a suspension bridge: the main deck. LEFT: assembled on rollers on either bank, was finally pushed out, RIGHT: supported by trolleys suspended from the main cables.

vertical piling beneath the anchors, plus secondary anchorages 75 feet behind the existing blocks designed to take the full horizontal load.

While this was going on, the span was steadily being built up on either side of the creek on rollers. When both sides were complete, they were simultaneously rolled out over the water, the two dangling ends supported by trolleys running along and suspended from the main cables, until the magical moment, nine months after erection began, when they met in the middle and could be bolted together. The erection supervisor was so excited he hurled himself into the grey waters forty feet below. The entire operation took just two hours.

After this, the bridge was soon completed. The deck was supported by steel cables (supplied by British Ropes Ltd, of Doncaster). The decking was installed: heavy sleepers of a durable ironwood called azobe, imported from the Cameroons in French West Africa. Meanwhile three miles of new bitumen road approaches were laid by the Ministry of Works. As soon as these were complete, Ron, who had been making regular visits throughout, christened them by landing on them in the Tri-Pacer. Finally, the bridge was finished in grey Miraculum graphite paint for protection against the sea air.

With the bridge's completion, one nerve-wracking task loomed – the testing. The Ministry of Works had specified two tests: a distributed overload test; and a concentrated load test. For the former, ten seven-ton tipper vehicles were evenly spaced across the suspended span, but right on one side of the carriage-way – an eccentric load equivalent to a central load of about 90 tons. The tipper trucks were left in position for twelve hours on each side of the bridge in turn. The second test consisted of a 40-ton load made up of a 15-ton Foden dump-truck towing a low-loader bearing a 20-ton Caterpillar D7 bulldozer. As

The Mtwapa Bridge: ready for opening, June 1958

these heavy loads were towed onto the bridge, the decking timbers rattled. The cables tightened and the deck visibly sagged. Everyone held their breath. All went well, however, and the bridge passed all the tests satisfactorily.

One task remained: settling the toll prices. For this, the Minister of Finance had to agree the rates that The Mtwapa Bridge Company wished to levy. At a meeting to discuss the matter, a scale was duly discussed and agreed, starting at ten cents for pedestrians, rising to ten shillings for special vehicles or very heavy equipment.[37] 'All government vehicles must pass free of charge,' finished up the minister – a blatant and shameless try-on. 'In that case, we'll

37 Pedestrians – 10 cents; bicycles – 20 cents; motorcycles – 50 cents; cars – 2 Kenyan shillings; Pick-ups, vans and station wagons – two shillings, 50 cents; lorries up to eight tons – 3½ shillings; buses or taxis carrying more than five passenger – 5 shillings; heavy lorries – seven shillings; special vehicles or heavy equipment (such as tankers or tractors) – 10 shillings. There are twenty shillings to a Kenyan pound.

have to charge more for everyone else, to balance the cost of the bridge,' said Ron. His demand was withdrawn and the tolls were left as agreed.

The opening ceremony was on Friday 20 June 1958. It was an afternoon of brilliant sunshine and more than a hundred attended. Clarence and Ron were there, of course, plus all the relevant dignitaries such as the provincial commissioner, the chairman of the Mombasa Municipal Board, the town clerk and district commissioner. 'Fluffy' Fowkes, resplendent in white linen jacket and regimental tie, now retired from the chairmanship of the Road Authority, made the first speech. He declared how much confidence the Road Authority had in the 'engineer responsible for the planning of the bridge, Ron Buxton' and congratulated him on the fact that not a single life had been lost during the erection of the bridge.

Then it was Ron's turn. Referring to the heavy ironwood planks of the bridge's decking, and the way they clanked noisily when a vehicle was driven onto the deck of the bridge, he told the crowd: 'Don't worry about the rattle; after a while it will settle down. And if you see the bridge bend in the middle, again, don't worry – because it is meant to bend.' Detailing the various tests the bridge had undergone, he said: 'The Ministry of Works tried their hardest to break the bridge, but it wouldn't break.'

With that, Fluffy tucked his walking stick under his arm and cut the tape across the south approach, and the new Mtwapa Bridge was declared finally and fully open. Then he and his wife, and the provincial commissioner and his wife, got into the first car to be driven across. The event was duly reported in the *Mombasa Times* next day: 'The finest bridge on the East African coast.'

The bridge was an immediate and triumphant success. Over a thousand tickets were issued within 60 hours of the opening, 500 of them for vehicles. Two hundred cars crossed on the Sunday following Friday's opening ceremony. In a small column entitled 'The Bridge of Wonder', all the way away in London, the *Daily Express* quoted a correspondent who had written in to report what a source of wonder the new bridge was to local inhabitants from as far away as Mombasa, who would make special trips out to see the new sight, and described the excitement of the 'first crossing' and the chance to see the Creek from a new angle. As the only crossing of the Mtwapa sea inlet that was near the coast, and being on the main Mombasa–Malindi road, the bridge had a captive market. And the huge improvement in convenience and cutting of journey times meant that soon it was generating its own traffic.

From the day it opened, the Mtwapa ferry lost almost all its business. In due course the government approached The Mtwapa Bridge Company to ask if they would allow bicycles and pedestrians to cross free if the government-run ferry were closed? This they agreed to do. The small amount of business lost was soon more than made up by the increase in overall traffic. The bridge itself cost very little to run. Minimal maintenance was required; Ron would

**WKES OPENS
BRIDGE OVER
TWAPA CREEK**

*Project of interest to Road
Authority for a long time*

E £100,000 suspension road bridge over Mtwapa Creek
—the finest to be built on the East African Coast —
yesterday officially opened by Maj.-Gen. C. C. Fowkes,
her chairman of the Road Authority.

Those present at the ceremony, which was attended by
guests, included Maj. Clarence Buxton and Mr. Ronald
ton, two of the directors of Mtwapa Bridge Ltd., the
ate enterprise which will control this toll bridge. Also
ent were the Provincial Commissioner and Mrs.
mond O'Hagan, the Chairman of the Mombasa Munici-
Board, Mr. P. F. Foster, the Town Clerk, Mr. A. V.
liff, and the District
missioner, and Mrs.
H. Wolff.

brilliant sunshine Gen-
es cut the tape at the south
a r o a c h to the bridge.
n, and Mrs. Fowkes, and
and Mrs. O'Hagan, entered
first car to be driven across
picturesque creek.

Two years since

n. Fowkes said it was very
to be invited back from retire-
to witness the finale of a
project which had been
interest to the Road Authority
very long time.

Is about two years since
Clarence Buxton and Mr.
ld Buxton came to see me
st forward the idea of this
e," Gen. Fowkes said.
"e then went to see Mr.
and much to my surprise

rattle, after a while it will settle
down. And if you see it bend in
the middle, again don't worry because it is meant to break."

After detailing the various
tests carried out on the bridge
he commented amid laughter:
"The Ministry of Works tried
their hardest to break the bridge,
but it wouldn't break."

Mr. O'Hagan said that Mtwapa
Creek, if not the most attractive
was one of the most attractive
creeks in East Africa, "and looking at that bridge I think it is
an addition to the creek."

Tarmac road

Gen. Fowkes, during his years
as chairman of the Road
Authority, had never failed to
give sympathetic consideration
to any representation the Coast
Development Committee put forward, and he never failed to

The Provincial Com-
missioner, Mr. Desmond
O'Hagan, was at the wheel
of the first car to be driven
across Mtwapa Bridge yes-
terday. With him was
Mrs. O'Hagan and Maj.-
Gen. C. C. Fowkes and Mrs.
Fowkes. On the right Gen.
Fowkes, former chairman
of the Road Authority, is
seen opening the bridge by
cutting a tape.

'The finest bridge on the East African coast' – the *Mombasa Times* reports the opening,
21 June 1958. In the right-hand photograph, RCB extreme left, while General 'Fluffy'
Fowkes cuts the tape.

'It's meant to rattle and bend … !'
Over the opening weekend, 1,200 toll tickets were sold.

visit twice a year to check the cables and tighten them up, but apart from this, and occasional painting, the structure looked after itself. Every year, Clarence and Ron would hold a party by the bridge, on the north side of the creek, to keep everyone on side. The main expense, it soon transpired, was embezzlement of toll cash by those collecting the money, or armed hold-ups at the toll booth. For a time these were so serious that, a year after opening, Ron seriously contemplated selling the bridge. Articles in the Kenyan and British Press reported the rumour with headlines like 'PSSST! WANNA BUY A BRIDGE? ONLY £100,000'. In the end, the situation was remedied by installing a local director, Wally Brown, as bridge manager at the end of 1959.

The talk of selling didn't go away, however. In August 1959 the Kenyan government passed the Mtwapa Bridge Bill, granting to The Mtwapa Bridge Company the right to operate the bridge for twenty years from 20 June 1958, subject to certain clauses entitling the government to buy the bridge, should it wish to, after 5, 8, 11, 14 or 20 years, on payment of a sum calculated at the rate of £3,000 for each year of the period unexpired at the date of purchase, plus £77,000. After 20 years, if the government still had not exercised its right to buy the bridge, the company would be allowed to operate the bridge 'for such further period as may be agreed and subject to such conditions, including an option to buy the bridge, as shall be agreed'. As it turned out, the government never did buy the bridge. It took five years for the company to pay off the 70,000 Kenyan pounds original construction costs, after which the tolls were almost pure profit. For twenty-five years the Mtwapa Bridge delivered a steady stream of income which, Ron would cheerfully declare in later years, paid his children's school fees.

In 1985 the Japanese government, as part of in international aid package, offered Kenya three new bridges. Two of these were vast civil engineering enterprises, replacing the Nyali Bridge in Mombasa and the Kalifi Bridge between Mombasa and Malindi. For the third bridge, the government chose to replace the single-track toll bridge at Mtwapa. The Mtwapa Bridge Company was compensated for their loss of revenue to the tune of 200,000 Kenyan pounds. Unfortunately, exchange controls meant it was impossible to get this money out of the country. Within two years the Kenyan pound had devalued from around 20 Kenyan pounds per £1 sterling to around 100. Meanwhile the bridge was dismantled and its constituent parts – mostly, for the third time – were recycled: a fitting end, perhaps, for a bridge that fell off the back of a lorry.

12

A Magnificent Landing

Ron's greatest flying adventure – like much of the Mtwapa Bridge – came about because of his nose for a bargain. During the summer of 1958, at the Nairobi Aero Club, he got wind of a plane for sale. As he took in the details, he sniffed a chance to turn a tidy profit for minimal effort.

The machine in question was nothing remarkable: an old-fashioned, high-winged, single-engined monoplane called an Auster Aiglet, very like the Piper Cub on which he had received instruction at Nairobi Aerodrome a few years earlier. The Aiglet was a robust little machine. This particular one had been used as a crop sprayer with Desert Locust Control until it was grounded in need of extensive repairs. Now it had recently emerged from a total rebuild, resplendent in a green and silver livery that made it look almost new. It came with a new Certificate of Airworthiness (a plane's MOT). Ron knew that in the UK such a machine would easily fetch £2,000, yet in Nairobi they were so common he could probably get it for less than half that. After some bargaining, he bought it for £700. All he had to do to collect his £1,300 profit was fly it home and flog it.

He decided to do this straight away – or as soon as the business of his present visit was complete – and his friend (and director of The Mtwapa Bridge Company) Michael Harley asked if he could join him. Having just got

Simple and sturdy – an Auster Aiglet like the one bought by Ron

his private pilot's licence, Mike was keen to experience flying outside Kenya. What better way to spend his annual holiday, then, than by joining Ron in flying back to the UK?

Ron made a few practice flights in his new purchase, to get used to the controls, and to try out the supplementary, long-range fuel reserve he had rigged up. This consisted of an old car petrol tank on the back seat which fed aviation gas into the Auster's main belly tank. On 11 July they took off for their 5,000-mile journey back to Britain.

From the start, it became clear it was going to be a long haul. The Auster was never intended for long distances. Its Blackburn Cirrus Minor engine generated just 100 hp, achieving a cruising speed of barely 100 mph. The slightest headwind made an enormous difference. However, so far as the route went, following his two previous 'ferry' flights, Ron was beginning to know it almost by heart.

The first leg of their journey was the most spectacular: the short leg to Kisumu on the shore of Lake Victoria. This took them across the Rift Valley, climbing to 9,000 feet to cross the Mau Escarpment on the far side, then dropping down to the lake at 3,000 feet. The next morning, leaving Kenya, they set off on the much longer 410-mile leg to Juba, in the Sudan, taking them over Tororo, then across Uganda's lakeland and a huge stretch of uninhabited bush until they caught their first glimpse of the Nile at Nimule. All went uneventfully, and at Juba, today capital of South Sudan, armed with a letter and a permit to cross Sudan, the authorities were helpful. After lunch with an old friend, Stuart, a game warden Ron had met through Jocky, they were once again on their way. They headed north, over the swamp-land of The Sudd formed by the White Nile, better known locally as the Bahr al Jabal – and better still, simply as 'The Bog' – gleaming like a gigantic mirror in the evening sunshine. They spent the night at Malakal in the Upper Nile Province.

Between Malakal and Khartoum they followed the White Nile as it gradually left the swamplands for the flat desert plain north of Kosti. By the time they reached Khartoum the midday sun was making the hot air choppy. An enforced 48-hour break followed while they awaited their permit to cross Egypt. Politically, their journey was rather less straightforward than the last time Ron had undertaken it in the Gemini, as diplomatic relations between Britain and Egypt had ceased with the Suez Crisis. Their permit was duly granted, however, routing them via Wadi Halfa on the Egypt-Sudan border. In searing midday heat they departed Khartoum, stopping to refuel about a third of the way along their route to Wadi Halfa, at Atbara.

From Atbara, it was still 340 miles to Wadi Halfa. The first part of this route followed the Nile to Abu Hamed, but after that the Nile makes a huge serpentine meander south-west before heading north again, so pilots follow the line of Kitchener's railway, built in 1900 for the re-conquest of the Sudan after the Mahdis' rebellion. Featureless rocky desert here extends indefinitely in all directions, the railway line almost surreal as the only man-made feature. (Jocky, as an experienced Fleet Air Arm pilot used to navigating vast featureless expanses, likened flying over the deserts of Sudan to flying over the sea.) In an account of this leg of their journey that he later wrote for *The Woking News and Mail* (because it had a bearing on the events that followed), Ron describes what happened next:

The railway crosses a waterless uninhabited stretch of desert with nameless stations known as No.1 to No.10 along its length. The wind was favourable so I decided to cut a corner of the railway and fly on a course which would intersect it twenty minutes later on. The visibility was hazy, giving the appearance of blown sand and a dreary landscape which was a monotonous succession of black rocky hills and endless sand. After 30 minutes' flying there was still no sign of this railway. I nudged Michael to see if he had seen anything, only to find he had been asleep. After 45 minutes I was really worried; could we have overshot it, or had we hit a sudden strong headwind, reducing our speed by half? We had a hasty consultation. There was only an hour to go to sundown and we had about eight gallons of fuel left. To go on, if we had crossed the railway, could land us in some remote corner of the Sahara, far from civilisation. The alternative was to change course completely and fly towards the Nile, which must be somewhere on our port side 50–100 miles away. We decided to fly for the Nile. After 45 minutes on a westerly course we saw the first glimmer of a reflection in the setting sun; five minutes later we were over the Nile and its configuration showed us to be only 30 miles south of Wadi Halfa. Thankfully we pressed on with all possible speed and the runway came in sight just as the sun touched the horizon. We landed to find an anxious aerodrome officer awaiting us and with only 1½ gallons in the tank.

What was going on? They discovered from other pilots at the aerodrome that what had almost certainly happened was they had passed through the Inter-Tropical Front (these days known as the Inter-Tropical Convergence Zone), an area of extreme turbulence encircling the area near the Equator where the world's northerly and southerly winds meet. This had drastically reduced their speed just after leaving the railway. By the time they finally landed at Wadi Halfa they found that they had been flying into a northerly headwind of nearly 30 mph.

*

The same northerly headwind dogged them as they battled north through Egypt, reducing their ground speed to little more than 60 mph and cutting visibility in places to less than two miles. Thus they made it to Luxor. The Egyptian authorities had routed them the same way Ron crossed the country last time in the Gemini: northwards from Wadi Halfa, via Luxor, to Cairo before heading west to Mersa Matruh on the north Egyptian coast. On their next leg, from Luxor to Cairo, the wind was so strong they were forced to land at Asyût, only just over half-way, for more fuel, and only made Embaba, the small strip west of Cairo, the following evening – a day late – by which time they were supposed to be on the north coast at Mersa Matruh.

Egypt was in a strange state. Despite the lack of diplomatic relations with Britain everyone seemed friendly enough, though the country was operating under a mass of regulations reminiscent of wartime Britain. There appeared to be almost no air traffic. The usually busy Cairo International Airport was deserted except for Egyptian Airline planes. (At Asyût, there had been so little flying that when he signed the 'landing log' incoming pilots have to complete, Ron noticed that his entry of two years before was only a single page back.)

In Cairo, after dinner at Groppi's (see chapter 9) and a round of cabarets, the following day they were underway after lunch for the easy leg west to Mersa Matruh, which sits on the North African coast between Alexandria and Tobruk (across the border in Libya). Keeping north of Alexandria to avoid the prohibited area covering the Western Delta, they reached this pleasant small coastal town without incident and booked into an excellent hotel. Then they went to the beach to sample the celebrated Mediterranean bathing. In the sea, they took the opportunity to check their emergency equipment for the next day's sea crossing: a couple of old yellow inflatable Mae West life jackets, and a small inflatable dinghy.

Afterwards, with maps, rulers and his flight calculator (a circular slide rule), Ron planned the next day's flight. The key decision on any air journey between Europe and Africa, at least one conducted in a single-engined plane, is always the same: where to cross the Med? On his first trip out to Africa in the Proctor with Jocky, in 1956, they had opted for the safest (which means shortest-over-the-sea) course: overland down the Italian coast to Sicily, then a 60-mile hop to Malta, followed by a longer, 180-mile hop from Malta to Tripoli: long enough, at an hour and a half over water, to focus the mind; but sustainable, with only about 15 minutes completely out of sight of land.

The second time Ron had flown himself across the Med, this time heading northwards from Africa to England, it was in the Gemini; with the reassurance of two engines and much longer range, he could afford to be bolder. He had cut his previous journey, with its innumerable fussy legs down the coast, by hundreds of miles, making the almost 400-mile sea crossing straight from Tripoli to Sardinia and proceeding north from there. This time, in the Auster, for a change (and, he later wrote, to 'give us a chance to see something of the Greek Islands on our way') he elected to make the crossing from a place called Sidi Barrani to Heraklion, on Crete. Sidi Barrani was on a small promontory about 80 miles further west along the coast from Mersa Matruh. This would cut out the tedious 800-mile haul along the North African coast, via Benghazi, to Tripoli. The drawback was that it meant longer over open sea: a good 240 miles, or, in a plane of the Auster's speed, an unsettling 2½–3 hours.

The decision as to which route to take was, of course, never really in question. Ron was an intrepid flyer. His log book now recorded almost 500 hours flying time, accumulated over dozens of countries and landscapes on several different types of machine. Why would he conceivably opt for a vastly longer, familiar route, when he could have a new, exciting, shorter one that also allowed him to squeeze in the Greek Islands?

The route forecast from Mersa Matruh Air Traffic Control gave them a wind reading of 15 knots north-west (i.e. blowing *from* the north-west) at 5,000 feet, becoming west-north-west at higher levels. With a full fuel load, running on a 'weak mixture' (with the carburettor set to make the air-fuel mixture as 'lean' as possible) this meant their maximum possible time in the air was six hours. Leaving Mersa Matruh at 12.30 on their first leg to Sidi Barrani, Ron confirmed by radio that the weather forecast they had been given was about right. Yes, crackled back the voice. Wind was 15-18 knots blowing from about 290°. Otherwise the sky was cloudless with brilliant sunshine. By the time they had arrived over Sidi Barrani, Ron had climbed to 5,000 feet. As he turned onto their seaward course, leaving Africa behind, his bearing for Heraklion allowed for easterly drift. It was 13.40. By 16.40, they would be well over land …

*

Flying over open sea in a single-engined aircraft, even for short stretches, is never entirely comfortable. Every tiny change in engine note or alteration in the sound of the propeller's roar as its tips encounter slightly different air quality, every bump or thump of midday turbulence due to thermal activity, acquires an unwelcome extra significance, tending to send the imagination spinning into a cascade of 'what ifs'. For the first half-hour since setting course for Crete, they could still, if they chose to twist their necks far enough behind them, see the North African coast.

After that, gradually, steadily, the blue sea beneath them and the blue midday haze around them swallowed them up, until their world shrank into just the confines of the cockpit in which they sat, surrounded by a vast featureless dome beyond.

All that connected them to the familiar world they had so recently left were the dials and instruments on the Auster's dashboard – fuel and engine temperature gauges, air speed indicator, compass, directional indicator,

[165]

artificial horizon – and periodic bursts of static in their headsets. The few air traffic reports or exchanges from other pilots on their frequency soon dried up, leaving them in a strange, private world with nothing to look at, and just the odd crackle and hiss of their headsets, and the roar of the engine and propeller, for company. There were no ships beneath, no birds, no clouds or aircraft in the sky around them. Just blue. Endless, murky blue.

After two hours of this disconcerting sensation, at 5,000 feet, they should have been able to make out land ahead. But there was nothing. Ron climbed to 7,000 feet, then 8,000, then 9,000 feet, and they strained their eyes into the blue, desperately trying to discern some hint of the brown mountains of Crete. Nothing. Just haze and murk, and the roar of the engine. Far below, tiny white streaks of foam, 'white horses' on the surface of the sea, indicated a strong headwind had set in, which, in turn, could mean a longer crossing. Another hour passed. From Ron's own account:

> Nothing was visible. We had now been over the water three hours and the complete absence of land was worrying. Things looked rather serious; should we turn back and attempt to reach the North African coast? We still had 1¾–2 hours of fuel left. We decided to carry on and brought the plane down to 1,000 feet in the hope of reducing the wind effect.
>
> At 1700 hours we spotted a ship, which turned out to be a tanker, heading east. We circled it and dropped a note on to the deck in a shoe, asking them to report our position to Air Traffic Control, and indicate the direction of land [by steering so that the ship pointed like an arrow]. Although the ship gave no sign of receiving our message we later learned that the tanker, *The British Vision*, did in fact get our message and reported to Athens Air Traffic Control.
>
> We then flew on, taking a more easterly course; 40 minutes later, with still no sign of land, the auxiliary tank ran dry and I knew that we had only three gallons left in the main, which would keep us up for 20–30 minutes at the best. Things looked really bad now ... There was clearly a strong wind blowing and the sea was rough with large and uninviting waves.

The situation was every pilot's nightmare. Everything had apparently been done right. A carefully-made plan had been followed exactly. Wide safety margins had been built in. And yet the world wasn't reacting as it should. Something was wrong: but what? Crete wasn't where it was supposed to be. And in that simple, chilling question mark, all existing plans collapsed and the survival clock began to tick. What should they do? Was there still time to correct their course, if the correct course could be found? And behind these thoughts, the acute, unspoken awareness that every second now brought closer the moment when the engine spluttered and fell silent and they would be alone, whereabouts unknown by anyone, over the open sea.

The first thing they needed was a ship, in case the worst happened. Yet they had seen only one on their entire journey, the tanker to which they had dropped the note. Ron began a visual 'box search', a standard technique employed by ships and Coastal Command during the war for searching large areas of featureless water. Nothing. By now the fuel gauge indicated they had a gallon left – about ten minutes. Finally, at 17.45, they spotted a ship – only the second of the last four hours – about five miles off. Ron made for it. Hoping fervently that the fuel gauge was accurately calibrated, that the engine would not stop just a few moments too soon, they saw it was another tanker.

Ron circled twice, while Michael hastily pencilled his second note of the day onto the back of a map: 'S.O.S. WE ARE LANDING IN THE SEA – PLEASE STAND BY TO PICK US UP.' He folded the map and pressed it into the toe of one of Ron's desert boots. Then he slid back the window. The roar of rushing air and the noise of the engine increased sharply. Ron flew low over the deck of the ship. As he did so, Michael took careful aim, and hurled the shoe towards the deck.

*

The chances of successfully hitting a moving ship's deck with an object thrown from a moving aircraft in a strong wind, and this for the second time, was absurdly against the odds.

Yet hit it he did.

As Ron circled once again – the fuel gauge needle was now off the bottom

Lifeboat – TMS *Wilhelmine Essberger*, much as Ronald would have seen her moments before ditching

of the red – the ship hooted. Their message had been received. It appeared to be slowing down and Michael reported activity round one of the boats. Next time round, Ron jettisoned the cabin door. ('How thankful I am that Austers provided the Aiglet with a dispensable door' he later wrote.) Meanwhile, he was thinking fast. Landing in the sea is a procedure few amateur pilots get the chance to practise. Fortunately, however, as he prepared to ditch, a conversation with Jocky a few weeks before came back to him. It was about recommended Fleet Air Arm procedures for landing on water. 'You come down into wind in the normal way,' Jocky had explained, 'but at the last moment you kick the plane round 90° with the rudders to land *with* the swell.' That way, in theory at least, the plane doesn't smash into the waves or overturn.

They were now low enough that the direction of the wind was all too obvious from the swell. Flying into it, Ron descended to about thirty feet, about 200 yards in front of the tanker's bows. He was so low, he could feel the strength of the gusts as he tried to hold the plane steady. The waves looked enormous. As his speed dropped off Ron lowered the flaps fully (standard procedure when landing, to allow the plane to remain airborne while flying as slowly as possible). As he sank almost to the height of the waves, he slammed his foot on the rudder, kicking the tail round until the plane's body was parallel with the swell, then he gently raised the nose until, tail first, she dropped into the water along the crest of a large wave. It was a perfect landing.

In Ron's own words:

We hardly felt any shock at all. By the time we had freed our safety belts water was pouring in and I just got out as the plane settled down to wing level. The next wave swept right over us and Michael struggled up through the water a few seconds later. The sea was very rough, the waves must have been 15 feet from trough to crest, and it was all we could do to hold on. I sat on a wing, putting my foot through the fabric to get a better hold as we floated down towards the ship. Someone threw us a line and lifebuoy, but it was blown back by the wind.

The plane was settling now and would clearly not float much longer, so with a great effort we managed to break in the top of the fuselage and extract our partially inflated dinghy. Just then she started to sink, the nose first, and soon only the tail was sticking out and that went shortly after. There was no chance of trying to salvage anything, our own position was far too hazardous in that sea. A boat was not long looming up and a few minutes later strong arms hauled us out of the sea.

They were probably in the water about half an hour. And fortunately, being the Med, it wasn't cold. But the waves seemed vast. By the time they reached the tanker, they were too exhausted even to climb the ladder. They had to be pulled up and, at the top, collapsed onto the deck.

The German crew spoke little English – fortunately just enough to understand the message – but they could not have been friendlier. Soon they were being revived with coffee and Scotch and later were provided with clothes, razors and toothbrushes. The ship, it turned out, was the TMS *Wilhelmine Essberger*, a German-registered oil tanker of the Essberger line from Bremenshaven, bound for Banias, in Syria, to load crude oil piped from Iraq.

*

And so the question posed itself – as, indeed, it had a couple of days before at Wadi Halfa – what had gone wrong? Where were they? The *Wilhelmine Essberger* chart room revealed the answer to the second question. They were 35 miles *west* of Crete. The wind was blowing from the north-east at force 5 – nearly 25 mph. Hardly the 15 knots (18 mph) from the WNW that had been forecast. Their forecast had been utterly wrong. Piecing together the facts, it

Happy landing – on board the oil tanker TMS *Wilhelmine Essberger* –
LEFT: Mike Harley and Ron in borrowed whites and sandals. RIGHT: the lifeboat is
re-hoisted.

seemed that what Mersah Matruh Air Traffic Control must have supplied was the local wind, rather than the route forecast. In any event, it was enough to see them blown 100 miles off course. 'A glance at the map will show what a large deviation is necessary to miss Crete completely, as we did, when aiming at the centre of the island,' wrote Ron later. The extent of their drift meant they were still heading for open sea when they ditched.

The ship's captain, Captain Becker, radioed Customs to report he had two extra people on board. However, on arrival at Syria, because of unrest there, the British consul wouldn't allow them to disembark. The Middle East was in a volatile state, exploding just a few days later in Iraq when King Faisal, the Crown Prince and the Prime Minister were all assassinated in a Nasserite army coup, prompting British paratroops to land in Jordan and American marines to go ashore in Beirut. Instead, Ron and Michael Harley were relegated to an indeterminate spell on board as, loaded with oil, the tanker set course for Bremen. The speed at which oil tankers travel varies according to the demand for oil. At the time there was no demand, so the tanker travelled exceptionally slowly, taking almost two weeks to reach Bremen. The time passed slowly. Although there were books on board, they were all in German. Ron tried to arrange for a helicopter to collect them as they passed through the Dover Straits, but in the end there was no need. The tanker docked at Bremenshaven, and Jocky flew down in the Gemini to collect them.

*

The 'Details of Flight' box of Ron's flying log book for 19 July 1958, usually reserved to record the names of places of departure and arrival, contains the unusual entry for an aircraft with a fixed-wheel undercarriage: 'Mersa Matruh – sea'. The 'Remarks' box, blank for the vast majority of flights, contains the bald amplification: 'Force landed Mediterranean 50 miles W. of Crete. Picked up by TMS *Wilhelmine Essberger*.' Ron's account of his adventure, requested by *The Woking News and Mail* three weeks after his return, was hardly less clipped; a template for stiff-upper-lipped understatement, ending with the almost comically bland exactitude: 'Experience of any sort is of value, and thanks to our friends aboard the *Wilhelmine Essberger*, we are still here to tell the tale.' Other newspaper accounts were less reticent. 'SOS IN A SHOE SAVES FLYER' led a piece in the *Daily Mail*, published before Ron got back, relishing the antics of the 35-year-old 'prospective Tory candidate for Leyton'. In this and other accounts, the erroneous wind forecast became translated into 'a very bad storm'.

H. Young & Company's underwriter, Mr Risely-Pritchard, called. 'Thank goodness you're both alive,' he said, in a rare expression of sentiment which made even Ron, for a moment, feel touched. 'You were both insured by the company for £5,000 each,' he continued. 'Had anything happened, the company would have been liable for nearly £11,000.' Otherwise, the fall-out was limited. When Michael Harley married the following year, he was banned by his new wife, Jill, whom he'd only just met, from flying again.[38] The insurers of the Auster had only one question: 'Are you in possession of a valid pilot's licence?' As the answer was yes, in due course they paid £1,000.

Das Boot – Ron's left desert boot, later recovered from the crew

So Ron ended up with a more modest profit on his bargain aeroplane, £300 rather than the £1,300 he had hoped for. More importantly, he acquired his finest flying story. 'It was a brilliant landing,' he would tell the innumerable people who asked him about his adventure down the years. 'A magnificent landing. I came down into wind then, at the last minute, just kicked her round to land with the swell. Fortunately I'd recently spoken to my brother-in-law Jocky who was in the Fleet Air Arm. He saved my life …'

38 When she died, in 2000, his flying resumed.

13

A House in the Country

A 'CHUMMERY' WAS the term which most exactly described 67, Ashley Gardens, the apartment near Westminster Cathedral which became Ron's London base from 1951 onwards – what the dictionary defines as bachelor quarters for 'chums'. The brick mansion block, just off Victoria Street, was popular with young MPs; Westminster was less than ten minutes' walk away, within the Division Bell. Ron's fourth-floor rooms were reached by a small hydraulic lift, operated by a porter, which had the unsettling habit, when the button was pressed, of sagging slightly before departure.

Once attained, however, the accommodation in Ashley Gardens was rambling and comfortable. Activity centred around two rooms off the hall. One had a big south-facing window through which the tops of the striped brick cathedral towers could be glimpsed, and a dining table the size of which made you wonder (lift journey still in mind) how on earth it got there. In the sitting room were a grand piano and a desk, with a fine watercolour of the House of Commons nodding to Ron's political aspirations. Every surface, including walls and floors, was decked with mementos of foreign travel: knick-knacks from corners of Kashmir and Burma, Sumatra and the Sudan: Indian silk, the rug Ron had wrapped himself in crossing France from Cairo, a leopard skin. Wooden skis leaned against the walls, unruly piles of papers and company reports jostled with teach-yourself-Swahili manuals.

There were four bedrooms, whose occupation varied on an almost daily basis, contributing a sense of flux and fluidity to the atmosphere. This, it said, is a base camp from which assaults on life are mounted on a rolling basis. Notes pinned on bedroom doors might say 'JOHN P ARRIVING 28TH' or 'EMPTY UNTIL 1ST APRIL'. Perhaps in response to the many friends and relations who had opened their doors to him, Ron's doors remained perpetually open to any friends or acquaintances who might be passing through. Each morning, around eight, the chink and clink of china and cutlery indicated that the housekeeper Mrs Anderson had arrived and was laying breakfast, a sound that was shortly supplemented by the invigorating smell of kippers or frying bacon. Soon, a turbaned head or Arab face might appear from the spare room doorway. You never knew who might be staying at Ashley Gardens.

After briefly sharing with Jean in Cheyne Row, Ron had taken rooms in St James's Place (for £4 a week) with his Cambridge friend, Charles Dalgleish. Friends from singing in Trinity College choir together, Dalgleish had stayed

Sibling revelry: Ron and Jean attend a wedding in the 1950s

on to complete a D. Phil. before taking up a junior fellowship at the college, while Ron joined up.[39] Reconvening after the war, by 1951, in their late twenties, they needed somewhere larger. Charles found Ashley Gardens and, for what seemed the astronomical sum of £200 'key money', they moved to their palatial new quarters. A third tenant was found, Dick Peskett, a Wykehamist timber merchant and, sometimes, a fourth too, in the shape of Geoff Bovill, a contemporary of Ron's from Eton. Thereafter Ashley Gardens became – and remained, after he bought the lease for £13,000 – Ron's centre of operations in London. Holywell was kept on merely for weekends and as a furniture store.

Weekends were devoted to rural pursuits. During the Fifties, Jo Gurney, Anthony's older brother, introduced Ron to hunting. Jo was five years older. They had met after the war, when Ron, as mentioned earlier, without any

39 Later he became chief chemist for Guinness in Dublin, and a Professor of Chemistry in the Sudan. He would become godfather to Ron's daughter Camilla, and Ron godfather to his son, Jonathan (now an airline pilot).

parents with whom to spend Christmas, would often join Anthony and Jo at the Gurney seat, Northrepps Hall near Cromer in north Norfolk. In due course, Jo bought a house twenty miles further south, near Barnham Broom, a village almost central to the great pan of East Anglia.

Mill House soon became a regular weekend pilgrimage for Ron – and pilgrimage it was. With no M11 or dual carriageways, the journey from the Lea Bridge works in Leytonstone, out through the north-east of London, could take four hours. If a tractor or milk lorry happened to be dawdling along the A11 Norwich road through Thetford Forest, with its endless kinks and inadequate straights, it could be longer still. Leaving this road ten miles short of Norwich, after the pretty market town of Wymondham (pronounced 'windom'), the Barnham Broom road began to snake and wind in wide, ever-lazier loops, as if to say: this is where time slows down. There was some woodland, then a set of wrought iron gates with painted lodges, followed soon after by a glimpse across parkland to a great brick mansion, indicating that the journey was near its end. This was Kimberley Hall, and after a humpback bridge the road passed a church marooned in the middle of a grass field, and Barnham Broom was just a mile further on. Mill House quickly became a byword for contented country weekending – and shabby, freezing accommodation.

Through the 1950s, this was Ron's second home. Northrepps Hall and the coast were less than 45 minutes away. With Jo, through the winter months when he was in England, Ron attended meets of the North Norfolk Harriers, acquainting himself with rural Norfolk, with its big skies and rolling sea mists, and underfoot its heavy clay, so responsive to the celebrated agricultural experimenters, Coke of Norfolk and 'Turnip' Townshend; so productive of the sugar beet which, since the German submarine blockades of the First World War, had become a staple of the Anglian landscape.

Hunting showed Ron the county, its remote farms, picturesque villages, long coastline and famous Broads. Its country houses, too, for Norfolk was a county of estates, dotted with important landmarks in the evolution of the classical country house: from Inigo Jones's Raynham (seat of 'Turnip' Townshend) to William Kent's Holkham Hall, Colen Campbell's Houghton and William Talman's Kimberley. Galloping across the heavy plough, hooves clinking the flints, he would have felt the Arctic blast of the north winds which bring more snow to this region of lowland Britain than any other. He learnt to recognise villages by their church towers – often round because of the lack of stone underfoot to build corners – little imagining that one day this knowledge would save his life (see later in the chapter).

No doubt, during their days in the saddle, he and Jo moaned about the shortage of jumpable fences and the low-lying nature of the country (which accounted for quite so much of it being paved with disused air bases). By

1952, one thing is certain: Ron had hunted enough to be bored with riding hirelings; what he wanted was a hunter of his own. Jo agreed to keep his ears open and soon reported that there was a horse available locally which might be worth checking out. It was owned by his colourful neighbour, Lord Kimberley.

*

The 18th baronet and 11th Baron Wodehouse, 4th Earl of Kimberley, was a jovial extrovert who might have emerged directly from the pages of his celebrated kinsman, P. G. Wodehouse. 'Johnny' to his free-spending, fast-living circle, 'the brightest blade in Burke's' to a delighted tabloid press, his reputation extended far beyond the Norfolk hamlet from which he took his name, chiefly because so many of his nocturnal antics (being caught naked by an irate husband in a hotel cupboard was a typical example) appeared in the following day's gossip columns. A member of the high-rolling Aspinall-Lucan set at the Clermont Club, this hard-drinking 'knight of the green baize table' (*Daily Express*) alternated a day-job of running a public relations business (clients included Gregory Peck, Robert Mitchum and 'that bald bugger' Yul Brynner) with nights spent losing heavily at chemmy and bedding as many women as possible.[40] It was an expensive lifestyle, so much so that since the war's end Kimberley had already had to sell off some 7,000 acres of family lands around Norfolk – and he was rumoured to be running up prodigious new debts.

In due course, Kimberley would achieve a measure of fame as the most married man in the peerage, working his way through five wives before settling down with the sixth, a former masseuse met on a beach in Jamaica. His serious side, meanwhile, was represented by championship tiddlywinks, membership of Britain's international bobsleigh team and regular speeches in the House of Lords about UFOs.

For the moment, however, it was still 1952. Johnny was twenty-eight, still on his third wife, Cynthia, with a horse for sale. Jo knew Johnny well. Godfather to his eldest son, he was a regular shooting guest at Kimberley over the winter. So one weekend, he and Ron drove over to have a look at the hunter. Ostensibly Ron and Johnny Kimberley had plenty in common. Both had been in the same year at Eton – Johnny's surname plain Wodehouse then. Johnny's father, like Ron's, had been killed in a German air raid, when he was seventeen. However, there the similarities ended ('he was in the "lag set",

40 Compare the following diary entries. John Wodehouse, 1st Earl of Kimberley, Liberal Statesman in Gladstone's government: '*6 August 1866*. Monday. Spoke in the H of Lords on the 2nd reading of the H. Corpus bill. My speech was well received tho I don't suppose many of their Lps much liked what I said, in their hearts'. John Wodehouse, 4th Earl of Kimberley, from his memoir, *The Whim of the Wheel* (2001), of his life in the 1950s: 'What motivated me was very simple. Sex … I just couldn't think of anything else.'

frightfully dim') and their divergent approaches to their careers meant their lives had rarely overlapped. Nevertheless, it was always interesting to inspect at close quarters a local landmark, and this was the first time Ron had turned off the Barnham Broom road between the two brick lodges, with their wrought iron railings and wide, faintly Italianate, roofs. The drive ran straight, wooded both sides, opening out after a quarter of a mile to reveal a classical mansion on a grand scale, complete with corner towers and symmetrical wings breaking forward either side.

A groom led out the object of their mission. Sir Humphrey was a compact and handsome bay gelding. A 'fabulous jumper', he had been ridden in the Grand Military Cup at Sandown by Johnny and in numerous point-to-points, Ron learnt. If he had a drawback, it was his size: at just 15½ hands, he was too small to carry a heavy rider for a long day. But Ron was no weight. After taking him for a short ride, the only mystery seemed to be why Johnny Kimberley only wanted £150 for him. Over drinks in a charming cottage by the great walled gardens, where Johnny and his latest wife were installed while builders were in the main house, Ron bought Sir Humphrey on the spot.

With Sir Humphrey, Ron's career as a foxhunter broke into a gallop. Now the only thing holding him back became the country he hunted. Norfolk, even viewed in the most affectionate light, was never going to rank alongside the best hunting country. There were few fences to jump. The country was just too low, too open, and the ground too heavy, rendered stickier by a general lack of pasture due to the largely arable farming. Norfolk was shooting, not hunting, country (Sandringham was not far away). The packs might be enthusiastic, but, for two young 'thrusters' like Jo and Ron, the West Norfolk Foxhounds, North Norfolk Harriers or Dunston Harriers had their limits. Greater things beckoned.

So, in 1953, Jo and Ron decided to try a season in the elevated sporting Elysium of Leicestershire. Towing the horses in a battered old trailer horsebox bought for an Army jeep, they billeted them with a farmer near Melton Mowbray and hunted whenever they could with the Quorn. The experiment was so successful they repeated it the following season, supplementing it on one occasion by flying out to Western Ireland for a weekend with the Galway Blazers. At other times, around Christmas especially, they continued to have days out with Norfolk packs.

These were happy times, filling his winter weekends away from Africa, but already Ron was casting around for new excitements. He did not have far to look. Many of his new hunting friends, come the spring, rode in point-to-points. Ron decided it was time for him to have a try. He entered two or three races around Norfolk, successfully completing the course, but unplaced. In 1955 he decided to raise his game. Sir Humphrey was entrusted to a well-known local trainer, Jack Bloom, a tall, jovial figure familiar to everyone in the Norfolk hunting scene. Bloom declared confidently that, under his guidance, Sir Humphrey could not only be placed in the prestigious Members' Race at the West Norfolk Harriers Point-to-Point in April – he could win.

The big Saturday dawned, 2 April, 'one of the finest days mid-Norfolk has enjoyed this year' the *Eastern Daily Press* later declared; a meeting which, as a result of such clemency, 'attracted the largest crowd for several seasons'. It would be an eventful afternoon. In the Ladies' Race, only two of the five starters finished the course, one suffering concussion, with 'a final thrill' when the leading rider made a clumsy landing at the last fence but 'retained her seat and came home an easy winner'. In the Adjacent Hunts' Lightweight, Johnny Kimberley led the field for most of the race, and 'was still well-placed when he fell heavily at the last fence'. The big event of the day, however, was the Members', Farmers' and Subscribers' Race, held mid-afternoon. There were five runners: Ron on Sir Humphrey and his friend Willy Bulwer-Long on Jane's Return (the only owner-riders). Favourite was Kempton Jane, ridden by Michael Bloom, Jack's son, plus, as unknown outsiders, a Mrs Thomas's Torrecht River and Colonel Shaw's Fitz Rodney. Ron's key adversaries, however, were the favourite and Bulwer-Long. Willy, he knew only too well, was a much more experienced race-rider, on a horse considerably larger than Sir Humphrey.

Weighed in and resplendent in his white breeches, top boots, racing cap and blue jersey, all too soon the tour of the paddock was over and they were under starter's orders. The first stages of the race passed in a blur of adrenaline. Somewhere in the excitement of the first circuit, Ron lost his hat, but soon he, Willy and the favourite had pulled away from the rest of the field. By the second circuit, it was looking like a two-horse race, between Ron and Willy. The last fence they took together, the favourite trailing two lengths behind. As Ron, hatless, and Willy galloped towards the finishing post, there didn't seem to be anything between them, crossing the line, as the *Eastern Daily Press* reported, 'to provide the finest finish to the Members' Race that many people could remember'. Photographs of the 'photo-finish' proved that Sir Humphrey was, in fact, the clear winner, and at the prize-giving later Mrs Quintin Gurney (Jo and Anthony's aunt), a cheerful figure clad in leopard skin and hairy tweed, presented Ron with the handsome silver Lockhart-Ross Challenge Cup. Jack Bloom had fulfilled his promise. The splash in Monday's *Eastern Daily Press* was headlined 'Sir Humphrey Home by Neck at Sparham'.

*

'Kimberley is for sale. We think you should buy it.' Three years later, in August 1958, Jo Gurney broke the astounding news to Ron that for months

'The finest photo finish many could remember' –
TOP: Ron wins the Members' Race at West Norfolk Harriers Point-to-Point, Sparham,
2 April 1955
BOTTOM: the challenge cup was presented by Mrs Quentin Gurney

had been the buzz of the county. For Ron, whose feet were barely dry from his adventure in the Med with Mike Harley, after months away overseeing the completion of the Mtwapa Bridge, it was the first he had heard of it. Johnny Kimberley, he discovered, had finally done it. He had run up debts so colossal – said to be over £100,000 – that his only option was to sell his birthright, the estate that had been in his family since the sixteenth century. 'And so he shed in a few years what had taken his family the best part of a millennium to accumulate' later wrote the *Guardian* in his obituary. Simultaneously, he had become bored of Cynthia, his third wife. Having moved her and the children out of the garden cottage into the newly-renovated main house, he then became aware of the difficulty of evicting her. 'Very well,' he had declared, to everyone's disbelieving delight, 'I'll sell the place over her head.' And this was what he had tried to do.

Except the place had not sold. The auction, it transpired, had come and gone – on 25 July 1958, at the Royal Hotel in Norwich – while Ron was enjoying his unscheduled cruise aboard the TMS *Wilhelmine Essberger*. If a single buyer could not be found, the estate was to be broken up into 91 lots and dispersed accordingly. And this is what had happened. The farms, cottages and most of the surrounding fields and woodland had been snapped up by the tenants (at an acreage rate of £55 an acre). The home farm had gone to Sir Humphrey's trainer, Jack Bloom. What was left, however, the heart and soul of this noble estate, the very first lot, 'The Mansion, Pleasure Gardens, Lake, Well-timbered Park, Arable, Woodlands, Buildings and Lodges; in all some 247 acres' as described by the particulars, plus the garden cottage where Johnny had been living, two acres of walled garden and some additional arable land and woodland, had all failed to find a buyer.

'Come on Ron, you've got to buy it,' said Jo. It was a plan enthusiastically endorsed by Jo's brother, Anthony Gurney. And it was true that Ron had been thinking about buying a house in the area for some time; they had all talked about it on numerous occasions. Well – here was his chance!

Even so, Kimberley ...

Still, wild as the idea might be, there was no harm taking a look. Ron sent for the particulars. By their sumptuousness alone, folio-sized and embossed with the Wodehouse arms, their presentation declared that this sale was something special. Eighty-five pages listed details of mansion and park, farms and cottages, rights and tenancies, yields and game bags, with coloured maps delineating woodlands, field names and parcels of outlying land, and all the other peripheries that make up a major estate.

Unfazed by his recent flying escapade in the Med, Ron decided to fly up in the Gemini to check the place out. With him, he took Jocky's sister Anne. Anne was married to Henry Gillespie, a consultant radiologist, and they had settled near Holywell. She had become good friends with Jean, leading to their travelling round Europe together. She was the automatic choice of companion when Ron flew up to inspect Kimberley. Anne recalled the flight only too vividly. Taking off early from Fair Oaks, in Surrey, in clear weather, as they proceeded north-east over East Anglia the ground began to disappear beneath thickening tendrils of fog, a state for which that sea-fringed flatland is only too renowned. This is never a happy situation for a pilot, partly

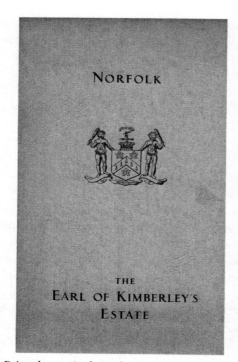
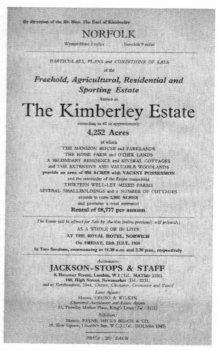

Princely particulars: the 85-page particulars that documented the Kimberley estate, to
be auctioned on 25 July 1958 at the Royal Hotel, Norwich

because of the difficulties it presents for navigation, with all the usual
landmarks hidden, but more importantly because there is the risk that the
destination airfield, on arrival, will also be buried. With every minute, the
blanket beneath thickened until they were flying over a sea of white in all
directions. The Gemini had no radio, so assistance from air traffic control was
not available.

The increasing seriousness of this situation, however, was not what was
preoccupying Anne, for through her passenger window she had noticed something else; something that seemed, to her, of even more pressing significance.
The object of her attention was a small screw on the wing, which she had
noticed was turning. The more she watched it, the more it seemed to be
moving, turning with the vibration of the engines. As the journey progressed,
she became increasingly fixated by the screw, unable to think about anything
else. Her chain of thought was simple: what happens when the screw falls out?
Would the wing fall off?

A loose screw was the least of Ron's worries, as he pressed boldly on. After
about fifty minutes it was impossible to know where they were, a state of
affairs sufficiently unsatisfactory that even Ron began to be concerned. Until,

with an exclamation of delight, he recognised the spire of Norwich Cathedral poking up through the fog. After that, the only visible way-points were church towers – a considerable test of Ron's powers of topographic recognition. Fortunately, his many days hunting across Norfolk, getting to know its villages, now paid off. Taking his bearing from Norwich Cathedral, he was able to recognise some other church towers looming out of the fog. In this way he managed to triangulate his way to roughly where Swannington, their destination airfield, must be.

Once overhead, however, his worst fears were realised. There was no sign of the ground. To make matters worse, the cloud level here had risen considerably, to over a thousand feet, well above the height of Swannington's church tower. This posed the critical question: was there clear air beneath, or did the cloud reach down to ground level? It was far too risky to try descending through the cloud, in case the latter proved to be the case. Ron did the only thing he could think of: he pressed northwards towards the coast, then out over the North Sea in the hope of finding a gap in the cloud through which he could descend, before heading back, beneath the cloud, to look for Swannington. That way, if the cloud did close in completely, he could always rise into clear air.

On and on they went, out over the sea, over what seemed to be an infinite expanse of cloud, until, at last, his hope materialised. He spotted a small gap in the cloud. He descended through it, found the air beneath clear, and turned back towards the land. Flying low, he skimmed landward beneath the cloud base until, after several tense minutes, they were racing over fields at (as Anne remembers it) telegraph pole height until, with inexpressible relief, Ron spotted the church towers of Oulton, Swannington and Attlebridge in the familiar line ahead. A few moments later they were safely on the ground greeting Jo, who had come to meet them. Anne vowed she would not set foot in an aeroplane with Ron at the controls again.

It was only a few years since Ron's last visit to Kimberley but, even allowing for the markedly altered circumstances, the place looked very different. There was an air of neglect as they drove up the drive. Even so, when the house came into view, flanked by its two wings, the spectacle was as imposing as ever ('giving the centre great scale', as the particulars put it). But the east wing, to the left when facing the Entrance Front, was in a shocking state, with evidence of water damage everywhere.

The door was answered by Cynthia, Countess of Kimberley number three, a buoyant figure wearing, Anne vividly recalled, cork wedge-heeled shoes, tangerine Thai silk trousers and a white blouse. The door led into a grand two-storey entrance hall with a generous wooden staircase ascending to a gallery. The hall led through to a large garden sitting room, into which light streamed from the three central windows of the Park Front. Despite its classical

Kimberley Hall, entrance (north) front: built in 1712 by William Talman, with the corner towers added around 1754 and the curved colonnades connecting the wings in 1835

grandeur, the house was essentially two rooms deep. From here a door lead through to a big drawing room. Cynthia pointed out the alcove which had contained the Snetzler organ, the best of its kind, sold by Johnny's mother to settle her bridge debts. Adjacent to the drawing room, back on the north side and entered from the entrance hall, was the equally formal music room, with elaborate plasterwork and carayatids by John Sanderson (a pupil of Adam's).

Left off the hall, down a short, airy passage was the dining room, opposite a new kitchen. The interior, Cynthia explained, had just been extensively rearranged, to rationalise a previously pretty odd lay-out. The front door, for example, hadn't been in the middle of the house, but off to the left, as was the main staircase. There had been no entrance hall or central stairs; all these were new. As part of this re-siting of the front door, the architect, Fletcher Watson, had added a white-painted classical porch made of timber.

Back in the garden sitting room, the central window opened up completely, like a door. Throwing it open, in her cork wedges, Cynthia led them down the stone steps to a wide grass terrace. Beyond a stone-balustraded parapet and ha-ha, parkland designed by Capability Brown swept down to a sheet of water closed and balanced at the edges by woodland, with glimpses of open country stretching to the horizon: an eighteenth-century vision of Paradise.

Strolling across the grass terrace and looking back at the house, this front was plainer than the Entrance Front. In fact, in comparison, it looked positively unfinished: blank brick, with no stone embellishment, articulation or ornament at all. Even the pediment was blank. It was as if whoever built it ran out of money by the end. The brickwork however, in colour somewhere between pale pink and fiery orange (when it caught the sun) radiated a gentle

'An eighteenth-century paradise': view from the central steps of the Park Front (winter)

warmth which countered any austerity. It was just possible to see where the four corner towers had been added some decades later, as the bricks were slightly larger and darker.

Going back inside, a long and chilly tour of the cellars followed, a labyrinthine subterranean warren extending not just beneath the main house, but also along a long vaulted brick passageway to the east wing. Originally, the particulars explained, this underground passage had been all that connected the kitchen beneath the east wing to the main house. The curved brick colonnades linking the wings to the main block came later, added after 1835. If nothing else, they asserted the princely scale on which the house was built. The architect responsible, William Talman – re-modeller of Uppark and Chatsworth amongst his other commissions – had done his work well. Upstairs, the 'Gallery Landing' above the entrance hall offered an even better view of the park and lake. 'There are thirty-three bedrooms' announced Cynthia brightly. Children rampaged around (Cynthia had three by her first marriage and two more by Johnny). The only place they were told they could not go was a bedroom on the first floor. 'There's a child asleep in there.'

The Park (South) Front, from the south-east, as featured in the sales particulars in 1958

'We'll come back' said Ron.

After leaving Cynthia, Ron, Jo and Anne wandered the garden and grounds. There was an avenue of ancient clipped yews and, near the woods to the south-east of the house a hidden, enclosed 'Bird Garden'. They walked down the back drive to the ford below the weir, and through the woods to the hopelessly overgrown walled garden, in all three acres of it. Nearby was the orchard and another secret walled garden of roses known as Lady Isobel's Garden. All that remained of the great glass house was the line where the panes met the brickwork. There were endless additional outbuildings and sheds – cart sheds, potting sheds, tool sheds, apple and fruit houses, sunken glass houses, store rooms and an ice house. Many were roofless, or falling in, or overrun with nettles and foxgloves. Windows were opaque with mould and thick with cobwebs. Almost every pane of the sunken glass houses was smashed.

They looked over The Garden Cottage which Ron had visited when he bought Sir Humphrey. More substantial than it sounds, this was where Johnny Kimberley had lived since inheriting, first as he awaited war reparations compensation, subsequently as he spent it doing the main house up. Kimberley had fared better than many houses during the war. The park was lined with Nissen huts for the Norfolk Regiment and, later, Italian prisoners of war, but the house, as the officers' mess, remained relatively unscathed. Even so, by the war's end it was badly run down and in need of

'Woodlands, buildings and lodges; in all some 247 acres ...'
The brick bridge over the Tiffey, from The Beds (winter)

modernisation. Once the work was done, however, it was only ever Cynthia who enjoyed the benefit, moving in with her five children. Her erstwhile husband remained at the Garden Cottage, having decided he was 'no longer able to stand the sight of her'.

Overall, the impression was one of sadness and desolation. Worst by far was the east wing (left of the Entrance Front). Bigger, by itself, than many a Georgian rectory, it was in a state of almost total dereliction. Water had clearly been pouring in for months and was still everywhere. The roof needed replacing completely: there was evidence of dry rot and wet rot. Everywhere was the smell of damp and mould and decay, with not a single room remotely habitable. And that was just one small part of the whole. It was a salutary reminder of the scale of a proposition like Kimberley.

On the other hand ... what a place! What an opportunity! What history and romance! Kimberley![41] The name had a pleasing cadence, and, of course, a familiarity, too; those three well-balanced syllables were, in another context, a household name, because they also belonged to the most famous diamond mine in the world, in South Africa. Yet it was the mining city that took its name from this nook of rural Norfolk, not vice versa, named after the first Earl of Kimberley, who was Colonial Secretary when the mine was discovered in 1873.[42] Accordingly, Kimberley was part of Britain's colonial history. More importantly, it was part of the history of British Africa, the continent to which Ron's career, and the name of the Buxton family, were indivisibly tied.[43]

Kimberley village lay over on the other side of the estate. A minute hamlet consisting of little more than a church and a handful of houses, it was now connected to the house only by the long back drive. This was picturesque, but seldom used, winding behind the lake and away through open country to emerge by the village church. Two large fields near the end of this drive had been sold at the Norwich auction, so now, psychologically at least, village and

---

41 When asked by Queen Victoria what title he would take for his earldom, the fourth Lord Wodehouse's initial request was 'Agincourt', because of a forebear who had fought with Henry V. The Queen said this might 'upset the French'. So Wodehouse took the name Kimberley, where his ancestors had built their family home.

42 How did the Kimberley diamond mine come to acquire the name Kimberley? When diamonds were discovered in the Northern Cape in 1873, it prompted a mad diamond rush. A new settlement sprang up in months. Lord Kimberley, in his position as Colonial Secretary, declared the place needed a name – one that was 'decent and intelligible'. This declaration followed a refusal to be associated with such 'vulgar' suggestions as 'New Rush', or the Boer Dutch alternative, 'Vooruitzigt', which, he said, 'he could neither spell nor pronounce'. With great diplomacy – or perhaps sycophancy – the Lieutenant-Governor's secretary's solution, which 'made quite sure that Lord Kimberley would be able both to spell and pronounce the name', was to name it 'after his Lordship'.

43 At least two other Kimberleys exist, named for similar reasons, in Australia and New Zealand.

View from the back drive: Looking across the lake towards the Park (South) Front, from *Seats of the Noblemen and Gentlemen of Great Britain and Ireland*, 1860

house were separated. Not that this mattered much, as the only road into Wymondham was reached from the main Entrance Front.

Was Kimberley a venture worth pursuing? Could it be a realistic proposition? There were good reasons why the house and park, the heart of the whole estate, had not sold. These were dark days for the country house. In crisis since the agricultural depression of the 1870s, many country estates had for decades existed in a state of chronic indebtedness, their rental income insufficient even to meet interest payments. The First World War had killed almost an entire generation of young men; not just first-in-line heirs, but often younger brothers and cousins as well, in the process racking up colossal death duties such that, among landed families, it was those who had sacrificed most who were hit hardest.

The Second World War had repeated the process. Johnny Kimberley had seen both his grandfather and father killed early on, presenting a double set of death duties – a by no means unusual occurrence. Meeting such dues, while hanging onto the estate, was often just not viable. As for the cult of country house life, with its leisured hours and armies of low-paid servants, it was now a thing of the past, along with the deferential culture that supported it.

Confronted with vast, leaking, vandalised piles, in parks transformed into prefabricated camps of Nissen huts, with no state grants available, no National Trust as we know today, no developed tourism or culture of venue hire or house subdivision, there weren't many options. 'It was a time', the architectural historian John Harris has written, 'when melancholy owners sat in their decaying houses awaiting the auctioneer, helplessly contemplating demolition.' The Destruction of the Country House Exhibition, which Harris helped curate at the Victoria and Albert Museum in 1974, prompted shocked headlines when it revealed that, in 1955, a major English house was demolished every two and a half days.

So it was with plenty to contemplate that Ron and Anne boarded the Gemini for the flight back. The fog had cleared by this time, and the sun was shining. Ron flew over Kimberley on his way south. Mad the whole idea might be, but there was no doubting that it was quite a place ...

The North (Entrance) Front

Over the following weeks, Ron consulted everyone he could think of. His cousin Christopher, a close friend of his sister Jean's and the son of their father's brother, Uncle Godfrey, was one. Christopher Buxton had recently set up a company, Period and Country Houses Ltd, specialising in the sensitive restoration and conversion of distinguished buildings into independent flats and apartments. His notable successes over the following years would include Kirtlington Park in Oxfordshire, a Palladian mansion where he retained the central part to live in himself, and Charlton Park in Wiltshire.

Six years younger than Ron, a Cambridge historian, his passion was country houses and finding new roles for them. He was immensely knowledgeable about all the potential pitfalls of ownership. A couple of weeks later, at the end of August, Ron flew him up from Fair Oaks. There was no fog this time, but like last time, for his passenger, the airborne part of the day came to eclipse all other aspects. Christopher recalls a 'rickety' plane and

[187]

The South (Park) Front faces SSW, just west enough to catch the setting sun

landing at an 'abandoned' airfield (Swannington). Of Kimberley, his chief impression of their visit was of Cynthia Kimberley, of how she made a determined play for Ron, and of her limited intentions of ever leaving the place if she could possibly help it. 'In property law', he advised his cousin, 'there's something called vacant possession, in which you acquire the place without anyone else still in occupation. I should make sure you get it.'

It was, however, the return journey that left an indelible impression. What with looking around, by time they got back to Swannington airfield it was getting late. There was certainly no time for refuelling if they were to have any hope of making it back to Fair Oaks in daylight, as they must. Approaching the outskirts of London, it seemed to Christopher a toss-up as to which ran out first: their fuel or the daylight. 'It wasn't at all funny,' he recalls. 'We could have got over London and run out of fuel, or got lost without enough light to find somewhere to land.' In the end, they made it ('via Luton' a mysterious note in Ron's log book adds) – but only just. A second of his passengers vowed never to fly with Ron again.

Ron made several more visits to Kimberley. By the last, Cynthia and the children had gone, leaving the house an empty shell. With no children in the place, not a stick of furniture, no curtains or carpets – literally, in fact, not a light bulb – the sheer, echoing emptiness of the place was daunting. The rooms seemed much larger; cavernous spaces, bare to their floorboards, which, now the rugs and carpets had been taken up, were revealed to be riddled with woodworm. In the garden sitting room, someone appeared to have taken a hammer to the marble fireplace, presumably trying to get it out. Outside, everywhere reeked of neglect. The empty fields were overgrown, reminding Ron he knew nothing about farming. Could he see himself here? Everyone, with the exception of Anthony and Jo (who naturally wanted their cousin and friend nearby), said buying the place would be insane.

But what was that, set against the feeling he had felt the first time he walked out onto the garden terrace and looked down towards the lake? Because he had certainly felt something. Yes, it might be a bit shabby and run down. But what were such trifles but opportunities in disguise? Here was a base, a home, a project to last a lifetime. Gardens, fields, woods; farming, shooting, riding, fishing. For someone young and practically-minded, with energy and an engineering mind, what were a few buildings to look after? As for farming, how hard could it be? And to have a river, complete with lake, weir, sluice and stone bridges: well, could an engineer ask for more? It was a once-in-a-lifetime opportunity to own one of the great country seats of England, in the heart of the county that meant more to him than any other.

He asked a surveyor friend, Philip Hall, to make a valuation. Hall went over every detail of the remaining lots, assessing the agricultural land, the trees for timber, the walled garden, the Garden Cottage, the lodges and outbuildings. He came up with a figure. The grounds, lodges, Garden Cottage, park, farmland and woods, he said, were worth £18,000. 'What about the house?' said Ron.

'The house? The house is worth nothing at all. Put it in at £2,000.'

It was September. On the 20th Ron was leaving on another flying trip, to Greece and Turkey, returning via Corfu and Florence. He spoke to Anthony Gurney. They agreed that Anthony, acting as Ron's agent, would put in a derisory bid of £22,000 for the lot, saying a rapid decision was required. 'Mr Buxton is leaving for Nigeria imminently and the offer will be gone.'

Gurney did as he was bid. A day or two later, the agents responded. His bid had been accepted by Lord Kimberley. 'I loved every inch of that house,' Johnny later confided to his diary. 'But selling was the easiest way to get rid of Cynthia. All I could think about was buying a new Aston Martin.' So the 'champion free-spender', as his *Guardian* obituary would put it, completed the disposal of his lands, 'shedding, in a few years, what his family had taken the best part of a millennium to accumulate'. And Kimberley Hall acquired a new owner.[44]

Everyone who knew Ron Buxton agreed. The 35-year-old entrepreneur had finally taken leave of his senses.

*

44 Decades later, documents revealed that the ground on which the house now stands was part of lands sold by a Squire Richard Buxton in 1640 – so Kimberley already had a Buxton connection.

There are certain inherent difficulties in running a house designed for a staff of twenty-three with a staff of one. Until 1940, the house and estate had run at a full and suitably lordly tilt: butler, footmen, valets, maids, parlour maids, cooks and so on: an inside staff of fourteen (accommodated in the east wing) and nine gardeners, this before estate workers were taken into account. For the last two years, as Johnny worked on ways to eject Cynthia, eventually concluding that the only way was by selling the floor beneath her feet, neither house nor grounds had received proper care or maintenance.

There was little that didn't need doing. By the time Ron returned from Nigeria a month later to take possession, it was to a palace of neglect. The central block of the house, although structurally reasonably sound, sat cold and forlorn. The parlous condition of the east wing, having done its work in deterring buyers, now became an urgent priority, heading a long list of outbuildings in varying states of decay. The ungrazed park was like a hayfield; sluices controlling the level of the lake were blocked or broken; the woods, fences and gates hadn't received attention for years.

The urgent priority was accommodation for a farm manager to take control of the land. Unfortunately, there were no cottages. All the estate cottages in Kimberley village and the neighbouring village of Carleton Forehoe had been sold off separately. This left three options. There was the west wing, which had previously contained room for grooms as well as horses and carriages, but which Johnny Kimberley had converted into a concrete granary. There were the two empty lodges at the end of the drive, both uninhabitable. And there was the ruinous east wing. Builders started work on a flat in the east wing.

In the meantime, Anthony Gurney's farm advisor, Jim Prior, helped Ron to organise the farm.[45] In due course a working farm manager arrived in the form of Jack Burroughs, the first (and, for the time being, only) member of the Kimberley staff. He was installed in Flat 1 of the east wing, and a new Fordson Major tractor, plus a selection of ploughs, harrows and other implements, was ordered for him to begin his work.

Having arranged a bridging loan from Barclays, Ron and Jean put Holywell on the market.[46] All the larger furniture, including Jean's, was brought up to Kimberley. Even so, and even once Ron's various pianos had also arrived, it was remarkable how empty the house still looked. There was just so much space to be filled, such expanses of bare walls, so many windows

45 Later Lord Prior, former MP, leader of the House of Commons and cabinet minister 1979–84 in Margaret Thatcher's Conservative government. His advice was good until some land adjoining Kimberley came up for sale – see chapter 16.
46 Chunks of Holywell's garden had already been sold off to developers to build houses, and soon the house itself would be demolished – replaced with two blocks of ten luxury flats, each 'with superb views out towards the Hog's Back and Guildford'.

crying out for curtains. It would be three years at least, and a small fortune, before the main downstairs rooms had curtains.

The so-called garden sitting room, now furnished with a grand piano and large book cases, was re-christened 'the library'. Its floor, along with that of the entrance hall and dining room, had all been carpeted. The removal of this carpet by the departing Kimberleys had revealed cheap deal softwood boards, starkly out of keeping with the high-quality plasterwork and mahogany doors. Ron replaced these with hardwoods brought from Kenya in the form of rough planks: *musheragi* (East African olive) for the library and dining room; *mahuhu* in the hall. Both timbers were planed and cut by Anthony Gurney's saw mill. The *mahuhu* in particular was so hard, he complained, that it blunted the machines.

A monumental mason was found to repair the library fireplace, using Siena marble. Until the furniture arrived from Holywell, a ping-pong table served as the dining table in Talman's elegant dining room. Stables were built in a courtyard behind the east wing and, in due course, a second flat was ready for another farm worker. (Thus, steadily, the east wing has been done up, until, today, it contains seven flats.) Roy Hardiment, who had started working at Kimberley straight from school in 1945, aged fourteen, moved into the east lodge as tractor driver. This was in due course done up, with the west lodge eventually becoming two bedrooms, later rebuilt to house a kitchen, bathroom and bedroom.

Structurally, the main house was reasonably sound. By selling off the lead on the roof to help pay his debts, replacing it with asphalt, Johnny Kimberley had actually made maintenance easier and cheaper. Fletcher Watson's make-over had added electricity, and also central heating to a central core of rooms on the ground floor, though not to any outlying bedrooms, the towers or the upper floors. As summer faded into autumn and the shooting season began, early guests learned to carry logs – the beginning of a working tradition for guests at Kimberley Hall that never ceased.

Meanwhile the delights of ownership of such a place could begin to manifest themselves: those little rites of passage that officially consecrated Ron's elevation to landowner, countryman and farmer. These included, as well as the shooting of his first pheasants and partridges, ducks and geese, the first shooting lunch round the ping-pong table. There were pike to be landed from the Tiffey. There was riding out from his own stables and even landing the Gemini on his own soil. And so it went on: his first crop of corn, his first herd of beef cattle, plus all those smaller but no less significant joys and satisfactions not itemised in the particulars, from the way the last rays of the setting sun always ignited the brickwork of the Park Front to that fiery orange, to the pair of kingfishers that nested by the weir, to the visiting swallows and house martins, in summer, and the greylag and

Canada geese as they came in to graze the water meadow in winter. All this lay ahead.

But for now it was the last week of October, Ron had returned to Kenya, and Kimberley, once again, was deserted – a gentle reminder, perhaps, that there was still one highly significant aspect of his life that was missing.

A 'Norfolk' Buxton: countryman, and Norfolk man, at last

14
'The Name's the Same'

PERHAPS IT WAS natural that the hunting field should be Ron's chosen arena for courtship. By 1958 what might be called his 'Hunting Period' was still at its peak. Despite having acquired a large, empty mansion in need of every kind of attention, the evidence was that, for Ron, a winter Saturday not spent hunting was a winter Saturday squandered. Accordingly, when he encountered a winsome 25-year-old woman whom he wished to impress, and she turned out to be both a capable rider and in possession of her own horse, he proposed the most romantic idea it was in his power to contrive – a hunting tour.

The person to whom this invitation was extended was nine years younger than Ron, and not quite so straightforward as she first appeared. Outwardly, here was a country girl moulded at the St Trinian's end of the educational spectrum, a system designed to supply capable, independent, outdoorsy, no-nonsense young women of the kind required to complement the empire-building males that every public school was still busily turning out. Phyllida had the rough-and-tumble confidence of someone who had grown up in a large family, and a don't-mess-with-me attitude that made her seem taller than her five feet eight-and-a-half inches. The odd nautical expression in her everyday speech hinted at a sailing or marine background.

Beneath her slim frame, however, and high cheek bones, clear skin and brown hair, was something less easy to place: a shy vulnerability. This, confusingly, combined with an international gloss, a cosmopolitan sophistication, altogether at odds with the bullet-proof Englishness. It was there in a taste for Spanish and Italian food, and an easy familiarity with those languages. The astute might have noticed a slightly faraway look, sometimes, in those brown eyes, a yearning for romantic adventure tinged, perhaps, with a conviction that in English country life she had low hopes of finding it. Her name was Phyllida Buxton, a distant cousin, and with her on the hunting field was her proudest possession: a dark bay gelding called Hostillius.

Now, were a template devised for a wife for Ron, it might go something like this. She would obviously have to ride and hunt, and love adventure, and not be averse to being flown in 'rickety' planes by someone with a breezy attitude to air safety procedures. She would need a romantic streak that tolerated – better still, enjoyed – non-conformism, who could see in a driven, independently-minded pragmatist an achiever who, almost by definition, would often seem unbelievably selfish and inconsiderate. She would need, herself, to be strongly independent and self-reliant, a coper, because for long periods that is what she would be doing, alone – certainly when it came to bringing up any children. She would need to enjoy wide-ranging company of all types and nationalities. Finally, perhaps most importantly, she would need to embody a sense of family for someone who had lost most of his own, while simultaneously valuing and properly appreciating the sheer, blessed good fortune of being attached to a Buxton.

*

Phyllida Dorothy Roden Buxton, known universally as Phyll, was Clarence Buxton's niece and Jocky's youngest sister. She was a third cousin, once removed, of Ron's (who was the same generation as Phyll's father). Born on 9 July 1932 at her paternal grandmother's house, 66 Eaton Place, she was the youngest of six. Her next closest sibling was Derry (Gerrard), five years older. Above him were Jocky (Jocelyn), eight years older, Elisabeth, ten years older, Anne, 12 years older, and Victoria, thirteen years older.

Her maternal great-grandfather, Colonel George Bennett, had had the distinction, while serving on St Helena in 1821, of seeing his dining table broken up to make Napoleon's coffin (it being the only decent piece of mahogany on the island). A passionate gardener and astronomer, after

Captain Roden Buxton, shortly before the war, and Dorothy,
probably taken in the 1930s. Married 7 December 1917.

retiring to Cape Town he created a garden on the slopes of Table Mountain and, in 1858, was the first person to spot and identify the brilliant, long-period Donati Comet (next due in the year 4000). On her paternal, Buxton side, like Ron, she was directly descended from the family's founding father, The Great Emancipator. He was Phyll's great-great-grandfather (an extra 'great' compared to Ron, due to being a generation younger). Her father, Captain Roden Buxton, RN, was the second son of the fourth baronet.

Two generations earlier, however, in the late nineteenth century, a schism of values had occurred within the family when the second son of The Great Emancipator (the first baronet) decided to plough his brewing fortune into building the vast Easneye Park. This move took him and his heirs (Ron's line) in a sharply different direction from their serious-minded, religious, high-principled (and, accordingly, much poorer) Quaker cousins (Phyll's line). In short, Phyll's side of the family missed out on the cash and the stately home, but retained the title and the moral high ground.

For Phyll's forebears, life was godly rather than worldly. There was no commerce, no drinking and certainly no cards ('the devil's book'). Thereafter, however honourably their entrepreneurial cousins, from whom Ron and Jean descended, might conduct themselves; however strong their social conscience (and several conscience-wracked members turned to God, or philanthropy, or both), they would forever be regarded by Phyll's branch as the 'Other Side' of the family, known as the 'Easneye Buxtons'. And their own side? Did they also have a nickname? I asked Anne as she was explaining this. 'I don't know. But we are *not* Easneyes.'

Phyll grew up at Greatbridge House, in the Test Valley, a mile north of the old market town of Romsey in Hampshire. With its warm brickwork, white-painted sash windows and hipped roof, set in a huge garden, it was a magical place. Her father had bought it in the late 1920s, to accommodate his rapidly expanding household. By the time Phyll was born he was in his forties and a commander in the Royal Navy. The location was a convenient compromise between the naval bases of Plymouth and Portsmouth, and the Admiralty in London.

The area was a rural Elysium, tranquil water meadows and ancient woodlands, dotted with mellow brick buildings, many still thatched. A tributary of the Test, that gin-clear and world-renowned chalk stream, ran through the garden. In fact, it ran past the kitchen window, from where the children could feed bread to the trout. In the nearby New Forest, over the heaths and unenclosed pastures and through the forest itself, there was marvellous riding.

Within this charming and still unspoilt world, Greatbridge was a kind of Eden, casting an unbreakable spell over the youthful Phyll. The Captain was a keen and knowledgeable gardener, so the large garden was full of rare trees

Greatbridge House, Romsey, Hampshire, bought by
Commander (later Captain) Roden Buxton in the late 1920s

and shrubs. There were old roses, which he taught Phyll how to prune, and an orchard he had planted with over a hundred varieties of fruit. Two tennis courts, one grass, one hard, stood side-by-side, and a bulge in the river had been dug out under her father's supervision to form an icy swimming pool for the summer.

The Captain was a strict and godly man, decorated in the First and Second World Wars, and the children were appropriately terrified of him. His severity, however, was offset by the warmth of Phyll's mother Dorothy, whose sense of humour meant she could, with a turn of phrase, defuse tense situations and make everybody laugh. The household also included a Welsh nanny (who would listen to the news on the nursery wireless in Welsh), a Labrador and a cat. To this happy throng, and the many charmed childhood memories that went with them (which included dockyard parties at Portsmouth where a girl, while being looked after by the sailors, could admire them in their romantic uniforms of blue, white and gold braid) there was but one blemish. It came in the form of the governess, who arrived after Nanny retired, Miss Crowe. Everyone hated 'The Crowe Bar'.

Despite her five siblings, Phyll might have been an only child: during term time, her much older brothers and sisters were all away at boarding school; in the holidays, if they went abroad, she was sent to stay with the Welsh nanny's nieces in Barry, or on a Welsh hill farm. Phyll was seven when the Second World War broke out. There was talk of sending her and Derry, now twelve, to Canada to some cousins of Dorothy's for the duration, but it didn't happen.

The summer of 1940 was fine and warm. Just as everyone was home for the

[196]

The Greatbridge Buxtons: Phyll (with wheelbarrow, aged 4), Anne, Captain Buxton, Jocky, Victoria, Elisabeth (standing), Mrs Dorothy Buxton, Derry

school holidays, the Battle of Britain began. Directly over their heads, they could watch electrifying dog fights between German and British fighters. Often, while they watched, a plane would come spiralling down to crash in flames. When this happened, Jocky and Derry would leap onto their bikes and pedal furiously off to search for the burning wreck. At night, sometimes, they would sleep in the garden without tents, watching the beams of the searchlights raking the sky. When they found a plane, the beams would rapidly converge and criss-cross, and the ack-ack would begin. Southampton was a regular target for the German bombers, so often on nights of particularly intense activity, everyone piled into Dorothy's bed to watch the city burning. Derry and Jocky joined the Home Guard in the holidays. The sisters were now away: Victoria in the Wrens (the Women's Royal Naval Service), Anne driving an ambulance and Elisabeth training to be a nurse.

Somehow, despite losing most of their prewar staff – cook, nanny, house maid and two gardeners – Dorothy kept the household going. There was a big vegetable garden, in which Captain Buxton busied himself whenever his leave allowed. There were bantams for eggs and bees for honey, for which the government allocated an annual sack of sugar. Once everyone returned to school, Dorothy would write to each of them, every week. Phyll's father was at the Admiralty in London most of the time (staying with his mother in Eaton Place). By then fifty, which was too old to captain a ship, he was Director of Combined Operations Personnel. In 1943 he accompanied Churchill to the top secret Quebec Conference between the British, Canadian and US governments that planned the invasion of France and Italy, and made the pact between Churchill and Roosevelt to share nuclear secrets.

In 1945, like her three sisters before her, the thirteen-year-old Phyll was despatched to Westonbirt, a girls' boarding school (where Anne had been head girl) set in a Victorian mansion in Gloucestershire next to the famous arboretum. From the start Phyll hated it, with its dreadful punishments and terrifying staff (for slouching, the gym mistress Miss Gibbs broke a girl's back by placing her knee against her spine and pulling her arms back). It felt far from Greatbridge, and petrol rationing meant her parents could make only one visit a term – lunch at the local Hare & Hounds Hotel, then a walk in the arboretum. For this reason, to her delight, her parents took her away after two and a half years and sent her to St Swithun's, near Winchester. This was far preferable: it was no distance from home and the girls were allowed into town on Saturdays, and to choose which church to attend on Sunday. In summer there was a two-mile walk down the River Itchen to St Cross, or to Winchester Cathedral. Phyll often chose the cathedral; she had developed a teenage crush on one of the preachers. He was a friend of her father's: the Bishop of Southampton.

*

After leaving school, now seventeen, for a few months Phyll went to Cornwall to work on a farm near Boscastle. While urban Britain tried to pick itself up after five years of war, clearing bomb-shattered town centres and contemplating its debts, farming, at least, went on much as it always had. There the pigs chewed contentedly at her Wellington boots and recalcitrant goats refused to deliver milk. There were ponies and riding and the sea, and she loved it all – except for the taste of goat's milk. Having to drink this put her off milk for good, so much so that she still drinks coffee black.

A Swiss finishing school followed; at the time a routine educational round-off for well-brought-up English girls, not unlike chalet-girling or art courses in Florence in later years. Mon Fertile (alumni later included Camilla, Duchess of Cornwall) consisted of three months from Christmas to Easter in the *Heidi*-like setting of the Swiss Alpine village Les Diablerets, at the foot of a glacier. Mornings were spent studying French (which had to be spoken all the time), afternoons skiing, later moving near Lausanne for the summer.

Soon, however, Phyll was back in Cornwall. On return from Switzerland, she enrolled in a secretarial college in Winchester. After two terms, when she was still equally hopeless at typing and shorthand, a post came up. Her father's friend Edmund Morgan, Bishop of Southampton, her crush at St Swithun's, was about to be appointed Bishop of Truro. He needed a new secretary. Phyll was plucked from her course and despatched to fill the post – with some reluctance, because she had recently acquired a boyfriend in Winchester, with whom she was much in love. She agreed to try it for a month.

Things got off to a bad start. At the end of her first day, at 8 p.m. she was still trying to decipher her shorthand. She began to despair of a future as a secretary. The bishop, however, turned out to be saintly – patient and kind. They took to each other. Phyll was installed in the Bishop's Palace with the bishop's widowed daughter-in-law and if, technically, she was there in an official capacity, as secretary and chauffeur, she was soon part of the family. Besides, the bishop had set himself the task of visiting every church in Cornwall in his first year (which he did), so her shorthand and typing were diluted with plenty of driving. On Sundays, for example, there was matins at one church, afternoon service at another and evensong at a third.

All in all, it was an interesting life, made more so by the touching faith the bishop seemed to place in her. For the Coronation in 1953, for example, there was to be an exhibition of Elizabethan church plate. Phyll was sent on a mission to collect up the antique gold and silver chalices and plates. Dutifully wrapping them in newspaper, she stuffed them, as requested, into the boot of the bishop's car. It was a responsible mission for a young girl barely out of her teens, as her cargo must have been irreplaceable and of immense value. Had anything happened, had she crashed or had the car been stolen, it could have meant the loss of untold millions. The bishop's faith was well-founded, however, and she assembled it all safely. In such ways, under his kind and trusting eye, Phyll's confidence grew.

Part of the bishop's charm was his ability to exhibit startlingly un-bishop-like qualities. One such occasion was a visit to Barbara Hepworth's studio in St Ives – part of the Festival of Britain exhibition. Hepworth's shapely Modernist forms were then still strikingly new and bizarre. The bishop had brought along his brother, a near-blind QC, who loved running his hands over the smooth surfaces. 'I call this one Antiphon' the sculptor was explaining, upon which the bishop dissolved into uncontrollable giggles. Strings of distinguished figures visited the Bishop's Palace, from conductors like Sir Adrian Boult and Sir Thomas Beecham, to Leonard Cheshire, who had just opened the first Cheshire Home at Culdrose Air Base. They all treated Phyll like family.

The bishop went out of his way to make opportunities for her to meet people of her own age, including buying her tickets for the local hunt ball. It was through his flexibility, too, that she learnt to sail. When a near neighbour, a Colonel Mulock, needed a crew member at short notice and asked Phyll if she would like to join them, the bishop readily agreed, granting her an unscheduled holiday.

Having never set foot in a sailing boat, Phyll embarked on a Channel-crossing in a force eight gale. She had to learn fast, and Colonel Mulock proved to be a demanding skipper. Everyone had to 'learn the ropes': what to pull, how to coil them neatly, what knots to tie and when to tie them. Orders had to be repeated immediately to show they were understood, and the meaning of every light on other boats or ships, and the sequences of flashes from lighthouses had to be learned. (This was still the time of dead reckoning, by map, compass and stars, long before the GPS. For communication, there was just a crackly old battery-powered radio for receiving the shipping forecast.) But Phyll, from a naval family, was unfazed by her new adventure. She was never seasick, however long spent in the galley brewing Bovril, and she took to nautical life immediately.

Colonel Mulock's boat was a thing of beauty: a 78-foot, wooden gaff-rigged ketch,[47] built in Norway in 1905 by Colin Archer. She was called *Asgard* and came with a remarkable history. Built as a wedding present for the writer-spy Erskine Childers by the father of his American bride Molly, the married couple had sailed her extensively in the Baltic (the area on which his classic novel, often cited as the first ever example of spy fiction, *The Riddle of the Sands*, was based). By 1914 Childers had become a fervent Irish nationalist, and he used *Asgard* to smuggle 1,000 Mauser rifles and 29,000 rounds of ammunition to the IRA from Germany, landing them at the fishing village of Howth, north of Dublin. (Childers's weaponry was eventually used against the British Army in the Easter Rising of 1916, for which Childers was executed by firing squad in 1922, after which *Asgard* was sold. Now restored, as a sacred relic of Republican history, she is exhibited at the National Museum of Ireland.)

Asgard slept six, and the canvas was so heavy it took four people to hoist the mainsail. But Phyll learnt quickly and plainly made a satisfactory shipmate because after that first voyage she became a regular crew member, sailing, in due course, around Brittany, to the Channel Islands, Spain and Portugal, criss-crossing the notoriously rough Bay of Biscay (three nights out of sight of land), encountering wild storms, dense fog and, most unnerving by far, crossing the crowded Channel by night. Over winter weekends she helped scrub and caulk the decks, polish the brass and varnish the woodwork.

---

47 Translation: a *ketch* has two masts: a main mast, and a shorter mizzen mast rearward of the main mast. A *gaff rig* is a configuration of sails in which the main sail is four-cornered, fore-and-aft rigged, controlled at its peak and, usually, its entire head by a spar (pole) called the *gaff*. The gaff enables a fore and aft sail to be four-sided, rather than triangular, which can as much as double the sail area carried by that mast and boom.

Asgard, the 1905 gaff-rigged ketch owned by the writer-spy Erskine Childers

So Cornwall, in the end, turned out fine. But Phyll knew, after four years, that if she didn't leave soon, she would still be there when she was fifty. By this time her Winchester romance had petered out (her *beau* met someone else and emigrated to New Zealand). So she handed in her notice, and joined a circus.

*

How does a well-brought-up young woman join a circus? The answer in this case is as follows. When Phyll was ten, Dorothy had bought her youngest daughter a very wild skewbald pony, Melka. The seller had shamelessly deployed every tactic to clinch the sale. 'If you don't take her, the circus will, and you know how they'll treat her,' she said, under which threat Melka had duly been purchased. She turned out to be completely unmanageable. After a month or so, there didn't seem much option but for Dorothy herself to write to the local circus. She held back from posting the letter, however, and it sat around the house for weeks while everyone wondered what to do. Eventually someone evidently posted it, for one day a man in a blue RAF uniform appeared at the door. 'I hear you have a pony for sale,' he said.

'We only bought it to save it from the circus,' Dorothy explained.

'Ah,' said the man. 'I *am* the circus.'

His name, it turned out, was Jimmy Chipperfield. The famous circus was based at Stockbridge, not far from Romsey.

Flushed with embarrassment, Dorothy asked Jimmy Chipperfield in. They hit it off immediately, and in no time were swapping stories round the kitchen table as if they'd known each other for years. Anne happened to be home on leave, and after that the family regularly visited the Chipperfields, getting to know the youngest son, Jonny, who looked after the horses, and Dick, the eldest, who looked after the lions and tigers. When Phyll was at a loose end after leaving the bishop, they suggested she spend the summer travelling with them. So she did. She went on the road with Chipperfield's Circus, from Doncaster to York, and on, sharing a caravan, helping wherever needed, from selling programmes and chaining up elephants to grooming the Liberty horses (which perform without harness or human touch) and riding the High School ones. When the circus was on the move, in the middle of Saturday nights, she even drove one of the vehicles.

As for Melka, she became more amenable. So much so, that in due course Phyll would ride her, alone, all day in the New Forest. She went with Phyll to Cornwall, and eventually she came to Norfolk, too, where she was ridden by Peter and Camilla. So she never did get sent to the circus.

*

In the autumn the circus packed up for the winter, so Phyll was left in search of a new adventure. Staying with friends in a cottage in Cerne Abbas when she was fourteen, she had come across a book called *Tschiffely's Ride*. Published in 1932, it was the account, by the writer A. F. Tschiffely (no, no one else can pronounce his name either) of an epic 10,000-mile ride through the Americas taken by the author, a Swiss schoolmaster, in the late 1920s. Tschiffely sets off from Buenos Aires with his two horses, Mancha and Gato ('the wildest of the wild'), on a route across the pampas of Argentina and the desolate wastes of Santiago del Estero, up through the high, wild valleys on the Bolivian border to the Altiplano. On the way he encounters ostriches, foxes that rid themselves of fleas by drowning them, swarms of locusts and pumas that are scared of donkeys. In Peru he sees Inca ruins before crossing the 16,500-foot pass and descending to Lima to cross deserts in which rain is unknown. There are quicksands, rainforests inhabited by the head-shrinking Jibaro Indians, live volcanoes, swamps and revolution-torn Nicaragua and Mexico. And so it goes on until, two-and-a-half years later, after encountering crocodiles, poisonous snakes and a horse-attacking spider, he finally makes it to Washington DC.

It was a longish book, but Tschiffeley wrote in a wonderfully readable style with vivid descriptions. It was an instant bestseller, inspiring a generation of teenage children (including a youthful Eric Newby, who, having read it under the bedcovers at school, later wrote a foreword to a paperback edition). Phyll was captivated by it in a way she had never been by a book before. So much so that when she had not finished it at the end of her week's holiday, she did something she had never done before. She pinched it. ('It's been on my conscience ever since.')

That August of 1955, when she was glancing through the personal columns of *The Times* (on the front page in those days) idly looking for a job, an advertisement caught Phyll's eye. It was for someone to teach English to the children of a family living in Argentina. Reminded of *Tshiffeley's Ride*, she applied, and a few days later a letter arrived asking her to attend an interview at Claridge's. The post on offer was to work for a wealthy Italian family, who lived most of the time in Argentina. There were six children, two sons and four daughters – ranging from twelve to a new baby. Phyll was interviewed by a formidable young Italian woman, the Contessa Mazzini, who spoke excellent English. The Contessa, it turned out, was interested chiefly in two things. Could she leave in two weeks? Could she stay for two years? Phyll was able to answer 'yes' to both questions. A few days later, she was offered the post. It later turned out there had been more than 150 applications, from which two were chosen: Phyll, and another young woman called Gillian Percy who would join Phyll in Argentina the following year.[48]

Everything happened quickly after that. Phyll was told to travel via the family's house in Rome, to collect the necessary medical and other certification. Her plane left Heathrow at 5 a.m. Before leaving Greatbridge for the airport with her father – to return … well, who knew when? – she had to say goodbye to her mother, Dorothy. For the first and only time in her life, Phyll saw her mother cry.

48 Gill subsequently became a close family friend and godparent to Camilla.

From Rome, after being sent north to Genoa to collect some document, Phyll proceeded to Naples to join eight cabin trunks bound, with her, for Buenos Aires. In Naples she hid in her hotel room, too terrified to venture out. Embarked on the *Conte Grande*, of the two thousand passengers Phyll was the only person who was English, on a journey lasting three weeks. As they departed from Naples, everyone was in inconsolable floods of tears. Within an hour, however, a remarkable recovery seemed to take place. Since they were all leaving to seek their fortune, there was a buoyancy and optimism in the air. This soon turned into a carnival atmosphere. Phyll paired up with a German girl, then with a Yugoslav and a Brazilian. The ship stopped over, a day at a time, at Genoa and Barcelona, Madeira and Dakar before the long Atlantic crossing began. When they crossed the Equator, an elaborate 'Crossing the Line' ceremony was held, in which everyone was dunked in soapsuds. In between, Phyll tried to teach herself Spanish.

The first port they called at having crossed the Atlantic was Recife, where a Brazilian diamond merchant on board bought everyone pineapples. Then they headed down the coast via Rio de Janeiro, Sao Paolo, Santos and Montevideo towards Buenos Aires. Everyone was unaware that a revolution was taking place in Argentina. On 21 September 1955, the President, General Juan Perón, was thrown out in a military coup. The country Phyll was about to arrive in was in turmoil.

At Buenos Aires they were greeted by chaos. The place was under military rule, and on the quayside this was manifest by a requirement for festoons of documentation, culminating in the taking of thumb prints. Fortunately someone from Ferrania arrived. Ferrania was a giant photographic company, like Kodak, that was owned by the family Phyll was working for. The man started dispensing biros – then an extraordinary novelty – to the customs officials, before snatching Phyllida from the mêlée. Everything was so new and strange: the people, the language, the currency, the food, the architecture. It was hard for a 23-year-old English girl to know what was normal and what was different because of the revolution.

She tried to settle in. The family's house was in the pleasant, leafy *barrio* of Belgrano in the north of the city. The children were friendly and fun and seemed to like her. But, struggling to master Spanish *and* Italian (although the Count and Contessa spoke English, no one else did), she felt completely isolated. Without a friend, in an alien culture, seven thousand miles from home, she had never felt so lonely. She visited the sights, queuing to go round the deposed President Perón's house, contemplating his wife Evita's hats and shoes, and the aeroplane in the garden. (A few months later the house was demolished and the space turned into a public park.) It was no substitute for Greatbridge and all her friends. For months she was so miserable that, given the chance, she would have taken the first available passage home.

At Christmas, however, things looked up a little. The family travelled for three weeks to Punta del Este, near Montevideo, in Uruguay. There the British consul invited Phyll to a Christmas lunch in a house with a spectacular view overlooking the Isola de Los Lobos, where the German heavy cruiser *Graf Spee* had been before it was scuttled in 1940. (Powell and Pressburger were about to start filming the story for *The Battle of the River Plate*.) Soon after, the Mazzinis, who spent winters in Buenos Aires and summers on their *estancia* in the pampas, moved to the vast, treeless plains so famous for their cattle ranching.

This was the South America Phyll had come to see. The pampas was something else, unimaginably flat and vast – it was like living in the middle of the ocean – teeming with cattle and the romantic gauchos, the cowboys she had read about in *Tschiffeley's Ride*. Here life was much more agreeable than in Buenos Aires. The Mazzini ranch, like most of Argentina's great *estancias*, had been established and fenced in the nineteenth century, and the building built under Spanish colonial rule. There was an old stone lodge, with a modern wing with a swimming pool around a garden and private golf course. Here the sun shone, the living was easy, the staff plentiful and the steaks vast. Life was exciting. The children, all of whom spoke Spanish, Italian, French and, increasingly, English, were fun. Exotic guests were constantly arriving and leaving. Private flying, still a novelty in most of the world, was routine out here. Friends of the family would arrive for weekends in small planes. One weekend it would be a tearful wife with her children, distraught because her husband would not leave his mistress. The next, it would be the mistress, wretched because, despite her lover's promises, he wouldn't leave his wife and children. There was racing, polo, the vast herds of cattle and, most importantly, ample time to enjoy them all. Every morning, while the children sat with their Italian governess, Phyll would go riding with the gauchos. 'Which horse for senorita today?' they would ask – from the forty available.

By the time the family returned to Buenos Aires for winter, things felt very different. Phyll would take the children to the opera and the cinema, and to dancing lessons. Her Spanish was improving, the family adored her, and she had fallen for both them and the country in general. There was an exotic, international glamour to it all. In any given room six different languages might be spoken. The Mazzinis' cosmopolitan existence was a world away from the stodgy expatriates of the Hurlingham Club. And so Phyll settled in. She had never been so happy.

Then, in the second week of December 1956, a telegram arrived for the Contessa. As she was away, and the telegram was in English, it was brought by a maid to Phyll for translation. It read: 'PLEASE BREAK NEWS PHYLLIDA BUXTON'S MOTHER DIED STOP'

It was utterly unexpected. Dorothy was barely sixty. The last time Phyll had seen her, when she kissed her goodbye before leaving to catch her plane to Rome, she had been glowing with health. It was impossible. As details emerged, however, it turned out that she had had cancer for some time, but the news had been kept from Phyll. In retrospect, had she been looking for it, a clue might have come in the fact that her last letter from home was from her sister Anne rather than Dorothy. But why should Phyll have suspected anything? There was no reason to. In any case, what difference did any of it make now? Her mother was dead. Phyll was inconsolable and cried for days.

The key question was: what to do now? Go home? It was already too late to make the funeral, even if she left immediately. And once home, what was there for her in England, compared to life in Argentina? She had been so happy that, until now, she had had no intention of leaving, at least, not yet. But if she stayed on, who would look after her father? Deep down she knew that as the only unmarried daughter in the family it was up to her to do so. He, she was only too aware, was completely incapable of looking after himself. After infinite agonising, she made up her mind. She gave notice. Then she tried to adjust to the idea of leaving.

The family was as saddened by her decision as Phyll. There would always be a place for her, they promised, if she changed her mind. But she knew – they all knew – that once she had left, there would be no return.

A passage had been booked for December, and as the machinery went into action to find her replacement, each day became more resonant. The kindness and generosity of the family almost made matters worse.

Phyll had a favourite horse, Hostillius, a dark bay thoroughbred gelding on whom she had won a bareback race against the gauchos (who took off their boots to save weight).

The surge of power as he went from a standing start to a gallop was like no horse she had ever ridden. They gave Hostillius to her, plus his passage home, plus a leather saddle hand-made to fit them both.

*

And so, Phyll prepared for her return. A month before she was due to sail, news arrived from home. Her father had remarried: his secretary.

This changed everything. If the Captain had remarried, then it meant he had someone to look after him. Which meant he no longer needed Phyll to do so. Which meant there was no reason for her to return.

What made this information appalling was that it was too late. Phyll's successor had been appointed. To make matters worse, Phyll knew her prospective stepmother – knew her only too well. Hilda, or 'the goldfish' as the children called her, on account of her reddish-gold hair, had been Captain Buxton's secretary at the Admiralty for years. And now here they were, married, less than a year after her beloved mother Dorothy had died. In a black

Surge of power – Phyll on Hostillius after bareback racing against gauchos

frame of mind, Phyll embarked on a ship of the Royal Mail Line for her three-week voyage home to Southampton. The atmosphere was very different from her outward passage. As she sailed north, away from the sunshine and warmth and happiness of Latin America towards the chilly winter skies of the Northern Hemisphere, she grew progressively more miserable.

She reached Southampton shortly before Christmas. The first news she learnt was that Greatbridge had been sold. The house stood cold and almost empty. Several loads of furniture had already been moved to a new house recently bought by her father in Norfolk: Smallburgh Hall, near Norwich. There, in the county of so many of his Buxton relations, he had chosen to establish a new life with his new wife. To Phyll and the children it seemed almost as if he wished to cut his ties with his previous life altogether. A few days after her return, a sale was held of the remaining effects at Greatbridge. The contents of Phyll's room had already gone, except for the rocking horse she had had since she was little. It was the only material memento of her childhood. She begged her father to save it. The Captain was adamant. Unfortunately, there simply was not room in the new house. It went for £6.

It was not the homecoming she might have wished for. Jocky, the sibling to whom, by dint of their both being single, she was closest, was in Africa. (The day they had all seen him off from Southampton Water on the Sunderland flying boat was still vivid in her memory.) She had no home to speak of.

Fortunately, her sister Anne came to the rescue and asked her to stay with her family for Christmas in Klosters. She had no job. The only thing she had to look forward to was the arrival of Hostillius on board the SS *Ledbury*. He arrived in Royal Albert Dock on 13 March.

The day before Hostillius was due, Melka arrived in London by train from Cornwall, where she had been staying while Phyll was away. A cousin, Polly Blount, drove down from Norfolk with her trailer and they collected Melka. Then they went on to Royal Albert Dock.

They arrived in a snowstorm, to find Phyll's beautiful horse in a crate on the deck. The sleek, powerful creature she had last seen in Argentina was unrecognisable; a ragged cipher of skin and bone, head hung low, covered in scars from being hurled against the sides of his crate by rough seas. In his thin summer coat he was shaking with the cold. A bowl of cornflakes had been left for him to eat. Supposedly travelling with a shipment of polo ponies, somehow he had got sent on alone, on a ship in which no one knew the first thing about horses. He had roasted in the tropics, then frozen in the North Atlantic. They drove him up to Norfolk, stopping in Newmarket to buy him a New Zealand rug (a warm horse blanket) on the way.

Now with the added appendage of Hostillius, Phyll started looking for jobs. She started with three interviews with BOAC to become an air hostess. It seemed the quickest way back to Argentina.

*

So this was the tall, winsome, slightly discombobulated, 23-year-old Buxton cousin, with her brown eyes and brown hair (with just a hint of Buxton red), who some time in 1958 caught Ron's eye. Possibly, in this instance, it was more due to her skill with horses and air of adventurousness than to her ironic eye and dry wit.

If she were a catch, so, undoubtedly, was he. At thirty-four, Ron was the embodiment of the young company chairman – handsome, a gifted business-man at the height of his powers, radiating energy, competence and zest for life. If he had the air of someone for whom no challenge was too great, well, it was backed up by his ownership of a thriving British company, a string of overseas ones, an aeroplane, a London flat and the country seat of an earl. And with political ambitions, who knew what might follow? Life with Ron Buxton might be many things, but dullness was not amongst them.[49]

Both Ron and Phyll are a little hazy about exactly when they met, having been vaguely aware of each other for years. Since leaving school, Phyll had

---

49 It was around this time, Anne remembers, that, arriving back from Africa, Ron produced two curious-looking green items from his luggage which he announced were delicious to eat. Nobody knew whether to believe him. They were called, he said, avocado pears.

Miss Buxton, and Mr Buxton: Phyllida, aged 26; Ronald, aged 35, both photographed in 1958

several times stayed at Ashley Gardens to go to parties in London. Then in 1954, aged twenty-two, she joined a canoeing trip with Ron and six others down the Wye. During this expedition, following heavy rain, the Wye rose six feet overnight. Capsizing into the swollen and muddy torrent, during her recovery Phyll became chilled to the bone. She was revived by ministrations of whisky from Ron – her first taste of the drink.

They probably also saw each other through Phyll's eldest sister, Anne. Having married, Anne and her (first) husband Henry Gillespie had settled near Holywell, where she and Jean, who were the same age, soon became close friends. They also met out hunting with the North Norfolk Harriers, and it was this setting that suggested to Ron a romantic plan. Why not spend a season taking a hunting tour of all the greatest packs of England?

So that's what they did: Ron on Sir Humphrey, Phyll on Hostillius. What followed was a kind of *Mr Sponge's Sporting Tour*. Through his season in Leicestershire, and membership of the masonic Foxhunters Lodge, Ron had acquired many new hunting friends.[50] Now, through them, he planned a season, moving, weekend by weekend, from one country house to another.

Starting with Philip Cazenove in Pytchley country, they moved on to 'Tommy' Beecham, son of the famous conductor, in Warwickshire; thence to

50 Ron joined the Foxhunters Lodge in St James's, London, in 1954, subsequently becoming its secretary for twenty years.

friends in Beaufort country, the Vale of the White Horse and so on. In all, they visited eight different packs, from the dry stone-walled Cotswolds, to the timber of Warwickshire, finishing in Belvoir country. Between hunting days, Phyll would look after the horses while Ron returned to Lea Bridge.

At the end of the tour, in March 1959, Ron asked Phyll whether, perhaps, they should carry on in some way? 'Oh,' said Phyll. 'How d'you mean?' – after all, the hunting season was now over. Ron said that what he meant was that, maybe, they should get married?

So Phyll considered this suggestion. And in due course ('It could have been a week, it could have been a month'), she said yes.

*

So it was that a Buxton became engaged to a Buxton, and wedding preparations began. Phyll had always imagined she would be married in Romsey Abbey, in the church she had attended every Sunday as a child. The trouble was, her home was no longer there. She certainly had no intention of getting married from the Norfolk house in which her father was now installed (and in some style, too, she noted, complete with the cook that her mother Dorothy had always had to manage without). Nor did anywhere else in Norfolk, Kimberley for example, appeal much; simply because Norfolk was not where her friends were. Finding somewhere available was also not without problems, as the date had to be fitted around Ron's trips to Africa, plus any prospective election plans, as by now he had been selected as Conservative candidate for Leyton. In the end, they compromised, and settled on London. Ron's new status as a parliamentary candidate qualified him to get married at St Margaret's, Westminster, on the green in Parliament Square. The church was duly booked for Saturday 20 June 1959.

The obvious person to perform the ceremony was Phyll's friend and former employer, the Bishop of Truro, but unfortunately he could not manage the date. Instead it was the Dean of Truro, Canon Jo Fison, who had also become a friend during Phyll's Cornwall years (and was now at St Mary's, Cambridge, later going on to become Bishop of Salisbury). He was assisted by Phyll's 79-year-old great-uncle, the Right Reverend Harold Buxton, former Bishop of Gibraltar and Chaplain of St George's Cathedral, Jerusalem. The big day was a scorcher, sunshine blazing from a cobalt June sky as they emerged onto the green, before a reception at the Senior United Services Club, 'the Senior', on the corner of Pall Mall and Carlton House Terrace.

As they emerged from the church, the newly married Mr and Mrs Buxton were photographed by the London *Evening Standard*. They appeared on the front page later that day, the splash headlined: 'The name's the same.'

*

Mr Buxton and Miss Buxton become Mr and Mrs Buxton. Ron's marriage was on the same day of the year, 20 June, as his parents' in 1920.

Their honeymoon was not a conventional one. When they left the reception, it was not for Heathrow or a swish hotel prior to catching a flight somewhere exotic. No, instead they drove to Stapleford Aerodrome, North London (roughly where, today, the M25 meets the M11), where the Gemini was waiting. An earlier draft of this manuscript recorded that Ron drank little at the reception in preparation for flying down to Lydd, in Kent, but this detail drew an indignant 'I don't know why you say that' from Phyll, 'he was swilling it back.' The plan was to stay overnight at a small airfield hotel before proceeding next day for the Mediterranean, to compete in a sporting event: the 11th annual Giro Aereo Internazionale di Sicilia, the International 'Tour of Sicily' air race.

Needless to say, the flight didn't go entirely according to plan. Perhaps Ron *had* drunk too much at the reception, for on landing at Lydd, he was ordered to the control tower for breaching air traffic procedures. The young bride checked into the airport hotel where, for an indeterminate period, she found herself alone, wondering what one was supposed to do on one's wedding night, in a remote and provincial hotel, in the absence of one's new husband. Ron, having negotiated his release, eventually reappeared.

The next morning they took off for Nice. Phyll was, fortunately, much more familiar with travelling in small planes than most people. In Argentina, she had learnt the basics of how to fly and had even been involved in a crash, when a Cessna's nose wheel caught in a viscacha burrow (a viscacha being a rabbit-like creature of the pampas). They made Nice without further incident and that evening joined an old friend of Phyll's from Truro, Guy Bowden, another canon of the Cathedral, for dinner. Thence it was to Naples, then on to Sicily.

The Giro di Sicilia was the most picturesque, popular and prestigious of European air races. Sicily's size, slightly larger than Wales, and setting in the Mediterranean Sea, made it an ideal island for racing around, whether by bicycle, motorbike, car or aeroplane. The race consisted of flying between timed markers: halfway round the island one day, half the next, with fifty or

From *Volo, Mensile di Vita Aeronautica*: the Giro di Sicilia. LEFT: Some sample planes. RIGHT: the competitors: Ron is number 10, third from the top, right-hand column.

more planes taking part. 'Most of the other competitors were up at five in the morning, polishing the edges of their wings,' recalled Phyll. At least one other couple, however, shared the Buxtons' more relaxed approach: 'At one point we were wing-tip to wing-tip with a French couple in a Jodel. They were swigging wine.'

On the evening of the last day there was a gala presentation dinner. 'Cups from a table groaning with silver were doled out. There was a cup for the winner in each class; a cup for the competitor who had come furthest – some bugger from Sweden – and so on. We came forty-seventh out of about fifty, so we weren't actually last. But pretty low.' Everyone who competed was given a case of wine.

After that they flew on to Djerba Island, on the African coast, where Ron had booked in at, in Phyll's words, 'a primitive hotel'. 'A carpet-seller came to our room and wouldn't leave until we bought a carpet.' As Phyll was swimming in her discreet new one-piece bathing suit, an Arab woman hurried up to cover her with a blanket. After that, via a few days in Malta, and a few more in Sardinia, they flew back up through France to Beauvais, then to Norfolk and their new life together.

*

For the month of July, with Kimberley still barely habitable, they alternated between Ashley Gardens and Holywell. In August, Jocky and Phyll went out to Lisbon to crew *Asgard* back to Britain (promised long before any thoughts of a wedding). Ron was less than thrilled to be parted from his new wife so soon, but as Phyll had pledged herself to the trip before their engagement there was no alternative.

For Phyll, it turned out to be her roughest voyage yet: crossing the Bay of Biscay, the sea was so big the dinghy was lost overboard. Worse, unknown to them, a newly-installed metal water tank was affecting the compass readings, so that when on the south Brittany coast they encountered dense sea fog they lost any exact idea of their position. In desperation, Tony Mulock bellowed 'Où sommes-nous?' at a French fishing boat with which they almost collided. It transpired they were thirty miles off course. After three weeks, Ron flew the Gemini out to Quimper to join them, replacing Jocky, who flew the plane back. He was repaid for his trouble by one of the roughest crossings of the Channel imaginable.

After that, a measure of normality, or at least regularity, settled over their lives. Most Friday nights would be spent making the three-and-a-half-hour journey to Kimberley, winding through the endless villages to Stevenage, then Bishop's Stortford, then Newmarket where they would have dinner at the Coach & Horses before the final leg to Wymondham. 'I'd just about have got the central rooms warm and the larder stocked by the time we had to return to London,' says Phyll.

In October Ron left for Africa and Phyll found herself alone in Kimberley without curtains or carpets: a vast echoing box in a county in which she knew almost no one. One night a south-west wind got up, and a ghostly howling scream began to reverberate through the entire house. It was a maddening din, insistent and unabating. It came from copper strips fitted round the windows to exclude drafts. The wind from that direction set them vibrating. By 8.30 in the evening it was unendurable. Phyll rang Jo Gurney, still living down the road in Barnham Broom, to ask if she could come and stay.

As autumn turned to winter, Kimberley's qualities as a giant freeze-box asserted themselves. The insides of their bedroom windows were routinely plated with rime ice in the mornings. (In later years Phyll would enjoy telling chilly-looking guests: 'If you want to warm up, I should go outside.') Even so, there was still a tingle of pleasure when they turned between the lodge gates and drove up to the great house, or unbolted the library window and wandered onto the terrace to watch the sun setting over the lake. At such moments, 'It was a pretty amazing place,' admits Phyll. 'I'd think: do I really live here?' These moments, however, were more than offset by others, of the will-we-ever-get-this-straight? kind. 'The five-year plan we made at the start has yet to be finished.'

By Christmas, Phyll was pregnant. 'It was a blow,' she says, having decided not to have children for years. They spent Christmas with the Gurneys at Northrepps Hall, in Elizabeth Fry's four-poster. 'It was hard to know whether

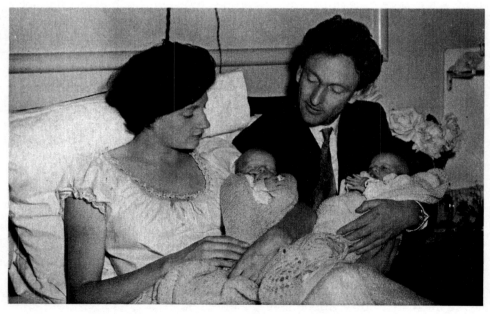

'It's twins': with Peter and Camilla, Welbeck Street nursing home, 19 June 1960

it was more or less uncomfortable than Kimberley. The bedding was unbelievably heavy. I counted nine wringing wet blankets'.

The baby was due in June and it was a large pregnancy; a situation explained three days before the due date when Phyll discovered she was in fact carrying twins. On 19 June 1960, they were induced. Phyll's lasting memory of the event is the comfort and cenrally-heated warmth of the nursing home at 27, Welbeck Street: 'So cosy'. When Ron appeared ('Luckily they didn't allow husbands anywhere near for the birth'), she was able to present him with a boy and a girl, the girl already showing the fiery red hair of her maternal grandmother, Dorothy, and her paternal great-grandfather, Barclay Buxton.

They named the boy Peter Hildred ('Hildred' after his paternal great-grandfather, Sir Hildred Carlile), and the girl Camilla Janet St John ('Janet' after Ron's mother, 'St John' after Phyll's mother). Children's cries were about to fill Kimberley once more.

15

'Put Your X against BuXton'

HIS PATERNAL GREAT-grandfather, 'The Liberator', had been an MP. His maternal grandfather had been an MP. Numerous Buxton cousins, close and distant, had been MPs. Why not Ron Buxton, MP? Ron's already latent interest in politics asserted itself in 1950. Horrified by Clement Attlee's postwar Labour government's wholesale nationalisations of major British industries – first the railways, then the coal mines, later steel – he offered to help Leyton's Conservative candidate, Peter Williams, for the forthcoming General Election.

Leyton was not a glamorous borough. 'The grey, drab, infinitely depressing wasteland ... it has the air of a Victorian East Berlin' is how the *Sunday Express* would later describe it; a 'grimy gateway to Greater London where voyagers to East Anglia by rail or road tend to become despairingly becalmed' said *The Times*. Other papers would have their own versions, but two adjectives cropped up again and again: 'grey' and 'grim'. Until the war, Leyton had been two seats. Leyton East was Conservative. West Leyton, full of highly unionised railway workshops, was Labour. But for the first postwar election in 1950, the two seats were combined. This was won for Labour by the MP for Leyton West since 1929, Reginald Sorensen, and retained in October 1952 with a majority of 16,000. Following these disastrous defeats, the existing Conservative candidate, Peter Williams, resigned, and the chairman of the local Conservative Association approached Ron to see if he would be interested in standing.

Being a candidate required getting to know the chairmen of each ward of the borough. In Leyton there were eight wards, and a candidate's duties between elections largely involved attending dinners and functions. Once an election was announced, obviously it involved mounting a campaign. Ron decided he had the time. H. Young's UK operation was running well and it gave him a base in the borough. If he didn't live there, his family had ties with the area going back centuries. His grandfather's grandfather had lived in Leytonstone in the nineteenth century and several roads and streets bore the family name. He could arrange his schedule to accommodate an election when it was announced. He even had a campaigning vehicle in the form of his trusty army jeep, the one he had driven to Morocco and with which he towed his old horse-box.

So, even if there were little hope of winning, why not? After going up to

Conservative Central Office to meet John Hare, he was formally adopted in October 1952 as the new Conservative candidate for Leyton. He was twenty-nine.

Ron made his first public address a couple of months later when Leyton Conservative Association organised a thousand-strong rally at Leyton Baths. Dr Charles Hill MP was the main speaker, Parliamentary Secretary to the Ministry of Food, but more famous for his weekly show as a radio personality, Radio Doctor. He welcomed Ron, who told his new constituents how much he was looking forward to getting to know them.

A General Election was still two years away, but the months flew by, as Ron adjusted himself to his new role, and got used to seeing his name and photograph in the local papers, now promoted from 'Prospective Conservative Candidate' to 'The Conservative Candidate'. He fitted what meetings and dinners he could around his trips to Africa. Sir Anthony Eden finally called the election for the late spring of 1955 and the moment he had been waiting for arrived.

Ron's campaigning style, as might be expected, was individual. 'During the campaign you will hear organ music recorded on a Leyton organ played back from the loudspeaker jeep' promised his campaign leaflets.

Photographs in his campaign literature, meanwhile, portrayed the young Tory candidate as an energetic man-of-action: at the H. Young drawing board, in the factory, winning Sparham point-to-point, paddling his canoe through dramatic rapids. ('His favourite summer sport is wild water canoeing.') His listed interests included mountaineering and other sports.

Exhorting his potential constituents not to be duped by Labour claptrap ('their heads ... so full of doctrinaire theories, such as nationalisation, controls and socialist planning'), he urged them to consider 'that all men and women should have the right to own their own houses, farms or shops, and not be serfs under the thumb of a despotic central government'. Jean was co-opted to write a section in his campaigning literature, 'To the women of Leyton'. With postwar austerity and rationing over, and a house-building boom and better times underway, as his slogan he chose: 'SAFEGUARD YOUR PROSPERITY'.

As polling day approached, this apothegm was replaced by the more urgently specific: 'PUT YOUR X AGAINST BUXTON'. And when the big day came, many of his constituents chose to do so. By the time counting was finished, and the Conservatives had been returned under Anthony Eden, Ron was still some way from winning his first election – but he had reduced Sorensen's majority from 16,000 to 10,000.

Little of Ron's campaign literature from the next election, in 1959, survives. By now, economic times were good. His previous 'Safeguard your prosperity' platform chimed well with the Prime Minister Harold Macmillan's famous

'SAFEGUARD YOUR PROSPERITY'

declaration, two years earlier, that 'Most of our people have never had it so good'. The country returned the Conservatives nationally for the third time running, and Ron managed to slash Sorensen's majority from 10,000 to just 3,900. Following such a dramatic result, he applied for the safe Conservative seat of South-West Norfolk. He made the final shortlist of four, but was pipped in the final selection.

By the 1964 election, the country had seen twelve years of Conservative government. Over this period Ron had evolved from a young, free and single, globe-trotting bachelor to a married father of three with a large house in the country. The twins, now four, had acquired a sister. Born in April 1962, Vanessa Anne Carlile was brown-haired and blue-eyed – and by October's General Election, Phyll was eight months pregnant again.

Change was in the air in the country, too. The death penalty was about to be abolished, and there was the general sense of being on the threshold of a new age: the nuclear age, the jet age (with supersonic Concorde on the drawing board) and now, with President Kennedy's pledge to put a man on the moon 'before this decade is out', the Space Age too. Science and technology were the new gods – the pill, instant food, the hovercraft, fibreboard, the Kenwood chef, the breeze-block, Formica, the Post Office Tower, colour supplements, the Mini, the miniskirt. The Sixties were in full swing. 'This is what 1964 can mean' Wilson thundered in his election campaign. 'A chance for change ... A chance to sweep away the grouse-moor conception of Tory leadership and refit Britain with a new image, a new confidence.' In place of the old Britain under the stodgy, archaic Conservatives, Labour would bring a New Britain born out of scientific revolution. 'A Britain', Wilson declared, 'forged in the white heat of this revolution.'

Ron waged his campaign on his now trusty platform of 'SAFEGUARD YOUR PROSPERITY' and 'KEEP IT GOING – VOTE FOR BUXTON' ('Labour still cling to their outworn ideology of more Nationalisation and State Control, hiding their purpose behind a smoke screen of double talk'). Phyll now wrote a section in his election leaflet on the family ('I am sure you will agree with me that women are often more practical than men ...') and his listed hobbies had mellowed from travelling, mountaineering and wild water canoeing to, perhaps more appropriate for a married man in his forties, music, riding and gardening. But this time, after so long under the Tories, the country swung away from them and Harold Wilson's new Labour government swept to power. Leyton's Labour majority climbed back to 8,000.

Any disappointment at this result was at least softened, six weeks later, by the birth of their next child, another boy: Robert Victor.

Having just fought an election, Ron might reasonably have expected a break for at least a couple of years from political campaigning. In fact, the opposite happened. Having hardly put down his megaphone, he was now asked to take it up again for a fourth trip to the polls. For certain events from the recent General Election had just caught up with the government, and as a result Leyton's long-standing Labour MP, Reg Sorensen, was to be replaced. At short notice, a by-election at Leyton was called.

*

The Leyton by-election would become one of the notorious political events of the era. It came about because the Prime Minister, Harold Wilson, did something rash: he promised a high-flying minister in his Cabinet a seat when he did not, technically, have one to offer.

By 1965 Wilson had assembled the most intellectually brilliant Cabinet ever to be brought together – more than nine members had first class degrees from Oxford or Cambridge. One of the brightest stars in this constellation was his Foreign Secretary, Patrick Gordon Walker. Gordon Walker's career was a story of almost faultless ascent. The son of a Scottish judge in the Indian Civil Service, at Wellington he had played rugby, cricket and hockey for his house. A regular forward in the first XV, he had won the half-mile and mile races in the school sports of 1925, taken the Athletics Cup, been Master of the Hunt and company sergeant-major in the Officer Training Corps. After an open scholarship had taken him to Christ Church, Oxford to read history, it was his sporting achievements, his regular rugby-playing, that had certainly contributed to his election as a fellow of the college (reasons cited alongside his 'admirable scholarship' included 'reliable games-playing'). In the list of eminent Christ Church dons in the *University Calendar* for 1932, his name appeared directly below that of Albert Einstein.

A year in Germany attached to Heidelberg and various other universities had left him fluent in German. As special correspondent for *The Daily Telegraph* there, he had reported on the final years of the Weimar Republic. Twice he had seen Goebbels, once at one of the gigantic Nuremberg rallies. ('Those who saw and heard Hitler never forgot the experience' he later reported. 'But Goebbels's words and arguments were longer remembered.') His familiarity with Germany brought Gordon Walker into close contact with the British Labour Party, which he joined in the early Thirties 'because the Conservatives had degraded the country I wanted to be proud of'.

Four years after winning the Midlands seat of Smethwick in 1945, Atlee promoted him to Cabinet Minister, aged 43. By 1958 the *Daily Express* was speaking of him as the next Labour leader, and when Hugh Gaitskell died in January 1963, Gordon Walker considered making a bid. As chief opposition spokesman on defence, his standing was high as a man of measured judgement. Of Labour's leading figures, only he and Harold Wilson had served as Cabinet ministers. The *New Statesman* called him 'the pipe-smoking exponent of moderating common sense ... one of the most decent men in British politics'. *The Sunday Times* pronounced him 'Baldwin-like' in his solidity: 'he conjures up a picture of the trusted family solicitor and everybody's favourite uncle.' He stood aside, however, and let George Brown, Harold Wilson and Jim Callaghan slug it out. The quick-witted Wilson soon saw off the other two, and promptly offered Gordon Walker the post of shadow Foreign Secretary. The choice was well received. His Cabinet experience was an asset, and when they returned from talks with American and Soviet leaders, Gordon Walker impressed the House with his expertise and a new note of authority.

But then, in the 1964 General Election, disaster struck for Labour's new golden boy. The reason was one completely new to British politics: race.

Gordon Walker's seat, the run-down industrial town of Smethwick, between Birmingham and Wolverhampton in the heart of the Black Country, had the highest concentration of Afro-Caribbean immigration of any county borough in England (between five and seven thousand in a population of 70,000). The newcomers, having at first been welcomed, began to be viewed with suspicion and distaste. Pubs, clubs, even barbers, were by the early 1960s operating a 'colour bar' – a British apartheid. The local paper, the *Smethwick Telephone*, was fiercely anti-immigrant. As the leader of Labour opposition to the Conservative government's Commonwealth Immigrants Bill, which sought to limit immigration, Gordon Walker became a target of racist campaigning tactics by the prospective Conservative candidate, Peter Griffiths.

Griffiths, a local headmaster and Conservative leader on the borough council, milked local suspicions that further immigration would push down property prices and increase competition for council houses and jobs. 'If you want a nigger for a neighbour, vote Labour' was one of the catchphrases of his campaign. Rumours were spread by his canvassers that many of the blacks had leprosy, and that two secret leper hospitals were being built in the town.

Even the Labour Party itself was not immune to prejudice. In a high profile own-goal, a party given by Smethwick's Labour headquarters for Gordon Walker himself banned coloured guests – a situation Gordon Walker got round by holding the event elsewhere. The damage this did to the Foreign Secretary's campaign was immense – and, as it turned out, irrecoverable. His slim majority was turned into a 1,174 vote defeat and he lost his seat to Griffiths. A swing of 3% to Labour nationally became a swing of 7% to Conservative in Smethwick. Harold Wilson called the result 'a disgrace to British democracy' and labelled Griffiths a 'parliamentary leper'.

Yet, despite no longer having a seat, Wilson used his special powers to retain his Cabinet star until a suitable safe Labour seat could be found for him. Labour Central Office went to work, and duly alighted on Leyton, where the much-loved old-timer Reggie Sorensen – 'old Reg' – was now 73. A life peerage was pressed onto him as a lord-in-waiting, and he was reluctantly 'promoted' to make way for Gordon Walker.

A by-election was called, for Thursday 21 January. Darkest winter, in the post-Christmas and New Year malaise, it was a stagnant time for news. The only other story was that the greatest statesmen of the age, Winston Churchill, lay dying after a stroke. So when the Foreign Secretary adjourned from the colonial grandeur of the Foreign Office to tread the grey streets of Leyton, complete with emergency red scrambler phone to the PM's office, the national media went with him.

But this wasn't the only reason for Press interest in the by-election. The scheduled date for polling day happened to coincide almost exactly with the new Labour government's first 100 days in power; a statistic that would doubtless have passed unnoticed had it not been singled out by Harold Wilson in his election campaign as a critical period of time for delivering on his promises. All Labour needed, he had claimed, was 'a hundred days of dynamic action', to show just what changes they could make to the country.

As Labour Central Office went to work, so, in Leyton Conservative Club, Ron discussed strategies for squaring up to his exalted foe. It was all too much for his timorous local chairman Percy Ayers. 'Oh, Ron, what are we going to do?' he whined, wringing his hands. 'We're going to win,' said Ron. 'It's a marvellous opportunity.'

*

And so the candidates lined up. As if to underline the anonymity of Gordon Walker's opponents, a *Times* piece on the campaign (at the end of the first week of January) muddled up the captions beneath the photographs of the three candidates; the Liberal candidate was labelled 'Mr R Buxton', and Ron was labelled 'Mr A Mackay'. Meanwhile, the patrician, liberal-minded, pipe-smoking statesman was portrayed in all his gloom, his mouth set into its default inverted half-moon. Against him – for this, if not a one-horse, was certainly no more than a two-horse race – the young Tory structural engineer: 'with his blue eyes, elegant, high-pitched voice and calculated bagginess of clothes, presumably as Old Etonian camouflage' noted *The Times*. But was he 'a bit ethereal', the paper wondered: 'Does he really have the resolution or the rind for a close contest?'

Much was made of the installation of Her Majesty's Foreign Secretary into

Red box and red scrambler phone – the Foreign Secretary in his temporary campaigning office, Leyton Town Hall

Room 169 of the Town Hall (one up, and turn right at the top of the stairs), whence he returned every lunch time to deal with international affairs. As for the red scrambler phone: was it really a special line to the Prime Minister, in case of emergency – or perhaps, as Ron suggested to one televised election meeting, 'to find out from him how to win the election'?

Much, too, was made of the Foreign Secretary's chosen campaign style, in particular the sight of him 'canvassing in a delightfully decrepit old furniture van, crying "I am Gordon Walker" before scuttling back to the mayor's robing room to open telegrams from Nigeria and Indonesia'. 'A mighty Caesar being brought down to democratic earth in this way', said *The Times*, 'is a spectacle as refreshing as that of the slave who rode beside a Roman conqueror to remind him that even if he had been made Foreign Secretary he was still mortal.' His attempts to interact and endear himself with his constituents were delightedly noted, in particular the way he awkwardly called one 'Brother' at a stone-laying ceremony.

Gordon Walker, unlit pipe clenched between his teeth, chose as his tack the 'mess' left behind by the Conservative government, and Labour's progress in clearing it up. Ron attacked the Foreign Secretary as a casual and inefficient MP foisted onto Leyton, berating Labour's strategy of using Leyton as a dumping ground for Cabinet ministers who couldn't get themselves a seat.

Mr. Buxton, the Conservative candidate, stops Mr. Ron Harris, a milkman on his rounds, yesterday to discuss local issues likely to affect the by-election at Leyton, which takes place on Jan. 21.

Portrait of Her Majesty's Foreign Secretary, seeking the votes of the electors of Leyton

LEFT: Ron buttonholes a milkman on his rounds: *The Daily Telegraph*, 6 January 1965; RIGHT: Gordon Walker canvassing on by-election day, 21 January, from the next day's *Daily Express*

But beneath the surface, the 'race issue' had not gone away – not by any means. The first, chilly, morning that Gordon Walker arrived at Leyton Labour headquarters, it was to find that overnight the windows and doors had been daubed with white swastikas. From that moment, race was an underlying, if often unspoken, issue. At his official nomination, Gordon Walker was greeted by a man with a face blackened with boot polish, posing as a nominee, bearing a placard reading: 'Walker Gordon – the race mixing candidate – MAKE BRITAIN BLACK' and Colin Jordan bawling: 'You are a disgusting racial traitor.' This was a reference not just to Smethwick, but to the fact that his wife Audrey, whom Gordon Walker had met at Oxford, was Jamaican (her father owned a coconut plantation) and that his daughters had married black men. Anti-immigration campaigners paraded outside Labour headquarters dressed in monkey suits and bearing placards reading: 'WE IMMIGRANTS ARE VOTING FOR GORDON WALKER'.

At the start, once it had become clear that Gordon Walker was to be put up as Labour's new candidate for Leyton, in November, it had seemed irresistible to make a little capital. But Ron soon discovered how easy it was to become sucked into a mire by the Press. Following a telephone conversation with a journalist at the *Observer* it was reported on 15 November that he had made claims that 'there is growing feeling on the immigrant question in the Leyton area'. The piece went on to quote him as saying that during his General Election canvassing 'many people complained about the immigration of coloureds'. 'They do not resent coloured people as such, but they do object to the blacks coming off the banana boats and taking Council houses that would be available for locals.' Such remarks unleashed a storm in the liberal Press, most notably the *Guardian* on 11 December, in an article headlined 'Mr Buxton And That 'Observer' Report'. This contained some rapid footwork by Ron to 'clarify' his position. 'Mr Buxton this week told the *Guardian*: "The *Observer*'s report was garbled in certain details and it appears to have created the wrong impression. It resulted out of a conversation over the phone with an *Observer* reporter. After seeing the story I decided never again to discuss such matters over the phone with journalists because of the danger of misrepresentation ..." Having explained that he did not use any of the phrases of which he was accused – "colour conscious", "blacks", "banana boats" – this, in turn, led to further questions as to why he had not submitted a letter to the *Observer* for publication pointing out the report's alleged misrepresentations.' And so it went on.

It is important to remember how novel discussion of race and immigration still was in 1964, and how, accordingly, the terms, and the language, of the debate were still largely unframed. It seems scarcely believable today, for example, that *The Telegraph* could publish (on 12 January 1965), when the man with a blackened face presented himself at the Leyton nominations, the following sentence: 'Dressed in traditional West Indian costume, he cried in the accents of a chocolate coloured coon: "De noo candidate".'

Conservative Central Office spotted this bear-trap for what it was, and moved quickly and completely to dissociate themselves. Ian Macleod (a powerful member of the Shadow Cabinet) called Ron: 'You're carrying the banner for the Party. You must not under any circumstances bring up the immigration issue. We must have clean hands.' Thereafter, despite daily radio meetings, television interviews and attempts by the left-wing Press, especially the *Daily Mirror*, to trick him, Ron was always careful and measured. Asked by the BBC, 'Do you think that coloured immigration is being made an issue here?', he replied: 'I think it's being deliberately brought into this constituency by people that want to make it an issue. Naturally, Mr Gordon Walker, by his connection with Smethwick, is likely to bring immigration issues here, and I'm afraid that many of his old enemies at Smethwick are deliberately creating this issue.'

And indeed they were. Gordon Walker's election meetings were routinely disrupted by scuffles and shouting. One of the most notable set-tos occurred at his first campaign meeting, at Leyton Town Hall, when the neo-Nazi campaigner Colin Jordan, leading a group of about 100 fascist demonstrators, invaded the stage with various heavies and bags of flour, receiving, for his pains, a left hook from Gordon Walker and another from the Defence Secretary, Denis Healey.

'PUNCH-UP POLITICS': the *Guardian* reports events of 7 January 1965

Race was considered enough of an issue by the second week of January that a BBC play entitled *The Fable*, which presented a fictional apartheid-in-reverse scenario in which England was under black rule and a white chauffeur was brutally dragged from his home and murdered by black police, was pulled until after the Leyton by-election. None of this, of course, did Ron's campaign any harm. The fact was, he didn't *need* to mention race; Colin Jordan was doing it for him. And when, in due course, a couple of papers picked up on the fact that he was a descendant of Sir Thomas Fowell Buxton, the great Liberator and abolitionist of slavery, it helped to distance him further from such thinking.

Meanwhile, for those on the streets, the campaigning was rarely less than eventful. A friend of Ron's, a stockbroker called Philip Darwin, brought his entire staff out of his office in the evenings to canvass and the 26-year-old Phyll was also pressed into service. Well-meaning, if something of a novice at such work, she vividly recalls the occasion when, after knocking on one door, the occupant took one look at her, shouted 'Fuck off', and slammed the door so hard a brick fell out of the lintel. Another time, at an evening meeting, thunder flashes were thrown onto the stage and everyone had to bolt for cover.

Ted Heath came down to speak, and Quintin Hogg (later Lord Hailsham). While the latter was on stage, Phyll – on the platform with Ron – remembers looking down to see that the entire audience were fighting, continuing until the police arrived to break things up.

And so the hustings proceeded. There were daily press conferences at Conservative HQ, as different issues came up. Labour, however, failed to grasp the scale of their problem until a fortnight before polling day. By the time they brought down their heavy hitters – notably George Brown – the damage, Ron believes, was done. On the Sunday before Thursday's poll, the vicar of Leyton held a special service for the three by-election candidates, filmed by the BBC. During the singing of the hymn 'God is working his purpose out, the time is drawing near' Ron watched the crew sneak up behind Gordon Walker and the Liberal candidate and place microphones directly behind them. Aware they would be doing the same to him, he took special care to sing well. The following night, *Panorama* broadcast a round-up about the Leyton by-election. All that was broadcast of Sunday's service was the hymn, with his two running mates each singing chronically, irredeemably flat.

*

Polling day, Thursday 22 January, 1965, dawned cold, grey and miserable. By lunchtime it was snowing. This was good news for Ron. Bad weather always reduced the voting turnout, and with its high proportion of old age pensioners this was even more the case in Leyton. A bad turnout would damage Gordon Walker more than Ron.

Counting began after the polls closed in the thirty polling stations at 10 p.m., by which time a considerable crowd of 150 or so had gathered outside the Town Hall. Once counted, the votes were sub-divided into bundles, which were tied with coloured tape; blue for Conservative votes, red for Labour. Periodically, officials would collect up the bundles and put them into racks. As the racks filled, the candidates and their agents – the only people allowed in the room apart from the sixty counters themselves – were able to see that both blue bundles and red bundles were very closely matched.

The first hint that high drama was in the air came shortly after 11.30 p.m., when the last bundles came in. Ron could see that there were more blue than red. This could only mean one thing: he had won. And indeed, the acting returning officer a few minutes later announced to the startled room that the first count showed Mr Buxton was in the lead by about 200 votes. It was a minute majority from a constituency of over 70,000, and the veteran Labour agent Wilfred Young, fighting his last campaign, immediately demanded a recount. In the maelstrom of excitement, Ron slipped out and whispered the news to his supporters outside. They, in turn, leaked the story to the Press and the BBC – and the touch paper was lit.

As midnight approached, the crowd around the Town Hall had increased to more than 400, and snow was falling in large flakes. At the front, a youthful David Dimbleby anchored live for the BBC's 11 p.m. *Gallery* programme. After the late evening news, there had been a round-up of the campaign. Beginning with the scuffles when Gordon Walker and Denis Healey landed blows on Colin Jordan ('The Minister of Defence and Mr Gordon Walker,' intoned a waggishly detached voice-over in the clipped pronunciation of the time, 'using conventional weapons, proved the ultimate deterrent.') The voice went on to describe the borough ('Leyton is in London's Far East. From the playing fields of Eton Manor, it's about half an hour to Waterloo. Beyond the dismal flatness of Hackney Marshes stand the spires and minarets of the Orient. Orient here means football – the local team almost the only thing by which Leyton is known to the larger world outside …'), before mentioning the Foreign Secretary's red scrambler phone and his eccentric campaigning style ('The Foreign Secretary preaches the word from the back of what looks like one of those Gospel vans used by the more flamboyant religious sects') ending with the flat rendering of 'God is working his purpose out' in Leyton church. ('The first week was to end as it began – on a discordant note'.)

News had already come in that at the Nuneaton by-election, happening simultaneously, the Labour candidate, Frank Cousins, Minister for Technology, had got in safely, albeit with a majority reduced by 6,000.

Finally, shortly after midnight, Leyton's Labour mayor, Councillor Terence Messenger, called silence to announce that the results of the recount were in, and that, as mayor of the Borough of Leyton, he could 'hereby give notice that the total number of votes recorded for each candidate at the election is as follows ...'.

'Buxton, Ron Carlile ... sixteen thousand, five hundred and forty four ...'

So anything less than 16,544 and Ron was in. The atmosphere thickened as Councillor Messenger unhurriedly read out the Disarmament Party's score of 5,382. At last, he came to the man that mattered. 'Gordon Walker, Patrick Chrestien ...'

'Labour' interjected an official voice.

Here the mayor paused, savouring his moment. 'Sixteen thousand ...'

The hall entered that state of heightened, deep silence only possible in the presence of a crowd. Would Ron's tiny winning margin hold up? Gordon Walker had to beat that extra 544. Even a single vote would be enough.

'... three hundred and ...'

The final 'thirty-nine' was drowned out by the roar. He was in. Ron Buxton had won the seat. The Conservatives had taken Leyton, by 205 votes on an electorate of 78,000. Chanting broke through as the doors were thrown open to the crowd outside: 'Walker out ... Walker out ...'

*

'Perhaps it was his Eton training which enabled him to remain outwardly calm,' reported the *Evening Standard* next day. Whatever it was, Ron, determined to enjoy his moment to the full, was in no hurry. After a jubilant wave to the crowd of his constituents and supporters around the Town Hall steps in the snow, he launched into an impromptu victory speech.

> 'This is a stupendous victory, a fantastic victory. After twelve years of work in this constituency and four campaigns, we are at last victorious. As I said at the last count, when we lost by 8,000 votes, never mind, we'll fight again. And we fought and conquered. Thank you to my supporters for this magnificent victory. And this victory belongs not only to us, the people of Leyton, but to the whole people of the whole country. People far beyond the walls of this town, the boundaries of this town, will rejoice with us ...'

While he spoke, the Foreign Secretary awaited his turn. Formalities dictated that the losing candidate, too, must second the winner's vote of thanks to the mayor. Pale and weighed down by exhaustion and defeat, Gordon Walker's default gloom had become a mask of misery. No doubt desperate for the evening to be over, unfortunately for him Ron was nowhere near finished.

'It has been shown that the first 100 days have been a failure, that the

'A stupendous victory, a fantastic victory ...': Ron takes the platform; behind him, the
Foreign Secretary's face tells *his* story

Conservative Party will come to the fore again, and that we shall get victory in the next election. Now may I, in saying these words, thank ...'

Ron proceeded to thank his supporters, and his friends and comrades, and the counters, who had apparently made only one vote difference in the recount, and ...

'... thank you all again ... all my supporters for this magnificent campaign ... a wonderful victory!'

Finally, it was Gordon Walker's turn. He made a short, statesmanlike speech, thanking the mayor and his supporters, and the formalities were over.

A swarm of Press surrounded Ron. How did he feel? What did he think was the reason for his victory? Modestly he pointed out that he thought Lord Sorensen's removal from the 'close family circle' of Leyton had been a major factor of his success. It had, he said, always been his ambition to become an MP but after twelve years of trying, the prospect had 'always looked rather far off'.

Outside, after waving to his supporters, Ron was buttonholed by David Dimbleby, who, determined to give the racial shenanigans a final airing, found he was already dealing with a consummate politician:

DIMBLEBY: There's been a lot of racialist intervention here which has dogged Mr Gordon Walker. Don't you think that's been to your advantage?

RON: I don't think so. Nobody in Leyton has raised the racial issue among the three major parties.

DIMBLEBY: But it has ... it has ... you don't think you really got in on that smear campaign that went on?

RON: I certainly don't, no. There is no reason to suggest that the racial issue was raised. It certainly wasn't by any of us.

The Foreign Secretary, during all this, made to leave, slipping away by a side door. He had got as far as a grey saloon outside the Town Hall before baying phalanxes of the Press coaxed him back inside, snow dusting the shoulders of his overcoat, to make a comment. 'I am rather tired and want to get along home. I have not given any thought about my future plans. I shall speak to the Prime Minister.' Asked about a telephone call he had made immediately after the result was declared, he said: 'I cannot say anything about it. You will have to ask the Prime Minister about whether it is possible for me to continue as Foreign Secretary.' Racism, he said, had nothing to do with his defeat. 'I do not want to pretend this has been a happy night for the Government, but I do not think it is a judgment on the first 100 days.'

Watching the proceedings, waiting quietly just inside the door of the Town Hall, was the man who had previously represented the voters of Leyton for over thirty years, Reg, now Lord, Sorensen. Behind his steel-rimmed spectacles, beret in hand, the collar of his long blue overcoat turned up against the cold, the 73-year-old was still blinking with shock and disbelief. As Gordon Walker, flanked by frowning party officials and detectives, came down the stairs to return to his official residence in Westminster's Carlton Gardens, the two politicians exchanged farewells. 'I'm sorry, Reg.'

'You were a wonderful candidate.'

'But not quite wonderful enough.'

Then, with a final, weary smile, Gordon Walker got back into his car and sped away.

Sitting at home, watching the television in his pyjamas, Richard Crossman[51] wrote in his diary: 'It was an awful evening ... I could see the Tory candidate not really believing his ears and watch Gordon Walker acting

---

51 Richard Crossman (1907–74), author, Labour politician (cabinet minister under Harold Wilson) and editor of the *New Statesman* who is now best known for his political diaries.

with melancholy dignity – and also revealing his deep inner defeatism. It was an awful evening. I felt an epoch had ended.'

*

The party went on until 4 a.m. Towards the end, because the pianist failed to show up, Ron himself took to the keyboard, thumping out 'Land of Hope and Glory'. In the next day's *Daily Sketch*, there he was, flanked by Phyll and Jean.

The following morning, Friday, with Ron bleary-eyed after Robbie had woken them at six after just a couple of hours of sleep, there were more than a hundred congratulatory telegrams. From Sir Alec Douglas-Home, Leader of the Opposition: 'Congratulations on magnificent result.' From Iain Macleod: 'Warmest congratulations on brilliant epitaph you have written for Mr. Wilson. I shall spend next 100 days chuckling.' *The Telegraph* made much of the scene at Ashley Gardens, nappies piled on a chair in the hallway, baby's cries competing with the telephone, ever more telegrams pouring in, and, radiating calm amid the chaos, Mrs Buxton. 'How, I wondered, would she cope with the additional responsibilities as wife of an MP? "I shall manage," she said through teeth clenched round a safety pin – she was in the middle of changing a nappy.'

The front pages of the morning newspapers told their own story: 'MR GORDON WALKER LOSES LEYTON' proclaimed *The Times*, conceding, a subhead or two lower down: 'DEEP DAMAGE TO GOVERNMENT'. The same thought was echoed by *The Telegraph* and most of the other papers. The shockwaves crossed both the Channel – 'A SERIOUS SET-BACK FOR MR WILSON' reported *Le Monde* in Paris – and the Atlantic: 'BRITISH LABORITES STUNNED BY DEFEAT: NEW GENERAL ELECTION MIGHT BE FORCED' announced the *Houston Chronicle*. The *Eastern Daily Press* proudly took the local angle: 'NORFOLK FARMER ROBS GORDON WALKER OF LEYTON SEAT.'

Edward du Cann, the newly-appointed chairman of the Conservative Party, told newspapers: 'The electors ... have shown quite clearly what they think of Mr Wilson's first 100 days.' And to prove that the race issue, whatever everyone said and hoped, was not far away, there were two other contributions: the South African *Sunday Times* reported that: 'If it was "Black Friday" for the Labour Party in Britain, it was a shining White Friday for the Nationalist Government in Cape Town', describing how the pro-apartheid South African government had taken the election victory to their bosom. And from the 'League of Empire Loyalists', a telegram to the Prime Minister: 'Are Leytonians lepers too?'

In the City, share prices jumped £1,000 million, the biggest single-day surge since May 1962 and the best day the market had had since the October General Election. Newspapers reported crowds gathering round the stands of

The Times and The Daily Telegraph main headlines, Friday, 22 January 1965

the steel, insurance and property share jobbers 'due to a growing belief that the Government will have to shelve its plans for steel nationalisation'.

Then it was off to Conservative headquarters in Leyton. As Ron and Phyll, after parking, took a handle each of the carry-cot of two-month-old Robbie, the press photographers spotted a photo opportunity and snapped away furiously. The picture would become one of the defining images of the campaign, from the *Evening Standard* that evening, to the *Daily Express* and the *Norfolk Daily Press*.

Patrick Gordon Walker, meanwhile, made his way to Buckingham Palace to resign from the Foreign Office. In newspapers in days to come he agreed that it had been, on the whole, a fairly conducted by-election and he he did not accuse the Tories of exploiting the racial angle. However, he did accuse the Press of deliberately portraying him as perpetually grim-faced and downcast. All in all,

Photo opportunity: Ron and Phyll carrying two-month-old Robbie to Conservative HQ in Leyton, which became a defining image of the campaign

it was a dignified departure. As someone would later say: 'Nothing became his career like his leaving of it.'

How could such an experienced politician have let an only three-month-old majority of 8,000 slip through his fingers? What was the real reason behind Ron's triumph? The matter was much discussed in the weekend's papers. A combination of factors, was the general agreement. The turnout of just 38% was dismal, and this massive abstention was the reason the Conservatives had been able to swing it. The terrible weather certainly contributed to this, plus general lack of knowledge or interest in the by-election. There was resentment in the constituency at having a Cabinet minister foisted on them and a respected senior member turned out. The Government was in a bad patch owing to the unpopularity of its mortgage programme and its attack on the aircraft industry. The smear which Gordon Walker brought from Smethwick probably accounted for the fact that the swing at Leyton was 8 per cent, rather than the 4.5 per cent it had been at Nuneaton. But most of all, even the right-wing papers agreed, Gordon Walker was just a lousy candidate. His

[233]

demeanour, 'intellectual fastidiousness, unrelieved by charm' as the *Sunday Telegraph* put it, and his 'lofty preoccupation with ideas' meant 'he could not help making it seem that he was indifferent to people'. No one, it was agreed, could have looked more miserable over the weeks of the hustings. And, of course, there was the final factor. Full of beans as ever, the Conservative candidate had fought an almost faultless campaign.

On Saturday morning, at 8 a.m., Winston Churchill died and Britain became a nation in mourning. 'Tonight', Harold Wilson told the British people in a televised address, 'our nation mourns the loss of the greatest man any of us have ever known.' Following the funeral, the *Observer* put things rather less grandiloquently: 'This was the last time that London would be the capital of the world ... the final act in Britain's greatness. After this the coldness of reality and the status of Scandinavia.' In this chilly new world, Ron prepared to embark upon his political career.

*

The first step for a newly elected Member of Parliament is to take his or her seat. Because Parliament was sitting, this could happen immediately, so Ron had arranged to do so the following Tuesday. Perhaps run down after his hard-fought campaign, plus the interrupted nights due to a new baby, Ron

NEW M.P. TAKES HIS SEAT

NOW he can add the initials M.P. after his name. Mr. Ronald Buxton, 41-year-old surprise winner of the sensational Leyton by-election, is pictured arriving at the Commons on Tuesday to take his seat. His sponsors were Mr. William Whitelaw, Opposition Chief Whip, and Mr. John Harvey, East Walthamstow M.P., and a close adviser of Mr. Buxton during the by-election campaign.

contracted a bronchial cold and retired to bed. There was a photograph of him in the *Daily Sketch*'s diary sitting up in bed, having medicine spooned into him by Camilla and Peter.

By Tuesday, however, he was up and ready for his friend, John Harvey, MP for East Walthamstow, to introduce him as a new member, rounding up friends to come down and support. After arriving in the lobby of the Commons, the procedure was to sign the members' book on the Speaker's desk in front of the prime minister and the mace. As Ron stepped forward, George Brown on the government front bench said loudly to Harold Wilson: 'He doesn't look any worse than the rest of them.' And so, a week after his victory, to a welcoming roar of Conservative cheers, Ron was officially inducted as an MP. It was reported (left) in the *Guardian* on 5 February.

Despite gleeful reports in the papers

that, having collected his sixth parking ticket of the week, 'it wasn't such a good start' to his career as an MP, it was, in fact, a great start. Aged forty-one, unlike most new members, Ron arrived to find he was known to every single person in the house. It was also a fun time to be in Parliament. The two parties were so finely balanced – Labour, following his victory, only held power by two seats – that the Conservatives always had a good chance of defeating the government's motions. It meant, unlike today, that the House was always well-attended. He also had plenty of friends: there were around thirty Old Etonian MPs (compared to nineteen in 2014), four of them from Ron's house.

On 15 April, a couple of months later, Ron made his maiden speech. Deliberately low key and anodyne, as maiden speeches always are, he described how the recent budget would affect his Leyton constituents and congratulated his predecessor Lord Sorensen on his familiarity with borough matters. Nevertheless, like his every move during this period, it made the papers ('Uncontroversial maiden speech on budget by Leyton Tory M.P.' – *Express*) and prompted congratulations from the Chancellor of the Exchequer, James Callaghan, at the end of his budget summing up.

The ensuing twelve months passed in a happy blur of division bells (the six-minute warning bell before a vote), two- and three-line whips, raising questions with ministers, taking distinguished guests round the Commons, sleeping in the Commons Library for important 3 a.m. votes, dealing with constituency business – and endless pictures and reports of his every movement in the newspapers. There was also the State Opening of Parliament and the 800th anniversary of the founding of the House of Commons and Lords to celebrate.

A typical day for Ron started at 8 a.m. in Ashley Gardens, with the morning devoted to a mixture of company and parliamentary business (constituency mail might consist of up to twenty letters). There were constituency matters to be dealt with, questions to be investigated and reports to read, from the proposed routing for the new M11 motorway (down the Roding Valley, or the Lea Valley?) to bringing the body of a Leyton soldier killed in Aden back home. (The Ministry of Defence refused to pay.) Then there was lunch at the Commons, showing groups round, and maybe a vote in the evening (usually at 10 p.m.). The sole thorn in his side over this period was the secretary of Leyton's Labour-controlled Borough Council, who, as the wife of a Labour MP, loathed Ron. She was as obstructive and unhelpful as his own company secretary, fortunately, was excellent.

In the summer, Ron joined a parliamentary delegation to observe the Ugandan elections. Consisting of two Labour MPs and two Conservatives, the deputation was led by his Conservative colleague, the Ulster Unionist Henry Clark MP, a former colonial district commissioner in Tanganyika (now Tanzania) who, like Ron, spoke Swahili. This nonplussed and thoroughly

Parliamentary delegation to Uganda, July 1965: front row, Shirley Summerskill MP, with Ron and the Mayor of Kampala. Behind, Reg Freeson MP.

wrong-footed their Labour consorts, Shirley Summerskill and Reg Freeson. Being abroad, they missed Edward Heath's election as Tory leader in place of Sir Alec Douglas-Home on 28 July.

Knowing that Ron was continually travelling on business, the Foreign Office took to asking him where he was going, in case it could be useful. Learning of a trip to the Sudan, in which he was also visiting Uganda, he was asked: 'Do you know anyone in the Sudan government?'

'I used to know the Prime Minister,' said Ron. It was true: he had met Sayed Muhammad Ahmad Mahgoub, previously an engineer and writer of Arab poetry, years before. The next thing he knew, in Uganda, a telegram from the Foreign Office arrived: 'Mr Buxton's appointment with the Prime Minister of Sudan ten o'clock Sunday'.

On arrival at Khartoum, Ron was met off the plane by the British ambassador, Roland Hunt. 'Can I come with you?' he asked. 'I haven't been able to get in to see the Prime Minister since I was appointed.'

'What are the issues?' said Ron.

'Overflying rights,' said Hunt. 'They've denied us overflying rights.'

So Ron took the ambassador with him (he had been a university professor, 'a very nice chap'). When Ron was ushered in to meet the Prime Minister, he was greeted warmly. In fact, his reception couldn't have been friendlier. After discussing various matters, Ron said: 'Could you do something to help us with the overflying rights?'

'I'll talk to my department.'

'Leyton's flying MP' flanked by RAF officers after landing a Shackleton Coastal Command bomber at Ballykelly, Northern Ireland, during a parliamentary tour of inspection, 25 November 1965

Soon after – not immediately, but soon – overflying rights were granted. The ambassador was delighted.

Trips to Kenya now meant meeting senior ministers of the Kenyatta government. In Rhodesia, where the Smith regime was in power, Ron made a speech in Bulawayo to defend the UK's position. Meanwhile, his interest in the armed forces meant he was sent on defence-linked missions – such as to see the Harrier jump jet, or to Northern Ireland to inspect search-and-rescue systems over the Atlantic. On such a day he might board a plane at RAF Northolt after breakfast, fly to Ballykelly, be taken on a trip in a new plane, have lunch, then be flown back in time to vote in the evening. Happy days ...

One of Ron's Leyton constituents, it turned out, was Clerk of Works of the Commons. He took Ron up to inspect the workings of Big Ben. The job of being MP, too, carried various perks. On top of delegations, fact-finding missions and tours of inspection, the most obvious was of little use to Ron: unlimited first class return tickets to his constituency. His annual salary was £1,750, rising, during his time in office, to £3,000.

It was a lively time to be in the House of Commons. The place teemed with colourful figures, from Bill Deedes to Lord Lambton, Sir Fitzroy Maclean to Robert Maxwell and Margaret Thatcher, all listed in *Vacher's Parliamentary Companion*. Ron was one of only three members who owned their own companies. The big issues of the time were the Southern Rhodesia Act, bringing in legislation to formally abolish all government institutions in the former colony of British Rhodesia following Ian Smith's Unilateral Declaration of Independence (UDI) on 11 November 1965; the other was the nationalisation of steel.

Prompted about this time, a wistful gleam entered Ron's eyes. 'So much happens around the House of Commons,' he said. 'People coming and going, others arriving from your constituency, or representing other interests ...' Twelve months whirled by, during which Ron had to live several lives simultaneously. In addition to his new parliamentary career, he was still chairman of H. Young & Company and its numerous subsidiaries, still making bi-annual trips to Africa. There was Kimberley and the farm to get into shape. And there was Phyll and the family: the twins, now rumbustious five-year-olds, plus Nessa and now Robbie. Asked how he balanced all these competing claims on his time, a smile of pure contentment came over him. 'I was very, very busy' – and it is as if no more idyllic state is conceivable.

*

Ron's political career was not an extended one: a day under fourteen months, to be precise. On 31 March 1966 a General Election was called. Ron stood again ('HE'S DOING A GOOD JOB, MAKE HIM YOUR MP AGAIN'), but sadly normal service resumed: Gordon Walker won back Leyton for Labour with a comfortable majority of over 5,000. The former Foreign Secretary became Education Secretary, but his career never flew again to the heights he had enjoyed before his first Leyton by-election disaster.

Ron stood again in 1970 ('THE MAN WITH LEYTON'S INTERESTS AT HEART'), but times had changed. He no longer fitted the prescribed Central Office profile. They were concerned he did not live in the constituency. 'Will you be selling your Norfolk estate, Mr Buxton?' inquired one member of the Selection Committee innocently. Ron applied again for one of the safe Norfolk seats, which, with his record, he would certainly have been granted under the old system. But again, the Select Committees knew of Kimberley. By then a new kind of self-made Tory was sought, epitomised by Edward Heath. The 'Old Guard', as Eton and Kimberley inevitably represented, no longer fitted. It was ironic that one of the party's most successful entrepreneurs should be damned as old school, traditional and hide-bound.

So Ron's political career was short, but spectacular. His victory at Leyton remains one of the most exciting glitches of mid-twentieth century British politics, for which he will always retain a footnote in the history books and a page on *Wikipedia*. It stands as proof that in politics anything can happen; that the British electorate can be led, exploited or spun so far, but, when they choose, they can still make an individual or a government a laughing stock. Asked, decades later, to say which was the most exciting day of his life, perhaps unsurprisingly his reply was Thursday 21 January 1965.

16

The Swimming Pool

KIMBERLEY WAS A paradise for children. There were fields and bluebell woods to explore, trees to climb, the lake and the River Tiffey to fish and swim in, and on which to mount boating expeditions. There were carrots and strawberries to pinch from the walled garden and bonfires to have round fallen trees in the park (Grandfather Roden, Phyll's father, now only twenty miles away, was an enthusiastic pyromaniac), with sausages on sticks to cook in the flames. There were ponies to ride and, in due course, take hunting with the Dunston Harriers and the West Norfolk Hunt.

Nine years after buying the house and park, Ron had acquired more land. The original purchase had included about 300 acres of pasture and arable land around the park. Now he added all the woodland and bought a farm beyond Kimberley village. Kimberley's policies now extended to 544 acres – not, perhaps, the tens of thousands of acres to which the estate once extended, nor even the 4,200 acres it was from the time Sir Philip Wodehouse built the present house until his descendant, Johnny Kimberley, disposed of it. Indeed, it was no longer enough, alone, to support the house. But it was a considerable holding nonetheless.[52]

In the house, Phyll, in between looking after four children under five, made the curtains, window by window, room by room, each set consuming fifteen metres of material before even considering the lining. Gradually the downstairs rooms were furnished. Ron, when he was in England, was adept at picking up big old carpets and bits of furniture at auctions and country house sales. As a result of his Uncle Hanbury, Sir Hildred Carlile's only son, being killed in action in 1918, much of the Ponsbourne furniture and portraits had come to Ron. The huge rug on the floor in the library came from Grandfather Hildred's yacht *Andrea*.

Jean had a flat on the top floor. The plan was that she would have a separate entrance of her own in the west front, so she could come and go as she pleased. Ever the opportunist, when St Thomas's Hospital, on the south

---

52 In the 1970s, a neighbouring landowner, David Cherry, offered to sell two large fields adjoining the Kimberley village side of the park. Cherry wanted £100 an acre, which Ron would happily have paid, but his farm advisor at the time, Jim Prior (see chapter 13), insisted this was too much. 'Offer £80 an acre' he said. This was rejected and the offer to sell was withdrawn, not to be repeated – to Ron's eternal regret. The moral, Ron became fond of declaring, is this: if offered land adjacent to your own, *buy it*, because it only comes up once in a generation.

of the Thames by Waterloo Bridge, was being rebuilt, Ron noticed that sections of the classical brick façade were being demolished. He acquired one of the big dressed stone doorways: a number of Portland Stone side and top stones for an opening about seven feet high. Then he and Jean arranged for the sculptor Michael Black (later well known for the thirteen new heads of emperors he carved for the stone pillars outside the Sheldonian Theatre in Oxford) to install it in the West Front. Black had been part of Jean's Oxford academic circle, first coming to Kimberley around 1960. 'They could have got contractors to do it, I suppose,' Black recalled. 'But they thought I could do it cheaper. And I suppose they were right, when I consider what I got paid.'

The twelve yews on the Park Front planted by the first Earl of Kimberley were clipped, and some first attacks were made on the jungle that was Lady Isobel's Garden. Ron continually fossicked about ways to make Kimberley pay for itself. More flats were created in the East Wing, often with their own foibles. One potential tenant, James Gilbey, remembers being taken round by Ron and, on entering the kitchen, becoming vaguely aware that something important was missing – until Ron, with a flourish, opened the door into the adjoining bedroom: 'And here …', he announced, '… is the cooker.'

Another idea was to use the walled garden to grow Christmas trees to sell in winter and strawberries in summer. The trees were duly planted, but the strawberries became the more successful venture. However, because they required pickers, they brought their own problems: chiefly their children, who ate prodigious amounts of fruit and needed frequent care. Accordingly, the operation was modified to 'Pick Your Own'. Here the enemy, due to the incompetence of a newly-hired gardener, were the rampant thistles shrouding the fruit, considerably reducing the enthusiasm of pickers. Undaunted, Ron and Phyll loaded the punnets themselves, distributing them to shops in Norwich and a roadside layby near Anthony Gurney's at Northrepps. Later, raspberries were added, sold by Ron at weekends using a brick as a counterweight on the old scales. Any surplus went down to London with Ron, to be sold from the back of his car in Leyton.

From the children's point of view, only one thing was lacking from this otherwise idyllic private world – their father. Ron was at Kimberley only at weekends, and for long parts of the year was away altogether. The children's memento of these times is vast numbers of postcards, invariably of the same thing – aeroplanes. Civilian passenger travel in the 1950s–60s had reached its glamorous apogee, the jet age bringing with it sleek silver 'airliners' like the De Havilland Comet and the Boeing VC10. Air travel was still sufficiently exotic for the airlines to issue passengers with free bags and postcards, and these latter, in large numbers, Ron sent to his children: 'Flying off to Kenya, seeing Sue, Lots of Love Daddy' or something similar, hastily scrawled in his unintelligible hand. Vanessa received so many she considered collecting them into a book and trying to publish them. Even when he was at home, at Kimberley, there was always so much to do that Ron seemed to be perpetually preoccupied. But there was one time when they could get their father's undiluted attention: holidays.

*

From the late Sixties, the family took two holidays a year. Having four children so close in age meant everyone could enjoy similar activities. From the late summer of 1968, for several years they went to Tiree, westernmost isle of the Inner Hebrides, flat, windswept and treeless, but with vast sandy beaches. The journey alone was an adventure, driving up via Uncle Derry, Phyll's brother, in Fife, then on to Oban where the car was hoisted onto the ferry, 'The Claymore', by crane. Then, via Tobermory on Mull, they reached Tiree. The accommodation was basic, a cottage set in the *machair* sand dune pasture, but from this base they had miles of beaches and coast to themselves, to look for shells, and go lobster-potting. There was a rubber Avon boat with an outboard, from which they went exploring coves and line fishing for mackerel.

Ron, only ever a sporadic angler, once managed to catch a 2½ lb trout on a river trip, bending his cane rod like a horseshoe in the process. After the fish was taken for weighing at the Scarnish Hotel, he was forever after acclaimed as a champion and expert. Another time, out sailing, they almost collided with a basking shark.

Then there was sand castle building. Ron, as an engineer, had strong views when it came to sand castles. His unvarying style consisted of a giant fort surrounded by concentric rings of ditch and wall, the outer moat to be

Tiree, Inner Hebrides, 1968: LEFT: From left to right: Peter, Camilla, Robbie and Vanessa with the nanny, Amanda Freer. RIGHT: The characteristic Ron Buxton sand-fort.

flooded. There was nothing whimsical about a Ron sand castle: they were practical, no-nonsense affairs, robust and defendable, and they became a trademark of the Buxtons at the seaside. As the children got older, the cottage on Tiree was exchanged for a lodge with trout and salmon fishing, then stalking and rough shooting at Kildermorie near Alness, and then at Borrobol, on the Helmsdale River in Sutherland. 'I don't think Dad much liked beaches,' said Robbie. 'We'd go to Tiree, but we never went to anywhere with warm water.'

In the winter, there was skiing. Aunt Anne, Phyll's older sister, and her second husband, Tom Hazlerigg, owned an apartment in Klosters where everyone would meet up for the Easter holidays. The Peugeot 504, with its three rows of seats, would be jammed to the roof with luggage, with more cases and skis strapped on the roof-rack. The journey out would take two days (there were fewer auto-routes then), with the car so overloaded that on one occasion, with six children and two adults, the tyre burst. Detours were made for cultural highlights not listed in the Baedeker guides, such as the blast furnaces around Metz.

Ron's skiing, everyone agrees, but Phyll puts into words, 'has to be seen to be believed'. His attire never varied: blue Parliamentary Ski Team anorak, blue trousers and engine-driver's cap. Skis were wooden, with poles of bamboo and basket-work – not that these were needed or used. His 'skins', for ski-touring, raised eyebrows even in the 1960s by being made of real sealskin. Stylistically, his arms remained straight out at all times, as did his knees: giving him a profile that was recognisable even as a dot on the horizon. There was, however, not a slope he could not negotiate. He led regular excursions off-piste (or 'off pissed', as he called it) on which, when the situation graduated from treacherous to dangerous, he would (in later years) produce a small bottle of Kirsch from his jacket, handing it round while making light of the situation. His mountain sense was acute, and on at least one occasion, in white-out, blizzard conditions when even the guide was lost, it was Ron who found the way down.

Ron with the Parliamentary Ski Team, Davos, 1966

A feature of these holidays engraved in the children's memories was the almost wartime level of frugality. At meals fruit drinks had to be shared and it went without saying that the cheapest item on the menu had to be ordered. (Later, once over sixteen, they were expected to pretend to be children.) Plates had to be cleared. Under no circumstances were fizzy drinks permitted.[53]

Despite these privations, the trips were a triumphant success. Not many families went abroad in the early 1970s, let alone skiing, and the joyous excitement of it all culminated every day with a reckless race in squadron formation down the woodland tracks to the town. Those early holidays implanted some of the children's happiest memories. For his part, Ron's most vital travelling companion, then as now, was his small transistor radio, on which, morning and evening, he would listen to the World Service. Truth be told, Ron liked his family holidays. But he liked his distractions, too.

*

Most of all, what Ron loved was a project. And projects, in unending succession, Kimberley had to offer. By 1970, the east wing had been converted into four (by 2013, seven) flats. The farm had a new herd of pedigree Lincoln Red cattle bought by Jim Prior. With a part-time keeper (shared with the neighbouring Cherrys at Park Farm), the shooting was improving. And the house and garden were under control. With the twins almost ten, Ness eight and Robbie six (the eldest three all boarding at preparatory schools), an important question now arose, one that was vexing many well-to-do families with country houses at the time. Tennis court? Or swimming pool?

Tennis courts – hard, maintenance-free asphalt surfaces enclosed within high perimeter fences – and heated outdoor swimming pools were by the end of the boom years of the Sixties the two novelty outdoor leisure accessories of the era. With so much room at Kimberley, there was really no reason to be restricted to one or other, other than *not* to be would be unconscionably extravagant. The vote came down in favour of a pool, as two neighbours had recently put in hard tennis courts. Accordingly, a grass tennis court was laid out near the garden entrance by the 'Gents'. It never proved very satisfactory, requiring constant rolling to counter the moles, while the surrounding netting proved an unexpected trap for hedgehogs.

For the pool, most people would have called in one of the many competing professional pool-builders. Not Ron. When Vanessa was born, they had employed a Spanish couple, José and Mañuella, to help cook, clean and look after the house. José, it turned out, had in a previous life been a builder. He

53 Anne's teenage daughter from her first marriage, Dana, would sometimes sing in the bars in the evening. She went on to be the folk, pop, rock and blues singer (45 albums by 2013), Dana Gillespie.

was also excellent at ironwork, blacksmithing and joinery. His motto was 'Todo se arregale menos la muerte' ('Everything can be mended except death'). Ron was an engineer. With Phyll, Mañuella and four children, there was both manpower and expertise aplenty under one roof. They would build the pool themselves.

Of all the projects over the years at Kimberley, the swimming pool is the one that is somehow most Ron. Here was a *grand projet* requiring chutzpah, ingenuity and engineering nous; a way of achieving a bargain and saving a packet. True, a pool would not actually earn money, but the final result would provide something Ron loved: swimming. The first question was where to build it. Swimming pools were ugly, so it should be hidden away. 'Lady Isobel's Garden', a former rose garden adjacent to the potting shed within the ten-foot walls of the kitchen garden area was selected as the ideal place. The pool, Ron decided, would be large by the standard of most pools (they were doing it themselves, so why not?), with a big shallow end because Robbie was still learning to swim. The shape would be oval, rather than the conventional rectangle, because this offered the maximum surface area for the minimum volume of water to heat (22,000 gallons).

After widening the opening into the garden to allow in a tractor, digging of the foundations began in the summer of 1970. The work was taken on by Ron's favourite local contractors, the father and son team of Syd and Roger Howard, aided and abetted by José. While Ron returned to work in London during the week, the Howards excavated, laid a concrete base and built up reinforced walls of block-work. This was lined with a heavy black butyl liner (the black colour supposedly to aid heat absorption).

The heating system was to be of Ron's own devising. Most British pools at the time – the warmer ones, anyway – relied on oil-fired boilers. A few companies, however, had started offering solar heating; cheaper to run, but expensive to install and questionably effective beneath overcast English skies. Ron plumped for solar, but decided he would adapt his own apparatus from a published design by Admiral Drax, an early pioneer of solar heating.[54] He contrived sheets of black-painted corrugated aluminium beneath a glass cover, south-facing, angled to 60° (the mean incidence of the midday sun between May and September). The water would then be pumped from the pool along a perforated 'sparge pipe' which trickled it slowly down the black corrugated sheets, warming as it did so, before being collected in a gutter at the base and returned to the pool.

---

54 Admiral the Hon. Sir Reginald Aylmer Ranfurly Plunkett-Ernle-Erle-Drax, KCB, DSO, JP, DL, whose name made him famous well beyond his naval career, and inspired some of the more colourful appellations employed by writers about the aristocracy, from P.G. Wodehouse to Evelyn Waugh.

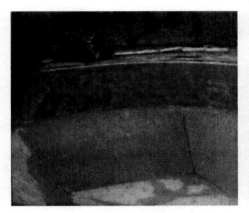

LEFT: The deep end blockwork; RIGHT: Roger applies black butyl liner in the shallow end

This, at least, was the theory. And, remarkably, it worked – up to a point, anyway. The great empty basin was gradually filled by hosepipe, taking a week. A wooden springboard was added at one end, and a set of professional-looking stainless steel ladder-steps at the other. The potting shed was converted into changing rooms and lavatory, with the fireplace becoming a chimneyed barbecue grill on which countless sausages would in due course be cooked and passed through the window to hungry swimmers. Phyll thatched the corner shed with Norfolk reeds (following instructions from a library book) to make an alluring summer house, and the metal swing seat from Holywell was brought in.

By June the pool was full, if chilly. By July the temperature was … well, if not exactly the 'warm tea' of certain oil-fired pools, at least appreciably warmer than it had been a month before. As for the colour of the water, it was an uncompromising black. If diving into this was a novelty compared to the crystalline, turquoise clarity of regular pools, then so be it. Everyone agreed: the pool was a triumph.

Ron's swimming pool rapidly became a byword for his resourcefulness and eccentricity. In hot summers, the water temperature frequently breached the 70 degree Fahrenheit mark. If higher temperatures remained elusive, it was simply because, the pool being so big, there was a lot of water to heat. Possibly, as Ron was the first to point out, the pitch of his 'solar panels' was a bit steep. The angle did not allow for the fact that most swimming takes place in June, July and August. During these months the sun is higher in the sky, so a shallower pitch would take fuller advantage of any rays on offer.

As for the blackness, after fifteen years the butyl liner was replaced with asphalt, and by popular consent this was painted turquoise, more in line with conventional pools. The result was to turn the water a definitely more inviting opaque green. The opaqueness remained irrespective of how many tubs of chlorine granules were added. Perhaps this was because the pool was so often filled directly from the river (by a four-inch irrigation pipe), and to the river state it constantly tried to return; perhaps it was because the solar heating apparatus was a perfect greenhouse for algae, the spores of which were conveyed directly to the pool. Whatever the cause, the solution was obvious and universally embraced: get used to murky water. The Kimberley pool gained a reputation for offering a bracing experience akin to loch or sea swimming, one which, despite consistent improvements over the years, it has never completely lost.

There would be more projects, plenty of them: the tree house (large enough to sleep in) in 1972; the trout pond, for which Robbie, aged eleven, spent ten hours a day carting spoil by tractor and trailer in 1974; a new steel boat house in 1988, to replace the one destroyed by the Great Storm of 1987; the dredging of the lake, requiring platforms like rafts for the diggers, in 1991,[55] the landing strip and hangar in 1995. But none, for sheer Heath Robinson ingenuity, engineering chutzpah, and overall pleasure given, could match the swimming pool.

*

In the summer of 1970, while the pool was being built, tragedy struck. In June, without warning, Jean was found dead at her home in London. Aged just fifty-three, she was only two years older than Ron. Now living in Chelsea, in the fashionable Little Boltons, apparently in the same rude health as Ron, she had been working on a book based on her D. Phil. thesis: 'The Religion of a Southern Sudan Tribe the Mandari' (1957).[56] The proofs were just going to press when, having failed to make a lunch appointment, she was discovered by a friend and Christopher Buxton, who rented the top floor of her house. The cause, it turned out, was a brain haemorrhage.

For Ron, it was the severest blow imaginable beyond something happening to Phyll or one of the children. Jean was his only shared blood, the only other human who knew the remoteness and exorbitant standards of his father, the trauma of losing first him, then their mother, so young. She was his witness to his success with the family business, his political triumph, Kimberley. For fifteen years, from his mother's death in 1942 until getting engaged to Phyll in 1959, Jean had been by far the most significant female presence in Ron's life.

55 Prior to dredging, Ron devised a novel system for controlling lakeside weeds: first he would raise the sluice gate by the dam to drain the water. This, after a few days, allowed the silt to dry out just sufficiently for him to cross it on skis. Thus bedecked, with a knapsack sprayer, the encroaching weeds could be confronted.
56 The book, *Religion and Healing in Mandari*, was published by the Clarendon Press in 1973 and remains the standard work on the subject.

They were each other's complete family. That Jean had never married only reinforced this connection. Forty years later, Vanessa, aged eight and away at school at the time, still vividly remembers the letter she received from Ron bringing the shocking news. 'It was so rare to get a letter from Dad at school that I couldn't work out who was writing it at first.' A single phrase stood out: 'She was my only sister ...' It was a fleeting acknowledgement of the depth of his internal anguish – addressed, as ever, by whirling, hectic activity.

As independent as Ron, as determined, and perhaps even cleverer too, or so Ron always said, Jean was a distinguished academic, a proto-feminist and a loner who guarded her emotions as closely as her brother did. Although she never held a formal teaching post, she lectured at the LSE. Did she sublimate the affection she lacked from her father or a husband on the Mandari, the subject of her studies and to whom she was plainly much attached? Perhaps significantly, after Jean left her house in The Little Boltons to Ron, he, in due course, passed it on to the girls of the family, Camilla and Vanessa. Her extensive collection of photographs of the Mandari was in 1988 donated by Ron to the Institute of Archaeology and Anthropology at the Pitt Rivers Museum, Oxford.[57]

*

Kimberley was large enough to accommodate most of Ron's interests. For a start, it provided a home for his ever-expanding collection of pianos. The best instrument was in the library, his grandfather's Steinway. Aunt Cicely had a story that it was made for the King of Greece, along with a mahogany-cased alternative (which he chose). Round this instrument, on winter evenings, the children would gather in front of the fire to sing while Ron played favourites like 'The Fox and the Geese'.

> The fox went out on a chilly night,
> He prayed for the moon to give him light ...

The library Steinway was complemented, in the music room, by the sturdy tropically-built Haake of Hanover grand, ferried from Saigon, via India; and a handsome Bechstein Aunt Cicely had left to Jean, which, when she died, reverted to Ron. In the drawing room was an antique forte piano (more *forte* than *piano,* the kind Beethoven would have played) made in 1808 by Thomas Tomkison – the nameplate engraved 'By Appointment to the Prince Regent' – plus a two-manual harpsichord (two keyboards) from the 1860s. In Ashley Gardens there was another baby grand.

The two pianos in the music room were kept for duets. Most of the time this meant Dr David Baker, organist at Wymondham Abbey and University of

57 Viewable at southernsudan.prm.ox.ac.uk/search/photographer/buxton/.

East Anglia librarian, but it was also in case Ron managed to snare a 'playing guest'. Music remained the one way, other than relentless activity, in which he could lose himself, and he made sure his children received thorough exposure. As well as the regular sing-songs, at bath time Radio Three would be playing, and all four children had piano lessons. Camilla would later receive a grand piano for her wedding present ('Even if you don't play it,' said Ron, 'it's somewhere to put the wedding photos.').

Then there was the organ. In 1965 Ron bought an electronic organ and installed it on the landing at the top of the grand staircase in the entrance hall. This was replaced with 'The Peterborough Console', a larger, mahogany instrument with ivory keys, in 1990 – formerly temporary organ at Peterborough Cathedral. It was not (as mentioned in chapter 13) the first time the house had had an organ. The alcove in the drawing room originally contained a Snetzler (one of the most distinguished organ-making names) in a classical mahogany case. The instrument in question, sold by Johnny Kimberley's mother to pay off her bridge debts, is now installed in the Wren Chapel at William and Mary College, Virginia, where it is the fourth oldest organ in the United States.

With the arrival of Ron's organ, the house occasionally acquired, at night, something of a *Phantom of the Opera* feel, as rousing hymns, haunting arias or great choral works rang out into the still Norfolk air. At other times, unsuspecting guests found themselves tootled, shaken or thundered awake

'My instrument really': playing the Peterborough Console on the first floor gallery

first thing on a Sunday morning as Ron practised church voluntaries for the 10.30 a.m. service at Carleton Forehoe (of which parish he was church warden as well as organist).

During the service the children were pressed to work pumping the organ. A weight on a string showed how much air was left, requiring redoubled efforts as it rose toward the line. Once, when Peter was ten, the handle fell off the pump and the organ conked out completely. The bellows are still not electrified.

The organ satisfied both Ron's love of music and his love of machines. Of all instruments, the organ is the most intensely mechanical. Every organ, unlike, say, the piano, is unique, with its own sound. An organ can – is designed to – imitate orchestras, with 'stops' (the stop-control which allows wind to flow into a given rank of pipes) such as 'flutes', 'oboes', 'clarinets', 'trombones' and so on. And while the sound is exactly predictable, continuing at the same pitch and loudness for as long as the key is pressed (unlike a piano, where each note is louder or softer according to how the key is pressed), making it despised by some keyboard musicians for its absence of subtlety, it also places immense resources at the organist's disposal. And no other instrument approaches an organ's power.

While this means the results of a mistake can be appalling, it also means there are an astonishing range of tone 'colours'. As well as all the orchestral stops there are dozens of others – diapasons, gemshorns, cornopeans. Playing a big cathedral organ has been likened to piloting a jumbo jet, and the flying analogy is no doubt apposite in Ron's case. Big organs require extraordinary multi-tasking abilities, with several keyboards (up to five) as well as pedal boards and hundreds of stops. Playing a morning service favourite, like Widor's *Toccata*, in which the tune is largely on the pedals, requires a physical and mental dexterity few can muster. (There are only a few thousand organists in the world.) Organists also know that there is a special, indescribable feeling to entering a church and climbing into wherever the console happens to be, getting organised, choosing what and how to play, then piercing the uncanny silence in a way that is, for a church or cathedral, so right.

Over the years, either through his attendance at the Incorporated Association of Organists' annual congress in one of Britain's cathedral cities, or the ten-day 'organ crawls' organised by Philip and Pam Carter across Europe, America and Canada, Ron has tried many of the best organs in the world. His favourites remain York Minster (arranged by his mother's sister, Aunt Dreda, and Uncle Tom, when he was staying on their estate at Grimstone Manor in Yorkshire during the war) and the seventeenth-century Snetzler organ in Eton College Chapel – a 'marvellous instrument' rendered better still by the chapel being 'a very resonant place'.

As Ron himself says of the organ: 'It's my instrument, really.'

The problem with being an organist, Ron soon discovered, was that it tied him down on Sundays; that, and the endless arguments with the clergy (which, he likes to point out, even Bach had to suffer). I discovered what this meant during the christening service at Kimberley church for Ron's grandson, Nat Buxton. Ron was organist, and the vicar, plainly pleased to have such an unusually large audience, proceeded to run through an interminable list of parish notices. After a few minutes he was cut off as the organ burst into life, and we were all piped briskly out of the church. I assumed, as everyone did, that this had been an error; that Ron, believing the vicar had finished, had set off a little early. Until, that is, Ron came up, his eyes gleaming. 'I warned him,' he said. 'He always does that. Prattling on, just as we all want to go.'

Often Ron was asked to play at friends' weddings, or those of their children. If, as was often the case, a preliminary inspection revealed the local church's instrument to be wanting, Ron would make arrangements to bring his own. Now an organ beats even a piano for sheer, cumbrous immove-ability; manhandling its vast weight down the slippery, polished wood steps of the entrance hall staircase, then outside and into the horse-box, was a quintessential Ron task. Four strong men would have to be marshalled at both ends. During the wedding service, Phyll or the children – Camilla and Peter especially, as they could read music – were press-ganged into page-turning duties. This was exacting work. 'Now!' Ron would say forcefully, and the page had to be turned – and not a split second later.

Incidents at these events, naturally, abounded. At the wedding of one friend, St John Agnew, with the service about to start, Ron realised he had left his music at Kimberley. The bridegroom's brother Bolton was despatched urgently to get it, with instructions that it was 'on the piano in the music room'. On arrival at Kimberley, however, Bolton, who had not been there before, found himself confronted by several rooms with pianos in, none with any music on them. Ron had to play without music …

One final bonus of having an organ at Kimberley was that it allowed Ron to keep up his other musical pleasure from Cambridge: choral singing. Twice a year, at Christmas and Midsummer, in conjunction with Wymondham Choral Society, 200 invitations would be sent out. Signs that the Big Day approached were to be found in packing cases of confectionery accumulating near the back door – wagon wheels, coconut snowballs, fig rolls, apparently delivered by Tardis. When the day arrived, the entrance hall would be thronged and the refrains of choral works – Handel's *Messiah* at Christmas, Handel's *Judas Maccabaeus*, Mozart's *Mass*, Fauré's *Requiem*, Mendelssohn's *Elijah* in summer – would waft out over the Norfolk countryside.

*

'What he likes is the machines': Havesting, Horse Park, 1990, Kimberley behind

So far as the farm went, too, it was not so much agricultural efficiency as love of machines that drove agronomic policy at Kimberley. Tractors, implements, combine harvesters, clearing the curved brick 'gun arches' of Capability Brown's land drains, converting an old combine into a mobile irrigation pump, installing a grain dryer in the east wing – these were the tasks he enjoyed. (And, always practically-minded, he had no compunction about cutting through old beams or eighteenth-century plaster mouldings to make way for pipes or practical requirements.) Phyll kept the cattle records and attended the birth of calves.

It was tremendously useful, of course, having a company steel works nearby in Wymondham (see next chapter), permanently on stand-by to fabricate whatever was needed for any new project. This might be a structure for a horse shelter, electric fence posts, supports for bridges, a prototype wood-burner to heat the entrance hall (still *in situ* today), a metal trolley and precisely-angled steel 'I' beam for the Little Boltons when a supporting wall was removed to enlarge the kitchen, and so on. Anything became possible.

This love of the technical and practical applied to most areas of Ron's life. Gardening was repeatedly mentioned as one of his hobbies in his political campaign literature, but neither plants nor landscape engaged him half as much as digging and sawing. When it came to food, an area in which he had little or no interest, he could still be delighted by gadgets, such as an egg boiling device, pressure cooker (a mark across the ceiling recorded the day it exploded) or apple peeler-and-corer.[58]

The critical part of serving game or poultry was the carving – 'you must have a knife with a good blade' – in order to produce wafer-thin slices in sufficient number that a single pheasant might feed five. No one but Ron was allowed near a Sunday roast – 'You'll ruin the joint'. Overcooked meat was detested because it was 'uncarvable'.

When home brewing kits appeared, Ron was immediately enthusiastic. He would mix vats of ingredients for stout, leaving them to ferment in a dustbin near the kitchen door. Naturally, this was routinely mistaken by everyone for *the* dustbin, with the result that an important part of the brewing process became the fishing out of crumpled paper, envelopes, tin cans and farm circulars from the mix. Over the year, empty bottles would be collected – the green Appelsaft bottles occasionally permitted on skiing trips were deemed ideal, because of their spring-loaded stoppers. Boxes of these would be brought back, clinking and rattling on the roof rack, ready for the final stage of the process. Once bottled, the brew would sit maturing next to the budgerigar cage in the kitchen. Periodically, in the Aga's warmth, bottles would explode, spreading broken glass across the kitchen and soaking the budgie.

Meanwhile, Ron's life remained as restlessly busy as ever, as if, like a migratory bird impatient to depart, to be still would be to be trapped forever. One small, documented glimpse of his scheduling survives in a letter from the distinguished architural historian Dorothy Stroud. In response to a letter from Ron requesting information for a school project by Vanessa on Capability Brown, the author of the famous monograph on the landscape gardener points out that not only have they not met, as Ron alleges, but, she continues primly: 'You kindly said that I might make a visit to Kimberley one day, but on making three different appointments with your secretary in London, she cancelled each of these in turn, either because you were having a shooting party or were otherwise engaged.'

*

Five or six times a year Ron would murmur darkly and disappear for strange meetings in London. Phyll and the children referred to these as his 'Mau-Mau meetings'. ('We never knew what went on and rarely asked.') These were formal, secretive occasions: for, following in his father's and grandfather's footsteps, in the 1950s, Ron found himself proposed for membership of Number Five Lodge – he was a mason.

58 He knew what food he liked, however, and it included sprats. Robbie recalls returning from a pike fishing expedition one day and throwing some left-over sprats into the dog bowl. Returning to the kitchen shortly later, he found Ron taking his discarded sprats out of the Aga and – still in the dog bowl – eating them with relish.

Meetings were held (as they were for all the masonic lodges in the London area) at the Freemasons' Hall, a huge, cathedral-like art deco building in Great Queen Street between Holborn and Covent Garden, headquarters of the United Grand Lodge of England and a masonic meeting place since 1775. Number Five Lodge consisted of London professionals – distinguished doctors, surgeons, lawyers and architects – and the ceremonies might number over 1,000 people. Having been admitted through the three initial degrees (apprentice, fellow, master) to become a full mason, over the next twenty years Ron had risen through the ranks to the 30th degree (the highest degree was 33rd).

These memberships were undoubtedly useful as meeting points. They introduced him to a friendly 'fraternity' he otherwise would not have encountered. His hunting tour with Phyll was arranged almost exclusively around people met through the Foxhunters Lodge. Similarly, when visiting a new country on business, being a mason provided an immediate entrée to the heart of things, and a deep understanding of the place. The Jersey Steel Company was set up entirely on the advice of someone Ron's father Murray had met, as a mason, in 1935. As for the handshakes, the passwords, the rituals and the secrecy? At this Ron smiles: 'The secret of freemasonry is that there is no secret.'

*

The practical effect of Ron's long absences was that Phyll brought up the children at Kimberley largely unaided, except by a succession of au pairs and boarding schools. Aged eight the children were despatched: Peter and Robbie to Summer Fields in Oxford, Camilla and Vanessa to Riddlesworth, near Diss. In the holidays, a *laissez-faire* approach operated. Everyone was free to run largely unchecked, on the condition they looked after themselves and didn't do anything too daft. It was a contract which suited everyone, even if it precipitated the odd crisis.

One summer holidays, for example, having built elaborate dens out of straw bales in a stubble field, Vanessa had the brainwave of communicating from one den to another by smoke signal. The resulting conflagration, when the bales went up, occurred so fast, with heat so intense, they were lucky to escape. As Ron and Phyll were out at the time, the children sent themselves to bed, drawing the curtains – knowing this would be their punishment.

Another time, in February, the river was up. The girls were out with the dogs, trying to walk across the weir of the lake. Normally a trickle, today it was like the Niagara Falls, and the dogs – Tewa and her daughter, Nazca, a pair of flat-coated retrievers – got washed over into the river. The dogs couldn't escape from the turbulence below the waterfall, so, thinking she had better rescue them, Camilla undressed to her bra and pants and waded in, followed by Vanessa, fully clad. Vanessa, being shorter, couldn't touch the bottom, and was being pulled relentlessly down until Camilla managed to drag her out. With the dogs still whirling helplessly, Camilla ran for help. The first person she encountered was Ken the gardener, who was so flustered at seeing a semi-naked, teenage Camilla, he ran in the opposite direction. Eventually Camilla found Phyll, who jumped on Blackie the pony, bareback with just a halter, and galloped to the rescue. By this time, of course, the dogs had got safely out by themselves.

One Christmas holidays Peter brought home a canoe he had made at Eton and it was decided to take it for a test on the river. Equipped with Christmas supplies of sweets and tangerines, everyone set off, radio playing cheerfully. Following heavy winter rain, the canoe was swept briskly along by the current. The weather, however, had brought trees and branches down across the river, which had to be ducked at intervals. All went well until, at one particular hazard, everyone ducked the same way. The canoe capsized, the crew went in, the radio was lost and a school of tangerines bobbed away downriver. Everyone traipsed home, soaked and freezing. The canoe had to be recovered from neighbouring land, an immaculately-kept racehorse gallops belonging to the Blooms (the trainer of Sir Humphrey, see chapter 13). In the soft ground, the rescue vehicle left a trail of deep, muddy ruts. The Blooms were furious.

Floods were not uncommon. When they were severe, such as in 1970, 1972 and 1976, the water was often deep enough for everyone to pile into boats and row over the fields – sometimes over wire fences.

In winter, if it froze hard enough, there was skating on the lake. Ron was an excellent skater, lacing on old-fashioned leather boots. Full of stories of how, at Cambridge, his grandfather had skated along the Cam to Ely, he would teach the children, showing them how to go backwards and even do pirouettes. Snow, meanwhile, in a county not noted for hills to toboggan down, required resourcefulness for full enjoyment. When it came, Phyll would improvise home-made harnesses for the ponies to tow the children's sledges. The ponies did not always take to this new role, so sledgers had to be ready for fast bail-outs when a terrified pony bolted. As the children got older, the sledges were replaced by skis, the ponies by Ron driving an old Daihatsu 4x4, towing the children like water skiers. It worked surprisingly well.

So Kimberley was a kind of giant adventure playground, presided over by parents who were up for almost anything. And as the children got older, the place adapted easily to every fresh enthusiasm. Which brings us to shooting.

*

Shooting – the sport of shooting reared or wild game birds such as pheasant, partridge, woodcock, or wildfowl, driven towards a line of placed guns – has long been akin to a religion for certain Buxtons. Norfolk, Buxton county, has always been pre-eminently a shooting county, with its great estates such as Holkham, Houghton, Raynham and Sandringham, and its vast coveys of partridges. 'It was largely the shooting that lured the Buxtons to North Norfolk,' wrote Aubrey, Lord Buxton, of The Emancipator, his great-great-grandfather. 'Thomas Fowell Buxton and his brother-in-law, Sam Hoare, rented or bought all the shooting they could lay their hands on, from Weybourne in the west to Trimingham in the east, and for some miles inland. It was an immense area...'[59]

Aubrey Buxton himself, conservationist, Anglia Television founder and assiduous royal courtier was (at least, in his early days) so mad about shooting and George VI that he wrote a book about the two.[60] Indeed, it is probably its shooting credentials more than anything (because so many Buxtons have been successful enough to buy country estates, and nothing consummates the country house ideal like the ritual of the shoot) that have singled out Norfolk as the family's chosen county.

Ron had done little shooting as a child, but had been in close enough proximity to be well aware of what it signified. At Britain's Lodge, in Sevenoaks, he had watched Murray put on tweeds on winter Saturdays to shoot with the Runges at nearby Montreal Park, where he had a gun, as well as, occasionally, at Easneye and Ponsbourne. But when they moved to Holywell, in Surrey, such countrified pursuits were not on offer, a change in circumstances which coincided with his entry to Eton where the shooting talk (with so many children from landed families) would have been incessant and inescapable. Given his impressionable age, did he, possibly, sense that his country credentials were lacking? It seems significant that, as an adult, he chose to dedicate his winter Saturdays to country sports, opting for the more exciting, active (and, of course, more readily accessible) hunting – engaging with the countryside in a way he perhaps felt he had not had the chance to as a child. Now, as the owner of a country seat, he was in the satisfactory position of having shooting of his own to offer.

Shooting is seldom just about shooting. The cult of the shooting weekend, at its heart, is the cult of the country gentleman. Here the rules of belonging to this august club are laid down, formalised and elevated to ritual. The shooting day offers, drive by drive, a tour of the estate, frequently with the seat at the

---

59 From the Introduction to *The Banville Diaries, Journals of a Norfolk Gamekeeper 1822–44* (1986) by Aubrey, Lord Buxton. Under Sir Thomas 'The Liberator' Fowell Buxton's instructions, Larry Banville, his keeper, was sent to Sweden to bring back capercaillie for release on Lord Breadalbane's Taymouth estate, where TFB was a regular visitor.
60 *The King in His Country* (1955).

estate's heart framed in the background. The offering and acceptance of hospitality; the execution of carefully presented birds (according to certain well-defined rules, which, to transgress, risks death, both socially and literally), the tipping of the keeper, the gift of the brace – the day is so larded with symbolism and sacrament that it is quasi-religious, each transaction offered or accepted as a mutual token of a shared ideal of education, class, politics and general outlook in life.

In this context, it is worth noting that one of Ron's most oddly endearing – and perhaps revealing – eccentricities has always been his insistence that Kimberley is not a large house. Following the death of Johnny, 4th Earl of Kimberley, in 2002, I drafted a light-hearted column about the dissolute peer for *Country Life*, mentioning that he, Johnny Kimberley, had described the place (in a piece in the *Daily Mail* on 30 July 1999) as 'a stately home the size of Blenheim'. When I showed the draft to Ron prior to publication, his only request was the deletion of this phrase. 'Why, out of interest?' I asked, to which his response, as if he were merely correcting a factual inaccuracy, was: 'Because it isn't big.'

Now, one can debate semantic niceties, and acknowledge that one of the charms of Kimberley is that, for all its grandeur, it is true, it doesn't feel excessively large. But the fact is that, even to those who have themselves grown up in large country houses, Kimberley indisputably ranks as a large house. When the children at Robbie's primary school in Barnham Broom were asked to count the number of chimneys their houses had, the vast majority answered 'One', a few rising to two or three. Robbie, when his turn came, was compelled to reply: 'Forty-five.' As Cynthia Kimberley had told Ron when he was looking round, there are thirty-three bedrooms. Does this reveal one of the impulses behind Ron's decision to buy Kimberley? Hinting, as it does, at a childhood sense of being the poor relation when visiting his relatives' great houses, Easneye, or Ponsbourne, as the vicar's grandson? Certainly, referring to Easneye, with its ten indoor servants and ten gardeners, he has regularly used the word 'Valhalla'. So it might be said that if the entire point and meaning of Kimberley could be distilled into a single event, that event would be the shooting weekend.

Shooting weekends, accordingly, were sacrosanct occasions. Shooting, Vanessa notes, *always* took priority over work commitments. There are signs, too, that shooting was significant in other ways. When Ron and Phyll eventually moved out of Kimberley, one of the few pictures they took to hang in the downstairs gents (along with an Eton house group, Ron's degree certificate from Cambridge and the framed front pages of his victory speech at Leyton) was a Victorian group photograph of six Buxton brothers on a shooting day in Norfolk in 1896.

There they are, gaitered, knickerbockered and bristling with tweed, eyes

Big shots: sons of Sir Edward North Buxton, 2nd Bt, after a shoot in Norfolk, 1896, and their Norfolk seats: LEFT TO RIGHT, STANDING: Charles Louis Buxton (Bolwick); Edward North Buxton (Knighton); Francis William Buxton (London). SITTING: Thomas Fowell Buxton, 3rd Bt (Warlies); Samuel Gurney Buxton (Catton): Henry Edmund Buxton (Fritton).

peering from shrubberies of whiskers, radiating self-assurance about their place in the world and Norfolk in particular. Yet contained therein is so much that is important to Ron: family, roots, shooting, Norfolk, all within a single picture.

Shooting offered a direct connection with Ron's Buxton lineage. Consequently any interest shown by his children in country sports was more than welcomed. The moment Peter showed an interest in fishing, Ron dug a trout pond. As soon as the girls were old enough, they were plonked on whatever ponies were available and taken hunting. But, always, shooting ruled. The keeper was detailed to instruct the children, the girls included. And the day he was allowed to stand next to his father in the duck butts by the lake was, Peter remembers, a critical rite of passage. When the girls continued shooting in later life, Ron was delighted – and even more so when Robbie, in line with Buxton tradition, proved completely obsessed.

This ultra-traditional side of Ron, rooted, perhaps, in a nostalgia for a childhood he never had, sits in contradiction with his non-conformity in other areas. Not that shoots at Kimberley ever followed entirely conventional lines. One guest recalls, at the pre-departure assembly of guns when the order of the day is announced, numbers are picked and safety reminders reiterated, being issued with but a single, unbreakable injunction, repeated for clarity: that the day was a 'cocks only' day. This meant that only cock birds – the males, easily identified by their larger size, darker plumage and longer tail feathers – were to be shot. Moments later, at the start of the first drive, the first bird of the day got up – plainly to all, a hen bird. It clattered passed Ron and was briskly dispatched.

Other sample anecdotes include Ron's inquiry of Peter's wife, Eleanor, having missed twice, 'Was that a cock or a hen?'

'Neither, Ron. It was a blackbird.'

Nor should be omitted the time, down by the lake, when Ron scored 'a left and a right' – a feat of marksmanship whereby a kill with the left barrel is followed immediately by a kill with the right, without the gun being lowered. Ron's 'left and right', it emerged, was of a pair of bats.

Ron's first shooting dog was a black Labrador called Dinka. As a retriever, Dinka was quickly recognised as a liability, a byword for disobedience, rushing after pheasants – anyone's, not just those shot by Ron – then hiding them or eating them. In between shooting days, Dinka frequently wandered, sometimes appearing at Barnham Broom village school (where Peter and Camilla were) or being handed in to the police (where, to reclaim him, Phyll once had to pay for a policeman's jacket which Dinka had chewed to pieces). Dinka was followed by a beagle, equally disobedient. After that, Phyll chose the dogs.

A shooting day at Kimberley usually began or ended down by the lake with 'duck-flighting'. For this, the guns had to steal quietly to camouflaged reed 'butts' to await unsuspecting fowl as, with the sun, they rose to depart at dawn or arrived back at dusk. The critical factor was silence, so the birds did not become aware of the guns until everyone was in position. Proceedings were always enlivened when a 'gun' in the semi-darkness straddled one of Ron's mains-wired electric fences. The bracing 240 volts, accompanied by screams of agony, invariably induced the clatter of departing birds without a shot fired.

As for shooting geese, which tend to take off before duck, here, in the excitement of the moment, it was Ron himself who had a tendency to open fire before the rest of the party had reached their butts. The result was the same.

*

As the children grew up, they started to become more aware of the ways their parents seemed different from those of their school friends. Two eccentricities were regarded as especially agonising. First was the ordeal of being picked up or dropped back at school. This formality was not conducted, as for many pupils, by a chauffeur in cap and uniform or, at worst, by a soberly-attired and innocuous-looking parent. Instead, it was done by Peter, the comprehensively-tattooed works driver for H. Young & Company – confirming in the Buxton children's eyes that their father was part of the criminal underworld.

The other cause of discomfort was Ron's habit, when out and about, of buttonholing dark-skinned strangers – usually waiters, or shop assistants – and inquiring where they came from, before saying something like: 'Jambo. Habari za jioni?' (Swahili) or, if they looked Asian, 'Assalam-o-alaikum, kya haal hain?' (Urdu) – languages in which (at least so far as he was concerned) Ron was fluent. Cringing with embarrassment, fearing for their safety, the children would pray for the ground to swallow them up. In fact, the usual response to Ron's greetings was delight at finding a white Westerner trying to address them in their own language. His attentions were also less random than his family probably imagined, as he knew from Jean and his travels exactly how to distinguish between say, a Tonga, a Nuer or a Kikuyu and had a knack for remembering obscure words in obscure languages.

As the girls' schooling drew to a close – Camilla went on to Branson's Tutorial College in Canada and Suffolk, while Vanessa transferred to Uppingham for her A Levels – Hugh Montgomery-Massingberd offered an appraisal of their qualities in a feature in *The Field*:[61]

'The daughters of these [Buxton] families are well-known for their good looks and their readiness to walk long distances beside their partridge-shooting men folk over heavy land in the teeth of the icy east wind. Sometimes, however, these tweed-clad sirens' love of animals may go a little too far: when, early this century, the pet lion of one family in the cousinhood killed their brother, they showed more concern for the lion than for the hapless youth, whom they reckoned had got what he deserved for teasing it.'

Meanwhile, the boys were finally beginning to earn their keep by bringing robust and energetic friends back to Kimberley who could be put to work about the place. Ron's recruiting drives were so notorious by the time Robbie was bringing his friends home – the commonest task being to be sent into the park to clear fallen or storm-damaged trees for the library fire – that the most regular recruits decided to form themselves into a club, 'The Loggers', which, even now its members have married, had children and scattered to all parts of the British Isles, continues to meet for an annual dinner.[62]

61 'Keeping Hold at Kimberley', 'Country Seats' series, *The Field*, 27 September 1986.
62 'The Loggers' were Robbie Buxton, Tom Coke, Nick Holmes, David Martineau, Charles Raymond and Damien Riley-Smith.

Aged eighteen, each of the children was given a car. Being granted such a freedom so early (and it was a decent car, too, worth £2,000, not a rattletrap of the kind Ron drove around in), Vanessa recalls, was uncommon even amongst her most privileged friends. Such uncharacteristic extravagance seemed less so when the reason was supplied: 'I thought if you had a car, you could be independent,' said Ron. He meant it, too. A couple of years later, aged twenty, Vanessa announced she would be taking her blue Ford Fiesta to Italy. 'Absolutely not,' said Phyll. 'Under no circumstances.'

Vanessa appealed to her father.

'Well, it's her car,' he said. 'She can do what she wants with it.'

*

As well as being the base for family, farming, shooting and music, Kimberley soon became the launch pad for the next stage of Ron's flying career. Since we left him in the cockpit of the Gemini in 1958, running short of fuel and daylight on the way back from Kimberley with Christopher Buxton, there had been no slackening in the incident rate.

A trip to Copenhagen started badly when, having been cleared to land at the international airport, and done so in about a quarter of the runway's vast length, Ron turned the Gemini round to find himself directly in the path of a four-engined airliner coming in to land. Despite taxiing hurriedly onto the grass to clear the way, the airliner aborted and went around again – avoiding calamity, but still making for the kind of incident over which jobs are lost and licences revoked. 'It's a pity you didn't clear the runway quicker,' said Air Traffic Control. 'It's a pity you let the DC6 in so close behind me' countered Ron. No more was said.

Landing the Gemini in the Avenue Field to the north-east of Kimberley, Ron discovered there wasn't really room to take off again. 'We took everything out: seats, surplus fuel, radio, everything, then took down a fence. We just made it; we *clipped* the top of the chestnuts.'

On a business trip to Jersey, descending through cloud, his passengers went into 'absolute panic' that they were going into the sea, until at 1,200 feet they popped out to see a huge liner heading into Cherbourg. It was the QE2. On another occasion, in 1960, Bridget Buxton recalls a day when Ron and Phyll flew up for lunch at Northrepps with Anthony Gurney, again in the Gemini, landing in a nearby field. After lunch John Buxton, Bridget's husband, accepted an offer from Ron for a quick aerial spin round Norfolk. Shortly after, strapped into the passenger seat, engines roaring ready for take-off, they didn't seem to be making any progress. Ron explained that unfortunately the plane was stuck in a rut. 'D'you mind awfully getting out and pushing?'

But now the Gemini was long gone. Ron's flying had paused in July 1964, as his parliamentary career had taken off. With not a spare moment to fly, by the time he lost his seat in 1966 his pilot's licence had lapsed. His trips to Africa were now more reliable if less adventurous affairs, aboard scheduled BOAC jets, in pressurised cabins high above the weather. As for the Proctor, in Sudan, and the Tri-pacer, in Kenya, the former had succumbed to woodworm (as all wooden planes in Africa do eventually) and the latter had been sold. Ron's love of flying, however, had not abated. And towards the end of the 1980s, a new opportunity presented itself when Robbie, myself and a friend, Roderick Corrie, the three of us motivated largely by Ron's flying stories, got together to investigate a new form of flying that was increasingly being reported in the newspapers: microlighting.

The word 'microlight' prompts conflicting responses. For many, these mopeds of the air are the last word in annoying, noisy, intrusions on a fine day. To others, with their open cockpits and 'by mail order' feel, they evoke the early days of aviation and a return to pure, seat-of-the-pants flying. The machine we chose was not most people's idea of a microlight (a hang glider with an engine): it had rigid wing-shaped wings, a propeller at the front and a tailplane at the back, and was controlled by a stick and rudder – 'Just like', as some were impertinent enough to note, 'a proper plane'. It had much in common with the earliest flying machines. Indeed, its layout was identical to Albert Santos-Dumont's 1909 'Demoiselle', a replica of which hangs in the Science Museum and was flown by the Frenchman in *Those Magnificent Men in Their Flying Machines*.

Both these aircraft were high-winged, monoplane tail-draggers, the main difference being that Santos-Dumont's had a bamboo frame with wings of

Santos-Dumont's 'Demoiselle' or 'Dragonfly': the template for the Australian Thruster

The Kimberley Syndicate – August 1993:
LEFT TO RIGHT: Antony Woodward, Dave Clarke (instructor), Robbie Buxton, Roderick
Corrie, Ron. BEHIND: The Thruster: Golf-Mike-Victor-Oscar-Yankee.

doped canvas, while ours had an aluminium frame stretched with Dacron
Terylene. Ours also had an Austrian two-stroke Rotax engine (designed for a
Snowmobile) with a pull-start; the seats were a pair of polypropylene,
stacking school chairs (as found in every 1970s classroom); and the tail-wheel
was from a shopping trolley. It had a wooden propeller and was designed in
Australia, where it was fitted with a klaxon to herd sheep. It was called a
Thruster.

The newly-formed 'Kimberley Syndicate' was instructed on its new flying
machine by Dave Clarke, a young microlight instructor who ran a flying
school out of RAF Swanton Morley, a grass landing field and RAF backwater
twelve miles north of Kimberley. Swanton Morley had the advantage, for
novices, of being the largest grass airfield in Europe. It also had, nearby, the
helpful landmark of East Dereham's funnel-shaped concrete water tower – an
indispensable orientation point in the otherwise almost featureless expanse of
East Anglia.

Having laughed loudly at Ron's tales of his flying misadventures, we now
found our own accumulating at a disconcerting rate – the non-Buxton
members of the syndicate particularly. Having booked two weeks' holiday to
make a start with the Thruster, we crashed her almost immediately. An engine
failure forced Roderick Corrie into standing corn, ending flying for the

summer. Soon after she had returned from a lengthy rebuild, the following year, it was my turn to write her off.

It was highly embarrassing confessing these cock-ups to Ron, the syndicate's elder statesman. ('What? Not *again*.') However, to our relief, his own incidents soon began to mount. After his maiden Thruster flight in July 1989, Ron regained his 'wings' – his full pilot's licence – thirteen months later, aged sixty-seven, well ahead of the rest of us. He was now free to take passengers, and Robbie, his most regular flying companion, vividly recalls one of these trips. Leaning out of the cockpit to inspect a field of standing corn below, Ron's helmet caught the slipstream and, as he had neglected to fasten his chin-strap, was unceremoniously plucked off, plummeting earthwards with the integral radio intercom, the map, and Ron's glasses. He and Robbie could only gaze helplessly as these items departed, leaving them to contemplate their interesting new situation, whereby the pilot-in-command could neither see nor hear. Somehow they got home. (The helmet was never recovered, though nor did Robbie's worst fears materialise: that, following this event, an irate farmer would call demanding compensation for the destruction of his brand new combine harvester.)

Taking Camilla up soon after, Ron decided to try a landing at Kimberley. Picking a big field of new stubble beyond the river, Horse Park, all went well until, shortly after touching down, the left-hand wheel caught a tractor rut.

Helmets and harnesses secure: Ron in the left-hand (flying) seat prepares for take-off with Robbie at Swanton Morley. 'I always seem to have the wrong glasses' he often observed at the controls. 'I can read the map, or see where I'm going, but never both.'

The Thruster span round and the wheel sheared off. Neither pilot nor passenger were hurt, however, and with Camilla's help Ron soon had the Thruster propped on a bale of straw to improvise a repair. From his workshop at the house, Ron found a bolt of a promising gauge, if rusty and a bit long. The four or five inches of surplus length to the point where the thread began he padded out with an assembly of nuts and washers of mixed size, origin and age – mostly, it appeared, from the workshop floor. The result, while serviceable enough to re-fix the wheel, was neither pretty nor high-tech. It got Ron back to Swanton, however, where I happened to be waiting with Dave Clarke.

As Ron taxied up, it was clear that something was wrong, as the Thruster crabbed badly to the left. Clarke was not impressed with Ron's makeshift repair, nor his airy assertions of 'a jury rig' that was 'perfectly sound'. Amateur aircraft modifications, he pointed out curtly, were illegal as well as potentially lethal.

'You know what this smacks of?' he said, clicking his tongue and cocking his head one way then the other as he inspected the makeshift repair. 'I'll tell you. It smacks of *Ron* …'

As was so often the case, the Thruster was more damaged than she looked, and she disappeared for another lengthy rebuild. As for us, despite cheerfully describing every bodged fix we came across after that as a 'jury rig', the truth is we were privately in awe of Ron's robustly self-reliant approach.

As the rest of us got our licences, the question of a permanent home for the Thruster at Kimberley arose. A wet January Saturday was spent pacing out parts of the park of varying degrees of unsuitability, until it became evident that the field where Ron had come to grief with Camilla, Horse Park, was much the most promising site. A grass strip was sown, a small steel hangar erected by Ron's Wymondham engineering works and, in due course, an orange windsock was raised on a telegraph pole.

The grass landing strip, visible bottom middle

The new airfield undoubtedly had character. Barely wider than a country lane, it had a pronounced gradient for two thirds of its length, then a slight hump, so that the two ends were never visible simultaneously. Approaching from the south-west, the landing was downhill – unsettling as the Thruster had no brakes. From the north-east, meanwhile, the combination of trees and the water of the trout pond guaranteed choppy air on the final approach. Intense concentration was required, especially as additional seasonal hazards included flooding at the downhill end in winter and absent-mindedly

The second Thruster, Golf-Mike-Zulu-Hotel-Alpha, outside the new hangar, 1997

placed straw bales in summer. Approaching from the west or south-west on a clear evening, however, the orange brick of Kimberley's Park Front caught the setting sun: a beacon visible from twenty miles away. To spot this, after a long trip, then see the tiny strip – often, in summer, running between standing barley rippling in the breeze – was flying Nirvana.

The Thruster's end came in a bright blue flash and a series of loud bangs and crunches, when Robbie and I entered the Round Britain Rally in 1996, and I flew her into some power cables near Lockerbie. Neither of us was hurt, but this time she was unequivocally beyond repair. ('You can't be too careful when it comes to wires,' said Ron. 'I remember once coming out of a dirt strip in Ol'Molog …') We replaced her with an updated model (with fuel gauge), paying more attention to the colour scheme this time: blue pod, blue and green wings, blue and green tailplane. 'My house colours' said Ron.

Ron eventually surrendered his pilot's licence in 2003, on his eightieth birthday. I asked him many times what exactly it was he liked about flying so much. His response was always the same, accompanied by one of his odd, slightly suspicious looks: 'I just like flying.'

*

Everyone knew that the only reason Kimberley worked was because of Phyll. Much as she enjoyed saying how much she disliked the place – not only the house, she liked to clarify, but the whole *county* of Norfolk, her home being the chalk streams around Romsey – it was viable only because, deep down, she embraced it so completely. At Kimberley, Phyll was in charge. Anyone forgetting this fact was set straight in the unambiguous language of a naval captain's daughter.

There was a tacit understanding that, with or without the necessary staff, Kimberley should continue to function as if the social changes wrought by two World Wars had not occurred. Thus there were dinner parties and house parties, barbecues and bonfire parties, shooting weekends, concerts and pony shows. Family, friends, friends' children, children's friends and guests arrived and departed in a never-ending stream. To make such an ambitious schedule possible, with minimal help, on a tight housekeeping budget (towards domestic matters, as to himself, Ron defaulted to a natural frugality) required feats of organisation and resourcefulness bordering on the biblical. It lead to occasional incongruous sights – for example, on a midsummer afternoon, a lone Phyll on hands and knees on the South Terrace lawn, engaged in the dauntingly labour-intensive task of transplanting bedding plants into the eight crescent-shaped borders around the rose-beds. ('Someone's got to do it. So I suppose it has to be me.')

With so much ground to cover, so many bedrooms to look after, so much catering constantly called for, Phyll devised her own ways to run her empire.[63] Certainly there was no room for indolence, incompetence or, Heaven forbid, obstruction from those around her. Nor, faced with them, did she shy from plain speaking – frankly, economically, and with total disregard of the consequences.[64]

Over the material infrastructure, undoubtedly, Ron's signature dominated. Everywhere there was evidence, past or present, of his enterprises. Turning in between the lodges, for example, for many years the first thing to confront any visitor was a push-button device on a long metal arm (not unlike the starter button at a car wash). Pressing this, once upon a time, activated an electric gate mechanism. But long after the mechanism had died or been disconnected, the button remained.

63 'Opening doors more or less at random, [Mrs Buxton] settled on a room containing two beds and a mountain of furniture stacked under dust sheets. There was a musty smell, which turned into the heavy scent of vanilla near the window. As she pulled the curtains on their noisy metal runners I glimpsed a branch of wisteria, laden with flowers, which had grown through the open top sash of one of the windows. It was at least an inch thick. "I don't think anyone's slept in here recently," she said. Her tone implied that this was to our advantage. Tugging on the frayed, plaited cord of an ancient electric fire to check it was plugged in, she flicked the toggle. Sparks fizzed from the middle section, where one of the ceramic bars had at some stage been broken, though the wire remained intact. "Make sure you switch it off," she said sternly. "The last person left it on for three months."' – *Propellerhead* (Harper Collins, 2001).
64 One summer, installed in the attic flat with Roderick Corrie for a fortnight's flying, night after night Phyll plied us with drink and home-cooking until we felt the least we could do was take her out for a meal. For a couple of hours, we glimpsed a Phyll unencumbered by her Kimberley task-list. She spoke of growing up during the war, of her family, of her time in Argentina before her mother died. When we got back, we parked outside the back door and mumbled cheery goodnights before heading upstairs. In the morning, a folded note was under the car's windscreen wiper. How delightful, we thought, finally to be in a position to *receive* thanks from Phyll. Her message was scrawled in firm capitals: 'SELFISH PARKING. THOUGHTLESS BEHAVIOUR MAKES LIFE A MISERY FOR OTHERS.'

Similarly, inside the house. Ron improvised a system of double-glazing consisting of polythene sheeting stretched across Talman's sash windows. And snaking pipes of sequential hot water systems converged upon every bath tub. Only by trying the taps could you ascertain which was current. Likewise, most bedrooms offered an assortment of round and square, two and three pin electrical sockets. As a child, Peter remembers, the house felt like a great ship, a liner, which to keep on course required constant trips by Ron into the boiler room, the cellars, the attics, the roof – to remedy problems and keep the place going.

Domestic matters, however, the running of the household, were Phyll's domain. The kitchen, accordingly, was the hub of Kimberley. It was the first room entered from the 'back' door (at the front, on the left); the everyday entrance. There, beneath a counter beside the Aga, rattling on long chains, resided two large flat-coated retrievers. Insanely affectionate, anyone who absently stood too close found a pair of paws planted on their chest. Kitchen implements included a vice mounted on the central island, and a fax machine. The dishwasher was raised a few feet off the floor to allow the relentless cycle of loading and unloading without bending down.

Other Buxton innovations included a two-door cat-flap opening directly onto the main food preparation areas, an 'Access All Areas' privilege not squandered by 'Breadboard', 'Woglet' and their successors. Most of the kitchen appliances carried caveats in red Dymo-tape: '5 AMP ONLY', 'USE ONLY LEFT SIDE OF TOASTER', 'DO NOT TURN UP TO FULL'. Other notices, 'DON'T WASTE WATER', or, above sockets with Lego-like accretions of adaptors, 'ONLY ONE AT A TIME', hinted at a fragile infrastructure. Sometimes a cryptic warning, accompanied by a curious smell, addressed the world in general: 'SOMETHING IN OVEN'. This could mean anything from shortbread to a slow-cooking rabbit, fur and all.

Yet these were the rules that kept the place running. Horizontal surfaces, apart from those bearing, say, wooden trays of fruit awaiting processing, heaps of pigeons awaiting plucking, crockery, jam jars or deliveries, were piled with paper: letters, magazines, circulars, copies of the *Eastern Daily Press*. Accordingly, any new piece of paper unthinkingly added to this litter was lost instantly and irretrievably. Of Ron and Phyll, it was Phyll (or so her sister Anne always said) who was the untidy one. Ron was tidy-minded; even if his desk at Ashley Gardens or Kimberley was not exactly clear, he always knew where everything was. Phyll's mind worked differently.

Take the chest freezer opposite the back stairs. Unwary visitors asked to fetch frozen items (usually involving pheasant) were often surprised to find packages labelled 'blue tit', 'blackbird', 'squirrel' or 'jay'. These creatures, tentative inquiry would reveal, had died of natural causes and were merely awaiting the taxidermist. When Vanessa's budgie died, it was only natural to freeze it as a reference for colour for the replacement. One visitor, encountering a large bag of frozen moles, was told that they would be surprised how many were needed for a single moleskin waistcoat (forty, in fact). When Phyll's handbag went missing and no leads were forthcoming, no one was especially surprised when, some days later, it was discovered in the chest freezer.

True, when it came to Ron's mechanical bits and bobs – car batteries, lavatory cisterns, folding kayaks – obviously there was no knowing when such items might be useful again, so it was only sensible to keep them. But the relentless accumulation of stuff for stuff's sake – that was Phyll. And so, like silt, it collected – in the kitchen, in the larder, along the corridor of the top floor. (One of the contrasts at Kimberley was always the relative emptiness of the formal rooms compared to the clutter of the domestic quarters.) Most of all, however, it occurred in that secret chamber, that holy of holies, the former strong room, that was Phyll's office. Here, past the chest freezer, was the perfect maelstrom, as if all the contents of all the handbags in the world had been simultaneously emptied into a single heap.

So, for the children, growing up at Kimberley was an unpredictable mixture of lordly grandeur and postwar improvisation to make ends meet – a lesson in self-sufficiency, self-reliance and fairy-tale romance. The confident, trusting, unmollycoddling, 'if-duffers-will-drown' nature of Phyll and Ron's parenting sometimes surprised the children's friends. Angus McCullough (now a QC) recalls the occasion he and Robbie returned from a microlight trip well after dark. Having safely landed after a delayed and harrowing final flight, necessitating hedgerow hopping at telegraph pole height to keep in sight of the ground through fast-forming mist and fading light, it struck him how demented with worry his parents would be under such circumstances – and what a row such a situation would prompt. Steeling himself for the inevitable dressing down as they entered the Kimberly kitchen, he was a little surprised to find that their absence had not even been noticed. 'Ah,' Ron hailed them cheerfully. 'You're just in time for an oyster.'[65]

---

65 Upon being reminded of this story, Ron was quick to point out that he has always *detested* oysters. The molluscs in question, it seems, were a present from friends just arrived from the north coast.

17

'Young's Steel Girders Span the World'

WHAT WITH ATTENDING to his new country seat, new wife, new family and new parliamentary career, it might seem that Ron had abandoned his business career. Not so. Although most of his energies were directed towards generating orders in Africa, plenty had also been going on in Britain.

H. Young & Company had joined the frenetic postwar building boom. The new era brought with it a whole new set of structural steel requirements: one was for the new towns, to house the rapidly expanding population being generated by the postwar 'baby boom'. Young's won a major contract for supplying Harlow New Town.

Another requirement was for entertainment. Where previously Young's had supplied steel for cinemas, now it was television that needed it, to build the towers that carried the broadcasting aerials. H. Young & Company got the order for the Manchester-Edinburgh link. By the end of the Fifties, the steel-frame was standard for buildings of every kind, almost everywhere. Fabricated sections and complete 'skeletons' in kit form streamed out of Lea Bridge and Durham Steel (its northern subsidiary) destined for factories, warehouses, department stores, bus stations, hospitals, bridges and almost every other kind of building across Britain and much of Africa. 'Young's steel girders span the world' trumpeted the headline to a feature about the company in Leyton's *Express and Independent* on 22 May 1959, handily timed for an election year (Harold Macmillan eventually called the General Election in October). By now more than 100 worked at the Leyton factory, surrounded at any given moment by more than 2,000 tonnes of mild steel, waiting to be cut, punched, drilled, riveted or welded.

There were many reasons for Young's healthy order book. One was that the company was continually coming up with new ideas. These included a 'collapsible building' hinged at the key intersections so that, without cranes or other heavy equipment, it could be pulled up by rope. In 1954, however, came their winner: they pioneered a system for curving girders without sacrificing strength, subsequently patented. A measure of the value of this technique, which they called 'curved construction' (and which was employed to fabricate the towers for the Mtwapa Bridge, Kenya) was that, in the five years following its conception, the company received more than £1 million-worth of orders for it.

Another reason for the company's success was the steadily increasing flow

From Leyton's *Express and Independent*, May 1959. A subtle, but timely, plug for Leyton's Conservative candidate with a General Election looming?

of orders from abroad. Ron had spotted, in postwar colonial Africa, a remarkable business opportunity. Everyone knew that one day the sun would set on Britain's imperial past. Independence, in the postwar world, was in the air, with Burma and India setting the example. Sooner or later the countries of 'British' Africa would follow. In the meantime, however, by a quaint historical anomaly, more of postwar Africa was 'pink', or under British control, than ever before. For British companies, this meant significant trading advantages, and as the vast majority of these territories had no access to structural steel, why not make the most of it?

By the Sixties, the five overseas outposts of H. Young & Company that Ron had started (or bought into), in Rhodesia, Kenya, Sudan, Nigeria and Zambia, were generating regular and increasingly large orders for the Lea Bridge works – eventually for huge projects such as factories, breweries and power stations as well as the more regular warehouses, schools and villages. (In Darfur, a province of the Sudan, one year the company handled the entire building programme.) Countless storage buildings were built along the Nile. In several countries Young's was the first and, for a time, only steel company. 'Recent orders, such as a hospital for Ghana or store houses for Nigeria now enable [the company] to talk of "Our man in Lhasa" as casually as the Foreign Office are reported to talk of "Their Man in Havana",' declared the *Express and Independent*.

'Their man' meant someone like Jocky Buxton in the Sudan. He would be responsible for generating sales, following up inquiries, and, once a building was commissioned, overseeing its fabrication, delivery and erection. In some offices, such as for the first couple of years in Nigeria, a single sales representative was enough. As orders began to multiply, or if a contract was large enough (such as Khartoum North Power Station), expatriate British engineers might be sent out from England to supervise. Local staff, obviously, fluctuated by the job. In difficult areas such as Zaire or Uganda, projects would be handled from the nearest neighbouring country.

The larger offices, such as Port Sudan for shipping materials into, Khartoum and Nairobi, gradually equipped themselves with transport equipment, trucks, cranes, winches and other plant, hiring additional kit as required. Small factories were fitted out for fabricating smaller jobs. Bigger contracts were designed, and even sometimes partly assembled, at Lea Bridge in London, then shipped. In several countries, such as Rhodesia, Kenya and the Sudan, where H. Young & Company were the first (or partners in the first) structural steel companies, there was no competition at all. Even when European companies started to arrive, Young's had the advantage of offering a complete service, from design through to erection.

None of the African companies was easy to run. The distances it was necessary to travel, especially in the Sudan, were vast, the roads appalling. There were never ready facilities on the ground; everything that could possibly be needed had to be provided; every eventuality catered for or coped with.[66] Corruption was endemic. When the Kenyan company H. Young (East Africa) got into serious financial difficulties, it was eventually revealed to be due to the Asian finance director embezzling £100,000 – then serious money. Soon after, the manager of the company was killed while on a trip to supervise an erection project in Zambia when his car went off the road in mysterious circumstances. Ron remains convinced he was murdered by someone tampering with the steering, for when he (Ron) got to the Nairobi office he was confronted by a suspiciously unanimous delegation refusing to work unless a particular, very second-rate, man was appointed as senior manager. These two factors together would spell the end for the company.

In the Sudan, a steel-hulled Nile boat was commissioned by the Mahdi family, the late-nineteenth-century rulers of the Sudan, in Khartoum. Having

66 Scheduled transport was so erratic in Africa that no opportunity could afford to be missed. When travelling from Zimbabwe to Zambia, Ron would get himself dropped off at Victoria Falls, then walk across the bridge into Zambia, carrying his trusty aluminium suitcase. On one occasion the managing director in Zambia was waiting for Ron (as arranged) at the Congo border. Having concluded he must have missed him, he was about to leave when a lorry carrying chickens pulled up. From the back emerged a dishevelled figure with a briefcase, dusting himself down and brushing off feathers – Ron, of course.

Ore-crushing plant, Zambia

Cotton ginnery, Egypt

fitted it up with the engine, the family visited because they said they wanted to take it for testing, then disappeared down the Nile and were never seen again. In Rhodesia, where the RESCCo (Rhodesia Engineering and Steel Construction Company) works had been fitted out to service Class 20 Garratt steam locomotives, business declined simply because Africans preferred diesel

Sugar refinery, Sudan

Grain bins, Fiji

Water tower, Nigeria

locomotives – because they could get commission on buying diesel, but not on buying coal. Backhanders were expected at every level. Collecting money was always difficult. The toll booth at the Mtwapa Bridge was continually being held up or embezzled, until an honest manager was found (and he was subsequently shot by robbers).

For all the difficulties in running them, however, the African operations were a huge success. Over the succeeding decades, where the British company's fortunes would inevitably have moved in lock-step with those of the boom-and-bust building trade (which, in turn, followed the general economy), the African contracts supplied a precious, steadying balance. Much work was grant-aided. At their peak, from 1960–70, the Nairobi works were employing as many as the London works – about 100 – while the Zambian operation employed 400 in four different fabrication works. RESCCo, in Bulawayo, employed over 1,000 and in forty-seven years the company built more than 3,000 railway wagons, tank cars and high-sided wagons on a highly-efficient production line run entirely by Africans.

By the 1970s contracts in East and Central Africa were beginning to involve more civil as well as structural engineering, involving concrete as well as steel work, such as large water towers or the aerial rope-way at Atbara cement factory, in the Sudan, to carry materials across the Nile. When the company did not know how to do something, specialised work was subcontracted. The most difficult project ever tackled was the erection of two giant ellipsoidal water towers in Northern Nigeria, both over 30 metres (100 feet) tall, the largest of which had a capacity of 1½ million gallons. The 1½ inch (3.8 cm) thick steel plates on the underside of the tanks had to be welded *in situ*, up in the air, an awkward and dangerous undertaking.

On another project, at Bukoba, in Tanzania, building the new Catholic cathedral in 1968, potential disaster was averted when Ron arrived to find the owner of the cathedral had cast concrete on the roof six inches (15 cm) deep instead of the specified design load depth of two inches (5 cm). Seeing that the girders had already stretched, Ron ordered the inspecting party off the roof, urgently, in case it collapsed. It certainly would have done, in time, but the steelwork was swiftly reinforced to carry the extra load.

The coming of independence was always going to be a threat to the African operations. After almost two decades, during which big contracts had arrived from Nigeria (such as the Guinness brewery at Enugu, Eastern Region) and nearby Ghana and Benin, in the 1970s the government instigated its policy of 'Nigerianisation'. This prevented foreign companies or interests from holding more than a 49 per cent share of Nigerian companies. Trading, already handicapped by the introduction of import duties, became pointless, sale the only option. Having completed the sale of Nigerian Steel Construction Ltd, however, in the early 1970s the purchaser went to the Nigerianisation agency, contested the value of the company, and ultimately not a penny was paid – the fate of many foreign companies operating in Nigeria at the time.

As British influence in Africa weakened through the 1980s, and dwindled in the 1990s, so political and financial operating conditions worsened. Ron had always known this was a risk, that his companies were windows of opportunity slowly, but steadily, closing. The new regimes that independence brought tended to wreak havoc for British companies. After the corruption issues with the Kenyan company, H. Young (East Africa) Ltd, in Nairobi, changes in government policy by President Moi's government finished it off in 1984. It went into liquidation, was bought by the president's family, and now flourishes – in the ownership of Moi's son. The Mtwapa Bridge was replaced in 1985 by a Japanese concrete dual carriageway. The company was compensated, but exchange controls and the fast-devaluing Kenyan pound meant the compensation soon melted away to almost nothing.

In Sudan, following Omar al-Bashir's *coup d'état* in 1989, and the rise of Islamic extremism (which included the government inviting Osama Bin Laden to base himself in Khartoum), finding a suitably qualified manager became impossible. The job specification would have required the applicant to be a qualified engineer, a good contractor as well as general manager, to speak Arabic and have the diplomatic skills to cope with Arab ways of business. Such people simply didn't exist, so after the last manager left, in 1992, the company was sold. By this time, the British embassy was almost under siege. H. Young & Company had the distinction of being the last British company in the Sudan.[67]

In Rhodesia, RESCCo, which had become by far the biggest company in which H. Young & Company had an interest, continued trading after 1965 when the white minority government under Ian Smith made its Unilateral Declaration of Independence (UDI) against the UK. It even continued trading through the civil war that followed, until the official independence agreement of 1979, brokered by the British government, when Robert Mugabe became president. In 1980, the year Rhodesia's independence was recognised as legitimate by Britain and the United Nations, RESCCo was floated on the Zimbabwean Stock Exchange (renamed the Zimbabwean Engineering Company, or ZECO). This had the effect of vastly diluting H. Young & Company's original one-third share, but at least allowed trading to continue. After this, however, a series of bad debts, poor management decisions, interest accruing at 30 per cent, and other financial difficulties effectively rendered the company bankrupt. Ron was the only original director still on the board in 1995, when closure became inevitable.

And so, leaving behind a remarkable legacy of development in a developing country, H. Young & Company's operations in Africa drew to a close. Everywhere, that is, except Zambia. Zambian contracts centred around the mines of the Copper Belt. In this region – around the towns of Ndola, Kitwe, Chingola, Luanshya and Mufulira – the local ore is so rich in copper that, since the nineteenth century, copper mining has been the defining industry, and copper Zambia's principal export. Ron and his Austrian-born partner Willi Eggar had bought two engineering companies in the 1950s, Raine

---

67 Jocky had left Khartoum when his daughters went to school in England.

Engineering and Trusteel, in what was then the British colony of Northern Rhodesia. Initially the companies were run from the RESCCo office in Bulawayo, but this was increasingly difficult after Northern Rhodesia's independence from the UK in 1964 when the Republic of Zambia was formed under President Kenneth Kaunda. In 1973 this became impossible, when the Zambia-Rhodesia border was closed, following Kaunda's establishment of training camps for guerilla fighters for Robert Mugabe's ZANU party, to assist in the civil war in Rhodesia. Willi Eggar, who had started out as an erection manager with RESCCo, became general manager in Zambia.

At its peak the copper mines generated so much business that the Zambian operation became one of the largest employers of H. Young's African subsidiaries, with eighty European staff. However, in the mid-1970s world copper prices plunged, and this, combined with the political and economic shenanigans of Kaunda's bellicose regime, began to cause chaos. With a lack of interest from other directors, Ron and Willi Eggar decided to buy the company from ZECO with revenues generated from four big contracts. By 1982, with corporation tax running at 40 per cent, the business was uneconomical. Kaunda, however, with Zambian agriculture in a disastrous state, had reduced tax on farming to 15 per cent. So Ron and Eggar came up with a new venture.

A holding of 500 acres was bought adjacent to Eggar's home at Musenga, near Chingola, and KSH Farms Ltd was set up. (The initials, which stand for K.S. Holmes Ltd, have no particular significance; they were taken from an electrical business Eggar had taken over.) Primarily the farm would ranch cattle, but also raise pigs. Despite having no farming experience, Eggar put his engineering nous to work – together with equipment from the steel company – and constructed dams and irrigation systems to improve the grassland. He built feed stores in preparation for difficult times.

Soon, administered with robust efficiency, the farm was absurdly more effective than the surrounding land farmed by Europeans. Several approached KSH Farms to ask if the company would be interested in buying their land. With new blocks either side of the Kafue river (a tributary of the Zambezi), the size of the managed acreage increased. More farmers approached wishing to sell, until now the operation consists of twenty-six farms in five separate blocks, covering 10,000 hectares (25,000 acres) in all – one of the biggest farms on the Copper Belt.

*

Back in Britain, the parent company H. Young & Company and its British subsidiaries had been having triumphs and troubles of their own. Through the Sixties, big high street names like Marks and Spencer, John Lewis and Cow & Gate (later Unigate) brought a steady flow of repeat business, with

[276]

'One of the biggest farms on the Copper Belt':
KSH Farms Ltd, near Chingola, with land either side of the Kafue river.
BOTTOM PCTURE: Ron (standing), Willi Eggar (sitting), on a visit in 2009.

[277]

warehouses and processing facilities as the commonest commissions. Demand during these years was so strong that sales offices were opened in Aylesbury and Guildford.

After buying Kimberley in 1958, Ron considered the possibility of a works serving East Anglia that would be near his country seat, yet have good rail connections to the region. In 1962 he built a new 'cold-rolling' mill on the eastern outskirts of Wymondham. The main building consisted of a dextrously recycled steel-framed hangar the company had just been contracted to take down at Jersey Airport. The new mill, called Eastern Sections Ltd, rolled or pressed chiefly standard, off-the-shelf, steel products such as 'Z' purlins. These ingenious structural members form an integral part of modern lightweight steel roofing, so-called because of their Z-shaped profile – lighter, for its weight, than a 'C' profile, stronger than an 'I' profile. Over the following years, 800 tonnes of Z-purlins were exported to build a new steel mill in Brazil. Other steel orders to the Wymondham company included a new port in Honduras, and exports to Africa, the Middle East, Indonesia, Russia and even Antarctica. In 1970 the works spawned an engineering division, manufacturing agricultural machinery such as the bale accumulators that farmers tow behind small balers, lorry bodies and trolleys for airport ground support equipment.

In 1971 H. Young & Company celebrated its centenary, establishing it as one of the oldest structural steel fabricators in the world. The following year, that century of experience was rewarded with their largest-ever commission: the Jumbo Jet Hangar Number 2 at Heathrow Airport. This vast building, designed by Z.S. Makowski & Associates and comparable in scale to the First World War airship hangars at Cardington, enclosed enough space for simultaneous servicing of two Boeing 747s and was only the second shed on such a scale in the UK. The 2,500-tonne roof structure, after final assembly on trestles at Heathrow, was jacked up 41 feet to its final position over four days using 56 jacks.

Changes to the company in the 1970s were driven, as for so much of British industry, by union problems and industrial disputes. By 1974, Durham Steelwork, the Gateshead works opened by Murray Buxton in 1937 to capitalise on government grants to regenerate the Tyneside area, became simply unworkable. The closed shop practices, whereby all employees were forced to belong to militant unions, were bedevilling almost every company in the area. Something had to be done to break their grip.

Secretly, the directors found and bought a site for a new factory near Thirsk in Yorkshire. (Ron chose the location at least partly for sentimental reasons: it was ten miles west of his cousins, the Brookeses, of Grimstone Manor, Gilling East, with whom he had stayed thirty-four years earlier when, as a sixteen-year-old Etonian, he had bicycled up the Great North Road in the summer of

ABOVE: before, and BELOW: after: the 747 Service Hangar, Heathrow, 1972, by Z.S. Makowski & Associates

1940.) Initially, the planning application was refused, but through his parliamentary connections Ron knew the recently-elected local MP, Leon Brittan.[68] Through Brittan, the application was pushed through.

In absolute secrecy, a brand new factory building was erected and equipped. When everything was ready, Ron and the board made their move. In a coup akin to Rupert Murdoch's union-busting switch of News International's publishing operations to Wapping, twelve years later, the closure of Durham Steelwork was announced. At the same moment, the new company, Thircon ('Thirsk Construction'), opened for business with about thirty new staff. The unions – the Construction and Engineering Union and the Boilermakers' Union

68 Lord Brittan of Spennithorne, QC, PC, DL (1939-2015).

The Thircon factory ('Thirsk Construction') in Yorkshire, which opened the
day Durham Steelworks, Gateshead closed in 1974, after building and
equipping in secrecy from the unions

– were furious. They had been outmanoeuvred. They promised to break the
company. Their threats were not realised, however, and the dodge succeeded
brilliantly. The new company went smoothly into production and all open
contracts running at Durham Steel were completed at Thircon.[69]

The new factory, over the next twenty years, took on orders from Lea
Bridge, Wymondham and the African companies. Thousands of tonnes of
Callender Hamilton sectional road bridge were fabricated and shipped to
Indonesia. The electrification of several railways, including the Glasgow
Suburban Line, brought in large contracts from Balfour Beatty. In addition,
there were all the usual retail, office, and commercial commissions, many
(such as big out-of-town supermarkets and distribution centres) reflecting the
changing lifestyles of the time. High profile contracts included the Motor
Heritage Centre at Gaydon, Warwickshire in 1991, the repairs to the roof of
Windsor Castle after the fire of 1992, and any number of Tesco stores.[70]

Union troubles in the end also did for the London works at Lea Bridge in
Leyton. Always an active presence, due to the big railway workshops in the

69 Phyll, she is at pains to point out, planted the trees.
70 Thircon was finally sold in 2010.

[280]

Motor Heritage Centre, Gaydon, Warwickshire, 1991 (600 tonnes)

St George's Hall, Windsor Castle, 1992: after Thircon steel made possible the roof restoration

borough, the Boilermakers Union and the Construction and Engineering Union were both exceptionally militant. By the early 1980s rising wage levels and restrictive practices were squeezing margins impossibly. As overseas orders dried up, a temporary stay of execution was provided by the building boom of the Thatcherite years. Once this frenzy tailed off, however, the familiar consequences of recession followed. The Aylesbury office was closed. There were lay-offs. Shortly after, the decision that everyone had been avoiding had to be taken. The successful establishment of Thircon had made it painfully clear how much cheaper a rural factory was to run than one in London. It was a difference too great to be ignored any longer. In 1983, the decision was taken to close Lea Bridge. For forty-five years it had been the heart and mainstay of H. Young & Company. The four-acre site was decommissioned and rented out as valuable commercial space.

In 1995 various subsidiaries were amalgamated and moved to the Wymondham works (renamed Hi-Span and Thircon Southern Ltd) which now became the Head Office. Here, again, by nimbly pre-empting the market, the company managed to prosper where others failed and fell away.

In the late 1980s architects began to favour a particular kind of truss-work and tubular steelwork that, as a result, could soon be seen in the roofing of almost any large out-of-town shopping centre. The Wymondham works became adept at fabricating these.

In the 1990s, when 'Design and Build' became the fashionable method of procurement in the construction industry (whereby, rather than going through an architect, a client could approach a single company for an all-in-one service) Young's were ready with a strong in-house computer-aided

Wymondham works – Hi-Span, Thircon Southern Ltd, and H. Young Structures Ltd are now based at the Norfolk cold-rolling mill established in an old aircraft hangar recycled from Jersey Airport in 1962

Before and after: the complex curved and barrel-vaulted roof construction for
Cambridge University Press's new printing works in the 1990s

drawing team. One prestigious 'Design-and-Build' commission in the region
was for Cambridge University Press, for a complex curved, barrel-vaulted
roof at its new printing works.

*

Two other ventures need mentioning, as they demonstrate two of Ron's great
entrepreneurial gifts – versatility and luck. In 1935 Murray, Ron's father, had,
with the help of his masonic connections, started the Jersey Steel Company.
Although the Channel Island promised some business opportunities, it was
chosen mainly for the tax advantages it offered: as a crown dependency outside
the United Kingdom, income tax was levied at a flat rate of just 20 per cent.
(This was why, in due course, the holding company for the Mtwapa Bridge
Company was also based in Jersey.)

Initially the company's Jersey base was a one-man sales office in La Motte
Street, St Helier, but it soon became clear that with no other steel company on
the island there was plenty of potential business to be had. After two years, a
second member of staff, a young draughtsman called Reg Dean, was sent
over. Trundling around the island in his Morris Eight, Dean visited architects
and builders and farmers and anyone else who might need steel-framed
buildings, drumming up business. When a contract was secured, Dean
designed the work, sent the details back to the Nine Elms yard in Battersea
(still the main London works until, after bombing in 1943, everyone moved
to Leyton), whence the fabricated steel would often be returned within a
week. The first modest contracts slowly but steadily grew into more
substantial ones, for farm and factory buildings, including the umbrella roof
of St Helier bus station. A small erection team was installed permanently on
the island.

The office was evacuated just before the Germans invaded in 1940. After the
war, however, Dean was sent back to resurrect the company. Soon, increasingly
prestigious contracts began to come through: the De Gruchy Shopping Arcade

[283]

in St Helier, a Jersey Airlines hangar and main hall at Jersey Airport, plus the usual hotels, department stores, hospital and schools. So much work was arriving by 1950 that Dean was charged with procuring a site for a new works. He found a four-acre plot in Goose Green Marsh, at Beaumont, midway between St Helier and the airport, and acquired a 99-year lease. Equipment was brought over from Lea Bridge. However, the works took up only a small portion of the site and four acres was a considerable area. What to do with the extra land? At the time, everyone in Jersey was growing tomatoes to supply the British markets. As the company was perfectly placed to erect a steel glasshouse, why, Ron thought, not have a go at that? A large greenhouse was duly erected and stocked, and Reg Dean's duties were extended to tomato-growing. H. Young & Company (Tomatoes Division) was not, it must be said, a success. Dean did his best, but he was an engineering draftsman, not a market gardener. With no full-time manager, tomatoes proved to be a product extension too far. After three years the venture was abandoned and the glasshouse dismantled.

This meant the company still owned the lease of a valuable piece of real estate which could be used for something. In 1975 Jersey Steel had made an ill-fated venture onto its Channel Island neighbour, Guernsey, acquiring a steel subsidiary there. With this had come a heating and plumbing department which, once it was closed down, meant Jersey Steel was left with a mass of plumbing equipment and merchandise. The solution? Open a bathroom supply centre.

Anxious to avoid making the same mistake as with the tomatoes, this time a dedicated general manager was hired. The idea worked well. From a small showroom selling bathroom suites to builders and the general public, by capable management and persistent salesmanship this soon grew into a thriving small company selling fitted kitchens too. Gradually, through the 1980s, the Beaumont Kitchen and Bathroom Company built and expanded its relationships with local architects and builders. The showrooms were extended, extended again, until the annual turnover exceeded

LEFT: Jersey Airport Terminal, 1968; RIGHT: The Springfield Grandstand, 1999, for which Jersey Steel Ltd supplied the cladding

£1 million. By the mid-1990s the company was employing fifteen staff, including six kitchen designers.

*

On 1 August 2003, just under three weeks before his eightieth birthday, Ron stepped down as chairman of the H. Young & Company group of companies. His career with his family business had spanned fifty-six years, fifty of them as group chairman. During this half-century the company had built power stations, cotton ginneries, sugar refineries, breweries, flour mills, processing plants, factories, depots, hotels, department stores, post offices, hospitals, water towers, schools and villages plus hundreds of warehouses, barns and sheds, not to mention specialist trollies and other steel goods. One of the founder members of the British Constructional Steelwork Association, the company had won numerous Structural Steel Design Awards, along with national accreditation for the quality of its management systems. Altogether, it was a remarkable record for a single chairman's watch.

Ron's style of executive leadership was refreshingly different from so many of today's corporate leaders, reflecting, perhaps, the strong Quaker ideals with which, however subconsciously, he was imbued – supplemented, perhaps, by the wartime values with which he grew up. Where today's successful company chairmen tend to reward themselves with million-pound salaries, chauffeurs waiting in Bentleys (Ron never even owned a new company car) and First Class Executive Lounge lifestyles, for Ron such trappings and indulgences would have been unthinkable.

True, at one stage H. Young & Company (East Africa) Ltd owned two company aircraft – the one area, undeniably, in which its chairman had a weakness – with ZECO owning another. But even these were no executive status symbols, merely workhorses demanded – well, almost, anyway – by practical necessity. Ron's works driver, the impressively-tattooed Peter, might occasionally drop the children back at school; John, the works mechanic, might service everyone's cars; and the staff of Hi-Span might periodically be put to work fabricating whatever contrivance the chairman needed, from boat house to hangar, at Kimberley. But that was the limit of company perks.

The corporate moments treasured by those who worked with and for Ron were lower key and altogether more colourful: the time his bulging suitcase burst open at Lusaka International Airport, revealing the contents to be not clothes or urgent company documents, but several dozen mangoes destined for the UK; or the chairman appearing at an important board meeting, soberly-suited and impeccable save for one of his grandchildren's Peter Rabbit sticking plasters on his forehead. On another occasion, with several kilos of frozen meat from the farm in Zambia packed in his case, it inadvertently got sent to

Frankfurt. By the time it returned to England, seeping blood and smelling, it looked as if a body were inside it.

Ron's achievements as a businessman are evident just by glancing at the photographs in this chapter. But teasing out the exact nature of his gifts is less easy. Obviously his head for figures and grasp of the anatomy of a balance sheet were a helpful start, especially when allied to his sharp nose for a business opportunity and huge tenacity. Those who have worked with him mention his energy, efficiency, natural optimism, self-discipline, pro-activity and uncanny ability to juggle many projects simultaneously. He also, plainly, had the commitment of an obvious workaholic who never really switched off. (Ron's working life epitomised the truism that, if you want something done, ask someone who is busy.)

His management style was essentially trusting, unflappable and *laissez-faire*. He had a knack for spotting a good person for a job, then, having chosen them, had the confidence to leave them alone. If occasionally a dislike of confrontation meant the wrong person remained in position too long, then that was a price worth paying. Similarly, his willingness to take risks, trying his hand at something new regardless of whether he knew the first thing about it, may have led to the odd failure (tomato growing), but more often led to great successes (the Mtwapa Bridge, the Beaumont Bathroom Centre, KSH Farms).

Underpinning these qualities is his Churchillian self-reliance. Does this arise from the moment when, as a schoolboy, he learned of his father's death, when the figurehead of the family company was suddenly removed at the top of his game? Was such an event, at the formative age of seventeen, a brutal declaration to Ron that now he was on his own? Whether so or not, Ron certainly possesses the loner quality which, to an extent, every leader must have. It is most poignantly evident in the photograph of him, aged seventeen, addressing the Lea Bridge workforce in 1940, at the opening of the new works canteen. (See last page of chapter 6.)

The African companies came and went. When Ron stepped down, handing over to Peter as Group Chairman, and Robbie on the parent company board, his legacy was a portfolio of streamlined companies and assets, ready for whatever the future might hold: three steel companies (H. Young Structures and Hi-Span at Wymondham, and the Jersey Steel Company), the Beaumont Kitchen and Bathroom Centre in Jersey and the commercial premises at Lea Bridge.

With them, of course, came just a single memento of the African years, but a substantial one: one of the biggest farms on the Copper Belt.

18

Ronstock

A ND SO TO the sociable Ron, the party-goer and giver. While never
approaching his social life with the determination of, say, a Johnny
Kimberley, there is no question that Ron enjoyed company. His children
noticed that, when asked for help by their father with tasks around the place,
this was seldom for any technical expertise they might bring; he just liked
having them around. Fortunately, in Phyll, he seemed to have found a like
mind. If an open-door policy had operated at Ashley Gardens towards
friends, relations and acquaintances collected along the way, it applied doubly
at Kimberley. Whether it was that the place cried out to be filled, due to some
deep sense of *noblesse oblige,* or in response to past kindnesses shown to
them, Ron's and Phyll's view of their new country home right from the start
seemed to be that it was a place to be shared. As a result, it was rare to find a
weekend when only family were present.

The company might take any form, be any age or nationality, be passing
through or resident in one of the flats. Sometimes their English was sparing
and they appeared to have little in common with anyone else, baffling family
as much as guests. I don't know who he is,' declared Phyll of one recent
arrival, 'but he says his name is "Shining Bird".' Most were interesting, and
often that interest manifested itself in unexpected ways. A renowned eye
physiologist inadvertently left a bag of eyeballs in the kitchen.[71] The
mountaineer Roger Mear gave abseiling lessons off the roof. The actress
Lesley-Anne Down floated round the lake in a boat. Perhaps the most exotic
guests were Sudanese friends such as Ibrahim, always resplendent in his white
robes and white Sudanese turban, or Ron's Armenian friend Vin Vanian. All
were received with the same easygoing hospitality, and cheerfully put to work
by Ron moving furniture or clearing fallen timber in the park. Meanwhile,
there was the regular round of birthdays (six a year) and other anniversaries
to be celebrated. Ron, a keen celebrator of his August anniversary, often
shared a party with his friend Jim Gurney who was the same age. There were
winter shooting weekends, summer house-parties, Choral Society meetings
and pony shows, interspersed with larger and more formal events such as
hunt balls or charity fundraisers like the Red Cross Ball. The Buxton children
grew up used to hosting on a grand scale.

71 Professor Nick Delamere.

This was certainly a contributory factor to the event which, a month before Ron's seventieth birthday in 1993, became the first of *the* Buxton parties: the prototype of what would over eighteen years grow into a three-day summer festival and make the name Kimberley more synonymous with dance music than a famous South African diamond mine. At its largest, in 2010, around 3,000 people, from Notting Hill to Namibia, in cars, caravans and camper vans could be found flocking to Norfolk during the second weekend of July. And locals became used to encountering eccentrically-dressed figures wearing coloured wrist-bands in the supermarket outside Wymondham.

How did the idea of a big annual summer party, held mainly underground, ever come about? By evolution is the answer. One of the wonders of Kimberley, though few knew about it, was the nether-world upon which it rested; a labyrinthine network of interconnected, vaulted brick chambers spreading like catacombs under the central block of the house and the east wing, where the original kitchens were. (The west wing has no such basement.) In the mid-1970s, a cousin, John Buxton, was the first to organise a party in the cellars, in aid of Voluntary Service Overseas (VSO). A wall was demolished as part of the preparations, and Pam Gurney painted murals of crocodiles in one room and buffaloes in another.

Then, in 1981, for Peter's twenty-first, shared with his equally music-obsessed friend Dominic Welby, the pair cleared out more of the cellars, enough to set up bars, a dance floor, a film show area and sitting-out dens.

After this, the cellars became a regular venue for dinners and parties. UEA students living in the attic held many a rowdy party there from the late 1970s. In 1983 Ron and Vanessa shared a joint 60th and 21st, with a sit-down dinner in the largest of the underground chambers, the potato room (so-called because it was once a potato store) beneath the music room.

So by a decade later, in 1993, the precedent for underground partying at Kimberley was well established. That year, Peter, now a married father aged thirty-three living in Wiltshire, was asked by a friend to join his cricket team, the Winchester White Hunters – on condition he help arrange a couple of country house matches in Norfolk. One of these fixtures consisted of a motley eleven assembled by Robbie.[72] Never that keen on cricket, Robbie devoted

---

72 The match bears description. In good time, the White Hunters arrived at the Marlingford Ground, immaculate in whites, and began practising – despite no sign of any opposition. In due course, an old farm Land-Rover rattled in and disgorged Robbie's Kimberley team – Robbie, Nick Evans-Lombe, Orlando Fraser, Ben Taylor, Charlie McMicking, Alf Rippingall, Ben Weatherall, Giovanni Amati, Tom Coke and Henry Whitbread – dressed in a mishmash of casual clothing, precious little of which was white. Their lateness, they apologised, was because the night before the UEA students in the east wing had thrown their annual summer party and Robbie's team had become fully engaged. In the process one of the Kimberley team, Jock Maxwell-Macdonald, had been mislaid, yet to be found – a severe loss given that Jock was their prize 'heavy hitter' – indeed, one of the few members of the side with much idea of the game (the Italian, Giovanni, for

most of his efforts to arranging the post-match party. Invitations were sent out for 'Psychoactive Subterranean Adventures', to be held in the Kimberley cellars. Helping Robbie was a young actor and DJ, Ben Taylor, a friend of Peter's following a school exchange scheme between Eton and Feltham Comprehensive. He was also deeply into the new electronic dance music scene sweeping London from the US. Together, they pounded out set after set of pumping house music.

What dedicated speleologists the young sportsmen turned out to be! For some, it was their first taste of the new dance music, with its tribal beats and swelling, euphoric crescendos. Dawn had arrived before the last adventurer emerged, blinking, into the light. It had been, it was agreed, a sporting fixture like no other. It must be repeated! Perhaps without the cricket ...

And so it was. What that first underground adventure grew into over the years that followed is said better by pictures than words (though for a fuller account, see Appendix I.) Through the efforts of a newly convened committee – Robbie and Iona, Ben and Pete, with, later, Vanessa and Ben's sister Poonie creating a holistic healing area – the summer party expanded, over two decades, into a three-day spectacular covering hundreds of acres, with six stages, more than 500 crew and over 150 acts. The spirit of those events chimed with something in the ether. The second half of the 1990s saw the genesis of numerous UK outdoor country house-based dance events and festivals, best-known of which was probably The Big Chill at Eastnor Castle, but which were followed by Bestival, The Secret Garden and many others. Kimberley offered comparable music, scale and staging, but in a much more intimate setting where the house itself was allowed to be used, and which was by invitation only, so many knew each other. It also had one other ingredient which none of the others could match.

Somewhere near the centre, always, were two unmistakeable – if unpre-dictably-clad – figures: Ron in characteristic pose, hands behind his back, resplendent in, say, scarlet vintage regimental tunic and fez, or straw hat with

---

example, had never played cricket before). Everyone was badly hung over. The White Hunters looked unsympathetic and unimpressed. What Robbie did not mention was that amongst his motley entourage were also Nick Evans-Lombe, formerly of the Eton First XI; Orlando Fraser, who had played for St Paul's; and Ben Weatherall, who, at 6 foot 8 inches tall, bowled like a catapult. Play commenced, the Hunters quickly notching up runs and with them an air of incontrovertible self-satisfaction. Around 5 p.m. Jock appeared, wearing jeans and tweed jacket, eyes swollen from cat allergies, reeking of alcohol. By the time it was Kimberley's turn to bat, the score to beat was 200. Robbie sent in two or three early cannon-fodder to cement the Hunters' complacency, before Nick Evans-Lombe took to the crease and the afternoon peace was broken by sharp reports of willow on leather ... on oak – as ball after ball was clouted into the branches of an ancient tree on the boundary. In minutes, he had scored 50 (the maximum permitted per man), before Orlando, then Jock, followed his example. The White Hunters' confidence evaporated. Even Giovanni scored a run. Kimberley won an easy victory.

Photo © The Jet Blondes all girls sky-diving team

Photo © Ben Cole

Britain's biggest private music festival: K2010, when numbers exceeded 3,000. The
love-heart with exclamation lines visible in front of the house in the top photograph,
became the logo, used for Saturday's 'team photo', shown below.

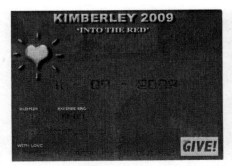

Photo © Greg Holloway   Photo © Greg Holloway

Ronstock revisited – TOP LEFT: The credit card invitation to 'credit crunch' K09.
TOP RIGHT: Smoke trails by the Red Bull Matadors. MIDDLE LEFT: 'Wizard's hat'
main tent. MIDDLE RIGHT: Sparks fly from the angle grinder. BELOW: Tipi village.

Welcome to the House of Fun: Paul Reynolds's dazzling projection mapping onto the
South Front, 2013

two-foot gold feathers; Phyll, taller and more voluble, recognisable despite
mask and striped sunglasses, glitter tee-shirt and silk patchwork coat. (Finding
exotic interpretations for the annual colour theme presented no problems for
such inveterate dressers-up.) Together they would wander the mêlée, radiating
a mixture of logistical concern, benign tolerance, and the occasional raised
eyebrow. (Ron, on encountering one young woman wearing little more than a
nipple ring: 'Is this what girls this year are not wearing?') Even those who had
never met Ron or Phyll – which, as the party got larger, inevitably meant many
– knew exactly who they were.

'Ronstock',[73] as the event quickly became known (further proof, were it
needed, of the event's ultimate centre of gravity) became for many the
unmissable date of high summer. Even if it was an event created and driven by
the children and Ben, ultimately it owed its warmth and character to Ron and
Phyll. However big it got, at heart it was still a family party, in a family home
– with the parents there to prove it.

Ron plainly enjoyed the party – or, as he called it, 'the rave'. The gathering
evidently appealed on a tribal level. More importantly, it was an almost miraculous source of free labour. One year, Vanessa, running one of her yoga
programmes, had booked a celebrated instructor from California (Madonna's
personal instructor, as it happened). The man in question was due at 4 p.m.

73 Also 'Toffstock' and 'Knobworth'.

and the yoga class had assembled to practise stretches on the lawn in readiness. Four o'clock passed, became four thirty, then five. Even the yogis were showing signs of impatience, and Vanessa, who had had confirmation that the great man had arrived, was pacing the house in frustration, wondering where he could be. Encountering Ron, she said: 'We're expecting our yoga teacher from California, Dad. You haven't seen him, have you?'

'No ... er ... no, no.'

Fifteen minutes later she bumped into Ron again. 'Dad, are you sure you haven't seen our yoga instructor? We know he's here somewhere.'

'No ... no.'

'You're *quite* sure? He was due at four. You haven't seen anyone around at all?'

'Er... well, there's a chap upstairs in the attic, giving me a hand.'

'Where is he now?'

'He's there, of course. He's helping me with the pipes.'

Ron's habit of pinching important members of the Kimberley crew – who

© Jörg Huber

Centre of the party: The K2002 invitation, the ninth Kimberley,
'Throw open the sluice gates and release your spiritual tsunami ...'

were invariably too polite or too intimidated to refuse him – eventually became such a liability that it was decided simply to assign him someone on permanent call, to prevent indispensable figures being hijacked at critical moments (such as Mark England, in charge of power and lighting for the entire site).

For survivors who made it through to the Monday morning, many Ronstocks ended with the same time-honoured ritual. This consisted of Ron, up fresh and early for the new week, driving around the campsites in search of Robbie. As the sun climbed above hushed and bleary campsites, Ron's unmistakeable drawl could be heard. 'Have you seen Robbie? Have you seen Robbie anywhere?' his voice carrying clearly over the quietly packing campers. 'I can't think where he's got to. He knows perfectly well we're doing the VAT returns today.'

*

In mid-November 2004, aged eighty-one, Ron fell mysteriously ill. After returning from his regular autumn trip to Zambia, making his way from Heathrow back to Kimberley by tube and train, on Saturday he complained (perhaps hardly surprisingly) of being tired. Then on Sunday, after a morning bath, he found he couldn't get out. After helping him back to bed and going to the Remembrance Day service, Phyll returned to find Ron feeling better. They watched the Cenotaph celebrations on the evening news. By Monday morning he was delirious, hallucinating that there were migrating big game out in the park. The doctor, who came after morning surgery, was baffled by his symptoms. On account of his soaring temperature, however, Ron was rushed by ambulance to intensive care at Norwich Hospital. (By bizarre coincidence, next to him there was his old friend Anthony Gurney, who, after driving his 82-year-old sister and dogs out to go for a walk, on their return had forgotten to put on the handbrake, and in diving to stop the car had been dragged backwards and eventually run over.)

With his raging fever, accompanied by blackouts and seizures, five doctors at Norwich Hospital were non-plussed by Ron's condition. By now Phyll had spoken to Vanessa who suggested a blood sample be sent urgently to the Hospital for Tropical Diseases in London. At 5 a.m. on Tuesday morning, now in a coma, Ron was taken by ambulance to their intensive care unit. There he was diagnosed with cerebral malaria; a severe complication of standard malaria. Untreated, it is a condition fatal in 24–72 hours. Even caught early, without further complications, it can be fatal in up to 80 per cent of cases.

Unfortunately, there were further complications: blackwater fever. This causes massive and rapid bursting of red blood cells in the bloodstream, releasing haemoglobin directly into the blood vessels and the urine (hence black water), leading to intense jaundice and, frequently, kidney failure. In most cases, death follows. Malaria and blackwater fever, of all tropical diseases, are the notorious killers of white men, the diseases that figure in the classic stories of the tropics. It transpired that on his trip to Zambia, Ron had not taken malaria pills. He never did, it turned out, believing he would be fine – as, before, he always had been. His children believed it, too. Now it looked as if the man who had built his career in colonial Africa was going to die a truly colonial African death.

For three days his condition worsened steadily. Unconscious, hooked up to monitors and drips, breathing by a tube attached to a ventilator, his condition was pronounced critical. He was checked every thirty minutes by two nurses in permanent attendance. Any visitor seeking admission had to scrub up and put on a sterilised gown and mask before entering his bubble. For the children, it was shocking to see their father, someone who was never ill – whom they had seldom even seen in bed – attached to the full apparatus of a contemporary intensive care unit. It was less the medical setting than the fact of his incarceration: the realisation, for the first time, that Ron was mortal.

By day six or seven it was becoming increasingly obvious that the situation was hopeless. The consultant took Phyll aside, confirming what everyone already suspected: Ron might not emerge from his coma. Camilla, after catching the sleeper down from Scotland (where she now lived) to see Ron, in desperation contacted a woman she knew who practised radionics (the 'black box'). The woman went to work on Ron the next day. Camilla also had the idea of taking in CDs of Ron's favourite music (Bach's *Preludes* and *Fugues in G Major* and *G Minor*, Bach's *Toccata*, Widor's *Toccata*) to play to him via headphones. Everyone took turns to be with him, changing the CD when it finished. Professor Fisher, head of intensive care at the hospital, roared into Ron's ears: 'Wake up, Ron! Wake up!'

None of it made any difference. On the way to the hospital one morning, Phyll paid a visit to All Souls, Langham Place. There she asked the rector to get in touch with John Stott, a former rector of the place, who had been at Cambridge with Ron, to ask him to visit him. Everyone prepared for Ron to die.

Yet, for some reason, he didn't. Ten days after he had fallen into a coma, Camilla (down again from Scotland) was sitting sadly by her father's bedside when the patient opened one eye. 'Why are you crying?' came a croak from the bed. The return to life was slow, but steady. After several more days in intensive care, Ron was moved to University College Hospital. There, finally allowed to join a ward, he remained in the 'high risk' category: of the four patients he was with, one died and another, a woman, screamed all night. Eventually Phyll got him moved to a private room. There, gradually, he learned to eat, and speak, again.

After a fortnight he returned to Norwich Hospital, where he remained for another week (Anthony Gurney had by this time been discharged), before being allowed to return to Kimberley. There, a ground floor bedroom was prepared in the dining room. Over the four months that followed his strength gradually returned. Somehow, the supreme survivor had done it again. By April, Ron announced, he was bored. He would be leaving shortly for his spring trip to Zambia.

*

For any great house or estate, the question of succession quietly looms, ever present, if seldom mentioned. For all his independent-mindedness, in some ways Ron was resolutely conventional. Male primogeniture was the rule by which country estates were traditionally kept together in England, so it was presumed that, in due course, Peter would take on Kimberley. In this case, there were additional reasons for such a presumption.

In 1987 Peter had married Eleanor Winch, the only daughter of a neighbouring landowner, Richard Winch, of Swannington Manor.[74] Swannington village was eleven miles north-east of Kimberley (and the location of the airfield Ron had so nearly not found when he flew up to look over Kimberley with Phyll's sister Anne in 1958). The Swannington estate comprised a thousand acres, with farms, cottages and woodland. From the perspective of a father-in-law as practically-minded as Ron, one can only guess at how satisfactory such a union must have seemed, promising, as it did, all the benefits of lands that almost marched together: of shared farm buildings and machinery, not to mention the strengthening of another Buxton foothold in Norfolk. Always looking forward, at their engagement party Ron's toast was not, as everyone expected, to the happy couple, nor even to Eleanor's parents, Richard and Frances, for having supplied the bride. The groom's father was far ahead. He raised his glass: 'To the next generation.'

Perhaps it was all too neat. Peter, by the mid-1990s, was well established in the family firm. After a skirmish with various businesses – creating holograms, starting his own marketing consultancy – in 1985 he had become a director of H. Young & Company. When he and Eleanor decided to leave London, furthermore, some instinct – perhaps some innate Buxton contrariness – took the couple westwards rather than towards Norfolk. Having fallen for the area around Avebury in Wiltshire, with its fishing on the Kennet, they had settled in Milton Lilbourne to bring up their children.[75] Norfolk and the land-owning, county life, they decided, was not for them. In due course, the Swannington estate was sold, and they decided not to take on Kimberley.

74 Their wedding day, 20 June, was the same day Ron and Phyll had married in 1959, and Ron's parents, Murray and Muriel, had married in 1920.
75 Laura, born 3 October 1990; and Freddie, born 2 June 1995.

Buxtons united: Peter marries Eleanor Winch, 1987; Robbie marries Iona Spens, 1996; Camilla marries Dominic Warre, 1997

Vanessa notes drily that this might have been the moment for her father to consider one of his daughters for the role of future chatelaine. Camilla, however, whom primogeniture would have favoured next, was by now married, to Dominic Warre (of the Warre port family) and was settled in Scotland with two young children.[76] Besides, it was never going to be an option as long as there was a male heir, and it became increasingly inevitable that it would be Robbie who would one day take on Kimberley. Besides, Robbie's heart was in the country – during the shooting season, at any rate. In 1996 he had married the dark-haired, doe-eyed architectural writer Iona Spens. Despite the couple being, for several years, something of a fixture on the London party scene, the prospect of children eventually made the number of stairs to their fifth-floor Earls Court garret seem excessive. Following the birth of their first child, Dorian, they completed a major overhaul of Kimberley Garden Cottage prior to leaving London permanently.[77]

Robbie and Iona's make-over of Kimberley Garden Cottage bears brief description, given that it was completed by the future taste-makers of Kimberley Hall. The house sits in a grassy clearing sheltered by ancient oaks alongside an old apple orchard and the walled garden. Revamped in 1880 in a vaguely Arts and Crafts style, it has a rustic timber porch, rustic eaves and a tiled roof rising to a clump of ornate terracotta chimneys. At some stage the brickwork had been painted a pale sugar-pink, so that the overall effect was of a gingerbread cottage in the Hansel-and-Gretel mould. As such, it chimed poorly with the urbane sensibilities of its new owners.

76 Rupert, born 2 January 1998; and Alice, born 19 December 1999.
77 Dorian, born 18 February 1999; Nat, born 27 January 2001; and Mala, born 17 April 2003.

Here mention needs to be made of a stubborn creative streak in Robbie's persona, belied by two years at Cirencester Agricultural College. Fostered during a spell at Chetwood Associates (Architects), it is an impulse that expressed itself in contented hours spent making a pair of sculptural steel racks to accommodate his expanding CD collection; cut, welded, shot-blasted and waxed using machinery in the company's Wymondham works. It was there, too, in an increasingly dandified dress sense, making him resemble, in John Doune's words, a 'scented popinjay'. It was most certainly there in the couple's alterations to their new country abode.

The changes to Kimberley Garden Cottage, inside and out, were considerable. In the new kitchen-cum-dining area, and the sitting room, silver-painted, riveted steel 'I' beams replaced supporting walls. (The beams provided the strength to carry a pair of frighteningly heavy bronze and steel panels by the sculptor Charles Hadcock, a friend, that were bolted to the ceiling.) Kitchen drawers were identified by panels of stained glass. Door-cases, fireplaces, cupboards and other furniture, all of dark, intricately-carved Indian hardwood, were shipped from Kerala where they had been chosen by Robbie and Iona on honeymoon. The most visible change, however, was to the exterior. Gone was the lickable, boiled-sweet pink, replaced by Dulux 'Garnet Symphony', a colour somewhere between beetroot and puce. It was, as intended, not to everybody's taste.

In 2006 Robbie and Iona moved into Kimberley Hall, and Ron and Phyll moved to The Garden Cottage. There Ron and Phyll have added a conservatory, and Phyll speaks of adjustments to the kitchen once Robbie and Iona's fashionable steel gas cooker has been replaced. The Garnet Symphony remains. Somehow it fits the cottage's new tenants almost as well as the old.

Ron runabout, 2012 – the latest in Ron's long line of disintegrating 4x4s.
(The fence post is to hold the door shut.)

Golden years: collage made by the children for Ron and Phyll's golden wedding
anniversary, June 2009

Buxtons at home, it seems to say, doing things their own way. Outside is
parked the latest of Ron's long line of 4x4s, not hard to recognise.

In June 2009 Ron and Phyll celebrated their golden wedding anniversary.
Everyone gathered in Jersey to celebrate; it seemed an appropriate setting, with
its long Buxton connection. For three days the sun blazed from cloudless skies.

In July 2012 Phyll celebrated her eightieth birthday.

Kimberley Buxtons: Taken at Phyll's eightieth birthday, July 2012.
RCB second row, one from the right.

Children and grandchildren – LEFT TO RIGHT: RCB, Phyll, Peter, Camilla, Vanessa, Robbie, Laura, Freddie, Rupert, Dorian, Alice, Nat, Mala

With eight grandchildren, the all-important 'next generation' is lining up, if not yet quite waiting.

Peter is now chairman of H. Young & Company and its associated companies and Robbie and Iona are overseeing a gradual makeover of the house as a venue for weddings, photo-shoots and artistic events in the hope of making the place, one day, pay its way. A longer, flatter, smoother grass landing strip now runs west from the top of the drive. Sometimes (depending what event is being hosted) exotic-looking aircraft and helicopters are parked on the apron. At ninety-two, Ron is about the place more than his hectic life has ever allowed before. He suffers painfully from *polymyalgia rheumatica* and other cruelties of age. But he can still explain as accurately as if it had happened yesterday the correct way to ditch a light aircraft in a heavy sea.

RCB – K2009, 'Into the Red', wearing the sunglasses which came free with Vanessa's *Tatler*.

Appendices

AS THE TRUCE IN POLITICS ENDS

"If only, Mr. Grimond, I could count on Labour supporters to give me the loyal and faithful support that <u>you</u> give me."

I
Chronology of Key Events

1921	Jean Carlile born, 10 June.
1923	RCB born, 20 August.
1927	Parents give up 51, Evelyn Gardens, Kensington and move to Britain's Lodge, Sevenoaks.
1932	RCB goes to Hawtreys Preparatory School. 9 July, Phyllida Buxton born.
1932–3	Grandfather Hildred moves to Bishop's Down Grange, Tunbridge Wells.
1935	Buxton family moves to Holywell, Woking. RCB aged 12.
1937–41	RCB at Eton.
1940	Monday 14 October, father, Murray Barclay Buxton, and uncle, Alfred Buxton, killed in air raid, London. Mother, Jean and RCB move to live with maternal grandfather, Sir Hildred Carlile, at Bishop's Down Grange, Tunbridge Wells.
1941–3	RCB at Trinity College, Cambridge.
1942	Mother, Janet Mary Muriel Carlile, dies.
1943	RCB comes down from Cambridge, joins Army – REME – but most of first year in England.
1944–7	Indian Army – IEME, hill stations, Burma, Indo-China.
1946	RCB's paternal grandfather, Reverend Barclay Buxton, dies.
1946	Iraq and Basra.
1947	RCB demobbed. Joins H. Young and Company.
1947–8	Trip to Africa with Jean.
1948	Starts Rhodesia Engineering and Steel Construction Company (RESCCo) and H. Young & Company (East Africa).
1950–2	Jean with Mandari in Sudan.
1952	RCB buys 67, Ashley Gardens, Victoria.
1953	Becomes chairman of H. Young & Company, aged 30. Starts Steel Construction Sudan Ltd, Khartoum, establishes Raine Engineering Ltd in Zambia.
1954	Starts Nigerian Steel Construction Ltd.
1955	Acquires Kenyan flying licence.
1956–8	Building of Mtwapa Bridge.
1957	Adopted as Conservative candidate for Leyton. Introduced to hunting.

	Phyll's mother Dorothy dies.
1958	21 June, Mtwapa Bridge opens.
	19 July, Auster plane crash into Mediterranean.
	September, buys Kimberley Hall. Sells Holywell.
1959	Marries Phyllida Buxton, 20 June.
	RCB fights General Election, defeated by Labour majority of 16,000.
1960	19 June, Peter and Camilla born.
1962	12 April, Vanessa born.
1964	September, contests Leyton for General Election. Reduced Labour majority to 6,000.
	22 November, Robert Victor born.
1965	January, wins Leyton by-election, defeating Foreign Secretary Patrick Gordon Walker. Takes seat in Parliament two weeks later.
1966	Loses seat.
1970	Swimming pool built. Ron's sister Jean – now Dr Jean Buxton – dies of brain haemorrhage. Captain Roden Buxton, Phyll's father, also dies.
1984	Silver wedding anniversary.
1989	Buys microlight.
1993	First 'Kimberley' party, Psychoactive Subterranean Adventures – soon to be christened 'Ronstock'.
2003	1 August, RCB steps down after 50 years as group chairman of Henry Young & Company. Peter Buxton becomes chairman. After 80th birthday, RCB surrenders pilot's licence.
2004	November, RCB develops cerebral malaria on return from Zambia.
2006	Robbie and Iona move into Kimberley Hall, Ron and Phyll move into The Garden Cottage.
2009	Golden wedding anniversary.
2012	Phyll's 80th birthday.
2014	RCB celebrates 91st birthday.

II

The Evolution of Ronstock

Hᴏᴡ ᴅɪᴅ ᴛʜᴇ post-cricket match celebrations of Robbie's Psychoactive Subterranean Adventurers in 1993 metamorphose into Britain's largest private dance music festival? The short answer is that it was driven by the dance music revolution sweeping the UK at the time.

It's hard to recall, now, how exciting computer-generated dance music was in the 1990s. By the late 1980s the electronic revolution that was about to usher personal computers onto every office desk and mobile phones into every pocket had already started to re-shape music. From America came a new kind of sound, based not on singing or performing, or even conventional instruments or vocals, but on tracks created electronically. Onto a baseline of machine-generated repetitive beats, synthesised melodies were hung, made easier by masses of new generation gizmos in the form of synthesisers, sequencers, samplers, drum machines and keyboards. With a tempo of 125-150 beats per minute and swelling baselines, this music (called 'house music' after one of the Chicago clubs, The Warehouse, where it began) was sensationally danceable. Like tribal drumbeats, at its best the new music had a unifying effect, bringing everyone on the dance floor together in a shared euphoria.

The folk heroes of the new scene were the DJs who mixed the tracks, seamlessly blending one into the next, judging and manipulating the mood of the floor as he or she brought everyone steadily up to a surging, euphoric crescendo, then pulled back the pace to gradually rebuild it again. Thus the best DJs could hold their crowd for hours. One sub-genre of this music, known as Trance, became the mainstay of the Acid House raves that started making British headlines in the late 1980s. This music rapidly became absorbed into the mainstream, however, with new clubs like the Ministry of Sound, and later super-clubs like Fabric, opening to cater for a new kind of all-night clubber for whom conventional pop or chart music was forgotten.

So when, with Ron and Phyll's blessing, their children set about organising the biggest party in Kimberley Hall's 282-year history, this was the background. The guest list would include many of Britain's most practised, committed and discerning partygoers, so the stakes were high. The event would take place, it was decided, over a weekend in July. Everyone would be asked for Friday night, to set up camp, paying a contribution to help cover costs. A thousand invitations were sent out to 'Flip and Turn at Kimberley'. (At the 1993 cricket match, after performing one of his characteristic nose-holding dives into the swimming pool, Ron had emerged from the water and announced his intention of taking a 'flip and turn' in the microlight. The phrase had stuck.)

The invitation consisted of a pen-and-ink cartoon of the house, drawn by Ben, surmounted by a smacking red love heart, complete with exclamation lines, rising like a bubble above it – to reflect the loved-up spirit of the times, in the wake of the so-called Second Summer of Love. A giant plywood heart, painted fluorescent pink, was duly attached to the central pediment of Kimberley's Park Front, facing the lake. The event had found its logo. Henceforward, that cartoon heart with its exclamatory lines, together with the word 'Give!' to evoke the new generosity and feel-good affection of the scene, would decorate every invitation, programme, sticker, badge, wrist-band and tee-shirt connected with the event.

The turn-out was complete. Someone placed Kimberley hearts on road signs all the way from London to guide everyone in. As tents, yurts and tipis sprang up, and caravans and camper vans grouped themselves around clumps of trees in the Terrace Field on Friday evening, the campers soon spilled over into the neighbouring field below, eventually reaching right down to the edge of the lake. The first of two mountainous timber pyres (constructed from fallen trees from around the park and woods) was lit as darkness fell by a flaming arrow shot from a bow wielded by a horned Mr Tumnus stilt-walking figure. Squealing rabbits bolted out as the flames spread. Around the fires, an assortment of stalls offered food and drinks, provided by Christoph Brooke, Mahmoud and Willie who ran the Foxtrot Oscar bar in Chelsea. Another friend of Robbie's, Rob Sawyer, who owned the Moroccan-themed Po-Na-Na chain of bars and clubs, set up a Bedouin-style, hand-blocked marquee, lined in red and green, selling cocktails beneath the starry July night sky.

On Saturday, the sun waxed shyly behind little fluffy clouds. There was swimming and snoozing round the pool, as knots of thirty-somethings, protected against the glare by sunglasses, dreadlocks, Afghan hats, kaftans, goatee beards and face paint, drifted about the park, river, bird garden and walled garden and one camping area and another, separating and re-joining continuously like wax in a lava lamp. Many of the camping areas had a practised, bush feel to them. There were smoke-blackened kettles, cushions, sofas, hammocks, sheepskin rugs and bunting, fresh herbs and iron cauldrons bubbling over wood fires. Dave Clarke offered 'flips and turns' in the microlight from the landing strip down by the lake. After a lazy day, during which many more arrived, supper was eaten perched on straw bales around another camp fire, even bigger than the one the night before. As the sun set over the lake, Robbie and his support crew prepared to set off the fireworks.

These were the days before legislation prevented untrained amateurs acquiring large calibre, Category Three, mortar-fired display fireworks. Robbie had driven over to Kimbolton Fireworks (founder and proprietor:

The Reverend Ron Lancaster) and picked out a selection of the largest, loudest and most colourful 100–150 mm shells, Roman candles and single ignition cakes The Reverend Lancaster could supply. This considerable magazine – complete with massive cardboard firing tubes like howitzer barrels – was ferried by boat across the lake to the island, where the tubes were set into the mud. As the display commenced, everyone, not least the amateur ignition team, was a little taken aback by the scale of The Reverend Lancaster's merchandise. When the odd mortar tube, stabbed too far into the mud, exploded at ground level, or, having slipped, sent rockets, pistils, and green and violet croisette rings fizzing and crackling horizontally, both ignition team and audience had to dive for cover. It was a display, everyone agreed afterwards, with just the right amount of danger.

During the fireworks, Robbie and others had tiptoed round behind the crowd to light an avenue of flares leading up to the now floodlit house. When the last firework exploded and died away into the darkness, and everyone turned round, they were greeted by a 'flaming runway' up to the main event. At the ha-ha, people were greeted by dancers and stilt-walkers and beating drums. Figures dressed like lizards abseiled down the walls of the house. Then it was into the cellars and the music room, where, on three stages, Ben and other DJs played in two-hour sets until dawn. (With the music room windows open, many discovered, it was even possible to move dance floors by jumping out of the window directly down the old wooden potato shoot into the potato room below.)

Sunday was more languid. After a late start (few had got back to their campsite before daybreak), as bleary-eyed figures gradually emerged from their tents to boil kettles or fry bacon for late brunch, a sound system and decks were set up in the open-sided Po-No-Na tent at the bottom of the Terrace Field. Around five p.m., the music fired up again. This time it was mellower, more chilled, funky beats, after the maelstrom of the subterranean night. People started dancing on the grass. Soon another party was in full swing, running late into Sunday night. Many decided not to decamp until Monday morning.

The following year (Kimberley '95 – 'Blast Off') the event was structured along similar lines, and a colour-theme – purple – was introduced. At five o'clock on Saturday afternoon there was a call for everyone, in purple, to assemble in the field in front of the house. There a 'team photo', carefully arranged in the shape of the Kimberley heart (complete with exclamation lines), was taken from the roof.

Everyone was disbanding from the photograph when there was a tremendous roar. Three Russian Yak aircraft and a Nanchang CJ6 (a 1950s Chinese fighter trainer) raced in low over the lake, pulling into a steep climb just over everyone's heads to narrowly miss the house. It was two flying friends of

Robbie's, Bob Davy and Tim 'Flash' Constance (plus, in latter years, another flying friend, Lee Mayall) who proceeded to perform an aerobatic display, the air vibrating and juddering as the giant nine-cylinder radial engines echoed off the front of the house. In the photograph, and the air display, the party had found two more of its indelible trademarks.

Each year after that first 'official' Kimberley party, in 1994, the scale and spectacle grew. By plundering their address books for talented friends, and friends of friends, a format was arrived upon which could steadily evolve. Friday became cabaret night, with the Medium Rare variety show, choreographed by a friend of Robbie's, impresario Matt Whitley. Some acts, such as Gunter the German Porn Star, were classics of their kind ('Really he's so funny, but you were embarrassed to laugh in case the person sitting next to you thought you understood the joke' said Phyll). The restaurant and food areas offered bars, fusion cooking (mainly barbecued) and a chai bar. There were tented villages and, as the guests got older (and wealthier), tipi villages, lavishly furnished with rugs, bedding, stoves and even beds.

In 2005 Vanessa set up the 'Healing Area', a separate tented village offering treatments from face massages and aromatherapy to reiki, yoga, meditation, pilates, ayurvedic medicine and tantric sex lessons. A children's area followed soon after. Saturday afternoon in the bird garden saw readings and live country music, and the air display graduated from accomplished amateurs to possessed professionals in the form of the Red Bull Matadors. The post-firework, pre-dancing, performance arts around the house became supplemented with laser shows, slide shows and, from 2009, dazzling architectural mapping projections by Paul Reynolds, transmogrifying the brick edifice into (amongst other things) an aquarium, pinball machine, computer game and ruined Greek temple, before seeing it rolled up, unzipped, conflagrated, demolished and resurrected.[78] The old concrete granary and tractor shed in the West Wing, as part of Robbie's improvements to the house as a 'venue', became the main dance-floor, re-christened the Tractor Shed, galleried, air-conditioned and sound-proofed.

Cousin Dana, Aunt Anne's daughter and Robbie's godmother, whom the Buxton children had watched singing in bars on their skiing trips (chapter 16), and who was now the acclaimed blues singer, Dana Gillespie, became a regular performer, launching Saturday night.[79] In 1997 Dana brought Rolf Harris along. His 2 a.m. rendition of 'Two Little Boys' on the back stairs had a cohort of sweat-sodden dancers wiping tears from their eyes.[80] Musically,

78 www.youtube.com/watch?v=dBtlLAohTvo.
79 Also co-founder, with Basil Charles, of the Mustique Blues Festival.
80 'How can anyone at the end of the twentieth century not have heard of either Houdini or Rolf Harris?' wondered Phyll out loud, on discovering that Ron's grip on popular culture was not the stranglehold it might have been.

the line-up improved every year, to include such international names as Dreadzone, One Giant Leap (Duncan Bridgeman), The Egg, Nick Warren, Seb Fontaine, Sancho Panzer (Matt Brown and Jimmy K-Tel), Jamie Cullum, Goldfish, Jackson Scott, as well as numerous lesser-known cult acts such as Terra Firma, Funky Porcini, Chocolate Harlots and North of Ping Pong.

The invitations tended to reflect the themes closest to the hosts' hearts: sometimes emphasising the spiritual coming together ('Throw Open the Sluice Gates and Release Your Spiritual Tsunami'), sometimes a more hedonistic take ('The Pink Portals of Pleasure', 'A Licentious Assault on the Senses'). Sometimes they acknowledged topical exterior events, such as, in 2000, the millennium bug (KY2K – 'Lube up and Let Go') or, in 2009, the credit-crunching 'Into the Red' with the invitation designed as a giant plastic credit card. A decade of Kimberleys was celebrated in 2003 with 'Perfect Ten'. And so on, up to 2011 ('Out of the Blue'), in which the holograms of the blue lenticular invitation card, of a water drop falling, merged, as the card was tilted, into a splash in the shape of the Kimberley heart – all too apt, as it turned out, for in response the Heavens opened, transforming park and campsites into a Glastonbury-style quagmire.

Once it was clear that Kimberley was an indelible fixture for a certain demographic of London's hard-working, hard-playing troubadours, clubbers, bon viveurs, barflies, City libertines, Notting Hill-billies and assorted flâneurs, poseurs, healers, music-lovers, rhino-huggers, White Mischievists, nomads, DJ-manqués and other aficionados of festival living, 'Are you going to Kimberley?' became the pack's rallying cry. The effect – driven by the strictly-enforced invitation policy of 'only friends, or named friends of friends' – was to ramp its exclusivity, guaranteeing a sell-out (despite pre-match nerves by the committee) year after year. Strenuous efforts to keep all mention out of the Press fuelled its elusive mystique, marking Kimberley as *the* hot date of high summer – and attracting, over the years, numerous celebrities. The list soon included Sting and Trudie Styler, Simon and Yasmin Le Bon, Sienna Miller, Nick and Nettie Mason, Damian Lewis, Bruce Parry, Tom Hollander, Orlando Bloom, James Blunt and Prince Harry.

In the two decades from 1993 to 2013, only two years were missed: 2001 (due to the foot and mouth epidemic) and 2012. Over those eighteen Kimberleys, couples met and separated, children were born, grew up and started coming to the party themselves, in what sometimes seemed like a single long summer of sunshine, dancing and happy hanging out – though, for all that, each forthcoming event never lost its ability to induce butterflies in even the most diehard regulars.

III
Acknowledgements and Select Bibliography

I<small>N</small> ADDITION TO Ron, Phyll, Peter, Camilla, Vanessa, Robbie and Iona, specific thanks are due to Michael Black, Father Grant Brockhouse, John and Bridget Buxton, Crispin Buxton, Christopher Buxton, Sir Jocelyn Buxton, Bt, Joe Buxton, Richard Buxton, Tom Coke, Roderick Corrie, Ed Douglas-Miller, Orlando Fraser QC, James Gilbey, Dana Gillespie, Anthony Gurney, Nick Harley, Anne Hazlerigg, Nick Holmes, Simon Kendall, Angus McCulloch QC, Tom Naylor, Carissa Nightingale, Guy Pease, Charlie Raymond, Damian Riley-Smith, Dave Stirling, Ben Taylor, my father Peter Woodward (as an organist who also happens to be exactly the same age as Ron) and the many others, too numerous to mention, who have furnished me with favourite Ron stories.

For pictures, thanks to Ben Cole, Vicky Couchman, Will Curtis, Greg Holloway, Jörg Huber and Paul Reynolds.

Thanks to Mark Girouard for allowing passages from *The Victorian Country House* and to John and Caroline Moorehead for the extract from Alan Moorehead's *No Room in the Ark* (1941).

The following selection of sources (many harvested from the shelves of Kimberley) represents only the tiniest sample of the voluminous writings by, or about, the indefatiguable Buxton or Carlile families. For those thirsty for more, there is a considerable Buxton archive at The All Nations Christian College, now based at the former family seat of Easneye Park, Hertfordshire – though much information has become available online while this book was being written.

Anderson, Verily, *The Northrepps Grandchildren* (1968).

Barclay, Oliver, *Thomas Fowell Buxton and the Liberation of Slaves* (2001).

British Constructional Steelwork Association Limited (BCSA), *A Century of Steel Construction 1906-2006* (2006).

Buxton, Andrew R., *The Rifle Brigade, A Memoir* (1918).

Buxton, B. Godfrey, *The Reward of Faith in the Life of Barclay Fowell Buxton 1860–1946* (1949).

Buxton, B. Godfrey, 'Murray Barclay Buxton, President of the Institution of Structural-Engineers', *The Structural Engineer*, Vol 18, Issue 6, 1 November 1940.

Buxton, Charles, *Memoirs of Sir Thomas Fowell Buxton* (1848).

Buxton, Doric, *The Liberator Sir Thomas Buxton* (2007).

Buxton, Edith, *Reluctant Missionary* (1968).

Buxton, Hannah, *Memorials of Hannah, Lady Buxton* (1883).

Buxton, Peter, *The History of H. Young and Company* (1996).

Buxton, Simon, *The Shamanic Way of the Bee* (2004).

Carlile, James (assembled by), *History of the Carlile Family (Paisley Branch)* (1909).

Carlile, James (the collection of), *A History of the Ancient Family of Carlisle* (1822).

Davies, R.E., *The Buxtons of Easneye: An Evangelical Victorian Family and Their Successors* (2007).

De Bunsen, Victoria, *Charles Roden Buxton, A Memoir* (1948).

Girouard, Mark, *The Victorian Country House* (1979).

Gordon Walker, Patrick, *Political Diaries 1932–1971* (1991).

Hatton, Jean, *Betsy: The Dramatic Biography of Prison Reformer Elizabeth Fry* (2005).

Hislop, Ian, 'When Bankers Were Good', BBC documentary.

Kennedy, Ludovic, *On My Way to the Club, An Autobiography* (1989).

Morris, David, *The Story of Easneye* (1976).

Morris, Jan, *Pax Britannica* trilogy (1968).

Pakenham, Thomas, *The Scramble for Africa* (1991).

Reffold, A.E., *Wilson Carlile and the Church Army* (1956).

Rose, June, *Elizabeth Fry, A Biography* (1980).

Rowan, Edgar, *Wilson Carlile and the Church Army* (1905).

Squibb, George D., *Belfield and the Buxtons* (1954).

Tillotson, Michael, *The Fifth Pillar, The Life and Philosophy of The Lord Bramall, KG* (2005).

Truman Hanbury Buxton & Co Ltd, *Trumans the Brewers, 1666–1966 The Story of Truman-Hanbury Buxton & Co Ltd*, London & Burton (1966).

Whitney, Janet, *Elizabeth Fry – Quaker Heroine* (pre-1923).

Woodward, Antony, *Propellerhead* (2001).

H. Young & Co promotional booklet, *H. Young & Co Ltd, from 1870* (c.1948).

AS THE TRUCE IN POLITICS ENDS

GORDON WALKER OUT AT LEYTON

CONSERVATIVE WINS AFTER RECOUNT

...S' MAJORITY ...DOWN

'No race issue' at Leyton

By A. J. Travers

LEYTON, Thursday.

SHORTLY before the Leyton by-election result was declared, it was evident that Mr. Gordon Walker had lost. While Mr. Buxton, the Foreign Secretary looked grim and unhappy. His wife, standing by his side, bit her lips.

News of the result quickly reached the crowd of about 100. There were prolonged cheers and cries of "We want Buxton." Mr. Buxton declared the result "fantastic and a complete surprise to me."

Mr. Gordon Walker, finding it difficult to compose himself, said the result was a very bitter disappointment. Asked if he would be continuing as Foreign Secretary this would mean the end of his political career, he answered...

From Landseer's lions

Young's steel girders

THEY PROVIDE THE 'BACKBONE' OF BUILDING

IN a noisy Leyton side-turning, off the Lea Bridge Road, there is a firm that deals in 'skeletons.'

Not, however, the skeletons used in medical studies — or even those kept locked up in family cupboards — but steel ones, which form the rough frame-work of modern buildings.

The firm is H. Young and Company Limited, the structural engineers of Burwell Road.

From their Leyton works have provided the 'backbone' that provide the 'backbone' of dozens of famous buildings and architectural landmarks throughout this country, and indeed throughout the world.

The firm started south, as the Thames, at Nine Elms, in 1871. From Nine Elms, Mr. Henry Young produced not only bridges and equipment but will not be stilled. It will remain, the rugs, fall. Queen Victoria and statues were very much in vogue.

THE VICTOR TAKES HIS SEAT

Mr. Ronald Buxton, the new Conservative Member of Parliament for Leyton, arrives to take his seat in the House of Commons today.

He defeated former Labour Foreign Secretary Mr. Patrick Gordon Walker, in the Leyton by-election.

A welcoming roar of Conservative cheers greeted him...

A second Tory cheer rose so he turned the...

DEEP DAMAGE TO GOVERNMENT

VERDICT ON THE 100 DAYS

POLITICAL CORRESPONDENT

...Gordon Walker, failed...

Parliament are a staggering setback for the Government. The loss of Leyton, quite apart from the fact that it reduces the Government's majority in the House to a mere three votes, is a personal disaster for Mr. Gordon Walker.

In little more than three months he has been rejected by two constituencies.

It is hard to see how he can remain Foreign Secretary with his authority impaired by such a glaring withdrawal of his countrymen's confidence.

On one principle that a sensible man should never reinforce failure it would be a mistake for Mr. Wilson to seek yet another seat for Mr. Gordon Walker. It he to remain in the Government, he will presumably be as a life Peer.

Statues were big business

Election. Of the £1,627 electorate 60.5 per cent. voted, compared with 60.1 per cent. at the General Election.

Labour's share of the total vote of 37,456 was 45.9 per cent. compared with 52.8 per cent. at the General Election.

The Conservative share was 34.9 per cent. (29.1 per cent.) and the Liberals share was 16.2 per cent. (18.1 per cent.).

The fall in the Minister of Technology's share of the vote is undoubtedly due to fears of redundancy abroad local aircraft and engineering workers and hires dropped several times by...

LEYTON

Walker, R. C. G. (C)
Mackay, P. C. G.
Lynch, A. ...
Dor...